普通高等教育"十二五"规划教材

汽车工程专业英语

第 2 版

张金柱　主编
张锦生　主审

化学工业出版社

·北京·

《汽车工程专业英语　第2版》是按照教育部颁布的"大学英语教学大纲",为高等院校车辆工程、汽车服务工程、交通运输及其他相关专业学生的专业英语课程编写的教材。

全书共分7章,第1章为发动机基本结构和工作原理,如发动机曲柄连杆机构、配气机构、燃油系、润滑系、冷却系和排放控制等;第2章为底盘和车身的结构和原理,如离合器、手动变速器、自动变速器、万向节、差速器、车架、悬架、转向系和制动系等;第3章为汽车电器结构和原理,如点火系统、启动系统、充电系统、防抱死制动系统、空调系统、安全气囊、电动助力转向、汽车通信技术等;第4章为发动机故障诊断与修理;第5章为底盘故障诊断与修理;第6章为汽车电器故障诊断与修理;第7章为汽车保养。

《汽车工程专业英语　第2版》可供高等院校车辆工程、汽车服务工程、交通运输及相关专业学生使用,也可作为从事与汽车相关专业的工程技术人员学英语的参考书。

图书在版编目(CIP)数据

汽车工程专业英语/张金柱主编 . —2版 . —北京:化学工业出版社,2014.9(2019.1重印)
普通高等教育"十二五"规划教材
ISBN 978-7-122-20855-2

Ⅰ.①汽… Ⅱ.①张… Ⅲ.①汽车工程-英语　Ⅳ.①H31

中国版本图书馆CIP数据核字(2014)第117850号

责任编辑:刘俊之　　　　　　　　　　装帧设计:韩　飞
责任校对:陶燕华

出版发行:化学工业出版社(北京市东城区青年湖南街13号　邮政编码100011)
印　　装:三河市延风印装有限公司
787mm×1092mm　1/16　印张15¾　字数390千字　2019年1月北京第2版第3次印刷

购书咨询:010-64518888　　　　　　　　售后服务:010-64518899
网　　址:http://www.cip.com.cn
凡购买本书,如有缺损质量问题,本社销售中心负责调换。

定　　价:35.00元　　　　　　　　　　　　　　　　　版权所有　违者必究

汽车工程专业英语

第 2 版

主　　编　张金柱
副主编　韩玉敏　吉淑娥　汪　伟
参　　编　李　鹏　王悦新　赵雨旸　胡世栋
主　　审　张锦生

前　　言

教育部颁布的"大学英语教学大纲"要求学生在完成基础阶段的学习任务，达到四级或六级后，都必须修读专业英语。学生应能顺利阅读有关专业的原版教科书、参考书及其他参考资料，能借助词典将有关专业的英语文章译成汉语。据此我们编写了《汽车工程专业英语》教材，以满足高等学校车辆工程、汽车服务工程、交通运输及其他有关专业学生的专业英语教学的需要，也可满足从事与汽车相关专业的工程技术人员学习英语的要求。

本书第一版自 2005 年出版以来，受到许多院校的欢迎，老师们对修订再版也提出了一些宝贵意见。修订版基本保留了原书的结构与框架，主要在以下几方面进行了修改：

1. 新增汽油缸内直喷、双离合器变速器、混合动力汽车结构、车辆网络等汽车新技术、新结构。

2. 增添课文插图。

3. 修改"传动系"，"手动变速器"和"自动变速器"课文的内容和插图。

4. 删除"化油器式燃油系"、"巡航控制系统"、"汽车导航系统"、"蓝牙技术在汽车上的应用"、"驾驶员辅助系统"等内容。

本书课文内容比较新颖，选取的原文资料反映现代汽车所具有的典型结构。主要文章选自国外汽车专业教材、网络文章等。为了适应专业英语教学的要求，书中内容既对学生学过的课程进行了必要的覆盖，又有所拓宽和延伸，既可提高读者英语阅读水平，又能使读者学到一些汽车专业知识。

全书共分 7 章。第 1 章为发动机基本结构和工作原理；第 2 章为底盘和车身的结构和原理；第 3 章为汽车电器结构和原理；第 4 章为发动机故障诊断与修理；第 5 章为底盘故障诊断与修理；第 6 章为汽车电器故障诊断与修理；第 7 章为汽车保养。

本书由黑龙江工程学院张金柱编写第 1～12 课，汪伟编写第 13～17 课，韩玉敏编写第 18～24 课，吉淑娥编写第 25～30 课，赵雨旸编写第 31～34 课，哈尔滨技师学院李鹏编写第 35～40 课，龙岩学院王悦新编写第 41～45 课，黑龙江工程学院胡世栋编写附录1及附录2.全书由东北林业大学张锦生主审。

衷心感谢对本书修订提出宝贵意见和建议的老师们。由于作者水平所限,疏漏和不当之处在所难免,敬请读者批评指正。

编 者
2016年4月

第一版前言

教育部颁布的"大学英语教学大纲"要求学生在完成基础阶段的学习任务，达到四级或六级后，都必须修读专业英语。学生应能顺利阅读有关专业的原版教科书、参考书及其他参考资料，能借助词典将有关专业的英语文章译成汉语。据此作者编写了这本《汽车工程专业英语》教材，以满足高等学校汽车工程、交通运输及其他有关专业学生的专业英语教学的需要，也可满足从事与汽车相关专业的工程技术人员学习英语的要求。

本书课文内容比较新颖，选取的原文资料反映现代汽车所具有的典型结构。主要文章选自汽车专业网站"icarumba.com"，"howstuffworks.com"等。为了适应专业英语教学的要求，书中内容既对学生学过的课程进行了必要的覆盖，又有所拓宽和延伸，既可提高读者英语阅读水平，又能使读者学到一些汽车专业知识。

全书共分七章。第一章为发动机基本结构和工作原理；第二章为底盘和车身的结构和原理；第三章为汽车电器结构和原理；第四章为发动机故障诊断与修理；第五章为底盘故障诊断与修理；第六章为汽车电器故障诊断与修理；第七章为汽车保养。

本书由黑龙江工程学院张金柱，韩玉敏，石美玉主编。参加编写的还有黑龙江工程学院齐晓杰，王悦新，东北林业大学张锦生，哈尔滨工程大学王立权。

由于作者水平所限，疏漏和不当之处在所难免，敬请读者批评指正。

编　者
2005 年 5 月

CONTENTS
目　　录

Chapter 1　Engine Construction 发动机结构 ··· 1
Lesson 1　Internal Combustion Engine Basics 内燃机基础 ··························· 1
Lesson 2　Engine Block 发动机缸体 ··· 5
Lesson 3　Crankshafts, Bearing Inserts, Connecting Rods and Pistons
　　　　　曲轴，轴瓦，连杆和活塞 ··· 10
Lesson 4　Valve Mechanisms 气门机构 ·· 15
Lesson 5　The Fuel Delivery System 燃料供给系统 ··································· 19
Lesson 6　Fuel Injection System 燃油喷射系统 ······································· 24
Lesson 7　Gasoline Direct Injection 汽油缸内直喷 ··································· 29
Lesson 8　The Cooling System 冷却系统 ·· 34
Lesson 9　The Lubrication System 润滑系统 ·· 38
Lesson 10　Turbochargers and Superchargers 涡轮增压器和机械增压器 ················ 43
Lesson 11　Emission Control System 排放控制系统 ··································· 48

Chapter 2　Chassis Construction 底盘结构 ··· 55
Lesson 12　Drivetrain 传动系 ··· 55
Lesson 13　How Does the Clutch Work 离合器如何工作 ······························· 60
Lesson 14　Manual Transmission 手动变速器 ·· 64
Lesson 15　Automatic Transmission 自动变速器 ····································· 70
Lesson 16　Differential and Final Drive 差速器和主传动器 ···························· 76
Lesson 17　Body and Frame 车身和车架 ··· 81
Lesson 18　Suspension 悬架 ··· 86
Lesson 19　Front Independent Suspension 前轮独立悬架 ······························ 90
Lesson 20　Steering System 转向系 ·· 94
Lesson 21　Wheel Alignment 车轮定位 ·· 98
Lesson 22　Hydraulic Brake System 液压制动系统 ···································· 105
Lesson 23　Disc Brake 盘式制动器 ·· 109
Lesson 24　Tires 轮胎 ·· 113

Chapter 3　Automotive Electric Equipments 汽车电器 ································ 118
Lesson 25　Ignition System 点火系统 ·· 118

Lesson 26	Starting System 启动系统	122
Lesson 27	Charging System 充电系统	125
Lesson 28	Battery 电池	129
Lesson 29	Antilock Brake System 防抱死制动系统	135
Lesson 30	Air-Conditioning System 空调系统	139
Lesson 31	Electric Car 电动汽车	144
Lesson 32	Hybrid Electric Vehicles 混合动力汽车	148
Lesson 33	Fuel Cell Car 燃料电池汽车	154
Lesson 34	Electric Power Steering（EPS）电动助力转向	158
Lesson 35	Vehicle Networks 车辆网络	162
Lesson 36	Air Bags 安全气囊	168
Lesson 37	Dual-clutch Transmission 双离合器变速器	173
Lesson 38	Automotive Communication Technology 汽车通信技术	178
Lesson 39	Intelligent Vehicle Applications 智能车辆的应用	182

Chapter 4 Engine Troubleshooting and Repair 发动机故障诊断与修理 … 187

Lesson 40	Overheating: Causes and Cures 发动机过热：原因和措施	187
Lesson 41	Diesel Diagnostics 柴油机诊断	193
Lesson 42	Engine Rebuilding Tips 发动机修理要点	199

Chapter 5 Chassis Troubleshooting and Repair 底盘故障诊断与修理 … 206

Lesson 43	A Guide to Four-Wheel Alignment 四轮定位指南	206

Chapter 6 Automotive Electrical Equipment Troubleshooting and Repair 汽车电器故障诊断与修理 … 211

Lesson 44	Toyota Fuel Injection System 丰田燃油喷射系统	211

Chapter 7 Automotive Maintenance 汽车保养 … 218

Lesson 45	Fall and Winter Service Checklist 秋季和冬季检查项目	218

附录 … 223

附录 1	Automotive Acronyms 汽车缩写词	223
附录 2	Automotive Tech Terms 汽车技术术语	234

参考文献 … 244

Chapter 1　Engine Construction
发动机结构

Lesson 1

Internal Combustion Engine Basics
内燃机基础

1.1　The Basics　基本结构

　　The engine is, of course, the heart of every car. At the most basic level, the engine develops the power to move the car. This section discusses the different types of engines in use, as well as the fundamental concepts behind internal combustion engine.

　　There are many types and variations of automobile engines. The most common type is the internal combustion engine. It is named so because combustion takes place inside the engine.

　　The engine is mounted to the car frame. An internal combustion engine is like a container into which we put air and fuel and then start them burning. The air and fuel is burned in the engine container, or cylinder. A cylinder is a metal tube closed at one end. A movable plug, called a piston, is installed inside the cylinder. There is a small space between the piston top and the top of the cylinder. This space, called the combustion chamber, is where the burning takes place. If several drops of gasoline are placed into this space, and the piston is pushed up in the cylinder, the gasoline and air in the combustion chamber will be tightly squeezed together. When the mixture is squeezed as tightly as possible, it is ignited by an electric spark. The burning, or combustion, increases the pressure in the combustion chamber and pushes the piston down the cylinder with great force. (See Figure 1-1).

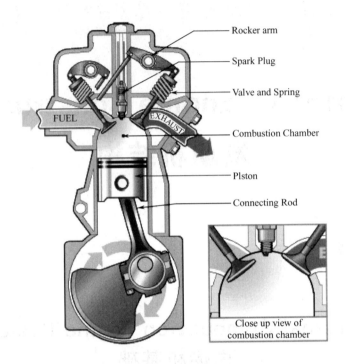

Figure 1-1 Automotive internal combustion engine

In order to use the power developed by the moving piston, the connecting rod is connected to the bottom of the piston. When the piston moves downward, this rod will move downward. The downward movement of the piston and connecting rod is changed to circular or rotary movement by a part called the crankshaft. The crankshaft is a shaft with its ends mounted in such a way that it can be rotated. The middle of the crankshaft is offset, and the lower end of the connecting rod is connected to the middle of the offset. The upper end of the connecting rod is joined to the piston by a pin called the wrist or piston pin. This pin allows the connecting rod to follow the motion of the crankshaft.

One additional part is required to complete a basic engine. Because it is necessary to push the piston down the cylinder more than once, in between down strokes it must be returned to the top of the cylinder. To do this, a heavy flywheel is mounted to the end of the crankshaft. When the piston is forced down, the crankshaft turns, and the flywheel turns with it. Because the flywheel is heavy, it does not slow down easily. Its momentum keeps the crankshaft turning. The rotation of the crankshaft then pushes the piston back up to the top of the cylinder. (See Figure 1-2).

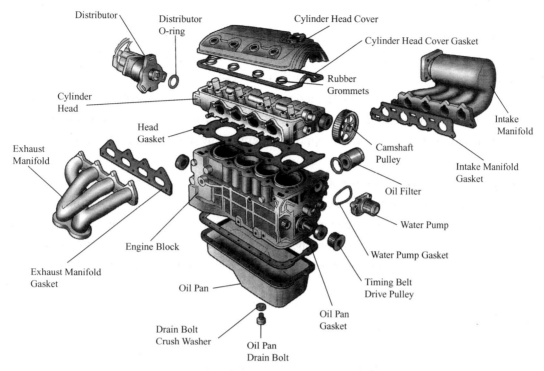

Figure 1-2 Engine components

1.2 Engine Design 发动机设计

Automotive engines may be classified in several different ways according to these design features:

Valve arrangement. Engines may be classified according to the location of the valves and the number of valves per cylinder. Many engines have the valves located in the cylinder head, and these engines are referred to as overhead valve engines. The majority of engines have two valves per cylinder, but engines with four valves per cylinder have become increasingly popular in recent years.

Camshaft location. Engines with a single camshaft positioned above the valve train on the cylinder head may be referred to as single overhead camshaft (SOHC) engines. Other engines have two camshafts located above the valve train in the cylinder head, and these engines are called dual overhead camshaft (DOHC) engines. V-type engines may have dual camshafts located above each cylinder head. Some SOHC engines, or DOHC engines have the camshaft located in the cylinder head rather than above the valve train. Other engines have the camshaft positioned in the cylinder block.

Ignition type. Engines may be classified as spark ignition (SI), and compression ignition (CI). In an SI engine, the air-fuel mixture in the combustion chamber is ignited by a spark at the spark plug electrodes. The air-fuel mixture in a CI engine is ignited by the heat of compression. Diesel engines use the CI principle, and these engines have much higher compression than SI engines.

Cylinder arrangement. The most common arrangements of engine cylinders are in-line, V-type, and opposed. An in-line engine has the cylinders mounted vertically and positioned in a line directly behind each other. V-type engines usually have 6 or 8 cylinders located in a V formation with an angle of 60 degrees or 90 degrees between the sides of the block. Other V-type engines have been used too; for example, one manufacturer is now marketing a V10 engine. In an opposed engine, the cylinders are positioned horizontally across from each other.

Number of cylinders. Engines are designed with 3, 4, 5, 6, 8, 10, or 12 cylinders.

Cycles. Most automotive engines operate on the four-cycle principle. Since the two-stroke engine is lighter and may be designed to produce more power than an equivalent size four-stroke engine, the two-stroke engine may experience widespread use in the near future. All of the big-three automotive manufacturers have two-stroke engines under development.

[词汇]

combustion	n.燃烧	cylinder head	气缸盖
fundamental	adj.基础的,基本的	overhead valve	顶置式气门
automobile	n.汽车	camshaft	n.凸轮轴
cylinder	n.气缸,柱面	valve train	气门组
piston	n.活塞	single overhead camshaft	单顶置式气门
combustion chamber	燃烧室	dual overhead camshaft	双顶置式气门
connecting rod	连杆	cylinder block	气缸体
crankshaft	n.曲轴	ignition	n.点火,点燃
piston pin	活塞销	spark plug	n.火花塞
stroke	n.冲程	electrode	n.电极
flywheel	n.飞轮	equivalent	adj.相等的,相当的,同意义的
momentum	n.动量		
valve	n.气门		

[注释]

1. Internal combustion engine 内燃机：燃料在气缸内燃烧的能量直接推动活塞,转子或透平运动的内燃机,如汽油机、柴油机、三角活塞旋转式发动机和燃气轮机等。

2. The big-three automotive manufacturers... 三大汽车制造厂。这里指通用、福特和克莱斯勒汽车厂。

[问题]

1. How does the internal combustion engine work?
2. How are the automotive engines classified?
3. What is the main difference between the SOHC and DOHC?
4. What is the characteristic of the opposed engine?

Lesson 2

Engine Block
发动机缸体

2.1 Engine Block Types 发动机缸体类型

In-Line Blocks. In an in-line block, the cylinders are positioned in a direct line behind each other, and the cylinders are mounted vertically. This type of engine usually has four or six cylinders, and one cylinder head mounted on top of the block. Since the cylinders are mounted vertically, the engine requires more underhood space. Therefore, the hood and front fenders must be mounted higher above the in-line engine. This body design reduces the aerodynamic qualities. (See Figure 2-1).

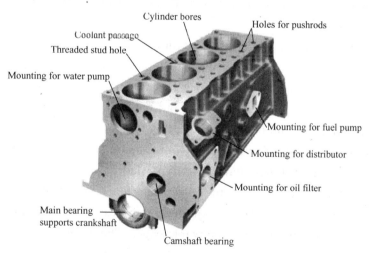

Figure 2-1 In-line engine cylinder block

V-Type Blocks. V-type engine blocks usually have six, eight, or ten cylinders arranged in two rows with an angle of 60 degrees or 90 degrees between the cylinder banks. This type of engine block has one crankshaft and a cylinder head mounted on top of each side of the V-block. Since the cylinders are mounted in a V configuration, a vehicle with this type of engine may be designed with a lower hood and improved aerodynamic qualities compared with a vehicle with an in-line engine.

Slant-Type Blocks. The slant-type engine is similar to the in-line engine, but the complete slant-type engine is slanted to one side. This type of mounting reduces the distance from the top to the bottom of the engine, and thus allows the engineers to design a lower hood with improved aerodynamic qualities.

Opposed-Type Blocks. In an opposed-type block, the pistons are mounted horizontally across from each other at a 180 degree angle. This type of engine has one crankshaft and a cylinder head mounted on top of the cylinders on each side of the engine. Since this engine requires very little vertical underhood space, it is often used in the vehicles with a rear-mounted engine.

2.2　Block Assemblies 缸体总成

Many engine blocks contain a cast iron alloy, but aluminum blocks are becoming more common. Some aluminum blocks have steel cylinder liners. The aluminum in other blocks is mixed with silicon so the silicon accumulates on the cylinder walls to provide a hard surface that does not require a sleeve. Cast iron blocks are heavier and more rigid than aluminum blocks. However, aluminum blocks have superior heat-conducting qualities compared with cast iron blocks. Aluminum blocks are more subject to distortion than cast iron blocks.

Many engine components are supported by the cylinder block. These components include the crankshaft, pistons, cylinder heads, valve lifters, camshaft, water pump, oil pump, and timing gear cover.

Cylinder Sleeves: The cylinders are cast integrally with the block in most engines. However, some heavy-duty engines have removable dry-type or wet-type replaceable cylinder sleeves. A wet-type cylinder sleeve is in contact with the coolant. This type of sleeve must be sealed in the block at the top and bottom. Since the sides of the wet-type sleeve are not supported by the block casting, this type of sleeve must be thicker. A dry-type sleeve is pressed into the block, which contacts and supports the sleeve. Therefore, the dry-type sleeve is cast thinner than a wet-type sleeve. If a cylinder wall is damaged, the sleeve can be replaced without having to replace the complete block.

Main Bearing Bores: The circular main bearing bores are located on the lower side of the block. These bearing bores have removable caps. The main bearing bores support the crankshaft in the block. Extremely high combustion forces are applied to the pistons, connecting rods, crankshaft, and main bearing bores. The main bearing bores must be strong enough to withstand these forces without distorting or stretching.

Camshaft Bearing Bores: If the camshaft is mounted in the block, it is supported in circular openings in the block. Circular bearings are pressed into the openings that support the camshaft. These camshaft bearings and bearing bores must support the load of the camshaft and valve train.

Valve Lifter Bores: When the camshaft is mounted in the block, the valve lifter bores are machined in the block directly above the camshaft lobes. Oil is supplied from the main oil gallery in the block to each valve lifter bore.

Coolant Jackets: Coolant jackets surround the outside of each cylinder wall in the block.

Coolant is circulated through each of these coolant jackets to cool the cylinder walls. A threaded coolant drain plug is positioned near the bottom of the coolant jackets in the block. In a V6 or V8 block, a coolant drain plug is located in each side of the block.

2.3 Engine Mounting Positions 发动机支撑位置

Front Engine Longitudinal. In many vehicles, the engine is mounted longitudinally at the front of the vehicle. Rear wheel drive (RWD) vehicles usually have this type of engine mounting with the transmission attached to the back of the engine. The differential is mounted under the rear of the chassis, and a driveshaft is connected between the transmission and the differential. This type of vehicle design has a somewhat higher weight on the front suspension compared with the rear suspension. However, this vehicle design provides satisfactory brake load distribution and steering force. A large underhood space is required by a longitudinally mounted engine, and the rear mounted differential reduces passenger compartment space. The engine, transmission, driveshaft, and differential may be removed individually on a RWD vehicle with a longitudinally mounted front engine too. Some front wheel drive (FWD) vehicles have a longitudinally mounted front engine too.

Front Engine Transverse. Many FWD vehicles have a transversely mounted engine at the front of the vehicle. The transaxle contains the transmission and the differential, and this transaxle is attached to the rear of the engine on the left side of the vehicle. Drive axles are connected from the transaxle to the front wheels.

With this engine and transaxle configuration, the rear-mounted differential and driveshaft are eliminated, assuming the vehicle is two-wheel drive (2WD). Transversely mounted engines and transaxles require less underhood space and reduce vehicle weight. The elimination of the rear-mounted differential and driveshaft allows increased interior space. The FWD transversely mounted engine and transaxle configuration has more weight on the front suspension than on the rear suspension. This weight distribution places a greater load on the front brakes and suspension.

Mid-Engine Transverse. The engine is always mounted transversely with a mid-engine mounting. With this type of engine mounting, the engine is positioned between the driver's seat and the rear wheels. Mid-engine vehicles often have a similar engine and transaxle configuration to a FWD vehicle. Drive axles are connected from the transaxle to the rear wheels.

The radiator is often mounted under the hood near the front of the vehicle, and the coolant is piped from the engine to the radiator. Since the engine is positioned between the driver's seat and the rear wheels, the front of the car can be designed with excellent aerodynamic qualities. The engine and transaxle intrude on the passenger compartment, and vehicles with this engine configuration are usually two-seater sports cars. A barrier is required to reduce engine heat, noise, and vibration transfer to the passenger compartment. Since the engine is positioned near the vehicle center of gravity, weight distribution between the front and rear wheels is much closer to being equal compared with other engine-mounting configurations. The mid-engine transverse design improves steering and handling characteristics.

2.4 Engine Measurements 发动机尺寸

Cylinder bore is the diameter of the cylinder measured in inches (in) or millimeters (mm). The crank throw is the distance from the crankshaft center line to the center line of the connecting rod journal. The stroke is equal to twice the crank throw. An oversquare engine generally delivers high rpm as required in many cars. If an engine is undersquare, it delivers excellent torque at low rpm, which is desirable in truck and tractor applications.

TRADE JARGON: If the cylinder bore diameter is longer than the stroke, the engine is referred to as oversquare.

TRADE JARGON: An undersquare engine has a stroke that is longer than the cylinder bore diameter.

[词汇]

block	n. 气缸体
cylinder	n. 气缸，圆筒，圆柱体
cylinder head	气缸盖
hood	n. 发动机罩
fender	n. 翼子板
aerodynamic	adj. 空气动力学的
bank	n. 气缸侧体
crankshaft	n. 曲轴
configuration	n. 构造，结构，配置，外形
slant	n. 倾斜，歪向
bearing	n. 轴承
bore	n. 气缸内径，口径，内径
mounting	n. 安装，安置，固定
cast iron	n. 铸铁，锻铁
alloy	n. 合金
liner	n. 里衬，衬垫，衬套
cylinder wall	气缸壁
silicon	n. 硅
sleeve	n. 套，套筒，套管
distortion	n. 扭曲，变形，曲解，失真
valve lifter	气门挺杆，气门升程
timing gear	n. 正时齿轮
cover	n. 盖
replaceable	adj. 可代替的
coolant	n. 冷冻剂，冷却液，散热剂
lobe	n. 凸角
gallery	n. 油通
jacket	n. 套
drain	n. 排泄，排出，排水
longitudinal	adj. 经度的，纵向的
longitudinally	adv. 纵向地
transmission	n. 变速器，变速箱
differential	n. 差速器
chassis	n. 底盘
transverse	adj. 横向的，横断的
transversely	adv. 横着，横切地，横断地
transaxle	n. 变速驱动桥
drive axle	主动轴，驱动轴
brake	n. 制动器，刹车，制动
suspension	n. 悬架
mid-engine	中置式发动机
radiator	n. 散热器，水箱
intrude	v. 闯入，侵入
sports car	跑车
barrier	n. (阻碍通道的) 障碍物，栅栏，屏障
millimeter	n. 毫米
journal	n. 轴颈，期刊，杂志
oversquare	n. 短行程
undersquare	n. 长行程
rpm	n. 每分钟转数
tractor	n. 车头，牵引车
jargon	n. 行话

[注释]

    1. some heavy-duty engines have removable dry-type or wet-type replaceable cylinder sleeves.　有些重载发动机采用可拆卸更换的干式或湿式缸套。

    2. Undersquare engine　缸径小于冲程的发动机：气缸直径小于冲程的发动机。

    3. Crank throw　曲轴半径：从曲轴轴线到曲柄销轴线的距离，等于活塞行程的一半。

[问题]

    1. What kinds of blocks have the engine?

    2. Where are the engines placed in the automobile?

    3. What's the meaning of front engine transverse?

    4. What's the cylinder bore?

Lesson 3

Crankshafts, Bearing Inserts, Connecting Rods and Pistons
曲轴，轴瓦，连杆和活塞

3.1 Crankshaft 曲轴

The crankshaft changes the vertical piston movement to rotary motion, and transfers this rotary motion to the drivetrain. Crankshafts may contain cast iron alloy or forged steel. Cast iron crankshafts are satisfactory in car and light-duty truck engines. However, forged steel crankshafts provide increased strength compared with those made from cast iron alloy. All the main bearing and connecting rod bearing journals are machined to a highly polished finish. Bearing inserts are located between the main bearing bores and the main bearing journals on the crankshaft. Connecting rod bearing inserts are mounted between the connecting rod bores and the crankshaft journals. The main bearing journals must be perfectly aligned with each other. Connecting rod journals are offset from the center of the crankshaft. Therefore, the connecting rod journals orbit around the main bearing journals. The crankshaft journals must be properly spaced so the pistons reach TDC in the correct order. (See Figure 3-1).

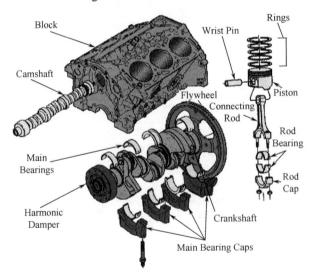

Figure 3-1 Engine main components

Oil passages are drilled from each main bearing journal to the connecting rod journals to assure adequate oil supply at the connecting rod bearings.

A flexplate, or flywheel, is bolted to the transmission end of the crankshaft, and a vibration damper and pulley are pressed onto the front of the crankshaft.

3.2　Bearing Inserts 轴瓦

Bearing inserts must have these characteristics:
(1) Embedability to absorb foreign particles which may scratch the crankshaft journal.
(2) Surface action to prevent bearing seizure to the crankshaft if the bearing insert momentarily contacts the journal surface.
(3) Conformability to allow bearing material to creep slightly and compensate for some misalignment between the bearing insert and the crankshaft journal.
(4) Fatigue strength to withstand severe explosion impacts from the combustion chamber, piston, and connecting rod.

Commonly used bearing insert materials include steel-backed Babbit, overplated copper, nonoverplated copper, overplated aluminum-cadmium, and nonoverplated aluminum.

Locking tabs on each half of the bearing insert fit into slots in the connecting rod or main bearing opening to prevent bearing rotation. Bearing inserts are designed so their curvature is slightly larger than the bore in which they are mounted. Therefore, when the bearing insert is installed it conforms exactly to the bore surface. This type of bearing insert design is called bearing spread.

When bearings are manufactured, they are designed so they are slightly longer than the bore in which they are installed; therefore, the edges of the bearing insert protrude a short distance from the bore. When the bearing cap is bolted in place, bearing crush forces the inserts to make complete contact with the bearing bore. Bearing crush and spread provide good heat dissipation from the bearing, and prevent bearing rotation in the bore.

A thin film of oil must be maintained between the bearing insert and the crankshaft journal. Correct bearing clearance is essential to maintain this film of oil.

3.3　Connecting Rods 连杆

Many connecting rods are steel-forged, tapered I-beam design. The connecting rod bore fits over the crankshaft journal, and the eye in the upper end of the connecting rod fits over the piston pin, and therefore the connecting rod connects the piston to the crankshaft. The connecting rod cap is bolted to the upper part of the rod.

The rod bore must be precisely machined to provide complete contact with the bearing insert. The piston pin may be pressed or clamped into the eye of the rod. In some applications, the piston pin fits through a bushing in the rod eye.

3.4 Pistons 活塞

Most gasoline engines are equipped with aluminum alloy pistons. Hypereutectic pistons contain aluminum mixed with 20% silicon. These pistons provide excellent strength, durability, and scuff resistance. Hypereutectic pistons are more wear resistant in the skirt, ring groove, and pin bore areas compared with other aluminum pistons.

The top of the piston is called the head, or dome. Pistons may have various top designs to match the combustion chamber design in the cylinder head. Piston ring grooves are cut into the sides of the piston just below the piston head. The ridges between the ring grooves are referred to as lands. Piston pin bores are machined through the piston, and these bores must be aligned with each other. The piston pin bore is usually offset in the piston to minimize piston slap against the cylinder wall when the piston moves from the compression stroke to the power stroke.

Pistons must be assembled on the connecting rods correctly, and the complete piston and rods assembly must be installed properly in the cylinder to maintain the pin offset in the correct position. The number of the cylinders is usually stamped on the connecting rod and cap, and an identification notch is placed on top of the piston. This notch usually faces to the front of the engine. The pistons and connecting rods must be assembled and installed according to the engine manufacturer's instructions in the service manual.

The piston skirt is the area from the lower ring land to the bottom of the piston. Automobile engines usually have slipper skirt pistons, whereas full-skirt pistons are used in heavy-duty truck and commercial engines. The slipper skirt piston is cut away in the pin bore areas to provide a lighter piston.

Piston clearance in the cylinder is critical. The piston must have sufficient clearance to allow a film of oil between the piston and the cylinder wall. If the piston clearance is too small, lack of lubrication causes piston scoring and seizure. When piston clearance is excessive, the piston will slap against the cylinder wall and cause an undesirable noise.

3.4.1 Piston Pins 活塞销

Piston pins are manufactured from hard steel, and they have a finely polished exterior surface. One of the most common methods of mounting the pin in the piston and connecting rod is to press the pin into the rod and allow it to rotate in the piston with a precise clearance. In some cases, the pin is clamped in the rod and rotates in the piston bores. Other connecting rods have a bushing in the rod eye, and the pin rotates in this bushing and in the piston. This type of pin mounting is called full-floating. A full-floating piston pin must have retaining clips at the outer edges of the pin bores. A set screw retains the pin in some pistons, and the pin then rotates in the rod eye bushing.

Regardless of the type of piston pin mounting, if the pin rotates in the piston pin bores or the rod bushing, the pin clearance is very important. There must be enough clearance between the pin and the piston pin bore or rod bushing to allow a film of oil between these components. When the piston pin clearance is insufficient, the lack of lubrication causes pin scoring and seizure. If piston pin clearance is excessive, the pin causes a knocking noise as combustion loads are applied to the piston.

3.4.2 Piston Rings 活塞环

The piston rings fit into the piston ring grooves and provide seals between the piston and the cylinder walls. Piston rings also control the amount of oil on the cylinder walls to prevent excessive amounts of oil from moving past the rings into the combustion chamber. Most piston rings are made from cast iron and nodular iron. Piston rings may be classified as compression rings and oil rings. Many pistons have two compression rings in the upper ring grooves and one oil ring in the lower groove.

The compression rings provide a seal between the piston and the cylinder wall. These rings are designed so the combustion and compression pressures force the rings against the cylinder wall and the lower surface of the ring groove. This action provides improved seals.

Some oil rings have an expander positioned between upper and lower side rails. Other cast iron oil rings have slots cut in the center of the rings and a thin expander behind the ring. Slots are cut in the oil ring grooves in the piston. The oil rings scrape the oil from the cylinder walls, and the excess oil flows through the ring and piston slots into the oil pan.

Piston ring technology now includes the use of low-tension piston rings in many engines. These piston rings have reduced tension against the cylinder walls, which lowers internal engine friction and improves fuel economy.

[词汇]

crankshaft	n. 曲轴	transmission	n. 变速器，变速箱
insert	n. 衬垫，代入，插入，衬垫，垫片	vibration damper	减振器
		pulley	n. 滑轮，滑车，皮带轮
rotary	adj. 旋转的	embedability	n. 压入能力，嵌入性
piston	n. 活塞，柱塞	foreign	adj. 外来的
drivetrain	n. 传动系	particle	n. 质点，粒子，颗粒
cast iron	n. 铸铁，锻铁	scratch	n. 擦痕，划痕，刮
forge	vt, vi 锻造		vt. 擦，刮，搔，抓，挖出
journal	n. 轴颈	seizure	n. 咬住
polish	v. 磨光，抛光，抛光剂	conformability	n. 一致性
finish	v. 精加工，光制，抛光	creep	n. 爬行，塑性变形
offset	n. 偏移，不重合，位移	misalignment	n. 失调
orbit	vt. 绕…轨道而行	fatigue	n. 疲劳
TDC	上止点	Babbit	n. 巴氏合金，巴比合金，轴承合金
passage	n. 流道，通道，孔口		

aluminum	n.铝	groove	n.沟，槽，针槽
cadmium	n.镉	dome	n.圆顶，圆盖，拱顶，穹圆顶，圆盖
tab	n.片，薄片，调整片		
curvature	n.弯曲，曲率	ridge	n.隆起物
spread	n.宽展，扩充，加宽，敷胶量，分布，刮胶	land	n.环岸
		slap	vt.& n.拍，掌击，拍击
crush	n.& vt.压碎，碾碎，压服，压垮，粉碎，（使）变形	stroke	n.冲程，闪击
		stamp	v.跺（脚），顿（足），压印
I-beam	n.工字梁	clearance	n.间隙
bushing	n.衬套，轴衬，轴瓦	lubrication	n.润滑
hypereutectic	adj.过共晶的，过低熔的	scoring	n.刮伤
durability	n.耐久性，持久性，强度	clip	n.夹子，回形针，子弹夹
scuff	n.磨损，拖着脚步，磨损处，咬接	nodular	adj.球状的，瘤状的，结节状的

[注释]

1. Flexplate （液力变矩器）柔性传动板（= flexible drive plate）
2. Babbit 巴氏合金：一种以锌、铜、锑和铅组成的合金，用于发动机轴承。
3. Bearing spread 轴瓦弹开（径向伸展）量（单片轴瓦自由状态下分离面宽度与承孔直径之差）。

[问题]

1. What's the function of the crankshaft?
2. What are the main characteristics of the bearing inserts?
3. What kinds of materials are used in the piston?
4. What are the main purposes of the piston ring?

Lesson 4

Valve Mechanisms
气门机构

Valve mechanisms vary depending on the camshaft location. When the camshaft is positioned in the engine block, valve lifters are mounted in openings above the camshaft. Pushrods are connected from each valve lifter to a pivoted rocker arm mounted above each valve. A lobe on the camshaft is positioned directly below each valve lifter. A typical camshaft drive has a sprocket bolted to the end of the camshaft, and a matching sprocket is attached to the end of the crankshaft. These two sprockets may be meshed together or surrounded a steel chain to have the camshaft drive. When the lower part of the camshaft lobe is rotating under the valve lifter, the valve spring holds the valve closed, See Figure 4-1.

4.1 The Principle of Camshaft and Valve Operation 凸轮轴和气门工作原理

On the intake stroke, the high point on the camshaft lobe rotates under the valve lifter, which forces the lifter and pushrod upward. This action moves the outer end of the pushrod upward.

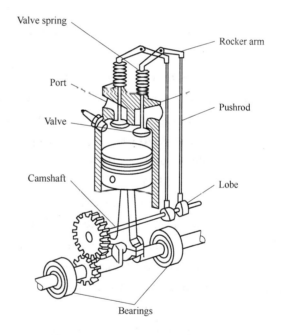

Figure 4-1 Parts of the valve train

Since the rocker arm is mounted on a pivot, the inner end of the rocker arm moves downward and opens the intake valve. When the lower part of the camshaft lobe moves under the valve lifter, the valve spring closes the valve, and the pushrod and valve lifter move downward. During the intake stroke, the crankshaft completed one-half a revolution, while the camshaft rotated one-quarter revolution.

During the compression stroke, both camshaft lobes are positioned with the lower part of the lobes under the valve lifters, and the valves remain closed. During the compression stroke, the crankshaft rotates for one-half revolution while the camshaft turns one-quarter revolution. On the power stroke, both valves remain closed until the piston is near BDC, and then the camshaft lobe opens the exhaust valve. On the power stroke, the crankshaft turns another half revolution, and the camshaft rotates one quarter revolution. The exhaust valve remains open as the piston moves upward on the exhaust stroke.

A few degrees before the piston reaches TDC on the exhaust stroke, the camshaft lobe opens the intake valve. When the piston is a few degrees after TDC on the exhaust stroke, the camshaft lobe closes the exhaust valve. During the exhaust stroke, the crankshaft completes another half turn, and the camshaft rotates one-quarter revolution.

Since the crankshaft rotates two revolutions to complete the four-stroke cycle, and the camshaft completes one revolution during this cycle, the crankshaft rotates at twice the speed of the camshaft. The crankshaft and camshaft sprockets are designed to provide the proper gear ratio and shaft speeds. The camshaft lobes are designed to open and close the valves at the correct crankshaft position. Camshaft lobes are also designed to provide the correct amount of valve lift, or opening, and these lobes also keep the valves open for the correct number of crankshaft degrees.

4.2 Camshaft Location 凸轮轴位置

Flathead or Side Valve. In some engines, the camshaft and valves are mounted in the block, and the end of each valve stem contacts a camshaft lobe. This type of engine may be referred to as a flathead, or side valve, engine. This engine design is not widely used at present.

Overhead Valve (OHV). In other engines, the camshaft and valve lifters are positioned in the block and the valves are mounted in the cylinder head. Pushrods are connected from each valve lifter to the pivoted rocker arms in the cylinder head. One end of the rocker arm contacts the valve stem, and the pushrod is mounted in a recess in the opposite end of the rocker arm. When the valves are mounted in the cylinder head, the engine is called an overhead valve (OHV) engine. In an OHV engine, a sprocket is bolted to the camshaft and another sprocket is pressed onto the crankshaft. A steel chain surrounds both sprockets to provide the camshaft drive.

Overhead Cam (OHC). In many modern automotive engines, the camshaft is mounted in or on the cylinder head. Camshaft followers, or lash adjusters, are mounted in one end of the rocker arms, which contact the valve stems. The opposite end of each rocker arm contacts the camshaft. In many OHC engines, the camshaft sprocket is driven by a cogged belt which surrounds the camshaft and crankshaft sprockets. A steel chain replaces the cogged belt in some OHC engines.

4.3 Camshafts 凸轮轴

Many camshafts are made from a hardened cast iron alloy. Hollow steel camshafts are now used in some engines. A lobe is positioned on the camshaft for each valve in the engine. The camshaft changes the rotary motion of this shaft to reciprocating motion of the valves. If the camshaft is mounted in the engine block, a valve lifter is positioned in a lifter bore directly above each camshaft lobe. A pushrod is located between the valve lifter and the pivoted rocker arm mounted on the cylinder head. The outer end of the rocker arm contacts the top of the valve stem. The valve spring holds the valve closed when the lowest part of the camshaft lobe is under the valve lifter. When the high part of the cam lobe moves under the valve lifter, the valve is opened by upward valve lifter movement and the action of the rocker arm.

Each cam lobe is positioned on the shaft so the lobe opens the valve at the proper time in relation to crankshaft rotation. Marks on the camshaft and crankshaft sprockets must be properly aligned before the timing chain is installed to time the camshaft in relation to the crankshaft.

Many overhead camshafts are mounted above the rocker arms in the cylinder head. These camshafts are usually driven by a cogged belt surrounding the crankshaft and camshaft sprockets. The timing marks on the camshaft sprocket must be aligned according to the manufacturer's recommended procedure prior to belt installation.

4.4　Valve Lifters 气门挺杆

A spring-loaded movable plunger is positioned in each valve lifter with a precision fit between the outer surface of this plunger and the lifter body. A check ball is located in the bottom of the lifter plunger. Since the bottom of the lifter is slightly convex, the lifter rotates as it contacts the camshaft lobe.

If the valve is closed, oil flows from the passage in the lifter bore through openings in the side of the lifter, and past the check ball into the lifter chamber under the plunger. Oil also flows through the opening in the cup on top of the lifter. This oil flows through the hollow pushrod to the rocker arm. As the higher part of the cam lobe moves under the lifter, the pushrod forces the plunger downward and seats the check ball. This action traps the oil under the plunger. Under this condition, the lifter body and plunger are forced upward to open the valve. The valve lifter maintains zero clearance between the rocker arm and the top of the valve stem.

4.5　Pushrods 推杆

In many engines with the camshaft mounted in the block, the pushrods are made from hollow steel. Each end of the pushrod has a round tip. The lower pushrod tip fits into the valve lifter cup, and the upper pushrod tip is located in a rocker arm recess.

4.6　Rocker Arms 摇臂

Rocker arms are usually manufactured from stamped steel or hardened iron alloy.

Some engines have individually mounted rocker arms, with each rocker arm mounted on a stud with a pivot and nut. On these rocker arms, the nut may be rotated to adjust the rocker arm.

[词汇]

mechanism	*n.* 机械装置，机构，机制	follower	*n.* 从动轮，随动机构
camshaft	*n.* 凸轮轴	lash	*n.* 间隙
block	*n.* 气缸体	adjuster	*n.* 调整，调节器，调整工
lifter	*n.* 挺杆	cogged	*adj.* 齿轮的，作弊的，骗人的
pushrod	推杆	reciprocate	*vt.* 往复，互给
rocker arm	*n.* 摇臂	timing	*n.* 定时，校时，计时
lobe	*n.* 凸角	mark	*n.* 标记，大潮水位标记，痕迹
sprocket	*n.* 链轮	plunger	*n.* 柱塞
chain	*n.* 链（条）	convex	*adj.* 表面弯曲如球的外侧，凸起的
intake	*n.* 进气，吸气，引入量		
stroke	*n.* 冲程，闪击	opening	*n.* 开度，开口
exhaust	*n.* 排气	recess	*n.* 凹座，凹穴，凹处
flathead	*n.* 扁平头；*adj.* 扁平头的	stud	*n.* 大头钉，纽扣，饰纽，柱头螺栓
stem	*n.* 杆，棒，柱		
overhead	顶置		

[注释]

1. Cogged belt   正时传动带：带齿的橡胶正时传动带。
2. A hardened cast iron alloy   淬火的合金铸铁

[问题]

1. How many components are there in valve mechanism?
2. How do the valves operate?
3. What's OHV?
4. What's the function of the camshaft?

Lesson 5

The Fuel Delivery System
燃料供给系统

The fuel delivery system consists of all the components which supply the engine with fuel. It includes the tank, all the lines, one or more fuel filters, a fuel pump (mechanical or electric), and the fuel metering components (carburetor or fuel injection system). (See Figure 5-1).

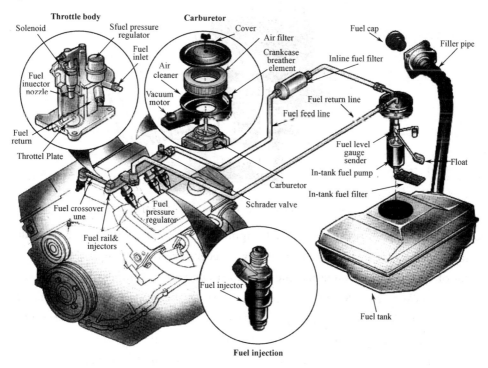

Figure 5-1　The engine fuel supply system

5.1　Fuel tank 油箱

Fuel tanks are normally located at the rear of the vehicle, although on rear or mid engine vehicles they are usually located at the front. The tank contains a fuel gauge sending unit, a filler tube and on most fuel injected vehicles, a fuel pump. In most tanks, there is also a fine mesh screen "sock" attached to the pickup tube. This is used to filter out large particles which could easily clog the fuel lines, fuel pump and fuel filter.

Since the advent of emission controls, tanks are equipped with a control system to prevent fuel vapor from being discharged into the atmosphere. A vent line in the tank is connected to an activated carbon or charcoal filled canister in the engine compartment. Vapors from the tank are stored in this canister, until they can be purged later for combustion in the engine. On many carbureted engines, the float bowl is also vented to this canister.

5.2 Fuel pumps 油泵

5.2.1 Mechanical pumps 机械泵

Mechanical pumps are usually found on carbureted engines or on engines that utilize a mechanical fuel injection system. (See Figure 5-2).

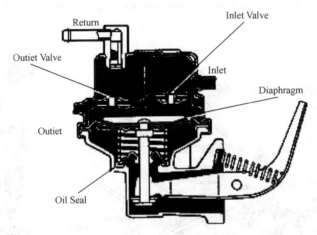

Figure 5-2 Cutaway view of a common mechanical fuel pump

Mechanical fuel pumps on carbureted engines are usually mounted on the side of the engine block or cylinder head and operated by an eccentric on the engine's camshaft. The rocker arm of the pump rests against the camshaft eccentric, and as the camshaft rotates, it actuates the rocker arm. Some engines use a pushrod between the rocker arm and camshaft eccentric. Inside the fuel pump, the rocker arm is connected to a flexible diaphragm. A spring, mounted underneath, maintains pressure on the diaphragm. As the rocker arm is actuated, it pulls the diaphragm down and then releases it. Once the diaphragm is released, the spring pushes it back up. This continual diaphragm motion causes a partial vacuum and pressure in the space above the diaphragm. The vacuum draws the fuel from the tank and the pressure pushes it toward the carburetor or injection pump. A check valve is used in the pump to prevent fuel from being pumped back into the tank.

Certain mechanical fuel injection systems also utilize a mechanical fuel pump, typically some diesel engines and early gasoline fuel injection systems. Many of them use a fuel pump essentially identical to the carbureted fuel system's. Some, however, use a vane type fuel pump mounted directly to the injection pump/fuel distributor assembly. The injection pump/fuel distributor assembly is driven by the timing belt, chain or gears which in turn drives the fuel pump. The vanes draw the fuel in through the inlet port then squeeze the fuel into a tight passage. The fuel then exits pressurized through the outlet port.

5.2.2　Electric pumps 电动泵

There are two general types of electric fuel pumps: the impeller type and the bellows type. Electric pumps can be found on all types of fuel systems.

The impeller type pump uses a vane or impeller that is driven by an electric motor. These pumps are often mounted in the fuel tank, though they are sometimes found below or beside the tank. The vanes or impeller draw the fuel in through the inlet port then squeeze the fuel into a tight passage. This pressurizes the fuel. The pressurized fuel then exits through the outlet port.

The bellows type pump is rare. This pump is ordinarily mounted in the engine compartment and contains a flexible metal bellows operated by an electromagnet. As the electromagnet is energized, it pulls the metal bellows up. This draws the fuel from the tank into the pump. When the electromagnet is de-energized, the bellows returns to its original position. A check valve closes to prevent the fuel from returning to the tank. The only place for the fuel to go now is through the outlet port.

5.3　Fuel filters 燃油滤清器

In addition to the mesh screen attached to the pickup tube, all fuel systems have at least one other filter located somewhere between the fuel tank and the fuel metering components. On some models, the filter is part of the fuel pump itself, on others, it is located in the fuel line, and still others locate the filter at the carburetor or throttle body inlet.

5.3.1　Inline and spin-on filters 串联旋装式滤清器

Inline and spin-on filters are located between the fuel pump and fuel metering components. They are connected to fuel lines either by clamps, banjo bolts, flare fittings or quick-disconnect fittings. Most are "throw-away" units with a paper element encased in a housing. Some have a clear plastic housing that allows you to view the amount of dirt trapped in the filter. Some filters consist of a replaceable pleated paper cartridge installed in a permanent filter housing. Their use is limited mostly to diesel and heavy-duty gasoline engines. (See Figure 5-3).

5.3.2　Carburetor/Throttle Body Inlet Filters 化油器/节气门体进口滤清器

Fuel filters can also be located in the carburetor or throttle body inlet.

For carburetors, they consist of a small paper or bronze filter that is installed in the inlet housing. They are extremely simple in design and are about as efficient as an inline type. The bronze filter is the least common and must be installed with the small cone section facing out. One type is held in place by a threaded metal cap that attaches to the fuel line and screws into the carburetor fuel inlet. On another type, the fuel filter threads directly into the carburetor.

On throttle body units, these filters are used as a supplement to the primary inline filter. They usually consist of a conical screen, similar in appearance to an air conditioning orifice tube. They can be accessed after removing the fuel line from the throttle body unit.

5.3.3 Fuel/water separator 油水分离器

This is usually found on diesel cars and trucks. It can either be part of the fuel filter housing or it can be a separate remote unit all together. Most operate as a two-stage filter. The lower stage removes dirt particles down to about 1 micron in size and allows the water to form large droplets. In the second stage, fuel freely passes through the filter, but water will not. Water collects in the bottom of the filter housing, and a drain plug on the bottom of the housing is usually provided. (See Figure 5-4).

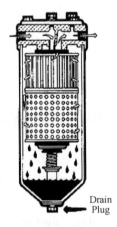

Figure 5-3　Some spin-on type filters have a replaceable cartridge

Figure 5-4　Some fuel/water separators are part of the filter housing assembly

The separate units are usually mounted next to the fuel tank. They collect water as it settles out of the fuel tank. Some may light a warning lamp on the dash when it requires draining.

[词汇]

filter	n.过滤器，滤光器，筛选	activated	adj.有活性的
metering	n.测量，计量，记录	carbon	n.碳，碳素
carburetor	n.化油器，汽化器	charcoal	n.木炭，活性炭，炭
injection	n.注射，喷射	canister	n.罐，金属罐，金属容器，滤毒罐
gauge	n.规，表，计		
mesh	n.网孔，网丝，网眼，圈套，陷阱，[机]啮合	float bowl	浮子室
		eccentric	n.偏心轮
screen	n.滤网	flexible	adj.挠曲的，可曲的，柔性的，韧性的，可弯曲的
advent	n.（尤指不寻常的人或事）出现，到来	diaphragm	n.薄膜，膜片
vent	n.通风孔，出口，开缝，出口，通风孔，通路	check valve	单向阀，止回阀
		vane	n.翼，叶片，风标

distributor	n. 分电器，配电器	encase	vt. 装入，包住，围
impeller	n. 叶轮，转轮，桨叶	pleat	vt. 使…打褶
bellows	n. 波纹管，波形膜，风箱	cartridge	n. 芯
electromagnet	n. 电磁铁	housing	n. 壳体
de-energize	vt. 断电，断开，关断	conical	adj. 圆锥的，圆锥形的
spin-on filter	旋装式机油滤清器	supplement	n. 补充，增补，添加物
banjo	n. 整体式，班卓琴，五弦琴	separator	n. 隔板，分离器，分离装置
flare	n. 喇叭管，端部斜展，锥度	droplet	n. 小滴，微滴
fitting	n. 装配，配件，接头		

[注释]

1. Impeller 驱动叶轮：用作离心泵的旋转元件，将机械能量转化为流体能量。
2. Separator 分离器：将流体中悬浮粒子分离出的装置，如将水从燃油或润滑油中分离出来的油水分离器。

[问题]

1. What are the main parts of the fuel delivery system?
2. How does the mechanical pump operate?
3. What kinds of filters are there in the engines?
4. How many types of feedback carburetors are there in automotive engines?

Lesson 6

Fuel Injection System
燃油喷射系统

6.1 General information 概述

Fuel injection systems have been used on vehicles for many years. The earliest ones were purely mechanical. As technology advanced, electronic fuel injection systems became more popular. Early mechanical and electronic fuel injection systems did not use feedback controls. As emissions became more of a concern, feedback controls were adapted to both types of fuel injection systems. Both mechanical and electronic fuel injection systems can be found on gasoline engines.

6.2 Multi-port fuel injections 多点燃油喷射

This is the most common type of fuel injection system found today. Regardless of the manufacturer, they all function in the same basic way. On these systems an equal amount of fuel is delivered to each cylinder. (See Figure 6-1).

These systems all use sensors which transmit operating conditions to the computer. Information from these sensors is processed by the computer which then determines the proper air/fuel mixture. This signal is sent to the fuel injectors which open and inject fuel into their ports. The longer the injector is held open, the richer the fuel mixture will be. Most fuel injection systems need the following information to operate properly:

Temperature sensors - this includes both air and coolant temperature. The computer determines how rich or lean the mixture should be. The colder the temperature, the richer the mixture.

Throttle position sensors or switches - the computer uses this information to determine the position of the throttle valve(s). Some vehicles use sensors which relay the exact position of the throttle valve(s) at all times. Others use switches which only relay closed and wide-open throttle positions (some may also use a mid-throttle switch). These switches and sensors help determine engine load.

Airflow sensors - these sensors also help the computer determine engine load by indicating the amount of air entering the engine. There are several different types of airflow sensors, but in the end, they all do the same job.

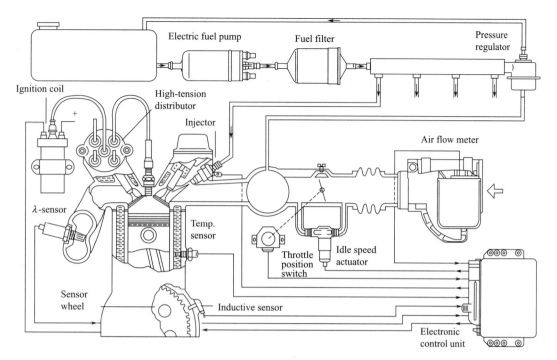

Figure 6-1 Common multi-point fuel injection system components

Manifold pressure sensors - if a vehicle is not equipped with an airflow sensor, it uses a manifold pressure sensor to determine engine load (Note that some vehicles with an airflow sensor may also have a manifold pressure sensor. This is used as a fail-safe if the airflow sensor fails). As engine load increases, so does intake manifold air pressure.

Engine speed and position sensors - engine speed/position sensors can be referenced from the crankshaft, camshaft or both. In addition to helping determine engine load, these sensors also tell the computer when the injectors should be fired.

These systems operate at a relatively high pressure (usually at least 30 psi). To control the fuel pressure, a fuel pressure regulator is used. As engine load increases, more fuel pressure is needed. This is due to the richer mixture (more fuel needed) and to overcome the increased air pressure in the ports. Any unused fuel is diverted back to the fuel tank using a return line.

The fuel injectors can be fired as a batch, a bank or sequentially. On batch fire systems, all of the injectors are fired simultaneously, usually at top dead center of the compression stroke for cylinder number one. Bank fire systems are divided into two separate injector banks. The first bank fires when cylinder number one is at top dead center of the compression stroke. The second bank is usually fired when the number one cylinder is at top dead center of the exhaust stroke. On sequential systems, each injector is fired as its cylinder is at top dead center of its compression stroke. This tends to be the most fuel efficient system.

Feedback fuel injection systems use an oxygen sensor to precisely monitor the air/fuel mixture. Using the signal generated by the oxygen sensor, the computer varies the pulse width of the fuel injectors. The longer the injector on time (longer pulse width), the richer the fuel mixture.

6.3 Central multi-port injection 中央式多点喷射

This system is very similar to the standard multi-port injection system. The main difference lies in the location and construction of the fuel injector(s). Instead of an injector positioned at each intake manifold port, the injector(s) is centrally located in the intake manifold plenum assembly (hence named central multi-port).

The main component of the system is the fuel meter body. This houses the fuel injector(s), pressure regulator and poppet nozzle/hose assemblies. A hose with a poppet valve extends from the bottom of the fuel injector(s). These hoses are routed to the individual cylinders. The poppet valves handle the atomization of the fuel rather the injector itself as in standard multi-port systems.

Early systems use one fuel injector for all the cylinders and is batch fired. Later systems use an injector for each cylinder and are fired sequentially.

6.4 Throttle body injection 节气门体喷射

The appearance of throttle body injection system is similar to the carbureted fuel system. Although not as efficient as multi-port systems, it does offer better driveability and lower emissions than carbureted systems. (See Figure 6-2).

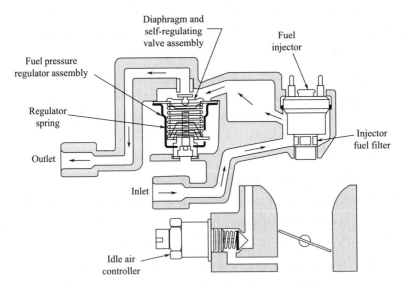

Figure 6-2 Common throttle body injection system operation

The fuel injector(s) are mounted vertically above the throttle plate(s). The throttle body assembly also houses the fuel pressure regulator. These systems typically run at lower pressure compared to multi-port systems. This is mostly due to the fact that pressure in the intake manifold does not have to be overcome. Since the injector (s) is mounted above the throttle plate, fuel is actually drawn into the intake system. Other than this, the actual operation of the throttle body injection system is similar to the multi-port system.

6.5 CIS System 连续燃油喷射系统

The Continuous Injection System (CIS) is an independent mechanical system. The basic operating principle is to continuously inject fuel into the intake side of the engine by means of an electric pump. The amount of fuel delivered is metered by an airflow measuring device. Some CIS systems are feedback controlled. (See Figure 6-3).

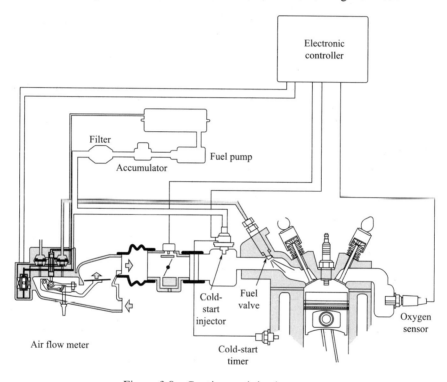

Figure 6-3 Continuous injection system

[词汇]

fuel injection system	燃油喷射系统	mixture	n.混合物，混合气
feedback	n.反馈	throttle valve	节气门
emission	n.发射，排放	relay	n.继电器，中继
multi-port fuel injection	多点燃油喷射	airflow sensor	空气流量传感器
sensor	n.传感器	manifold pressure sensor	歧管压力传感器
injector	n.喷射头，喷油器，喷注器	fail-safe	失效保护
		crankshaft	n.曲轴
port	n.口，港，汽门，港口，水门，左舷，舱门	camshaft	n.凸轮轴
		psi	磅每平方英寸
		regulator	n.调节器，调压器

batch	*n.* 成批，一批，程序组	plenum	*n.* 充实，送气通风，压力通风系统
bank	*n.* 气缸侧体	poppet	*n.* 菌状活门
sequentially	*adv.* 顺序地，序贯地	atomization	*n.* 雾化
stroke	*n.* 冲程，打击	driveability	*n.*（汽车的）驾驶性能，操纵性能，操纵灵活性
top dead center	上止点		
oxygen sensor	氧传感器		
pulse width	脉冲宽度	continuous injection system	连续喷射系统

[注释]

  Fuel injection system　燃油喷射系统：通过位于各部位的传感器，将所采集到的信息反馈输入到一个微电脑中进行处理，并由它发出指令来控制混合气中空气与燃油的比例，使所供给的混合气能适应发动机在各种工况的需要。

[问题]

1. How does the fuel injection system work?
2. What kind of sensors has the fuel injection system?
3. What's the central multi-port injection?
4. How is the fuel injection system classified?

Lesson 7

Gasoline Direct Injection
汽油缸内直喷

Several vehicle manufacturers such as Audi, Mitsubishi, Mercedes, BMW, Toyota/Lexus, Mazda, Ford, and General Motors are using gasoline direct injection (GDI) systems, which General Motors refers to as a Spark Ignition Direct Injection (SIDI) system. A direct injection system sprays high-pressure fuel, up to 2,900 PSI, into the combustion chamber as the piston approaches the top of the compression stroke. With the combination of high-pressure swirl injectors and modified combustion chamber, almost instantaneous vaporization of the fuel occurs. This combined with a higher compression ratio allows a direct-injected engine to operate using a leaner-than-normal air-fuel ratio, which results in improved fuel economy with higher power output and reduced exhaust emissions. See figure 7-1.

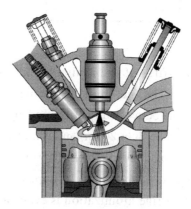

Figure 7-1 A gasoline direct-injection system injects fuel under high pressure directly into the combustion chamber

Bosch's high-pressure injection system for gasoline engines is based on a pressure reservoir and a fuel rail, which a high-pressure pump charges to a regulated pressure of up to 120 bar. The fuel can therefore be injected directly into the combustion chamber via electromagnetic injectors (Figure 7-2).

The air mass drawn in is adjusted through an electronically controlled throttle valve and is measured with the help of an air mass meter. For mixture control, a wide-band oxygen sensor is used in the exhaust, before the catalytic converters. This sensor can measure a range between $\lambda = 0.8$ and infinity. The electronic engine control unit regulates the operating modes of the engine with gasoline direct injection in three ways:

- stratified charge operation-with λ values greater than 1.
- homogeneous operation-at $\lambda = 1$.
- rich homogeneous operation-with $\lambda = 0.8$.

Compared to the traditional manifold injection system, the entire fuel amount must be injected in full-load operation in a quarter of the time. The available time is significantly shorter during stratified charge operation in part-load. Especially at idle, injection times of less than 0.5 milliseconds are required owing to the lower fuel consumption. This is only

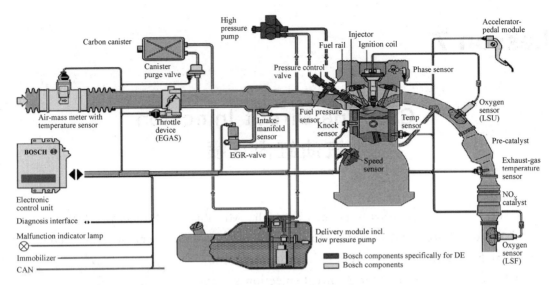

Figure 7-2 Bosch DI-Motronic

one-fifth of the available time for manifold injection.

The fuel must be atomized very finely to create an optimal mixture in the brief moment between injection and ignition. The fuel droplets for direct injection are on average smaller than 20μm (micrometres, i. e. a millionth of a metre). This is one-fifth of the droplet size reached with the traditional manifold injection and one-third of the diameter of a single human hair. It improves efficiency considerably. However, even more important than fine atomization is even fuel distribution in the injection beam. This is done to achieve fast and uniform combustion.

Conventional spark ignition engines have a homogeneous (well mixed up!) air/fuel mixture at a 14.7 : 1 ratio, corresponding to a value of $\lambda = 1$. Direct injection engines, however, operate according to the stratified charge concept in the part-load range and function with high excess air. In return, very low fuel consumption is achieved.

Fuel injection just before the ignition point and injection directly into the combustion chamber is to create a stratified (layered) mode (Figure 7-3). The result is a combustible

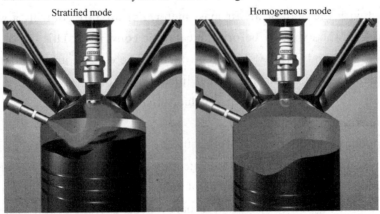

Figure 7-3 Operating modes

air/fuel mixture cloud on the spark plug, cushioned in a thermally insulated layer, composed of air and residual gas. This raises the efficiency level because heat loss is avoided on the combustion chamber walls. The engine operates with an almost completely opened throttle valve, which avoids additional charge losses.

With stratified charge operation, the lambda value in the combustion chamber is between about 1.5 and 3. In the part-load range, gasoline direct injection achieves the greatest fuel savings, with up to 40% at idle compared to conventional gasoline injection processes.

With increasing engine load, and therefore increasing injection quantities, the stratified charge cloud becomes even richer and emission characteristics become worse. As in diesel engine combustion, soot may form. In order to prevent this, the DI-Motronic engine control converts to a homogeneous cylinder charge at a predefined engine load. The system injects very early during the intake process to achieve a good mixture of fuel and air at a ratio of $\lambda = 1$.

As is the case for conventional manifold injection systems, the amount of air drawn in for all operating modes is adjusted through the throttle valve according to the desired torque specified by the driver. The Motronic ECU calculates the amount of fuel to be injected from the drawn-in air mass and performs an additional correction via lambda control. In this mode of operation, a torque increase of up to 5% is possible. Both the thermodynamic cooling effect of the fuel vaporizing directly in the combustion chamber and the higher compression of the engine with gasoline direct injection play a role in this.

For these different operating modes, two central demands are raised for engine control:

- The injection point must be adjustable between 'late' (during the compression phase) and 'early' (during the intake phase) depending on the operating point.
- The adjustment for the drawn-in air mass must be detached from the throttle pedal position to permit unthrottled engine operation in the lower load range.

However, throttle control in the upper load range must also be permitted. With optimal use of the advantages, the average fuel saving is up to 15%. In stratified charge operation the nitrogen oxides (NO_x) segments in the very lean exhaust cannot be reduced by a conventional, three-way catalytic converter. The NO_x can be reduced by approximately 70% through exhaust returns before the catalytic converter. However, this is not enough to fulfil the ambitious emission limits of the future. Therefore, emissions containing NO_x must undergo special treatment. Engine designers are using an additional NO_x accumulator catalytic converter in the

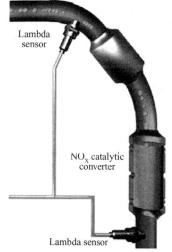

Figure 7-4 NO_x catalytic converter

exhaust system (Figure 7-4). The NO$_x$ is deposited in the form of nitrates on the converter surface, with the oxygen still contained in the lean exhaust.

The capacity of the NO$_x$ accumulator catalytic converter is limited. As soon as it is exhausted, the catalytic converter must be regenerated. To remove the deposited nitrates, the DI-Motronic briefly changes over to its third operating mode (rich homogeneous operation with lambda values of about 0.8). The nitrate together with the carbon monoxide is reduced in the exhaust to non-harmful nitrogen and oxygen. When the engine operates in this range, the engine torque is adjusted according to the accelerator pedal position via the throttle valve opening. Engine management has the difficult task of changing between the two different operating modes, in a fraction of a second, in a way not noticeable to the driver.

The continuing challenge, set by legislation, is to reduce vehicle emissions to very low levels. Bosch is a key player in the development of engine management systems. The DI-Motronic system, which is now used by many manufacturers, continues to reflect the good name of the company.

[词汇]

PSI	abbr. 磅/平方英寸（pounds per square inch）	droplet	n. 小滴，微滴；小水珠
swirl	n. 漩涡	combustible	adj. 易燃的，可燃的
vaporization	n. 蒸发；汽化	thermally	adv. 热地
pressure reservoir	蓄压器	soot	n. 煤烟，烟灰
fuel rail	燃油分配管，燃油轨	detach	vt. 分离；派遣；使超然
catalytic converter	催化转化器	segments	n. 段，节；部分
homogeneous	adj. 均质的，均匀的	ambitious	adj. 有雄心的；有野心的；有抱负的；炫耀的
manifold	n. 歧管	accumulator	n. 蓄能器；储能器；蓄压器
atomize	v. 将…喷成雾状	nitrogen	n. 氮
micrometer	n. 微米，百万分之一米（长度单位，符号为 μm）	nitrate	n. 硝酸盐
		monoxide	n. 一氧化物
millionth	adj. 百万分之一的；第一百万的	stratified charge	层状充气

[注释]

1. Gasoline Direct Injection (GDI) 汽油缸内直喷：类似于柴油发动机的供油技术，通过一个活塞泵提供所需100bar以上的压力，将汽油提供给位于汽缸内的电磁喷射器。GDI技术采用了两种不同的注油模式，即分层注油和均匀注油模式

2. λ 读作"lamda"，表示实际空燃比除以理想空燃比得出的比值，小于1表示混合气浓，燃油过量；大于1表示混合气稀，空气过量。

3. DI-Motronic 德国博世（Bosch）公司的汽油直喷系统：由高压油泵、高压油轨、高压喷油器、高压压力传感器、电控单元等组成。

[问题]

1. What is the main difference between the gasoline direct injection and diesel fuel injection?

2. Why the NO_x catalytic converter is needed in the gasoline direct injection?

3. What are the advantages of the gasoline direct injection?

4. Please describe the main components of the DI-Motronic system.

Lesson 8

The Cooling System
冷却系统

8.1 Introduction 引言

Your engine needs a cooling system to protect it from self-destruction. Burning gases inside the cylinders can reach a temperature of 4500°F (2500°C) and produce enough heat to melt a 200 lb. engine block.

About one-third of the heat produced in the engine must be carried away by the cooling system. Some is utilized for heating the passenger compartment. Moreover, strange as it seems, your vehicle's air conditioner produces heat in the process of cooling and dehumidifying the air. This heat must also be dispersed by the cooling system.

8.2 How does the cooling system work 冷却系统如何工作

The main parts of the engine cooling system are the radiator, pressure cap, hoses, thermostat, water pump, fan, and fan belt (except on electric fan engines). See Figure 8-1. The system is filled with coolant, which should be a 50-50 mixture of antifreeze and water. No matter where you live or how hot or cold the weather becomes, the mixture should be maintained the year around.

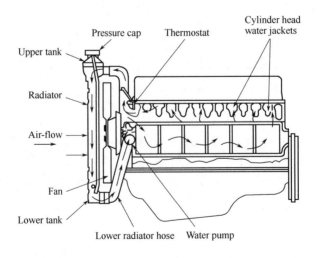

Figure 8-1 Parts of the coolig system

The water pump and engine cooling fan are mounted on the same shaft and driven by a belt connected to the engine. The pump draws coolant from the bottom of the radiator and forces it through passages surrounding the hot area——the cylinders, combustion chambers, valves and spark plugs. From there the coolant flows through a hose into the top of the radiator, then downward through tubes attached to cooling fins and surrounded by air passages. Heat is transferred from the coolant to air forced through the radiator passages by the fan and the forward motion of the vehicle.

8.3　Controlling the temperature 控制温度

It's important to get the coolant up to normal operating temperature as quickly as possible to ensure smooth engine operation, free flow of oil, and ample heat for the occupants. When the engine is cold, the thermostat blocks the passage from the cylinder head to the radiator and sends coolant on a shortcut to the water pump. The cooling fluid is not exposed to the blast of air from the radiator, so it warms up rapidly. As temperature increases, the thermostat gradually opens and allows coolant to flow through the radiator.

Cooling systems on older vehicles were limited to a maximum temperature of 212℉ (100℃)——the boiling point of water. To get rid of the extra heat generated by more powerful engines, automatic transmissions, and air conditioning, modern vehicles have pressurized systems using a 50-50 mixture of antifreeze and water which enables them to operate at temperatures up to 263℉ (129.4℃) without boiling. At this temperature, plain water alone would boil away.

8.4　Transmission oil cooler 变速器油冷却器

Automatic transmission oil is cooled by a small, separate radiator, usually located in the lower tank or alongside the main radiator. While the only purpose of the engine coolant is to keep the block and upper engine components cool, the transmission oil has three functions. It hydraulically operates the transmission, lubricates the transmission internal components and also keeps the transmission within proper operating temperature range.

Most vehicles can benefit from the installation of a transmission oil cooler, especially if the vehicle is used to pull a trailer or for some other kind of heavy service.

8.5　Engine oil cooler 发动机机油冷却器

Some vehicles, particularly high performance or diesel engines, are equipped with an engine oil cooler. The oil cooler can be located in one of the radiator tanks (similar to the transmission oil cooler), or mounted separately, near the front of the engine, on aftermarket applications. Also, there is usually an adapter mounted between the engine block and the oil filter. If the cooler is mounted in a radiator tank, heat is dissipated from the oil to the coolant. A separate oil cooler usually looks like a small radiator and heat is dispersed from the tubes and fins in the cooler to the air passing through the cooler. The purpose of the cooler is to reduce the temperature of the oil, preventing oxidation and increasing the oil's lubricating and protecting properties.

8.6　Electric cooling fans　电动风扇

Many late model vehicles are equipped with an electric cooling fan or an auxiliary electric cooling fan. These fans are usually operated by a thermostatically controlled switch located in the cylinder head, radiator tank, or intake manifold. When the thermostatic switch reaches a specified temperature, the contacts close providing current to the motor. As the temperature lowers to the specified range, the contacts open thus shutting off the cooling fan. (See Figure 8-2).

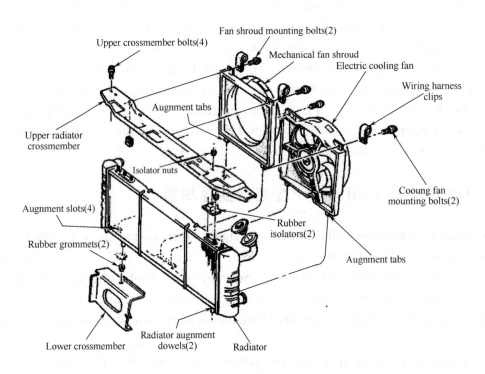

Figure 8-2　Typical auxiliary electric cooling fan mounted next to a mechanical fan

The thermostatic switches may be used to complete the ground side of the fan motor, they may trigger a relay to provide power to the fan motor, or they may send a signal to a computer to energize the fan motor.

On some air conditioner equipped vehicles, the fan motor is energized at all times the air conditioner is operating. This increases the airflow through the air conditioning condenser and the radiator.

[词汇]

cooling system	冷却系统	warm up	暖机
self-destruction	自毁	automatic transmission	自动变速器
passenger compartment	乘客室	trailer	n.挂车,全挂车,拖车
air conditioner	空调器	oil cooler	机油冷却器
dehumidify	vt.除湿,使干燥	aftermarket	n.贩卖修理用零件的市场
disperse	v.(使)分散,(使)散开,疏散	adapter	n.接头
radiator	n.散热器,水箱	fin	n.散热片,鳍状物,稳定器叶片,稳定筋,稳流筋,翅
pressure cap	压力式盖		
hose	n.软管		
thermostat	n.节温器,恒温器	oxidation	n.氧化
water pump	n.水泵,抽水机	thermostatically	adv.热静力学的
fan	n.风扇,风车	thermostatic	n.恒温的
belt	n.带,皮带	trigger	vt.引发,引起,触发
coolant	n.冷却液	relay	n.继电器
antifreeze	n.防冻剂	energize	vt.使活跃,加强,给予...电压
ample	adj.充足的,丰富的		
shortcut	n.捷径	condenser	n.冷凝器,电容器
blast	n.一阵(风),一股(气流),爆炸,冲击波	air conditioning	空调

[注释]

1. Radiator 散热器:用于冷却从水套流出来的热水。
2. Thermostat 节温器:用于改变冷却液的流量和循环路线。

[问题]

1. What's the purpose of the cooling system?
2. How does the cooling system work?
3. How many components are there in the cooling system?
4. How is the electric fan driven?

Lesson 9

The Lubrication System
润滑系统

9.1 The Basics 基础

The engine lubrication system supplies oil to all the friction surfaces between the engine moving parts. If the lubrication system did not supply these moving components with oil, friction would quickly destroy these surfaces. The oil reduces friction between moving components, which increases engine power and efficiency. Engine components are lubricated, cooled, cleaned, and sealed by the oil in the lubrication system. The oil also reduces wear on engine components to a minimum.

The purpose of the lubrication system is to circulate oil between moving engine parts. Oil between the parts prevents metal-to-metal contact, which causes friction and wear. The circulating oil has other important jobs. It carries heat away from engine parts, cleans engine parts, and helps the piston rings seal in compression pressures.

An oil pan is bolted to the bottom of the engine. The deep part of the oil pan houses an oil pump and pick-up screen. The pan also collects oil that runs off engine parts after lubrication. A plug in the bottom of the oil pan is used to drain the oil at required intervals.

Oil is circulated through the engine by an oil pump. Most oil pumps have two small gears that mesh with each other. A pressure-regulator valve in the pump is used to prevent the lubrication system from reaching too high a pressure. The oil pump pulls oil up from the oil pan through the pick-up screen. The screen collects any large particles of dirt so that the oil entering the pump is fairly clean. The pump then directs the oil through an oil filter, which strains any remaining dirt out of the oil; the oil entering the engine lubrication passages should be clean. The oil filter assembly is located on the outside of the cylinder block where it can be replaced easily. After the oil passes through the filter element, it reenters the engine block and is then circulated into the lubrication passages. The oil filter is equipped with a bypass valve assembly. The bypass valve is used to protect the engine from a clogged filter (See Figure 9-1).

When the oil leaves the filter assembly, it enters the passages in the cylinder block. These passageways, or main galleries, run the length of the cylinder block. Oil flows down from the main galleries to the crankshaft main bearings. It lubricates these and then flows through the hollow crankshaft, lubricating each of the connecting-rod bearings.

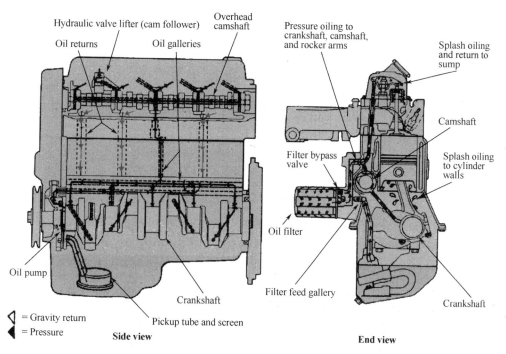

Figure 9-1 A typical engine design that uses both pressure and splash lubrication. Oil travels under pressure through the galleries (passages) to reach the top of the engine. Other parts are lubricated as the oil flows back down into the oil pan or is splashed onto parts.

Oil also travels up from the main gallery, through the block to the camshaft bearings, to each of the cam lobe areas, and into each of the valve lifters. It is routed through the lifters and up the hollow pushrods. Finally, it goes out the top of the pushrods, where it provides lubrication for the rocker arms and valve stems.

The rotating crankshaft throws off oil, which hits the cylinder wall. The piston and piston rings receive oil and distribute it over the cylinder wall for lubrication. This oil then runs back down into the oil pan to be used again.

9.2 Engine Oil 机油

Engine oil has several important jobs in the engine. First, it must be circulated between moving engine parts to prevent metal-to-metal contact. Without oil, metal-to-metal contact produces wear. Oil between moving parts allows them to move easily, with less friction. The lower the friction of an engine is, the more power it can develop.

The circulating oil also cools the engine by carrying heat away from hot engine components, and cleans or flushes dirt and deposits off the engine parts. Finally, oil circulated on the cylinder walls seals the rings, improving the engine's compression.

Friction is caused when two metal parts rub on each other. You could demonstrate friction if you were to push a wrench along a bench top. The resistance you feel is due to friction. The rougher the bench and the wrench surface, the greater the friction, because the two surfaces tend to lock together. If you use a heavier wrench, it takes even more effort to move it across the table. As the amount of pressure between two objects increases, their friction increases.

We want the friction between engine parts to be as low as possible. As you can see from our wrench example, friction takes power to overcome. The lower the friction between engine parts is, the more power an engine can develop. Friction between two objects also causes them to heat and to wear. You can demonstrate this by rubbing your hands together fast. The heat you feel is caused by the friction between the skin on your hands.

Engine oil is used to reduce friction on engine parts. Friction cannot be eliminated completely, but it can be reduced so that longer engine life may be expected. We can demonstrate this with our wrench example. If you were to pour oil on the bench top and try to push the wrench again you would see that the tool moves much more easily. The friction between the wrench and bench top has been reduced. The oil forms a thin layer, called a film, under the wrench that lifts it off the bench top surface.

An oil film is formed to prevent friction from metal-to-metal contact in an engine. A shaft is supported by a bearing. There is a small space, usually only 0.002~0.003 inch or 0.05~0.08 millimeter, between the bearing and shaft. Because this space is for the oil to flow, it is called the oil clearance. Oil is directed under pressure into the oil clearance area between the bearing and the shaft. The oil pressure and the rotation of the shaft cause a film of oil to wedge between shaft and bearing. The shaft is lifted slightly so that it rests on an oil film rather than on the bearing. When the oil film wedge is formed, there is no metal-to-metal contact. Oil is used in this way to reduce friction between all the moving parts in the engine.

9.3 Oil SAE Viscosity Ratings SAE 机油黏度等级

When you change or add oil to an engine you must select the type with the correct viscosity rating for the car you are working on. Viscosity is the thickness or thinness of a fluid. High viscosity fluids are thick and flow sluggishly. Thick pancake syrup is an example of a fluid with a high viscosity. Low viscosity fluids flow very freely. Oils used in engines must flow freely in cold conditions but have enough thickness during times of high temperature.

Viscosity ratings for oil are set up by the Society of Automotive Engineers (SAE). Thin oil gets a low viscosity number, like SAE 10, and thicker oil gets a higher number, like SAE 50. The viscosity number is printed on the side of the oil container. The owner's manual for the car specifies what viscosity should be used.

Say the viscosity of the oil is SAE 30. This oil has a single viscosity rating, so it is called a single viscosity oil. Other common single viscosity oils are SAE 10, SAE 20, SAE 40, and SAE 50. The higher the viscosity number, the better the protection when the engine is hot. The lower the number, the more freely the oil flows when the engine is cold.

Most newer cars require multiple viscosity oils. Multiple viscosity oil is rated by more than one viscosity number, as in SAE 10-40. This means it flows freely like SAE 10 when the weather is cold, but protects like SAE 40 when it is hot. An automobile operated in different climates needs multiple viscosity oil. A viscosity rating with a W after it, like SAE 20W, means the oil is rated for cold temperature operation.

9.4 Oil API Service Ratings API 机油使用等级

Engine oil is also rated by how well it holds up under severe service conditions in the engine. The service ratings are set up by the American Petroleum Institute (API). The car manufacturers determine which of these ratings are acceptable to meet their engine protection standards. The new car warranty can be considered void if a lower classification of oil is used.

[词汇]

lubrication	n. 润滑
efficiency	n. 效率，功效
minimum	n. 最小值，最小化
circulate	v. (使) 流通，(使) 运行，(使) 循环，(使) 传播
piston ring	活塞环
oil pan	油底壳
oil pump	机油泵
pick-up screen	集滤网
interval	n. 间隔，距离
pressure-regulator valve	压力调节阀
oil filter	机油滤清器
strain	vt. 过滤
cylinder block	缸体
filter element	滤芯
bypass valve	旁通阀
clog	v. 障碍，阻塞
passage	n. 通道，通路
passageway	n. 过道，出入口
main gallery	主油道
crankshaft	n. 曲轴
connecting-rod bearing	连杆轴承
lobe	n. 凸角
lifter	n. 挺杆
pushrod	n. 推杆
rocker arm	摇臂
stem	n. 杆
rub	v. 擦，摩擦
wrench	n. 扳钳，扳手
bench	n. 座，台，工作台，架，台座
wedge	n. 楔块，楔子板，斜铁
viscosity	n. 黏度
rating	n. 等级
sluggish	adj. 行动迟缓的
pancake	扁平形的，薄饼，渣饼
syrup	n. 糖浆，果汁
thickness	n. 厚度，浓度，稠密，(一) 层，浑浊
thinness	n. 瘦，稀，淡薄
Society of Automotive Engineer	汽车工程师学会
multiple viscosity	多黏度
the American Petroleum Institute	美国石油学会
warranty	n. 担保，保证，根据
void	n. 空间，空旷，空虚，怅惘
classification	n. 分类，分级

[注释]

Pick-up screen 集滤网：滤除较大的机械杂质，有浮式和固定式两种。

[问题]

1. What's the purpose of the lubrication system?
2. What are the main components of the lubrication system?
3. How does the oil circulate in engines?
4. What is the meaning of SAE 20W?

Lesson 10

Turbochargers and Superchargers
涡轮增压器和机械增压器

10.1 The Basics 基础

A turbocharger or supercharger may be used on a relatively small engine that provides adequate fuel economy when driven at normal cruising speeds. However, the turbocharger or supercharger increases engine power to provide the faster acceleration desired by the driver.

10.2 Turbocharger Principles 涡轮增压器原理

A turbocharger contains a turbine wheel and a compressor wheel mounted on a common shaft. (See Figure 10-1). This shaft is supported on bearings in the turbocharger housing, and both wheels contain blades. The exhaust gas from the cylinders is directed past the turbine wheel, and the force of the exhaust gas against the turbine wheel blades causes the turbine wheel and shaft to rotate. Since the compressor wheel is positioned on the opposite end of this shaft, the compressor wheel must rotate with the shaft.

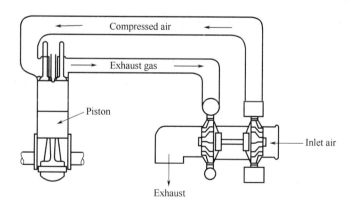

Figure 10-1 Basic turbocharger with turbine and compressor whells

The compressor wheel is mounted in the air intake, and as the compressor wheel rotates it forces air into the intake manifold. Since most turbocharged engines are port injected, the fuel is injected into the intake ports. The rotation of the compressor wheel compresses the air and fuel in the intake manifold, creating a denser air-fuel mixture. This increased intake manifold pressure forces more air-fuel mixture into the cylinders to provide increased engine power.

Turbocharger wheels rotate at very high speeds in excess of 100000 rpm. Therefore, turbocharger wheel balance and bearing lubrication is very important. The turbocharger shaft must reach a certain rpm before it begins to pressurize the intake manifold. Some turbochargers begin to pressurize the intake manifold at 1250 engine rpm and reach full boost pressure in the intake manifold at 2250 rpm.

10.3 Boost Pressure Control 增压控制

If the turbocharger boost pressure is not limited, excessive intake manifold and combustion pressure may damage engine components. Many turbochargers have a wastegate diaphragm mounted on the turbocharger. A linkage is connected from this diaphragm to a wastegate valve in the turbine wheel housing.

The diaphragm spring holds the wastegate valve closed. Boost pressure from the intake manifold is supplied to the wastegate diaphragm. When the boost pressure in the intake manifold reaches the maximum safe limit, the boost pressure pushes the wastegate diaphragm and opens the wastegate valve. This action allows some exhaust to by-pass the turbine wheel, which limits turbocharger shaft rpm and boost pressure.

On some engines, the boost pressure supplied to the wastegate diaphragm is controlled by a computer-operated solenoid. In many systems, the PCM pulses the wastegate solenoid on and off to control boost pressure. Some computers are programmed to momentarily allow a higher boost pressure on sudden acceleration to improve engine performance.

10.4 Supercharger Principles 机械增压器原理

TRADE JARGON: A supercharger may be called a blower.

The supercharger is belt-driven from the crankshaft by a ribbed V-belt. A shaft is connected from the pulley to one of the drive gears in the front supercharger housing, and the driven gear is meshed with the drive gear. The rotors inside the supercharger are attached to the two drive gears (See Figure 10-2).

The drive gear design prevents the rotors from touching. However, there is a very small clearance between the drive gears. In some superchargers, the rotor shafts are supported by roller bearings on the front and needle bearings on the back. During the manufacturing process, the needle bearings are permanently lubricated. The ball bearings are lubricated by a synthetic base high-speed gear oil. A plug is provided for periodic checks of the front bearing lubricant. Front bearing seals prevent lubricant loss into the supercharger housing.

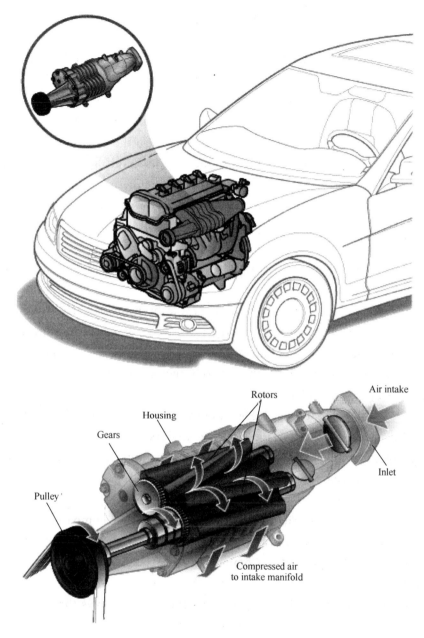

Figure 10-2 Supercharger components

10.5 Supercharger Operation 机械增压器使用

Many superchargers have three lobe helical-cut rotors for quieter operation and improved performance. Intake air enters the inlet plenum at the back of the supercharger, and the rotating blades pick up the air and force it out the top of the supercharger.

The blades rotate in opposite directions, and they act like a pump as they rotate. This pumping action pulls air through the supercharger inlet and forces the air from the outlet.

There is a very small clearance between the meshed rotor lobes and between the rotor lobes and the housing.

Air flows through the supercharger system components in the following order:

Air flows through the air cleaner and mass air flow sensor into the throttle body. Air flow enters the supercharger intake plenum. From the intake plenum the air flows into the rear of the supercharger housing. The compressed air flows from the supercharger to the intercooler inlet. Air leaves the intercooler and flows into the intercooler outlet tube. Air flows from the intercooler outlet tube into the intake manifold adapter. Compressed, cooled air flows through the intake manifold into the engine cylinders.

If the engine is operating at idle or very low speeds, the supercharger is not required. Under this condition, air flow is by-passed from the intake manifold adapter through a butterfly valve to the supercharger inlet plenum.

The by-pass butterfly valve is operated by an air by-pass actuator diaphragm as follows:

When manifold vacuum is 7 inHg or higher, the by-pass butterfly valve is completely open and a high percentage of the supercharger air is by-passed to the supercharger inlet.

If the manifold vacuum is 3 to 7 inHg, the by-pass butterfly valve is partially open and some supercharger air is by-passed to the supercharger inlet, while the remaining air flow is forced into the engine cylinders.

When the vacuum is less than 3 inHg, the by-pass butterfly valve is closed and all the supercharger air flow is forced into the engine cylinders.

On some superchargers, the pulley size causes the rotors to turn at 2.6 times the engine speed. Since supercharger speed is limited by engine speed, a supercharger wastegate is not required.

Belt-driven superchargers provide instant low-speed action compared to exhaust-driven turbochargers, which may have a low-speed lag because of the brief time interval required to accelerate the turbocharger shaft. Compared to a turbocharger, a supercharger turns at much lower speed.

Friction between the air and the rotors heats the air as it flows through the supercharger. The intercooler dissipates heat from the air in the supercharger system to the atmosphere, creating a denser air charge. When the supercharger and the intercooler supply cooled, compressed air to the cylinders, engine power and performance are improved.

A Ford supercharged 3.8-L engine provides 210 hp at 4000 rpm and 315 ft lb of torque at 2600 rpm. A Ford turbocharged 3.8-L engine provides 190 hp at 4600 rpm and 240 ft lb torque at 3400 rpm. Therefore, the supercharged engine produces more horsepower and torque at a lower rpm.

[词汇]

turbocharger	n. 涡轮增压器	lag	n. 滞后,延迟,落后
supercharger	n. 增压器	hesitation	n. 犹豫,迟缓

diaphragm	n.隔膜,隔板,膜片	interchangeable	adj.可互换的
wastegate	n.排气阀门	synthetic	adj.合成的,人造的,综合的
ingestion	n.吸收,摄取,空气的吸入	periodic	adj.周期的,定期的
plenum	n.压力通风系统,进气增压,增压的	helical	adj.螺旋状的
intercooler	n.中间冷却器	blade	n.转轮叶片,导叶叶片,刀片
butterfly	n.蝶形阀	inlet	n.进口,入口,进入,引入线,引入
dense	adj.密集的,浓厚的	horsepower	n.马力,功率
boost	v.增压,抬高		

[注释]

1. Turbocharger 涡轮增压器：涡轮增压器是由涡轮室和增压器组成的机器，涡轮室进气口与排气歧管相连，排气口接在排气管上；增压器进气口与空气滤清器管道相连，排气口接在进气歧管上。涡轮和叶轮分别装在涡轮室和增压器内，二者同轴刚性联接。

2. Wastegate 排气阀门：当涡轮增压器增压压力达到要求值后，或避免涡轮增压器超速而将排气排出的阀门。

3. Intercooler 中间冷却器：对增压后的空气进行冷却的热交换器。

[问题]

1. Why is the turbocharger used?
2. What's the turbocharger principle?
3. How is the boost pressure controlled in the turbocharger?
4. How does the supercharger work?

Lesson 11

Emission Control System
排放控制系统

When the first emission controls were first introduced back in the late 1960s, they were primarily "add-on" components that solved a particular emission need. When positive crankcase ventilation (PCV) became standard in 1968, the recycling of crankcase vapors eliminated blowby emissions as a major source of automotive pollution. When evaporative emission controls were added in 1971, charcoal canisters and sealed fuel systems eliminated fuel vapors as another factor that contributed to air pollution. Exhaust gas recirculation (EGR) was added in 1973, which lowered harmful oxides of nitrogen (NO_x) emissions. But the most significant add-on came in 1975 when the auto makers were required to install catalytic converters on all new cars.

The catalytic converter proved to be a real breakthrough in controlling emissions because it reduced both unburned hydrocarbon (HC), a primary factor in the formation of urban smog, and carbon monoxide (CO), the most dangerous pollutant because it can be deadly even in small concentrations. The converter slashed the levels of these two pollutants nearly 90%!

The early "two-way" converters (so-called because they eliminated the two pollutants HC and CO) acted like an afterburner to reburn the pollutants in the exhaust. An air pump or an aspirator system provided the extra oxygen in the exhaust to get the job done. Two-way converters were used up until 1981 "when three-way" converters were introduced. Three-way converters also reduced NO_x concentrations in the exhaust, but required the addition of a computerized feedback fuel control system to do so.

Unlike the earlier two-way converters that could perform their job relatively efficiently with lean fuel mixture, the catalyst inside a three-way converter that reduces NO_x requires rich fuel mixture. But a rich fuel mixture increases CO levels in the exhaust. So to reduce all three pollutants (HC, CO and NO_x), a three-way converter requires the fuel mixture that constantly changes or flip flops back and forth from rich to lean. This, in turn, requires feedback carburetion or electronic fuel injection, plus an oxygen sensor in the exhaust to keep tabs on what's happening with the fuel mixture.

Like the earlier two-way converters, three-way converters also require extra oxygen from an air pump or aspirator system, and some "three-way plus oxygen" converters are designed so air is routed right to the converter itself for more efficient operation.

11.1 CONVERTER REPLACEMENT 转化器更换

Original equipment converters are designed for going 100000 plus miles-which many do provided they aren't poisoned by lead, silicon or phosphorus. When leaded gasoline was still available, fuel switching to save money caused the premature demise of many a converter. Lead coats the catalyst rendering it useless. Silicon, which is used in antifreeze and certain types of RTV sealer, has the same effect. Coolant leaks in the combustion chamber can allow silicon to enter the exhaust and ruin the converter. Phosphorus, which

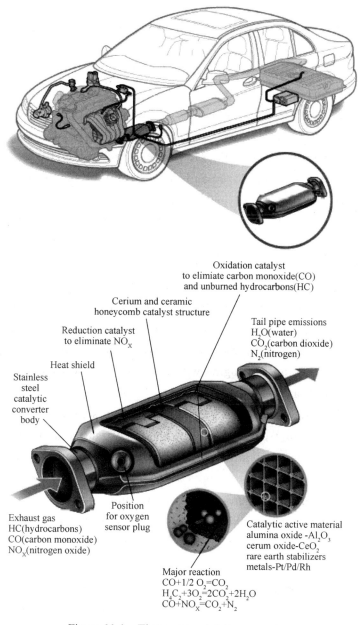

Figure 11-1 Three way catalytic converter

is found in motor oil, can foul the converter if the engine is burning oil because of worn valve guides or rings (See Figure 11-1).

Converters may also fail if they get too hot. This can be caused by unburned fuel in the exhaust. Contributing factors include a rich fuel mixture, ignition misfire (a fouled spark plug or bad plug wire) or a burned exhaust valve that leaks compression. Fuel in the exhaust has the same effect as dumping gasoline on a bed of glowing embers. Things get real hot real fast. If the converter's temperature climbs high enough, it can melt the ceramic substrate that supports the catalyst causing a partial or complete blockage inside. This increases backpressure, preventing the engine from exhaling and robbing it of power. Fuel consumption may shoot up and the engine may feel sluggish at higher speeds. Or, if the converter is completely plugged, the engine may stall after starting and not restart.

There's no way to rejuvenate a dead converter or to unclog or clean out a plugged converter, so replacement is the only repair option. Up to model year 1995, converters were covered by a 5 year/50000 mile federal emissions warranty (7 years or 70000 miles in California). In 1995, the warranty jumped to 8 years and 80000 miles.

Replacement converters must be the same type as the original (two-way, three-way or three-way plus oxygen), EPA-approved and installed in the same location as the original.

A new converter will solve a plugged or dead converter problem. But unless the underlying cause is diagnosed and corrected, the replacement converter may suffer the same fate. Other items that should also be inspected include the air pump and related plumbing, oxygen sensor and feedback control system.

A sluggish oxygen sensor, for example, may not allow the fuel mixture to change back and forth quickly enough to keep the converter working at peak efficiency. Though this might not lead to a meltdown, it could cause enough of an increase in pollution to make the vehicle fail an emissions test. If the oxygen sensor has died altogether, the fuel mixture will remain fixed and the engine will probably run too rich causing an increase in fuel consumption as well as emissions.

Many auto makers recommend inspecting the oxygen sensor at specific mileage intervals to prevent this kind of trouble. Some vehicles (primarily imports) have a reminder light that illuminates every 30000 miles or so to remind the motorist to have his oxygen sensor checked or replaced.

A leading supplier of oxygen sensors (Bosch) recommends replacing oxygen sensors for preventative maintenance at roughly the same interval as the spark plugs, depending on the application. Unheated 1 or 2 wire O_2 sensors on 1976 through early 1990s applications should be replaced every 30000 to 50000 miles. Heated 3 and 4-wire O_2 sensors on mid-1980s through mid-1990s applications should be changed every 60000 miles. And on 1996 and newer OBD II equipped vehicles, the recommended replacement interval is 100000 miles.

11.2 PCV 曲轴箱强制通风

PCV valves are generally considered a maintenance item like spark plugs, and should be inspected and replaced periodically (typically every 50000 miles). The PCV valve siphons blowby vapors from the crankcase into the intake manifold so the vapors don't escape into the atmosphere. One of the beneficial effects of PCV, besides eliminating blowby emissions, is that it pulls moisture out of the crankcase to extend oil life. Moisture can form acids and sludge which can cause major engine damage. So if the PCV valve or hose plugs up, rapid moisture buildup and oil breakdown can result. (See Figure 11-2).

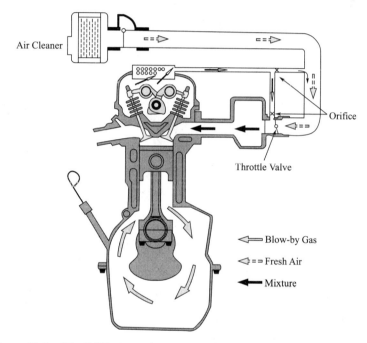

Figure 11-2 The PCV system is used to capture and reburn crankcase gases

11.3 EGR 废气再循环

The EGR valve has no recommended replacement or inspection interval, but that doesn't mean it won't cause trouble. EGR reduces the formation of oxides of nitrogen by diluting the air/fuel mixture with exhaust. This lowers combustion temperatures to keep it under 2500 degree F so little NO_x is formed (the higher the flame temperature, the higher the rate at which oxygen and nitrogen react to form NO_x). As an added benefit, EGR also helps prevent detonation. (See Figure 11-3).

The heart of the system is the EGR valve. The valve opens a small passage between the intake and exhaust manifolds. When ported vacuum is applied to the EGR valve diaphragm, it opens the valve allowing intake vacuum to siphon exhaust into the intake manifold. This has a same effect as a vacuum leak, so EGR is only used when the engine is

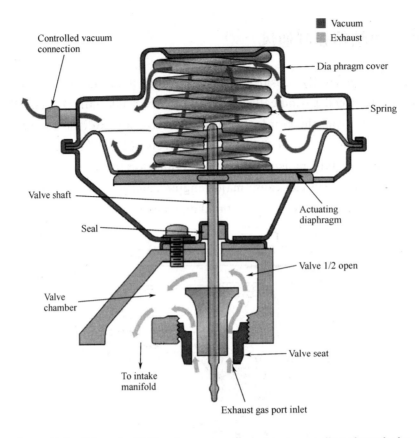

Figure 11-3 When the EGR valve opens, the exhaust gases flow through the valve and into passages in the intake manifold.

warm and running above idle speed.

Some vehicles have "positive backpressure" EGR valves while others have "negative backpressure" EGR valves. Both types rely on exhaust system backpressure to open the valve. But the two types are not interchangeable.

The vacuum control plumbing to the EGR valve usually includes a temperature vacuum switch (TVS) or solenoid to block or bleed vacuum until the engine warms up. On newer vehicles with computerized engine controls, the computer usually regulates the solenoid to further modify the opening of the EGR valve. Some vehicles even have an EGR valve that is driven by a small electric motor rather than being vacuum-actuated for even more precise control of this emission function.

EGR valves do not normally require maintenance, but can become clogged with carbon deposits that cause the valve to stick or prevent it from opening or closing properly. An EGR valve that's stuck open will act like a vacuum leak and cause a rough idle and stalling. An EGR valve that has failed, refuses to open (or the EGR passageway in the manifold is clogged) will allow elevated NO_x emissions and may also cause a detonation (spark knock) problem. Dirty EGR valves can sometimes be cleaned, but if the valve itself is defective it must be replaced.

11.4 EVAP 燃油蒸发排放控制

Evaporative emissions from the fuel system (fuel vapors) are trapped and store in a charcoal canister. Later, a purge valve opens allowing the vapors to be sucked into the engine and reburned. The EVAP system usually requires no maintenance. The fuel filler cap is also part of the EVAP system, and is designed to keep fuel vapors from escaping into the atmosphere. A leaky or missing fuel filler cap may cause a vehicle to fail an emission test. (See Figure 11-4).

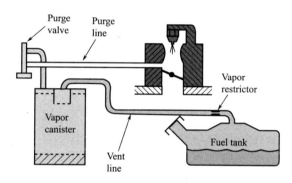

Figure 11-4 The EVAP system includes all of the lines, hoses, and valves, plus the charcoal canister.

[词汇]

PCV	n. 曲轴箱强制通风	phosphorus	n. 磷
recycle	v. 再循环	demise	vt. 让渡，遗赠，转让
evaporative	adj. 成为蒸气的，蒸发的	antifreeze	n. 防冻剂
charcoal	n. 活性炭，炭	contributing	adj. 贡献的，起作用的
canister	n. 罐，金属罐，金属容器，滤毒罐	dumping	n. 应急放油，卸除，卸减
EGR	废气再循环	backpressure	n. 反压力，背压，吸入压力
oxide	n. 氧化物	plumb	v. 查明，了解
nitrogen	n. 氮	sluggish	adj. 行动迟缓的
breakthrough	n. 突破	siphon	v. 用虹吸管吸出或排出
slash	v. 猛砍，鞭打，砍伤，大量削减	sludge	n. 软泥，淤泥，泥状沉积物
afterburner	n. 后燃室，补燃器	dilute	v. 冲淡，变淡，变弱，稀释
aspirator	n. 吸气器，抽气器	passageway	n. 过道，出入口
flip flop	触发	vaporization	n. 蒸发

[注释]

1. Backpressure 背压：管道中阻碍气流流动的压力，如排气管背压。
2. Three-way converter 三元催化转化器：外形像一个排气消声器，实际上也起到消声器的作用。壳体用耐高温的不锈钢制成，内部的蜂巢式通道上涂有催化剂，催化剂的成分有铂、钯和铑等稀土金属，当汽车废气通过净化器的通道时，一氧化碳和碳氢化合物就会在催化剂铂与钯的作用下，与空气中的氧发生反应产生无害的水和二氧化碳，而氮氧化合物则在催化剂铑的作用下被还原为无害的氧和氮。所谓三元催化转化器是指汽车废气只要通过净化器本身，就可同时将废气中的三种主要有害物质转化为无害物质的一种高效率净化器。

[问题]

1. What kinds of emission control systems are applied in automobiles?
2. What are the purposes of three-way converter?
3. How does the EGR valve work?
4. What's EVAP?

Chapter 2　Chassis Construction
底盘结构

Lesson 12

Drivetrain
传动系

12.1　General drivetrain arrangement 常见传动系布置形式

The general drivetrain is shown diagrammatically in Figure 12-1. The engine is at the front, with its crankshaft parallel to the axis of the vehicle. From the engine, the drive is transmitted through a clutch and a short shaft (c) to the gearbox. In cars, this short shaft is almost invariably integral with the primary gear in the gearbox but, in some commercial vehicles, it is a separate component, generally with flexible or universal joints at each end and, in some instances, with a sliding joint at one end. From the gearbox, a 'propeller shaft' or 'cardan shaft' - also with a sliding joint at one end and a universal joint at both ends-takes the drive to a live back axle. A live axle is one through which the drive is transmitted, while a dead axle is one that does not transmit the drive. Bevel or worm gearing (g) within the axle turns the drive through 90 degree, and *differential gears* divide it equally between the two drive shafts, or *halfshafts* (j), which take it out to the wheels.

　　The functions of the components are as follows. A clutch is used for disconnecting the engine from the driving wheels and it must also enable the driver to connect the engine, when it is running, without shock to the driving wheels. Since the clutch is kept in engage-

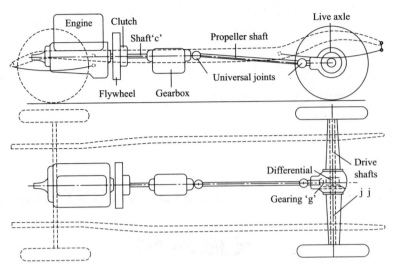

Figure 12-1 General drivetrain arrangement

ment by a spring-loading mechanism and is disengaged by pressure of the foot on a pedal, it cannot be disengaged except when the driver is in the vehicle. Therefore, when the driver wants to leave the vehicle with the engine running-and preferably for starting the engine, too-he has to disconnect the engine from the driving wheels by use of the gear-shift lever, which he sets in a 'neutral', or gears-disengaged, position.

The principal function of the gearbox is to enable the driver to change the leverage between the engine and driving wheels to suit the prevailing conditions-gradient, load, speed required, etc. As the propeller shaft transmits the drive on to the back axle, the universal joints at its ends allow both the engine-and-gearbox assembly and the back axle to move relative to one another, as their spring elements deflect. The sliding joint, usually integral with one of the universal joints, accommodates variations in length of the propeller shaft as its rear end rises and falls vertically with the back axle and its front end pivots about the universal joint just behind the gearbox. Gearing (g), in what is called the *final drive* unit, turns the drive through 90° and reduces the speed in a ratio of about 4 : 1, since the driving wheels must rotate much more slowly than the engine. Within the final drive unit too is the differential gearing, which shares the driving torque equally between the two road wheels while allowing them, nevertheless, to rotate simultaneously at different speeds while the vehicle is cornering.

In Figure 12-1, the gearbox is shown as a separate unit, but two other variants of this front engine rear-wheel-drive layout are in use. One is a 'unit construction' -almost universal on cars-in which the gearbox casing is either integral with or bolted rigidly to the clutch 'bellhousing' which, in turn, is similarly secured to the engine crankcase. This has the advantages of cleanliness, lighter weight, neatness of appearance and lower manufacturing costs. Its chief disadvantage is relative inaccessibility of the clutch. In addition to accessibility of both the clutch and gearbox, the layout in Figure 12-1 enables a shorter, and therefore lighter, final drive propeller shaft to be used, thus obviating potential problems associated with whirling and other vibrations. The second variant entails incorporation of the gearbox into the back axle, to form what is now widely called a *transaxle* unit. For three main reasons, this arrangement is used only rarely: first, it tends to be significantly more costly than the others; secondly, it entails the use of either a dead axle or an axleless transmission; thirdly, it is extremely difficult to mount a heavy transaxle in such a way as to accommodate the motions, torques, and forces of the input and output driveshafts yet to isolate it to prevent the transmission of noise and vibration to the vehicle structure. With certain types of gearbox-notably epicyclic-the clutch action is performed within the gearbox itself, to which the drive from the engine is therefore transmitted either directly by a shaft or through a fluid coupling or torque converter. The shaft can be either separate or integral with the gearbox mechanism.

Live axles are built in several forms. That in Figure 12-1 is called a *single reduction axle*, because the reduction in speed between the propeller shaft and final drive is effected in one stage, in the final drive at (g). In some heavy trucks, because the reduction ratio may have to be much higher, this reduction is done in two or even three stages, a *double-* or even *triple-reduction axle* being used.

12.2 Four-wheel-drive transmission 四轮驱动传动装置

Typically in a four-wheel-drive transmission layout, Figure 12-2, a transfer box is interposed between the gearbox and back axle unit. The function of transfer box is to transfer the drive from the main gearbox to both the front and rear axles.

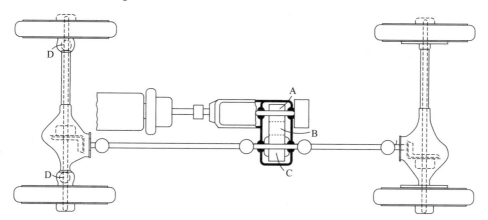

Figure 12-2 General arrangement of four-wheel driven chassis

In this box is a pinion A, driven by a coupling from the gearbox output shaft. The pinion, through an intermediate gear B, drives a third gear C, mounted on the cage of a differential gear assembly. From the differential gears, one shaft is taken forward to the front axle and the other rearwards to the back axle. Both the axles house their own differentials and final drive gears, but that at the front carries at its outer ends the universal joints D, which are necessary to allow the front wheels to be steered.

The differential at C, in the transfer box, is necessary to distribute the drive equally between the front and rear axles and to allow for the fact that, when the vehicle is driven in a circle, the mean of the speeds of the front wheels is different from that of the rear wheels and therefore the speeds of the two propeller shafts must differ too. Other factors include different rolling radii of the tyres owing to, for example, manufacturing tolerances, different degrees of wear and, perhaps, different tyre pressures.

Provision is usually made for locking this differential out of operation, to improve the performance and reliability of traction when the vehicle is driven on slippery ground. For vehicles intended mainly for operation on soft ground, the central differential may be omitted from the drive line, but some means of disengaging four-wheel drive, leaving only one axle to do the driving, is generally provided for use if the vehicle is required to operate on metalled roads.

Since the steered front wheels always tend to roll further than the wheels on the fixed-geometry rear-axle, because their radius of turn is always the larger, a one-way clutch, or freewheel can be substituted for the inter-axle differential, See Figure 12-3. In practice, this usually takes the form of two freewheels, one on each front hub, on which there are rotary controls by means of which they can be locked by the driver, but, of course, he has to stop and get out to do so. As soon as he again drives his vehicle on firm ground, however, he must remember to unlock the hubs. Should the rear wheels lose traction, on the other hand, and therefore tend to rotate further than the front ones, the drive will automatically be transferred to the front wheels even if they are in the free-wheeling mode.

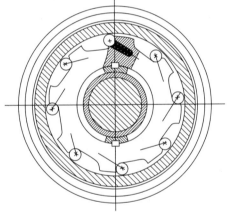

Figure 12-3 Roller-type freewheel, with rollers retracted against their springs

In four-wheel drive, the overall-frictional resistance throughout the transmission is higher than in the two-wheel-drive state, and of course the transmission shafts and gearing will progressively wind up and become highly stressed so long as the wheels on the two axles are rolling different distances. On soft ground, when this wind-up becomes too high the wheels can slip and thus relieve the stresses, but this may not be possible on metalled roads, and a fractured shaft may be the result.

With independently-sprung wheels, the transmission is the same, except that the final drive units are carried on the frame, or structure, of the vehicle. Consequently, universal joints have to be used on both ends of the driveshafts to the road wheels.

Four-wheel-drive offers two main advantages. First, there is the increased traction obtainable from four driven wheels, which is especially useful on soft or slippery ground. Secondly, if the front wheels drop into a ditch they tend to climb out, whereas with rear-wheel drive they tend to be forced downwards, except when the vehicle is driven in reverse, in which case, of course, the disadvantage of the lower traction of two-wheel drive remains. The principal disadvantages are increased weight, bulk and cost.

[词汇]

diagrammatically	adv. 用图解法地；图表似地；概略地	gearing	n. 传动装置
axis	n. 轴；轴线；轴向	final drive	主传动器
clutch	n. 离合器	bellhousing	钟形外壳（bell + housing）；钟形罩；外壳
gearbox	n. 变速器	cleanliness	n. 清洁
universal joint	万向节	neatness	n. 干净，整洁
sliding joint	滑动连接；滑动接头	inaccessibility	n. 难达到；难接近；无法理解
propeller shaft	传动轴	accessibility	n. 易接近；可亲；可以得到
cardan	n. 万向节	epicyclic	adj. 行星的；周转的
cardan shaft	万向节传动轴	fluid coupling	液力耦合
axle	n. 车桥	torque converter	变矩器
live axle	驱动桥	single reduction axle	单级主减速器
dead axle	从动桥	double reduction axle	双级主减速器
differential	n. 差速器	triple reduction axle	三级主减速器
halfshaft	n. 半轴	transfer box	分动器
engagement	n. 啮合	pinion	n. 小齿轮
preferably	adv. 较好；宁可，宁愿；更适宜	provision	n. 规定；条款；准备
		reliability	n. 可靠性
gear-shift lever	换挡杆	steer	v. 转向
neutral	n. 空挡	fixed-geometry	固定（几何）形状
leverage	n. 杠杆，杆系，杆件	freewheel	n. 自由轮，可单向自由转动
prevailing	adj. 流行的；一般的，最普通的；占优势的；盛行很广的	fracture	n. 破裂，断裂
		ditch	n. 沟渠，壕沟
		bulk	n. 体积，容量；大多数，大部分；大块
gradient	n. 梯度；坡度；倾斜度		
variation	n. 变化	metalled road	碎石路面

[注释]

1. Drivetrain 传动系，也称 powertrain。传动系的基本功用是将发动机发出的动力传给汽车的驱动车轮，产生驱动力，使汽车能在一定速度上行驶。传动系一般由离合器、变速器、万向传动装置、主减速器、差速器和半轴等组成。

2. Inter-axle differential 轴间差速器（亦称中央差速器）：安装在分动器内，通过它的作用，能使分动器的两根输出轴在必要时产生不同的转速。

3. One-way clutch 单向离合器：作用是只允许导轮单向旋转，不允许其逆转。

4. Transaxle 变速桥（transmission + driveshaft）。

[问题]

1. Please describe the main components of the drivetrain.
2. What is the meaning of the single reduction axle?
3. Please describe the arrangement of the four wheel drive transmission.
4. What are the advantages of the four wheel drive?

Lesson 13

How Does the Clutch Work
离合器如何工作

The clutch is a device to engage and disengage power from the engine, allowing the vehicle to stop and start.

A pressure plate or "driving member" is bolted to the engine flywheel and a clutch plate or "driven member" is located between the flywheel and the pressure plate. The clutch plate is splined to the shaft extending from the transmission to the flywheel, commonly called a clutch shaft or input shaft. (See Figure 13-1).

When the clutch and pressure plates are locked together by friction, the clutch shaft rotates with the engine crankshaft. Power is transferred from the engine to the transmission, where it is routed through different gear ratios to obtain the best speed and power to start and keep the vehicle moving.

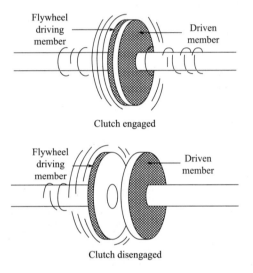

Figure 13-1 Clutch engagement and disengagement

13.1 The flywheel 飞轮

The flywheel is located at the rear of the engine and is bolted to the crankshaft. It helps absorb power impulses, resulting in a smoothly-idling engine and provides momentum to carry the engine through its operating cycle. The rear surface of the flywheel is machined flat and the clutch components are attached to it.

13.2 The pressure plate 压盘

The driving member is commonly called the pressure plate. It is bolted to the engine flywheel and its main purpose is to exert pressure against the clutch plate, holding the plate tight against the flywheel and allowing the power to flow from the engine to the transmission. It must also be capable of interrupting the power flow by releasing the pressure on the clutch plate. This allows the clutch plate to stop rotating while the flywheel and pressure plate continues to rotate.

The pressure plate consists of a heavy metal plate, coil springs or a diaphragm spring, release levers (fingers), and a cover.

When coil springs are used, they are evenly spaced around the metal plate and located between the plate and the metal cover. This places an even pressure against the plate, which in turn presses the clutch plate tight against the flywheel. The cover is bolted tightly to the flywheel and the metal plate is movable, due to internal linkages. The coil springs are arranged to exert direct or indirect tension on the metal plate, depending upon the manufacturer's design. Three release levers (fingers), evenly spaced around the cover, are used on most pressure plates to release the holding pressure of the springs on the clutch plate, allowing it to disengage the power flow.

When a diaphragm spring is used instead of coil springs, the internal linkage is necessarily different to provide an "over-center" action to release the clutch plate from the flywheel. Its operation can be compared to the operation of an oilcan. When depressing the slightly curved metal on the bottom of the can, it goes over-center and gives out a loud "clicking" noise; when released, the noise is again heard as the metal returns to its original position. A click is not heard in the clutch operation, but the action of the diaphragm spring is the same as the oilcan. (See Figure 13-2).

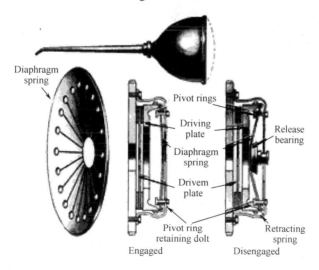

Figure 13-2 The operation of a diaphragm spring-type pressure plate can be compared to the effect of pressing the bottom of a can of oil

13.3 The clutch plate 离合器片

The clutch plate or driven member consists of a round metal plate attached to a splined hub. The outer portion of the round plate is covered with a friction material of molded or woven asbestos and is riveted or bonded to the plate. The thickness of the clutch plate and/or facings may be warped to give a softer clutch engagement. Coil springs are often installed in the hub to help provide a cushion against the twisting force of clutch engagement. The splined hub is mated to (and turns) a splined transmission shaft when the clutch is engaged. (See Figure 13-3).

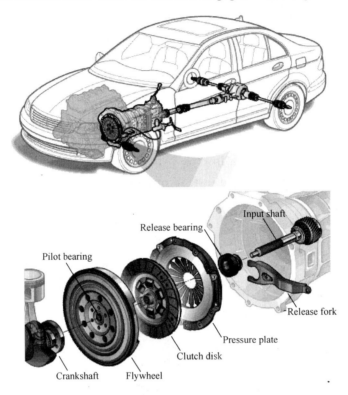

Figure 13-3　The clutch assembly

The release bearing

The release (throw out) bearing is usually a ball bearing unit, mounted on a sleeve, and attached to the release or throwout lever. Its purpose is to apply pressure to the diaphragm spring or the release levers in the pressure plate. When the clutch pedal is depressed, the pressure of the release bearing or lever actuates the internal linkages of the pressure plate, releasing the clutch plate and interrupting the power flow. The release bearing is not in constant contact with the pressure plate. A linkage adjustment clearance should be maintained.

13.4　Power flow

13.4.1　Power flow disengagement

The clutch pedal provides mechanical means for the driver to control the engagement and disengagement of the clutch. The pedal is connected mechanically to either a cable or rods, which are directly connected to the release bearing lever.

When the clutch pedal is depressed, the linkage moves the release bearing lever. The release lever is attached at the opposite end to a release bearing which straddles the transmission clutch shaft, and presses inward on the pressure plate fingers or the diaphragm spring. This inward pressure acts upon the fingers and internal linkage of the pressure plate and allows the clutch plate to move away from the flywheel, interrupting the flow of power.

13.4.2　Power flow engagement 动力啮合

While the clutch pedal is depressed and the power flow interrupted, the transmission can be shifted into any gear. The clutch pedal is slowly released to gradually move the clutch plate toward the flywheels under pressure of the pressure plate springs. The friction between the clutch plate and flywheel becomes greater as the pedal is released and the engine speed increased. Once the vehicle is moving, the need for clutch slippage is lessened, and the clutch pedal can be fully released.

Coordination between the clutch pedal and accelerator is important to avoid engine stalling, shock to the driveline components and excessive clutch slippage and overheating.

[词汇]

engage	vt. 从事，啮合，约束，接合		指针
disengage	vt. 分离，使分离	cover	n. 盖
pressure plate	压盘	linkage	n. 连杆系，连接
driving member	主动件	oilcan	n. 油壶，油罐
driven member	从动件	hub	n. 毂，轮毂
spline	vt. 用花键联接，开键槽	sleeve	n. 套，套筒，套管
momentum	n. 动量	stalling	n. 失速，脱流停车，抛锚汽车停车场
impulse	n. 冲动，冲击，冲量		
crankshaft	n. 曲轴	driveline	n. 动力传动系统
transmission	n. 变速器，变速箱	coordination	n. 协调
diaphragm spring	膜片弹簧	accelerator	n. 加速器
release lever	分离杠杆	slippage	n. 滑动，滑移，滑程
finger	n. 指，手指，抓手，手指，		

[注释]

1. Clutch　离合器：离合器位于发动机和变速箱之间的飞轮壳内，用螺钉将离合器总成固定在飞轮的后平面上，离合器的输出轴就是变速箱的输入轴。在汽车行驶过程中，驾驶员可根据需要踩下或松开离合器踏板，使发动机与变速箱暂时分离和逐渐接合，以切断或传递发动机向变速器输入的动力。

2. Pressure plate　压盘：在弹簧的作用下，压盘压向有摩擦衬片的从动盘，从而使发动机转矩传给传动系。

[问题]

1. What's the function of the clutch?
2. What are the main components of the clutch?
3. How does the clutch work?
4. Please describe the configuration of the clutch plate.

Lesson 14

Manual Transmission
手动变速器

A manual transmission (also known as a stick shift, straight drive, or standard transmission) is a type of transmission used in automotive applications, See Figure 14-1. Manual transmissions often feature a driver-operated clutch and a movable gear selector, although some do not. Most automobile manual transmissions allow the driver to select any gear at any time, but some, such as those commonly mounted on motorcycles and some types of race cars, only allow the driver to select the next-highest or next-lowest gear ratio. This second type of transmission is sometimes called a sequential manual transmission.

Manual transmissions are characterized by gear ratios that are selectable by engaging pairs of gears inside the transmission. Conversely, automatic transmissions feature clutch packs to select gear ratio. Transmissions that employ clutch packs but allow the driver to

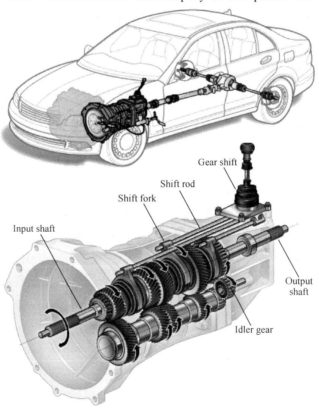

Figure 14-1 Manual transmission arrangement

manually select the current gear are called semi-automatic transmissions.

Contemporary automotive manual transmissions are generally available with four to six forward gears and one reverse gear, although manual transmissions have been built with as few as 2 and as many as 7 gears. Some manuals are referred to by the number of forward gears they offer (e.g., 5-speed) as a way of distinguishing between automatic or other available manual transmissions. In contrast, a 5-speed automatic transmission is referred to as a 5-speed automatic.

Other types of transmission in mainstream automotive use are the automatic transmission, semi-automatic transmission, and the continuously variable transmission.

Manual transmissions come in two basic types: simple unsynchronized systems, where gears are spinning freely and their relative speeds must be synchronized by the operator to avoid noisy and damaging "clashing" and "grinding" when trying to mesh the rotating teeth; and synchronized systems, which eliminate this necessity while changing gears.

14.1　Unsynchronized transmission 非同步变速器

The earliest automotive transmissions were entirely mechanical unsynchronized gearing systems. They could be shifted, with multiple gear ratios available to the operator, and even had reverse. But the gears were engaged by sliding mechanisms or simple clutches, which required skills of timing and careful throttle manipulation when shifting, so that the gears would be spinning at roughly the same speed when engaged; otherwise the teeth would refuse to mesh.

When upshifting, the speed of the gear driven by the engine had to drop to match the speed of the next gear; as this happened naturally when the clutch was depressed, it was just a matter of skill and experience to hear and feel when the gears managed to mesh. However, when downshifting, the gear driven by the engine had to be sped up to mesh with the output gear, requiring engagement of the clutch for the engine to speed up the gears. Double declutching, that is, shifting once to neutral to speed up the gears and again to the lower gear, is sometimes needed. In fact, such transmissions are often easier to shift from without using the clutch at all. The clutch, in these cases, is only used for starting from a standstill. This procedure is common in racing vehicles and most production motorcycles.

Even though automotive transmissions are now almost universally synchronised, heavy trucks and machinery as well as dedicated racing transmissions are still usually nonsynchromesh transmissions, known colloquially as "crashboxes", for several reasons. Being made of brass, synchronizers are prone to wear and breakage more than the actual gears, which are cast iron, and the rotation of all the sets of gears at once results in higher frictional losses. In addition, the process of shifting a synchromesh transmission is slower than that of shifting a nonsynchromesh transmission. For racing of production based transmissions, sometimes half the dogs on the synchros are removed to speed the shifting process, at the expense of much more wear.

14.2 Synchronized transmission 同步变速器

A modern gearbox is of the constant mesh type, in which all gears are always in mesh but only one of these meshed pairs of gears is locked to the shaft on which it is mounted at any one time, the others being allowed to rotate freely; thus greatly reducing the skill required to shift gears, See Figure 14-2.

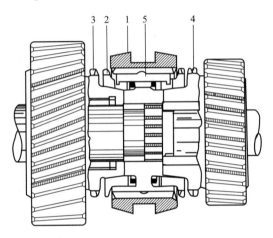

Figure 14-2 A conventional baulking ring type of synchromesh
1, synchronizer sleeve ; 2 , bronze baulking ring ; 3, dog clutch, third-speed gear ;
4, dog clutch, fourth-speed gear; 5, spring-loaded shifting plate

Most modern cars are fitted with a synchronised gear box, although it is entirely possible to construct a constant mesh gearbox without synchromesh, as found in motorcycle for example. In a constant mesh gearbox, the gears of the different transmission speeds are always in mesh and rotating, but the gears are not directly rotationally connected to the shafts on which they rotate. Instead, the gears can freely rotate or be locked to the shaft on which they are carried. The locking mechanism for any individual gear consists of a collar on the shaft which is able to slide sideways so that teeth or "dogs" on its inner surface bridge two circular rings with teeth on their outer circumference; one attached to the gear, one to the shaft. (One collar typically serves for two gears; sliding in one direction selects one transmission speed, in the other direction selects the other) When the rings are bridged by the collar, that particular gear is rotationally locked to the shaft and determines the output speed of the transmission. In a synchromesh gearbox, to correctly match the speed of the gear to that of the shaft as the gear is engaged, the collar initially applies a force to a cone-shaped brass clutch which is attached to the gear, which brings the speeds to match prior to the collar locking into place. The collar is prevented from bridging the locking rings when the speeds are mismatched by synchro rings (also called blocker rings or balk rings, the latter being spelled "baulk" in the UK). The gearshift lever manipulates the collars using a set of linkages, so arranged so that only one collar may be permitted to lock only one gear at any one time; when "shifting gears", the locking collar from one gear is disengaged and that of another engaged. In a modern gearbox, the action of all of these components is so smooth and fast it is hardly noticed.

14.3　Manual transmission principle 手动变速器原理

14.3.1　Shafts

Like other transmissions, a manual transmission has several shafts with various gears and other components attached to them. Typically, there are three shafts: an input shaft, a countershaft and an output shaft. The countershaft is sometimes called a layshaft.

The input and output shaft lie along the same line, and may in fact be combined into a single shaft within the transmission. This single shaft is called a mainshaft. The input and output ends of this combined shaft rotate independently, at different speeds, which is possible because one piece slides into a hollow bore in the other piece, where it is supported by a bearing. Sometimes the term mainshaft refers to just the input shaft or just the output shaft, rather than the entire assembly.

In some transmissions, it's possible for the input and output components of the mainshaft to be locked together to create a 1 : 1 gear ratio, causing the power flow to bypass the countershaft. The mainshaft then behaves like a single, solid shaft, a situation referred to as direct drive.

Even in transmissions that do not feature direct drive, it's an advantage for the input and output to lie along the same line, because this reduces the amount of torsion that the transmission case has to bear.

Under one possible design, the transmission's input shaft has just one pinion gear, which drives the countershaft. Along the countershaft are mounted gears of various sizes, which rotate when the input shaft rotates. These gears correspond to the forward speeds and reverse. Each of the forward gears on the countershaft is permanently meshed with a corresponding gear on the output shaft. However, these driven gears are not rigidly attached to the output shaft: although the shaft runs through them, they spin independently of it, which is made possible by bearings in their hubs. Reverse is typically implemented differently, see the section on Reverse.

When the transmission is in neutral, and the clutch is disengaged, the input shaft, clutch disk and countershaft can continue to rotate under their own inertia. In this state, the engine, the input shaft and clutch, and the output shaft, all rotate independently.

14.3.2　Dog clutch

The gear selector does not engage or disengage the actual gear teeth which are permanently meshed. Rather, the action of the gear selector is to lock one of the freely spinning gears to the shaft that runs through its hub. The shaft then spins together with that gear. The output shaft's speed relative to the countershaft is determined by the ratio of the two gears: the one permanently attached to the countershaft, and that gear's mate which is now locked to the output shaft.

Locking the output shaft with a gear is achieved by means of a dog clutch selector. The dog clutch is a sliding selector mechanism which is splined to the output shaft, meaning that its hub has teeth that fit into slots (splines) on the shaft, forcing it to rotate with that shaft. However, the splines allow the selector to move back and forth on the shaft, which happens when it is pushed by a selector fork that is linked to the gear lever. The fork does not rotate, so it is attached to a collar bearing on the selector. The selector is typically symmetric: it slides between two gears and has a synchromesh and teeth on each side in order to lock either gear to the shaft.

14.3.3 Synchromesh

If the teeth, the so-called dog teeth, make contact with the gear, but the two parts are spinning at different speeds, the teeth will fail to engage and a loud grinding sound will be heard as they clatter together. For this reason, a modern dog clutch in an automobile has a synchronizer mechanism or synchromesh. Thanks to this mechanism, before the teeth can engage, a frictional contact is made which brings the selector and gear to two parts to rotate at the same speed. Moreover, until synchronization occurs, the teeth are prevented from making contact, because further motion of the selector is prevented by a blocker ring. When synchronization occurs, friction on the blocker ring is relieved and it twists slightly, bringing into alignment certain grooves and notches that allow further passage of the selector which brings the teeth together. Of course, the exact design of the synchronizer varies from manufacturer to manufacturer.

The synchronizer has to change the momentum of the entire input shaft and clutch disk. Additionally, it can be abused by exposure to the momentum and power of the engine itself, which is what happens when attempts are made to select a gear without fully disengaging the clutch. This causes extra wear on the rings and sleeves, reducing their service life. When an experimenting driver tries to "match the revs" on a synchronized transmission and force it into gear without using the clutch, it is actually the synchronizer that makes up for any discrepancy in RPM, deceiving the driver into an exaggerated sense of how much human skill was involved.

14.3.4 Reverse

The previous discussion applies to the forward gears. The implementation of the reverse gear is usually different, implemented in the following way to reduce the cost of the transmission. Reverse is also a pair of gears: one gear on the countershaft and one on the output shaft. However, whereas all the forward gears are always meshed together, there is a gap between the reverse gears. Moreover, they are both attached to their shafts: neither one rotates freely about the shaft. What happens when reverse is selected is that a small gear, called an idler gear or reverse idler, is slid between them. The idler has teeth which mesh with both gears, and thus it couples these gears together and reverses the direction of rotation without changing the gear ratio.

Thus, in other words, when reverse gear is selected, in fact it is actual gear teeth that are being meshed, with no aid from a synchronization mechanism. For this reason, the output shaft must not be rotating when reverse is selected: the car must be stopped. In order that reverse can be selected without grinding even if the input shaft is spinning inertially, there may be a mechanism to stop the input shaft from spinning. The driver brings the vehicle to a stop, and selects reverse. As that selection is made, some mechanism in the transmission stops the input shaft. Both gears are stopped and the idler can be inserted between them.

[词汇]

clutch pack	离合器组件	blocker ring	锁环
mainstream	n. 主流	balk ring	摩擦环
unsynchronized	adj. 非同步的	baulk	n. 错误;失败;障碍(等于balk)
synchronized	adj. 同步的	countershaft	n. 中间轴
clashing	adj. 碰撞做声的,撞击的;	layshaft	n. 变速器副轴,中间轴并置轴
grinding	adj. 刺耳的,吱嘎的	mainshaft	n. 主轴
upshift	vt. 换入高挡	direct drive	直接挡
downshift	vt. 换入低挡	dog clutch	齿式离合器;爪形离合器
declutch	vt. 分离	spline	n. 花键
nonsynchromesh	n. 非同步啮合	collar bearing	环轴承;环式止推轴承;环肩止推式滑动轴承
colloquially	adv. 口语地;用通俗语		
crashbox	n. 冲击型变速器	symmetric	adj. 对称的,匀称的
brass	n. 黄铜;黄铜制品;铜管乐器;厚脸皮	clatter	vt. 使咔嗒地响
		synchronizer	n. 同步器
breakage	n. 破坏;破损;裂口;破损量	momentum	n. 动量;动力;冲力
sideways	adv. 向侧面地;向一旁	exaggerate	vt. 使扩大;使增大
circumference	n. 圆周,周长;胸围	reverse gear	倒挡
blocker	n. 妨碍者,阻拦者,阻挡者;堵塞物,阻塞物	synchronization	n. 同步

[注释]

1. Stick shift 手扳变速器。
2. Sequential manual transmission 顺序换挡手动变数器:用在摩托车或高档汽车上,按依次顺序换挡,不能跳入某一指定挡位。
3. Synchronizer 同步器:利用摩擦原理实现同步的,现代汽车上广泛使用的是惯性式同步器,可以从结构上保证待啮合的接合套与接合齿轮的花键齿在达到同步之前不可能接触,可以避免齿间冲击和噪音。

[问题]

1. What kinds of manual transmissions are used in automobiles?
2. How does the manual transmission operate?
3. Please explain the construction of the manual transmission.
4. What's the function of the synchronizer?

Lesson 15

Automatic Transmission
自动变速器

The basic purpose of an automatic transmission is to provide a forward and reverse driving range that increases the torque between the engine and the drive wheels, See Figure 15-1. Rather than having a solid conventional clutch as in a manual transmission, automatic transmissions utilize a fluid coupling device called a torque converter to transmit power from the engine to the transmission. Hydraulic pressure in the converter allows power flow from the torque converter to the transmission's input shaft. The only time a torque converter is mechanically connected to the transmission is during torque converter lockup, generally at relatively high speeds (highway speeds) and no load. The input shaft of the automatic transmission drives a planetary gearset which provides different forward gears, a neutral position, and reverse. Power flow through the gears is controlled by multiple-disc clutches, one way valves and friction bands. These friction elements either hold or turn the gear sets to provide different gear ratios. The control valve assembly (valve body) controls the hydraulic pressure required to operate the clutches and bands that shift the gears automatically. By holding different parts of the planetary gearset, different gear ratios are obtained. When the gear selector is moved to a given forward driving range, the "drive" posi-

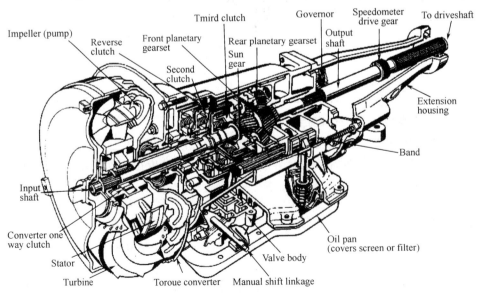

Figure 15-1 Cutaway view of a typical 3-speed automatic transmission

tion for example, the transmission shifts itself up or down depending on vehicle speed, throttle position and engine load. Electronically controlled automatic transmissions were first introduced in the mid-1980s, with electronics used to control the timing and length of shifts, as well as to engage and release the clutches.

Newer advances in automatic transmissions include continuously variable transmissions (CVT), which do not use specific gear ratios, rather an infinite number of ratios based on a belt moving on a variable diameter spool. Continuously slipping torque converters are also gaining popularity as they improve fuel economy. As automatic transmissions employ a fluid coupling between the engine and transmission, they have always been at a fuel economy disadvantage to manual transmissions, which employ a solid clutch coupling.

15.1 Planetary Gear System 行星齿轮系统

Automatic transmissions use a gear system that does not require gear shifts to change gear ratios. A simple planetary gearset is made up of three elements, the sun gear, the planet carrier assembly and the internal ring gear, See Figure 15-2. The sun gear is so called because it is at the center of the gearset. The other gears revolve around it like planets around the sun. The planet carrier assembly holds the planet pinions within a cage, or carrier. The pinions rotate on pins and are meshed with the sun gear at all times. The internal ring gear has its teeth cut on the inside of the gear, and these teeth are constantly in mesh with the pinions, See Figure 15-3. This planetary system rotates on the same axis, with input and output power on this same axis, so that the gears are never disengaged to change ratios. By causing one of the planetary gearset members to be stationary, and the other two still turning, a different output ratio is obtained. The holding of one member is done by a band or clutch pack using hydraulic pressure routed by the valve body. Each gearset member is attached to an input or output shaft in order to transfer power when the gear ratio is changed.

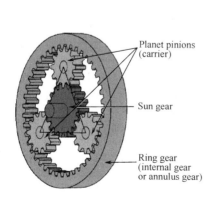

Figure 15-2 A typical planter gear set showing the terms that are used to describe each member

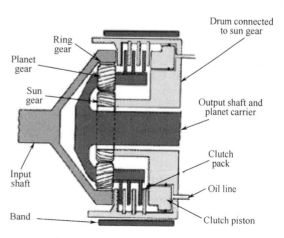

Figure 15-3 Planetary Gear System

71

15.2 Holding Devices 接合装置

There are two elements used to hold members of the planetary gearset, so another member can provide the output drive. These devices are transmission bands and multiple-disc clutches, also called clutch packs, See Figure 15-4. Transmission bands tighten around the outside of a drum and keep the drum from turning, See Figure 15-5. The drum is engaged with a member of the gearset, so if the drum does not turn, that member of the gearset does not turn. The band is anchored at one end and mechanical action against the other end is activated by hydraulic pressure via the valve body, which tightens the band. Multiple-disc clutches hold one or more members of the planetary gearset, via a hydraulically activated piston that locks the clutches together when hydraulic pressure is applied to the piston. The inside diameter of the clutch pack is splined to an input or output shaft. Multiple-disc clutches are used more than any other type of holding device in an automatic transmission. There may be as many as six different clutch packs in an overdrive transmission. Overdrive is a gear ratio in which the output shaft turns faster than the input shaft, which provides very low torque, but very good high speed fuel economy.

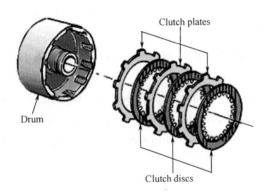

Figure 15-4　The multiple-disc clutch

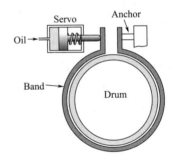

Figure 15-5　The band

15.3 Torque Converters 变矩器

The torque converter couples and uncouples the engine and the transmission. Converters use impellers and turbines, with vanes, to develop fluid flow and the transfer of torque, See Figure 15-6. In addition to an impeller and turbine, torque converters use a stator to accelerate the flow of fluid from the impeller to the turbine and back to the impeller, thereby multiplying torque. Whenever the impeller moves faster than the turbine, torque is multiplied. A torque converter consists of:

- An impeller (pump, or driven member)
- The turbine (driven member)
- The stator (reaction member)

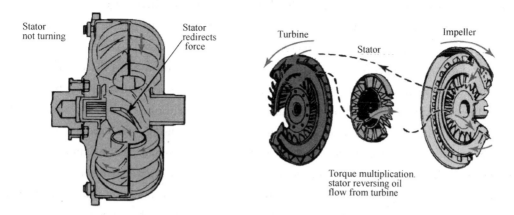

Figure 15-6 Torque multiplication occurs when fluid leaving the turbine strikes the front of the stator vanes and is redirected back to the impeller

The torque converter housing is filled with fluid by the transmission pump. The impeller is the driving member with its curved vanes picking up fluid in the converter housing and directing it toward the turbine. The turbine is the driven member, having vanes that receive fluid from the rotating impeller. With sufficient fluid flow from the impeller, the turbine rotates to turn the transmission input shaft. The stator is the reaction member whose curved vanes multiply the fluid force being sentback to the impeller by the turbine. The impeller is attached to the crankcase via a flexplate or flywheel, and the turbine is attached to the front of the transmission input shaft. Fluid is pumped into the torque converter housing by the transmission pump. As the impeller is turned by the engine, its vanes pick up fluid in the housing and throw the fluid outward toward the turbine. As the fluid moves, it follows two flow paths:

• Rotary flow: The oil flow path, in a torque converter, that is in the same circular direction as the rotation of the impeller (engine crankshaft rotation).

• Vortex flow: The oil flow path, in a torque converter, that is at a right angle to the rotation of the impeller and to rotary flow.

Three elements of a torque converter are curved backward to boost the acceleration of the oil flow as fluid leaves the impeller. The turbine vanes are curved on their inlet sides, back toward the impeller to absorb as much energy as possible from fluid moving through the turbine. Turbine vanes also curve to absorb shock and a loss of power whenever there is a sudden change in oil flow between the impeller and the turbine. Turbine vanes are curved to take advantage of the basic hydraulic principle that the more the direction of a moving fluid is diverted, the greater the force exerted by the fluid on the diverting surface. Stator vanes curve in the opposite direction from impeller and turbine vanes. Since the stator is located between the impeller and the turbine, its curved vanes multiply the force returning to the impeller from the turbine. Fluid that leaves a moving impeller to enter a turbine does not exit as rotary flow or vortex flow. It exits as a combination of both. Fluid from the impeller strikes the vanes of the turbine. When the speed and force of the fluid hitting the turbine vanes is great enough, the turbine rotates. Rotary flow and vortex flow moving through the turbine vanes at the same time create resultant force, which is the combined force and flow direction in the torque converter.

The stator is the reaction member whose curved vanes multiply fluid force being sent back to the impeller by the turbine. The stator is mounted on a one-way overrunning clutch that is splined to a stationary extension of the oil pump assembly. This extension is called the reaction shaft or stator support. The hub at the rear of the torque converter housing, which is the back of the impeller passes over the stator support and through the front seal into the oil pump. The converter engages the drive gear or rotor of the pump to drive it. Because the converter hub is part of the housing that is bolted to the engine, the oil pump is turning and pumping fluid whenever the engine is running. Because of the complexity of fluid flow through the converter, there is a great deal of stress on the fluid in the automatic transmission. The converter serves as a direct link between the engine and drive wheels of the vehicle. Typically, the converter has no means of draining the fluid it contains, which is why less than 50 percent of the transmission fluid is changed during a conventional drain and refill service.

15.4 Valve Body 阀体

The valve body is where many of the hydraulic valves are housed. This is where fluid is channeled and directed throughout the transmission to determine when shifting of gear ratios occurs, See Figure 15-7. This is accomplished in relation to engine load and throttle position.

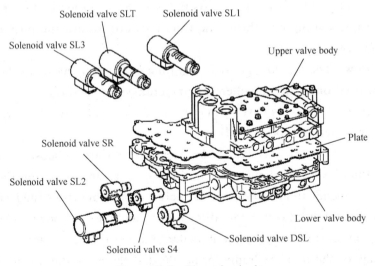

Figure 15-7 The valve body

[词汇]

planetary gearset	行星齿轮组	multiple-disc clutch	多片离合器
forward gear	前进挡	one way valve	单向阀
neutral position	空挡	friction band	摩擦带

gear ratio	传动比	uncouple	*vt.* 解耦
valve body	阀体	impeller	*n.* 泵轮
infinite	*adj.* 无限的，无穷的；无数的	turbine	*n.* 涡轮
spool	*n.* 线轴，线管；线轴状物	vane	*n.* 叶片
slipping	*adj.* 打滑的	stator	*n.* 定子
sun gear	太阳轮	reaction	*n.* 反作用
planet carrier	行星架	member	*n.* 构件，部件
ring gear	齿圈	flexplate	*n.* 柔性盘
planet pinion	行星小齿轮	vortex	*n.* 涡流；漩涡
cage	*n.* 保持架	overrunning clutch	超越离合器
pin	*n.* 销轴	stationary	*adj.* 不动的，固定的；静止的
couple	*vt.* 耦合		

[注释]

1. Torque converter 变矩器：由泵轮，涡轮，导轮组成。安装在发动机的飞轮上，以液压油（ATF）为工作介质，起传递转矩、变矩、变速及离合的作用。

2. Lockup 锁止：带锁止离合器液力变矩器的特点是，汽车在变工况下行驶时（如起步、经常加减速），锁止离合器分离，相当于普通液力变矩器；当汽车在稳定工况下行驶时，锁止离合器接合，动力不经液力传动，直接通过机械传动传递，变矩器效率为1。

3. Band 带式换挡制动器：是将内侧粘有摩擦材料的钢带卷绕在制动鼓外表面上，故又称外束带式制动器。它由制动鼓、制动带、推杆、活塞等元件组成。制动带的一端固定在自动变速器壳体上，另一端与控制油缸的推杆相连接。不制动时制动带与制动鼓之间有一定间隙，此间隙可用调整螺钉调整。

[问题]

1. How does the automatic transmission operate?
2. What's the construction of the clutch pack?
3. What's the purpose of the torque converter?
4. What kind of gear is used in the automatic transmission?

Lesson 16

Differential and Final Drive
差速器和主传动器

On FWD cars, the differential unit is normally part of the transaxle assembly. On RWD cars, it is part of the rear axle assembly. A differential unit is located in a cast iron casting, the differential case, and is attached to the center of the ring gear. Located inside the case are the differential pinion shafts and gears and the axle side gears.

The differential assembly revolves with the ring gear. Axle side gears are splined to the rear axle or front axle drive shafts. (See Figure 16-1).

When an automobile is moving straight ahead, both wheels are free to rotate. Engine power is applied to the pinion gear, which rotates the ring gear. Beveled pinion gears are

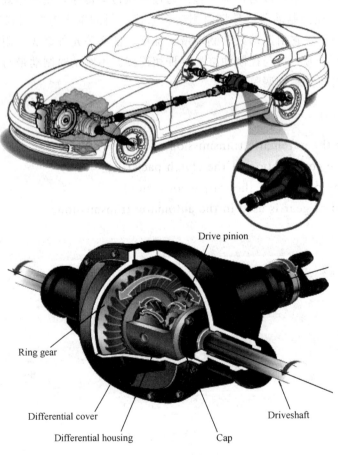

Figure 16-1 Differential

carried around by the ring gear and rotate as one unit. Each axle receives the same power, so each wheel turns at the same speed.

When the car turns a sharp corner, only one wheel rotates freely. Torque still comes in on the pinion gear and rotates the ring gear, carrying the beveled pinions around with it. However, one axle is held stationary and the beveled pinions are forced to rotate on their own axis and "walk around" their gear. The other side is forced to rotate because it is subjected to the turning force of the ring gear, which is transmitted through the pinions.

During one revolution of the ring gear, one gear makes two revolutions, one with the ring gear and another as the pinions "walk around" the other gear. As a result, when the drive wheels have unequal resistance applied to them, the wheel with the least resistance turns more revolutions. As one wheel turns faster, the other turns proportionally slower.

To prevent a loss of power on slippery surfaces, a differential lock is often used to lock the two axles together until the slippery spot is passed, at which point they are released. These differentials are referred as to limited-slip or traction-lock differentials. When the car is proceeding in a straight line, the differential gears are locked against rotation due to gear reaction. When the vehicle turns a corner or a curve, the differential pinion gears rotate around the differential pinion shaft. The differential pinion gears allow the inside axle shaft and driving wheels to slow down. On the opposite side, the pinion gears allow the outside wheels to accelerate. Both driving wheels resume equal speeds when the vehicle completes the corner or curve. This differential action improves vehicle handling and reduces driving wheel tire wear.

16.1 Differential Bearings 差速器轴承

At least four bearings are found in all differentials. Two fit the drive pinion shaft to support it and the other two support the differential case and are usually mounted just outboard of the side gears. The drive pinion bearings are typically tapered-roller bearings and the case bearings are normally ball bearings.

Different forces are generated in the differential due to the action of the pinion gear. As the pinion gear turns, it tries to climb up the ring gear and pull the ring gear down. Also, as the pinion gear rotates, it tends to move away from the ring gear and pushes the ring gear equally as hard in the opposite direction. Because of these forces, the differential must be securely mounted in the carrier housing. The bearings on each end of the differential case support the case and absorb the thrust of the forces.

The pinion gear and shaft are mounted on bearings to allow the shaft to rotate freely without allowing it to move in response to the torque applied to it. All of these bearings are installed with a preload to prevent the pinion gear and ring gear from moving out of position.

16.2 Differential Case 差速器壳

The differential case is supported in the carrier by two tapered-roller side bearings. This assembly can be adjusted from side to side to provide the proper backlash between the ring gear and pinion and the required side bearing preload. This adjustment is achieved by threaded bearing adjusters on some units and the placement of selective shims and spacers on others.

16.3 Transaxle Final Drive Gears and Differential 变速驱动桥的主减速器和差速器

Transaxle final drive gears provide the means for transmitting transmission output torque to the differential section of the transaxle.

The differential section of the transaxle has the same components as the differential gears in a RWD axle and basically operate in the same way. The power flow in transversely mounted power trains is in line with the wheels and therefore the differential unit does not need to turn the power 90 degrees.

The drive pinion, ring gears and the differential assembly are normally located within the transaxle housing of FWD vehicles. There are four common configurations used as the final drives on FWD vehicles: helical, planetary, hypoid, and chain drive. The helical, planetary, and chain final drive arrangements are usually found in transversely mounted power trains. Hypoid final drive gear assemblies are normally used with longitudinal power train arrangements.

The drive pinion gear is connected to the transmission's output shaft and the ring gear is attached to the differential case. Like the ring and pinion gearsets in a RWD axle, the drive pinion and ring gear of a FWD assembly provide for a multiplication of torque.

The teeth of the ring gear usually mesh directly with the transmission's output shaft. However on some transaxles, an intermediate shaft is used to connect the transmission's output to the ring gear.

Backlash is the clearance or play between two gears in mesh. It is the amount one of the gears can be moved without moving the other.

On some models, the differential and final drive gears operate in the same lubricant as the transmission section of the transaxle. On other designs, the differential section is separately enclosed and is lubricated by different lubricant than the transmission section. These designs require positive sealing between the differential unit and the transmission to keep the different lubricant from mixing. All transaxles use seals between the differential and the drive axles to prevent dirt from entering the transaxle and to prevent lubricant from leaking past the attachment point of the drive axles.

16.4　Helical Final Drive Assembly 螺旋线主减速器总成

Helical final drive assemblies use helical gearsets that require the centerline of the pinion gear to be at the centerline of the ring gear. The pinion gear is cast as part of the main shaft and is supported by tapered-roller bearings. The pinion gear is meshed with the ring gear to provide the required torque multiplication. Because the ring is mounted on the differential case, the case rotates in response to the pinion gear.

16.5　Planetary Final Drive Assembly 行星齿轮主减速器总成

The ring gear of a planetary final drive assembly has lugs around its outside diameter. These lugs fit into grooves machined inside the transaxle housing. These lugs and grooves hold the ring gear stationarily. The transmission's output shaft is splined to the planetary gear set's sun gear. The planetary pinions are in mesh with both the sun gear and ring gear and form a simple planetary gear set. The planetary carrier is constructed so that it also serves as the differential case.

In operation, the transmission's output drives the sun gear, which, in turn, drives the planetary pinions. The planetary pinions walk around the inside of the stationary ring gear. The rotating planetary pinions drive the planetary carrier and differential housing. This combination provides maximum torque multiplication from a simple planetary gearset.

16.6　Hypoid Final Drive Assembly 准双曲面齿轮主减速器总成

Hypoid gears have the advantage of being quiet and strong because of their thick tooth design. And due to their strength, hypoid-type gears can be used with large engines that are longitudinally mounted in vehicles. This type of final drive unit is identical to those used in RWD vehicles.

16.7　Chain Drive Assembly 链传动主减速器总成

Commonly used in automatic transaxles, chain drive final drive assemblies use a chain to connect a drive sprocket——connected to the transmission's output shaft——to the driven sprocket, which is connected to the differential case. This design allows for remote positioning of the differential within the transaxle housing.

[词汇]

differential	n. 差速器	pinion gear	行星小齿轮
transaxle	n. 变速驱动桥	bevel	n. 斜角，斜角规，倾斜，斜面
casting	n. 铸件，铸造		

	v.使成斜面	shim	n.垫片
stationary	adj.固定的	helical	adj.螺旋状的
proportionally	adv.按比例，配合着，相应地	planetary	adj.行星式的，行星齿轮的，轨道的
slippery	adj.滑的，光滑的	hypoid	n.准双曲面的
limited-slip	防滑	chain drive	链传动
traction-lock differential	牵引力锁止差速器	gear set	齿轮组
bearing	n.轴承，支承，承载	multiplication	n.倍增
tapered-roller bearing	锥形滚柱轴承	lubricant	n.滑润剂
carrier	n.托架，支持物，载体	backlash	n.启动，间隙，拉紧
adjuster	n.调停者，调节器	lug	v.拖拉
preload	n.预加载，预压，预先加料	housing	n.壳体，罩壳

[注释]

1. Final drive　主减速器：汽车传动系中减小转速、增大扭矩的主要部件。对发动机纵置的汽车来说，主减速器还利用锥齿轮传动以改变动力方向。现代汽车的主减速器，广泛采用螺旋锥齿轮和双曲面齿轮。双曲面齿轮工作时，齿面间的压力和滑动较大，齿面油膜易被破坏，必须采用双曲面齿轮油润滑，绝不允许用普通齿轮油代替，否则将使齿面迅速擦伤和磨损，大大降低使用寿命。

2. Hypoid gear　准双曲线齿轮：主动轴和从动轴成直角，但不在同一平面上的锥形齿轮，齿面有相对滑动，广泛用于主传动器。

[问题]

1. How does the differential work?
2. Why is the limited slip differential used?
3. What kinds of final drives are used in the automobile?
4. What's the backlash?

Lesson 17

Body and Frame
车身和车架

17.1 Body 车身

The body on the first automobiles was little more than a platform with seats attached. Today, the automobile body allows the driver and passenger to ride in total comfort. But the body is much more than a comfortable, attractive place to sit. It has evolved into a structure that protects the driver and passengers in a crash. Body design now takes into account much that has been learned about safe construction through crash testing.

In addition, automotive body designers have become concerned with wind resistance. The wind pushed by the front of the moving car creates drag. Thus the body is now carefully designed and tested to achieve the smallest possible drag. It is now possible to design and produce a body with little drag, or one that is very aerodynamic. The less drag created by the body, the less engine power that is required to move the car down the road. Low drag results in higher fuel mileage.

Weight has become very important in body design. Every pound saved on a body results in better fuel mileage. Older vehicles were made from thick steel panels. Now, thin sheets of steel are welded together to form a body that is both light and strong. Plastics and other lighter materials are replacing steel to further reduce weight.

Car bodies come in many shapes and sizes. They are grouped by a measurement called wheelbase, which is the distance from the center of the front wheel to the center of the rear wheel. The smallest automobiles are called subcompacts. The next size is called a compact. An intermediate-size car is larger still. Full-size cars have the largest wheelbase.

We also group car bodies on the basis of their body style. One of the oldest body types is the sedan. The sedan has a post, called a pillar, that goes down from the roof to the body. A sedan may have two or four doors. The hardtop is a design without this pillar. The hardtop may have two or four doors. The convertible has a roof made from vinyl that can be raised or lowered. The hatchback or liftback is a more recent design. It has a large rear door that provides access to the rear luggage compartment. Hatchbacks are available in three- and five-door models. The station wagon body has a long roof and a large interior for carrying passengers. Wagons can have two or four doors. The popularity of the station wagon has dropped recently in favor of the van. This vehicle is available as a full-size van or as a smaller minivan. Vans have many different door and seating arrangements. Pick-up trucks are also available in many sizes—— from full-size to mini. (See Figure 17-1 and 17-2).

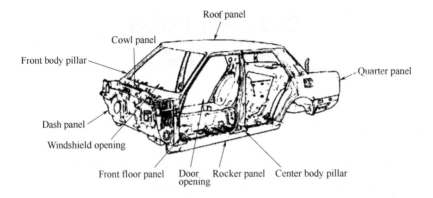

Figure 17-1　Main body components for a body-over-frame-design

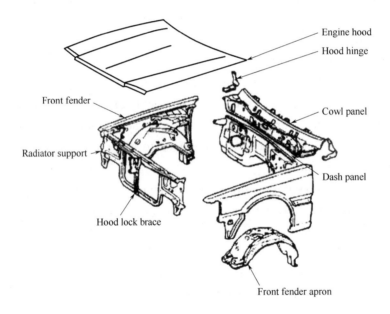

Figure 17-2　Main front body components

17.2　The Frame 车架

The body is either attached to or made in one piece with the car frame. The frame is a strong steel structure that must support the weight of the entire car. Along with the body, it must protect the driver and passengers during a collision.

The oldest design is to make the body and frame in two parts. This is called body-over-frame construction Currently, this design is limited mostly to light duty trucks. The frame for the body-over-frame design is made up of a number of members welded together. Two large rails run beneath the sides of the automobile and there are a number of connecting pieces called cross members. The body is bolted on top of the frame. Rubber pads, which help prevent road noise from entering the body, fit between the frame and the body.

Each major section of the body has a name. Large sections of the body are often called panels. Many body parts as well as many mechanical parts are described as being on the left or right side of the car. Left or right on a car is determined as if you were sitting in the driver's seat. This is how technicians describe the location of parts or damage on an automotive body.

The parts of the body-over-frame body assembly are welded together to form one structure. The bottom panel is called the floor pan. A rocker panel runs along between the floor pan and the door openings. The top is called the roof panel. The main center support is called the center body pillar. The cowl panel and dash panel are welded to the front of the body structure. Front pillars extend up from the cowl to the roof. The rear fender area is called the quarter panel.

The front panels of the body-over-frame-type construction are typically bolted to the dash and cowl panel area. The engine hood is often attached by hinges to the cowl panel or at the front of the car at the radiator support. The two front fenders are usually bolted onto the front radiator support and rear dash panel. Separate fender aprons are bolted to the inside of the fenders to provide support.

A newer design uses the sheet metal of the body and the body floor to form the support structure. The body is welded directly to the floor pan, and the other components are attached to the body floor-pan assembly. Small subframe assemblies may be used at the front and rear for more support. This design is called a unitized body or monocoque design. This design reduces vehicle weight, lowers production costs, and allows a lower floor. It is important to reduce weight because lighter cars are more efficient and use less fuel.

The unitized body structure extends to the front of the vehicle. The fender aprons and front crossmember are welded the cowl assembly. The panels, assemblies, and pillars have the same names on the unitized body as those on the body-over-frame construction.

The rear structural components are essentially the same on both types of body designs. The luggage compartment door is mounted to a door hinge arm. The door hinge arm is typically mounted to an upper back panel. A lower back panel provides the rear support for the side quarter panels.

The door assemblies are essentially the same on both designs. The front of the door is held in place on an upper and lower hinge. The hinges for front doors are attached to the front body pillars. Rear door hinges are attached to the center body pillar. Doors are constructed from an outer and inner panel, which is often welded together. A rubber weatherstrip fits around the door to provide a weatherproof seal when the door is closed.

The outside of the doors, fenders, and quarter panels are protected and decorated with trim and molding. The molding may be made from metal or plastic. The molding and trim parts can be attached to the body with adhesives or clips and screws.

The most common material used for the construction of body panels is steel. Steel can be easily welded for the body structure, but has the disadvantage of being subject to rusting. Therefore, steel body panels have to be coated with materials that prevent rust. Steel also has the disadvantage that it deforms when impacted.

The disadvantages of steel have led to an increased use of plastics in body construction. Many replaceable parts have been made from plastics because they are less expensive, lighter, and not subject to rusting. Manufacturers are also beginning to use plastics in large panels such as doors and fenders. Large plastic panels have the advantage that, if they are hit in a minor collision, they bounce back into shape, usually without any paint damage.

[词汇]

body	n. 车身	station wagon	旅行车
aerodynamic	adj. 空气动力学的	frame	n. 车架
mileage	n. 里程，里数	cross member	横梁
panel	n. 钣金	rocker panel	n. 车门下围板
wheelbase	n. 前后轮之车轮轴距离，轴距	cowl	n. 发动机罩
subcompact	n. 微型小客车，微型汽车	fender	n. 翼子板
pillar	n. 柱，支柱，囊轴	apron	n. 车身围裙前的围板，挡泥板上的橡皮板
roof	n. 车顶	subframe	n. 副架
sedan	n. 轿车，小轿车	monocoque	n. 硬壳式结构
hardtop	n. 汽车硬质顶盖，带顶盖汽车	weatherstrip	n.（门、窗的）挡风雨条
convertible	n. 敞篷车；有活动摺篷的汽车	trim	n. 修饰，装饰
vinyl	n. 乙烯基	molding	n. 成型
liftback	n. 提升式流线型后背车身汽车		
hatchback	n. 有舱门式后背的汽车		

[注释]

1. Cowl　前围上盖板：前围板和仪表板之间的盖板。

2. Dash panel　前围板：发动机舱和乘客舱之间的隔板。

3. Station wagon　旅行车：早期的四轮运货车，后演变为载人休闲的风格，刚性结构车顶，车厢有较大空间，有2排以上座位，4个侧门，或增加一个后门。

4. Unitized body　承载式车身：没有刚性车架，只是加强了车头、侧围、车尾、底板等部位，发动机、前后悬架、传动系的一部分等总成部件装配在车身上设计要求的位置，车身负载通过悬架装置传给车轮。这种承载式车身除了其固有的乘载功能外，还要直接承受各种负荷力的作用。

[问题]

1. What's the function of the car body?
2. How is the car body classified?
3. What's the unitized body?
4. What's the meaning of the rocker panel?

Lesson 18

Suspension
悬　　架

Most suspension systems have the same basic parts and operate basically in the same way. They differ, however, in the way the parts are arranged. The vehicle wheel is attached to a steering knuckle. The steering knuckle is attached to the vehicle frame by two control arms, which are mounted so they can pivot up and down. A coil spring is mounted between the lower control arm and the frame.

When the wheel rolls over a bump, the control arms move up and compress the spring. When the wheel rolls into a dip, the control arms move down and the springs expand. The spring force brings the control arms and the wheel back into the normal position as soon as the wheel is on flat pavement. The idea is to allow the wheel to move up and down while the frame, body, and passengers stay smooth and level. There are four basic types of springs used in suspensions: coil, torsion bar, leaf spring, and air spring. The coil spring is the most popular type of spring in both front and rear suspension systems. It is simply a round bar of spring steel that is wound into the shape of a coil. Usually, the top and bottom coils are closer together than the middle coils. The advantages of the coil spring are its compactness, lack of moving parts, and excellent weight supporting characteristics.

The disadvantage of a coil spring is its weakness in supporting side-to-side or lateral movement. When coil springs are used at the drive wheels, heavy traction bars or torque tubes are often required to maintain axle housing alignment.

A number of vehicles use a torsion bar spring. It is a long, solid steel shaft that is anchored at one end to the suspension's control arm and at the other end to the vehicle's frame. Torsion is the twisting action that occurs in the bar when one end is twisted and the other end remains fixed. When a vertical impact on a wheel is transmitted through the control arm to the torsion bar, the bar twists to absorb the impact. The bar's natural resistance to twisting quickly restores it to its original position, returning the wheel to the road.

A torsion bar can store a significantly higher maximum amount of energy than either an equally stressed leaf or coil spring. The torsion offers important weight savings and it is adjustable. In addition, it requires significantly less space than a coil spring.

The leaf spring is made of several layers of spring steel stacked one upon the other. Usually, there is one main leaf that uses spring eyes for locating and fastening the spring toe frame or underbody. Several other progressively shorter leaves are placed on the main leaf, and the assembly or leaf pack is held together in the middle by a center bolt and on the ends by rebound clips. Some spring packs use fiber or plastic pads between leaves to reduce the internal leaf friction. Some vehicles use a single leaf instead of a buildup of multiple leaves. One manufacturer is using a leaf spring manufactured from a nonmetal composite. Leaf springs are usually arched so that the ends are higher than the center when viewed from the side. (See Figure 18-1).

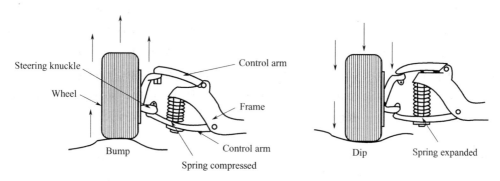

Figure 18-1 Basic suspension system parts and operation

The leaf spring is usually mounted in three places. A bushing is installed in each of the spring eyes. A bolt through the bushing in the rear spring eye attaches the rear of the spring directly to the vehicle frame. A shackle assembly is attached to the front spring eye and bushing and is then mounted through a shackle bushing to the frame. The shackle assembly allows the leaf spring to pivot up and down. A pair of U-bolts and a tie plate are used to clamp the front or rear axle assembly to the leaf spring.

The main advantage of leaf springs is their ability to control vehicle sway and lateral movement. For these reasons, leaf springs are often used on the rear suspension of rear drive vehicles.

Many late-model luxury cars use air springs. The spring is essentially a rubber bag or bladder full of air. A piston is attached to the lower control arm. Movement of the lower control arm causes the piston to move into the air bladder and compress the air in the bladder. Air pressure is used to regulate how easy or hard the bladder can be compressed. The air bladder is usually connected to an air compressor, which regulates the action of the air spring based on road conditions.

All suspension systems use a shock absorber at each wheel. When the coil, torsion bar, leaf spring, or air spring is deflected, it can oscillate (bounce up and down) uncontrollably, possibly causing the tires to lose contact with the road. This could cause the car to bounce up and down without any control. To prevent this from happening, shock absorbers are used, not to absorb shocks, but to control spring rate and dampen spring oscillations.

The shock absorber is a hydraulic device. One end of the shock absorber is attached to a wheel assembly and the other end is attached to the vehicle frame. Shock absorber movement is limited by forcing fluid inside the shock absorber through passages or orifices. This causes the shock absorber to compress or extend at a slow rate.

When the wheel goes over a bump, the shock absorber compresses. When the wheel goes into a dip, the shock absorber extends slowly. This action dampens spring rate and controls spring oscillation.

As we mentioned previously, the suspension system is designed to provide comfortable, safe ride control. For safety, especially in cornering, the suspension system must keep the wheels upright, or nearly upright, under all conditions of driving; a tire can deliver maximum force to the ground only when its tread is flat on the road. Therefore, the tire should be upright when the car is accelerating and cornering, especially the outside wheel that is carrying most of the load; when braking as the front of the car dips and the rear rises; and finally, when it is deflected up or down by road irregularities.

[词汇]

suspension	n.悬架	stack	n.堆，一堆，堆栈
steering knuckle	转向节	underbody	n.车身下体
coil spring	螺旋弹簧	rebound clip	回弹夹
lower control arm	下控制臂	pack	vt.包装，拼，装填，压紧
frame	n.车架	fiber	n.纤维，丝，硬化纸板
pavement	n.路面，人行道	shackle	n.吊耳
torsion bar	扭力杆	bushing	n.衬套，镶套
leaf spring	钢板弹簧	shock absorber	n.减振器
air spring	空气弹簧	oscillate	v.振荡
compactness	n.紧密，简洁	dampen	vt.使潮湿，减振，使减幅，使衰减
lateral	adj.横（向）的，侧面的		
traction	n.牵引	oscillation	n.摆动，振动
alignment	n.对准，调整，定位	orifice	n.量孔，小洞
anchor	n.锚，支座，固定，吊钩	cornering	转弯
adjustable	adj.可调整的	irregularity	n.不规则，无规律

[注释]

1. Suspension 悬架：用于连接车桥和车架；传递两者之间的各种作用力和力矩；抑制并减小由于路面不平而引起的振动，保持车身和车轮之间正确的运动关系。

2. Coil spring 螺旋弹簧：是现代汽车上用得最多的弹簧。它的吸收冲击能力强，乘坐舒适性好。

3. Leaf spring 钢板弹簧：多用于厢式车及卡车，由若干片长度不同的细长弹簧片组合而成。

4. Torsion bar 扭力杆：是利用具有扭曲刚性的弹簧钢制成的长杆。一端固定于车身，一端与悬架上臂相连，车轮上下运动时，扭杆发生扭转变形，起到弹簧的作用。

[问题]

1. What types of springs are used in suspensions?
2. What are the advantages of the torsion bar?
3. Please describe the configuration of the leaf spring.
4. How does the shock absorber work?

Lesson 19

Front Independent Suspension
前轮独立悬架

Most suspension systems utilize a spring and shock absorber. Suspension systems differ in the type and arrangement of the linkages used to connect these elements to the frame and wheel.

The unequal length control arm or short, long arm (SLA) suspension system has been common on American vehicles for many years. Because each wheel is independently connected to the frame by a steering knuckle, ball joint assemblies, and upper and lower control arms, the system is often described as an independent suspension. The short, long arm suspension system gets its name from the use of two control arms from the frame to the steering knuckle and wheel assembly. The two control arms are of unequal length with a long control arm on the bottom and a short control arm on the top. The control arms are sometimes called A arms because in the top view they are shaped like the letter A.

The short, long arm suspension is designed so that the wheel and tire assembly tends to rise and fall vertically as it goes over bumps in the road. The unequal length control arms compensate for jounce (upward movement of the wheels) and rebound (downward movement of the wheels). For example, if the front wheels hit a bump, the wheel and tire assembly move upward in a jounce movement. To offset this movement, the upper control arm is made shorter so the arc it travels is shorter than that of the lower control arm. This causes the top of the wheel to lean inward as the wheel rises. Any side-to-side movement of the tire that could cause scuffing and result in tire wear is eliminated by the short, long arm design.

If the control arms are of equal length, the wheel will move in an arc as it passes over irregular road surfaces. The short, long arm suspension is designed to allow each wheel to compensate for changes in the road surface while not greatly affecting the opposite wheel.

In the short, long arm suspension system, the upper control arm is attached to a cross shaft through two combination rubber and metal bushings. The cross shaft, in turn, is bolted to the frame. A ball joint, called the upper ball joint, is attached to the outer end of the upper arm and connects to the steering knuckle through a tapered stud held in position with a nut. The inner ends of the lower control arm have pressed-in bushings. Bolts, passing through the bushings, attach the arm to the frame. The lower ball joint is usually pressed into the control arm and connects to the steering knuckle through a tapered stud that is held in position with a nut. A ball joint is used on the control arms because it allows movement in more than one direction. It allows the up-and-down motion required as the wheels pass over dips and bumps. This type of joint also allows side-to-side motion as the wheels are turned back and forth for turns.

For the upper and lower ball joint, the ball stud in the ball joint is a tapered stud at one end with a ball-shaped end. The ball end is supported in a similarly shaped housing called a socket. The shape of the housing allows the ball stud to turn around or move side to side. A plastic or sintered iron bearing is positioned between the ball and socket. The bearing allows the ball stud to turn in relation to the housing for steering. The tapered stud and nut hold the ball joint in position in the steering knuckle.

Grease is used to prevent wear between the ball stud and bearing. A rubber seal is held in position around the ball stud by a seal retainer. The seal holds in the grease and prevents the entrance of dirt or moisture. The steering knuckle assembly is used to mount the wheel and wheel bearing assembly to the control arms. A spindle is usually forged in one piece with the steering knuckle. The wheel spindle is the unit that carries the disc rotor hub and bearing assembly. Through the wheel bearings, it carries the entire wheel load. The wheel bearings have a large inside bearing and a small outer bearing. The disc rotor hub is designed so that the center plane of the wheel is closer to the center plane of the larger inside bearing. The inside bearing supports most of the wheel load.

A coil spring is commonly used on the short, long arm suspension system. Some cars have the spring mounted from the frame to the upper control arm. In either case, the shock absorber is mounted through the center of the spring. Most short, long arm systems use a stabilizer bar between the two sides of the suspension. The sway bar connects both lower control arms to the frame crossmember. Movements affecting one wheel are partially transmitted to the opposite wheel through the frame to stabilize body roll. The sway bar is attached to the frame crossmember and lower control arms through rubber insulator bushings to reduce noise and vibrations. Sway bar end bushings and crossmember bushings are permanently installed on the sway bar.

MacPherson Strut Front Suspension 麦佛逊式短柱前悬架

The MacPherson strut suspension has become very popular on both imported and American vehicles. The MacPherson strut suspension uses a single lower control arm connected to a long, tubular assembly called a strut. The shock absorber, strut, and spindle are a combined unit that is supported by the coil spring at the upper end and by the lower control arm at the bottom. A ball joint is attached to the lower part of the spindle. The lower control arm is sometimes referred to as a track control arm, or transverse link. The lower arm is held in position by a sway bar and frame-mounted rod called a strut rod, or by a stabilizer bar that functions as a combined strut rod and sway bar.

In the strut assembly, the shock absorber is called a cartridge and fits inside the strut housing. A metal dust cover is used on some units to protect the strut cartridge assembly. A coil spring is held in place by a lower spring seat welded to the strut housing and an upper spring seat bolted to the shock absorber piston rod. The upper mount is bolted to the vehicle body, through two or three studs that go through the vehicle shock tower or fender well. A rubber bumper fits on the piston rod and protects it in case the shock absorber is compressed to its limit.

Some vehicles use a suspension system described as a modified MacPherson strut. This suspension has a lower control arm and coil spring similar to that used on the short, long arm suspension. Instead of an upper control arm, a strut assembly connects the top of the steering knuckle to the body. In this case, the strut does not have a spring attached to it. The strut acts as the upper control arm and shock absorber. (See Figure 19-1).

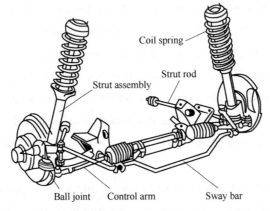

Figure 19-1　A MacPherson strut front suspension system

[词汇]

suspension	n.悬架	crossmember	n.横梁
shock absorber	减振器	sway bar	防倾斜杆
linkage	n.连接,交联,连锁	MacPherson	麦佛逊式悬架
unequal	adj.不平等的,不同的,不平衡的,不胜任的	tubular	adj.管状的
		strut	n.控制臂撑杆,制动反应杆,支撑,支柱,斜杆
steering knuckle	转向节		
ball joint	球铰	spindle	n.轴,心棒
independent suspension	独立悬架	track	vt.循路而行,追踪,通过,用纤拉
jounce	v.颠簸		
rebound	v.回弹	transverse	adj.横向的,横断的
scuffing	n.磨损,拖着脚步,磨损处,咬接	stabilizer bar	稳定杆
		cartridge	n.座,芯,筒
sinter	vt.使烧结	tower	n.柱,杆
retainer	n.保持器,护圈,挡板	fender	n.翼子板

[注释]

1. Independent suspension　独立悬架:独立悬挂系统使得每一个车轮都能垂直地移

动，而不影响到其他车轮。现在，几乎所有的轿车和轻型卡车都采用独立悬挂，因为它没有穿过车身的车轴所以能提供更多的空间容纳发动机。独立悬挂系统也减少了方向盘的振动，改善了车身的侧滚刚度和乘客的舒适感。

2．MacPherson　麦佛逊式悬架：又称滑柱摆臂式。有下横臂和减振器-弹簧组两个机构连接车轮与车身，它的优点是结构简单，重量轻，占用空间小，上下行程长等。

[问题]

1. What are the characteristics of the long and short suspension?
2. What's the role of the sway bar?
3. Please describe the construction of MacPherson suspension.
4. Why MacPhers on if used widely?

Lesson 20

Steering System
转向系

Inspection and maintenance of the steering system is important because a steering problem can lead to an accident. The steering system has two critical inspection and maintenance areas: the steering gear and the steering linkage. Two basic types of steering gears are in use. One is the recirculating ball type and the other is the rack-and-pinion type. Both may be operated manually or with the aid of hydraulic power. The next sections describe the parts and operation of the manually operated steering gears. (See Figure 20-1).

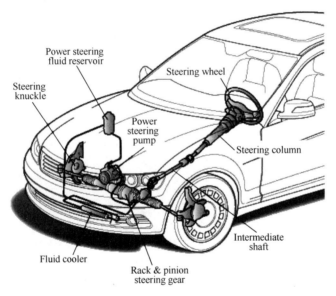

Figure 20-1 The steering system

20.1 Recirculating Ball and Nut Steering Gear 循环球和螺母式转向器

The larger and heavier the car is, the more difficult it is to steer. Most large American cars are equipped with a recirculating ball-type steering gear. This type of steering gear is very low in friction and provides a good mechanical advantage for a heavy vehicle.

The recirculating ball and nut steering gear consists of several parts contained in a steering gear housing. The steering gear shaft is connected to the steering wheel either directly or through some type of flexible joint. There is a worm gear at the end of the steering gear shaft. A cross (Pitman) shaft is mounted in the housing in a position 90 degrees to

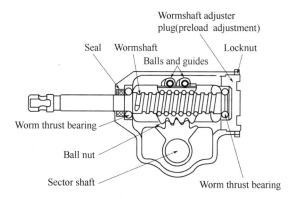

Figure 20-2 The balls are recirculated through the ball guides

the worm gear. A ball nut rides on the worm gear and a gear on the cross (Pitman) shaft, called the cross shaft sector, is engaged with this nut. (See Figure 20-2).

Ball or roller bearings are used to support both ends of the worm gear and are adjustable to remove end or side play from the worm gear. The cross (Pitman) shaft is supported by bushings, needle bearings, or a combination of the two, and provision is made to control the worm and cross shaft clearance. All parts are enclosed in a cast housing that is partly filled with lubricant. Seals are used to prevent the entry of dirt or the loss of lubricant. Provision is made to bolt the steering gear housing to a rigid area, usually the frame.

The ball nut has internal threads that are meshed to the threads of the worm with continuous rows of ball bearings between the two. The ball bearings are recirculated through two outside loops, called ball guides.

The sliding ball nut has tapered teeth cut on one face that mate with teeth on the sector. As the steering wheel is rotated, the nut is moved up or down on the worm. Because teeth on the nut are meshed with the teeth on the sector, the movement of the nut causes the sector shaft to rotate and swing the steering linkage connected to it.

The recirculating ball construction results in a friction-free contact between the nut and the worm. When the steering wheel is turned to the left, the ball bearings roll between the worm and the nut and work their way upward in the worm groove. When the ball bearings reach the top of the nut, they enter two ball guides and are directed downward into the worm groove at a lower point. When the steering wheel is turned to the right, the ball bearings circulate in the opposite direction.

20.2 Rack-and-pinion Steering Gear 齿轮和齿条式转向器

The recirculating ball steering gear has the disadvantage that it occupies a good deal of space, usually in the engine compartment. The rack-and-pinion steering gear was first developed for compact cars in which the engine compartment space was limited. The rack-and-pinion system has worked so well that it is currently being used in both imported and

American compacts and intermediate size cars.

The steering wheel and steering shaft are connected to a pinion gear. The pinion gear is in mesh with a straight bar that has gear teeth cut into one side. The toothed bar is called a rack. When the driver turns the steering wheel, the pinion gear turns, causing the rack to move. This movement, in turn, is connected to a linkage that moves the front wheels.

The rack-and-pinion gear is mounted in a rack housing assembly. The steering linkage consists of two inner tie rods and two tie rod ends. The inner tie rod ends are attached to the steering rack ends. The outer tie rod ends are attached to the suspension arms on the steering knuckles. Rubber boots are used to cover and protect the inner tie rod assemblies from road splash.

20.3 Steering Linkage 转向拉杆

With a rack-and-pinion steering gear, the rack is connected by linkage directly to the steering knuckle. Recirculating ball-type steering gears require a more complicated linkage to change the rotary output of the sector shaft to the back-and-forth movement of the wheels. A steering linkage consists basically of a steering gear Pitman arm, a centerlink, and a tie rod assembly connected to each other by ball sockets. The Pitman arm is splined on the steering gear sector shaft. When the sector shaft turns, the Pitman arm swings in an arc. The swinging end of this arm is connected to the center link.

The center link (also called drag link or relay rod) transfers the swinging motion of the gear arm to a linear or back-and-forth motion. It can also change the direction of the sector shaft arm motion, depending on the type of linkage. The center link is connected to the tie rods. These transmit movement of the relay rod to the steering arms. The steering arms are part of, or attached to, the steering knuckle spindle assemblies. When the steering arm moves, the steering knuckle assembly rotates on the suspension control arm ball joints.

Tie rod ends are used to connect the tie rods to the center link and to the steering arms. They are also used on the end of the sector shaft arm and the idler arm. Adjustment of the tie rod length is provided in threaded sleeves that are locked by clamps.

A tie rod end is a ball located in a socket. The ball is attached to a tapered stud. A spring or plastic spacer holds the ball in position in the socket. The tapered stud fits into a taper in a steering arm and is held in position by a threaded nut. The ball and socket allows up-and-down movement between the tie rod and the steering arm as the car goes over bumps. The ball and socket also allows back-and-forth movement as the driver turns the steering wheel. Grease is held between the ball and socket with a grease seal.

In most steering linkage arrangements, one end of the center link is supported in the Pitman arm. The other end is supported by a frame-mounted idler arm. The idler arm pivots in a support attached to the frame when the steering linkage moves back and forth.

Warning: All steering linkage parts are manufactured from malleable materials and will bend, distort, or deflect rather than fracture under extreme shock loads. This toughness and malleability are necessary to avoid the complete loss of control that would occur if any part of a steering linkage were to break. Steering linkage parts must never be heated during a repair because this could cause them to lose their malleability and, as a result, fracture.

[词汇]

steering system	转向系统	nut.	n. 螺母，螺帽，难解的问题
steering gear	转向器	provision	n. 供应，（一批）供应品，预备，防备，规定
steering linkage	转向杆系		
recirculating ball	循环球	thread	n. 线，细丝，线索，思路，螺纹
rack	n. 齿条，滑轨	loop	n. 环，线（绳）圈，弯曲部分，回路
rack-and-pinion	齿轮和齿条	guide	n. 导杆
steering wheel	方向盘	mate	v. 啮合
flexible	n. 柔性的，可弯曲的	groove	n. 沟，槽
worm gear	n. 蜗轮	tie rod	横拉杆
pitman	n. 转向垂臂	socket	n. 窝，穴，孔，插座，牙槽
housing	n. 套，壳，卡箍	malleability	n. 有延展性，柔韧性，柔顺
sector	n. 部分，部门，扇形	malleable	adj. 有延展性的，可锻的

[注释]

1. Recirculating ball-type steering gear 循环球式转向器：这种转向装置是由齿轮机构将来自转向盘的旋转力进行减速，使转向盘的旋转运动变为涡轮蜗杆的旋转运动，滚珠螺杆和螺母夹着钢球啮合，因而滚珠螺杆的旋转运动变为直线运动，螺母再与扇形齿轮啮合，直线运动再次变为旋转运动，使连杆臂摇动，连杆臂再使连动拉杆和横拉杆做直线运动，改变车轮的方向。

2. Rack-and-pinion steering gear 齿轮齿条式转向器：齿轮与齿条直接啮合，将齿轮的旋转运动转化为齿条的直线运动，使转向拉杆横向拉动车轮产生偏转。

3. Idler arm 转向传动机构的中间摆臂：将转向器输出的力和运动经中间摆臂两端的拉杆传递到距转向器较远的转向轮。

4. Ball and socket 球头销和球头座：球头销在球头座中能自由转动的机械连接，多用于悬架和转向杆件的连接。

[问题]

1. What kinds of steering systems are there in the car?
2. How does the recirculating ball steering gear operate?
3. What are the advantages of the rack and pinion steering gear?
4. Please describe the main components of the rack and pinion steering gear.

Lesson 21

Wheel Alignment
车轮定位

21.1 Two Wheel Alignments 两轮定位

In its most basic form, a wheel alignment consists of adjusting the angles of the wheels so that they are perpendicular to the ground and parallel to each other. The purpose of these adjustments is to maximize tire life and a vehicle that tracks straight and true when driving along a straight and level road.

This article begins with information that any motorist should know; We will cover various levels of detail with the deepest levels containing information that even a wheel alignment technician will find informative.

If you know anything about wheel alignment, you've probably heard the terms Camber, Caster and Toe-in.

21.1.1 Camber 车轮外倾

Camber is the angle of the wheel, measured in degrees, when viewed from the front of the vehicle. If the top of the wheel is leaning out from the center of the car, then the camber is positive, if it's leaning in, then the camber is negative. If the camber is out of adjustment, it will cause tire wear on one side of the tire's tread. If the camber is too far negative, for instance, then the tire will wear on the inside of the tread.

21.1.2 Caster 主销后倾

When you turn the steering wheel, the front wheels respond by turning on a pivot attached to the suspension system. Caster is the angle of this steering pivot, measured in degrees, when viewed from the side of the vehicle. If the top of the pivot is leaning toward the rear of the car, then the caster is positive, if it is leaning toward the front, it is negative. If the caster is out of adjustment, it can cause problems in straight line tracking. If the caster is different from side to side, the vehicle will pull to the side with the less positive caster. If the caster is equal but too negative, the steering will be light and the vehicle will wander and be difficult to keep in a straight line. If the caster is equal but too positive, the steering will be heavy and the steering wheel may kick when you hit a bump. Caster has little affect on tire wear.

21.1.3 Toe-in 前束

The toe measurement is the difference in the distance between the front of the tires and the back of the tires. It is measured in fractions of an inch in the US and is usually set close to zero which means that the wheels are parallel with each other. Toe-in means that the fronts of the tires are closer to each other than the rears. Toe-out is just the opposite. An incorrect toe-in will cause rapid tire wear to both tires equally. This type of tire wear is called a saw-tooth wear pattern.

If the sharp edges of the tread sections are pointing to the center of the car, then there is too much toe-in. If they are pointed to the outside of the car then there is too much toe-out. Toe is always adjustable on the front wheels and on some cars, is also adjustable for the rear wheels. (See Figure 21-1).

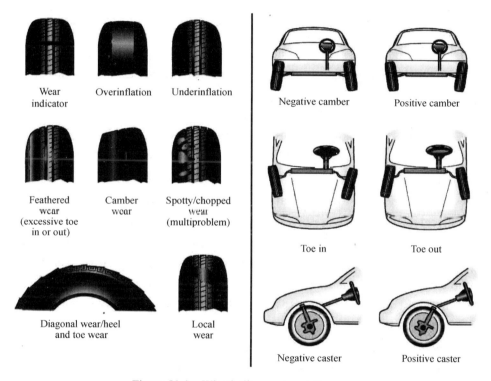

Figure 21-1 Wheel alignment and tire wear

21.2 Four Wheel Alignments 四轮定位

There are two main types of 4-wheel alignments. In each case, the technician will place an instrument on all four wheels. In the first type the rear toe and tracking is checked, but all adjustments are made at the front wheels. This is done on vehicles that do not have adjustments on the rear. The second type is a full 4-wheel alignment where the adjustments are first made to true up the rear alignment, then the front is adjusted. A full 4-wheel alignment will cost more than the other type because there is more work involved.

Below is a list of the alignment settings that are important for a wheel alignment technician to know about in order to diagnose front end problems.

21.2.1 Camber 车轮外倾

When camber specifications are determined during the design stage, a number of factors are taken into account. The engineers account for the fact that wheel alignment specifications used by alignment technicians are for a vehicle that is not moving. On many vehicles, camber changes with different road speeds. This is because aerodynamic forces cause a change in riding height from the height of a vehicle at rest. Because of this, riding height should be checked and problems corrected before setting camber. Camber specs are set so that when a vehicle is at highway speed, the camber is at the optimal setting for minimum tire wear.

For many years the trend has been to set the camber from zero to slightly positive to offset vehicle loading, however the current trend is to slightly negative settings to increase vehicle stability and improve handling.

21.2.2 Caster 主销后倾

Positive caster improves straight line tracking because the caster line (the line drawn through the steering pivot when viewed from the side) intersects the ground ahead of the contact patch of the tire. Just like a shopping cart caster, the wheel is forced behind the pivot allowing the vehicle to track in a straight line.

If this is the case, then why did most cars have negative caster specs prior to 1975. There are a couple of reasons for this. In those days, people were looking for cars that steered as light as a feather, and cars back then were not equipped with radial tires. Non-radial tires had a tendency to distort at highway speed so that the contact patch moved back past the centerline of the tire (Picture a cartoon car speeding along, the tires are generally drawn as egg-shaped). The contact patch generally moves behind the caster line causing, in effect, a positive caster. This is why, when you put radial tires on this type of car, the car wanders from side to side and no longer tracks straight. To correct this condition, re-adjust the caster to positive and the car should steer like a new car.

21.2.3 Toe 车轮前端

Like camber, toe will change depending on vehicle speed. As aerodynamic forces change the riding height, the toe setting may change due to the geometry of the steering linkage in relation to the geometry of the suspension. Because of this, specifications are determined for a vehicle that is not moving based on the toe being at zero when the vehicle is at highway speed. In the early days prior to radial tires, extra toe-in was added to compensate for tire drag at highway speed.

On some older alignment machines, toe-in was measured at each wheel by referencing the opposite wheel. This method caused problems with getting the steering wheel straight the first time and necessitated corrective adjustments before the wheel was straight. Newer machines reference the vehicles centerline by putting instruments on all four wheels.

21.2.4 Steering Axis Inclination (SAI) 主销内倾

SAI is the measurement in degrees of the steering pivot line when viewed from the front of the vehicle. This angle, when added to the camber to form the included angle (see below) causes the vehicle to lift slightly when you turn the wheel away from a straight ahead position. This action uses the weight of the vehicle to cause the steering wheel to return to the center when you let go of it after making a turn. Because of this, if the SAI is different from side to side, it will cause a pull at very slow speeds. Most alignment machines have a way to measure SAI; however it is not separately adjustable. The most likely cause for SAI being out is bent parts which must be replaced to correct the condition. SAI is also referred to KPI (King Pin Inclination) on trucks and old cars with king pins instead of ball joints.

21.2.5 Included Angle 内外倾总角

Included angle is the angle formed between the SAI and the camber. Included angle is not directly measurable. To determine the included angle, you add the SAI to the camber. If the camber is negative, then the included angle will be less than the SAI, if the camber is positive, it will be greater. The included angle must be the same from side to side even if the camber is different. If it is not the same, then something is bent, most likely the steering knuckle.

21.2.6 Scrub Radius 转向主销内倾内置量

Scrub radius is the distance between where the SAI intersects the ground and the center of the tire. This distance must be exactly the same from side to side or the vehicle will pull strongly at all speeds. While included angle problems will affect the scrub radius, it is not the only thing that will affect it. Different wheels or tires from side to side will cause differences in scrub radius as well as a tire that is low on air. Positive scrub radius is when the tire contact patch is outside of the SAI pivot, while negative scrub radius is when the contact patch is inboard of the SAI pivot (front wheel drive vehicles usually have negative scrub radius).

If the brake on one front wheel is not working, with positive scrub radius, stepping on the brake will cause the steering wheel to try to rip out of your hand. Negative scrub radius will minimize that effect.

Scrub radius is designed at the factory and is not adjustable. If you have a vehicle that is pulling even though the alignment is correct, look for something that will affect scrub radius.

21.2.7 Riding Height 离地间隙

Riding height is measured, usually in inches, from the rocker panel to the ground. Good wheel alignment charts provide specs, but the main thing is that the measurements should be within one inch from side to side and from front to rear. Riding height is not adjustable except on vehicles with torsion bar type springs. The best way to fix this problem is to replace the springs (Note: springs should only be replaced in matched pairs). Changes in riding height will affect camber and toe so if springs are replaced or torsion bars are adjusted, then the wheel alignment must be checked to avoid the possibility of tire wear. It is important to note that the only symptom of weak coil springs is a sag in the riding height. If the riding height is good, then the springs are good.

21.2.8 Set Back 向后移动

Set back is when one front wheel is set further back than the other wheel. With alignment equipment that measures toe by using only the front instruments, any setback will cause an uncentered steering wheel. Any good 4-wheel aligner will reference the rear wheels when setting toe in order to eliminate this problem.

Some good alignment equipment will measure set back and give you a reading in inches or millimeters. A set back of less than 1/4 inch is considered normal tolerance by some manufacturers. More than that and there is a good chance that something is bent.

21.2.9　Thrust Angle 推力角

Thrust angle is the direction that the rear wheels are pointing in relation to the center line of the vehicle. If the thrust angle is not zero, then the vehicle will "dog track" and the steering wheel will not be centered. The best solution is to first adjust the rear toe to the center line and then adjust the front toe. This is normally done during a 4-wheel alignment as long as the rear toe is adjustable. If the rear is not adjustable, then the front toe must be set to compensate for the thrust angle, allowing the steering to be centered.

21.2.10　Steering Center 转向中心

Steering center is simply the fact that the steering wheel is centered when the vehicle is traveling down a straight and level road. A crooked steering wheel is usually the most common complaint that a customer has after a wheel alignment is performed. Assuming that the steering wheel stays in the same position when you let go of the wheel (in other words, the car is not pulling), then steering center is controlled by the front and rear toe settings. When setting steering center, the rear toe should be set first bringing the Thrust Angle as close to the vehicle centerline as possible. Then the steering wheel is locked in a straight ahead position while the front toe is set. Before locking the steering wheel, the engine should be started and the wheel should be turned right and left a couple of times to take any stress off the power steering valve. After setting the toe, the engine should be started again to be sure that the steering valve wasn't loaded again due to the tie rod adjustments. Of course, you should always road test the vehicle after every alignment as a quality control check.

Another problem with steering center has to do with the type of roads that are driven on. Most roads are crowned to allow for water drainage, and unless you drive in England, Japan or another country where they drive on the left side of the road, you usually drive on the right side of the crown. This may cause the vehicle to drift to the right so that the steering wheel will appear to be off-center to the left on a straight road. The best way to compensate for this is as follows:

If there is a difference in caster, it should be that the left wheel is more negative than the right wheel, but not more than 1/2 degree. Check the specs for any specific recommendations on side-to-side differences.

If there is a difference in camber, then the left wheel should be more positive than the right wheel. Check the specs to see what the allowable difference is.

21.2.11　Toe Out on Turns 转弯时的后束

When you steer a car through a turn, the outside front wheel has to navigate a wider arc then the inside wheel. For this reason, the inside front wheel must steer at a sharper angle than the outside wheel.

Toe-out on turns is measured by the turning angle gauges (turn plates). Those are a part of every wheel alignment machine. The readings are either directly on the turn plate or they are measured electronically and displayed on the screen. Wheel alignment specifications will usually provide the measurements for toe-out on turns. They will give an angle for the inside wheel and the outside wheel such as 20W for the inside wheel and 18W for the outside wheel. Make sure that the readings are at zero on each side when the wheels are straight ahead, then turn the steering wheel so that the inside wheel is at the inside spec, then check the outside wheel.

The toe-out angles are accomplished by the angle of the steering arm. This arm allows the inside wheel to turn sharper than the outside wheel. The steering arm is either part of the steering knuckle or part of the ball joint and is not adjustable. If there is a problem with the toe-out, it is due to a bent steering arm that must be replaced.

[词汇]

alignment	n. 定位	measurable	adj. 可测量的
camber	n. 车轮外倾	scrub radius	转向主销内倾内置量
caster	n. 主销后倾	riding height	离地间隙
toe-in	n. 前束	rocker panel	车门下围板
tread	n. 胎面	chart	n. 图
steering wheel	转向盘	torsion bar	扭力杆
suspension	n. 悬架	sag	n. 下垂
bump	n. 凸起	set back	向后移动
saw-tooth	锯齿状	aligner	n. 定位仪
specification	n. 技术规格	tolerance	n. 规定公差
intersect	vi. (直线)相交,交叉	thrust angle	推力角
cart	n. 手推车	crooked	adj. 弯的
radial tire	子午线轮胎	power steering	动力转向
wander	v. 跑偏	tie rod	横拉杆
geometry	n. 几何参数	crown	v. 隆起
tire drag	轮胎滚动阻力	water drainage	排水
necessitate	v. 成为必要	toe-out on turns	转弯时的后束
steering axis inclination	主销内倾	steering arm	转向臂
king pin inclination	主销倾斜	steering knuckle	转向节
included angle	内外倾总角		

[注释]

1. Caster 主销后倾:站在车身左侧,观察车的左前轮,我们会发现主销是向后倾倒的。这样做的主要目的是为了让主销的延长线与地面的交点在车轮触地点的前面。这种设计是为了使车轮在滚动的过程中保持稳定,不致左右摇摆。

2. Steering axis inclination 主销内倾:站在车的后部,观察车的右前轮,我们发现主销向左倾倒,也即向内侧倾倒。

3. Thrust angle 推力角：推力线与汽车几何中心线间的夹角。

[问题]

1. Please explain following words: camber, caster, toe-in.
2. What's the difference between toe-in and toe-out?
3. What's scrub radius?
4. How is riding height measured?

Lesson 22

Hydraulic Brake System
液压制动系统

When you step on the brake pedal, you expect the vehicle to stop. The brake pedal operates a hydraulic system that is used for two reasons. First, fluid under pressure can be carried to all parts of the vehicle by small hoses or metal lines without taking up a lot of room or causing routing problems. Second, the hydraulic fluid offers a great mechanical advantage-little foot pressure is required on the pedal, but a great deal of pressure is generated at the wheels. The brake pedal is linked to a piston in the brake master cylinder, which is filled with hydraulic brake fluid. The master cylinder consists of a cylinder containing a small piston and a fluid reservoir. (See Figure 22-1).

Modern master cylinders are actually two separate cylinders. Such a system is called a

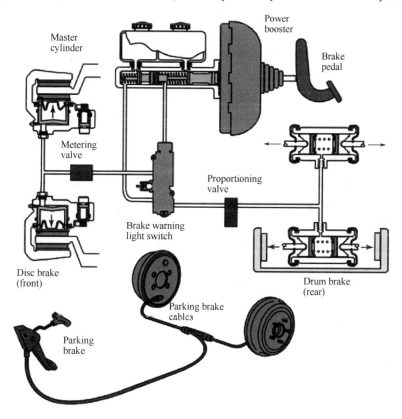

Figure 22-1   Typical brake system components

105

dual circuit, because the front cylinder is connected to the front brakes and the rear cylinder to the rear brakes. (Some vehicles are connected diagonally.) The two cylinders are actually separated, allowing for emergency stopping power should one part of the system fail.

The entire hydraulic system from the master cylinder to the wheels is full of hydraulic brake fluid. When the brake pedal is depressed, the pistons in the master cylinder are forced to move, exerting tremendous force on the fluid in the lines. The fluid has nowhere to go, and forces the wheel cylinder pistons (drum brakes) or caliper pistons (disc brakes) to exert pressure on the brake shoes or pads. The friction between the brake shoe and wheel drum or the brake pad and rotor (disc) slows the vehicle and eventually stops it.

Also attached to the brake pedal is a switch that lights the brake lights as the pedal is depressed. The lights stay on until the brake pedal is released and returns to its normal position.

Each wheel cylinder in a drum brake system contains two pistons, one at either end, which push outward in opposite directions. In disc brake systems, the wheel cylinders are part of the caliper (there can be as many as four or as few as one). Whether disc or drum type, all pistons use some type of rubber seal to prevent leakage around the piston, and a rubber dust boot seals the outer ends of the wheel cylinders against dirt and moisture.

When the brake pedal is released, a spring pushes the master cylinder pistons back to their normal positions. Check valves in the master cylinder piston allow fluid to flow toward the wheel cylinders or calipers as the piston returns. Then as the brake shoe return springs pull the brake shoes back to the released position, excess fluid returns to the master cylinder through compensating ports, which have been uncovered as the pistons move back. Any fluid that has leaked from the system will also be replaced through the compensating ports.

All dual circuit brake systems use a switch to activate a light, warning of brake failure. The switch is located in a valve mounted near the master cylinder. A piston in the valve receives pressure on each end from the front and rear brake circuits. When the pressures are balanced, the piston remains stationary, but when one circuit has a leak, greater pressure during the application of the brakes will force the piston to one side or the other, closing the switch and activating the warning light. The light can also be activated by the ignition switch during engine starting or by the parking brake.

Front disc, rear drum brake systems also have a metering valve to prevent the front disc brakes from engaging before the rear brakes have contacted the drums. This ensures that the front brakes will not normally be used alone to stop the vehicle. A proportioning valve is also used to limit pressure to the rear brakes to prevent rear wheel lock-up during hard braking. (See Figure 22-2).

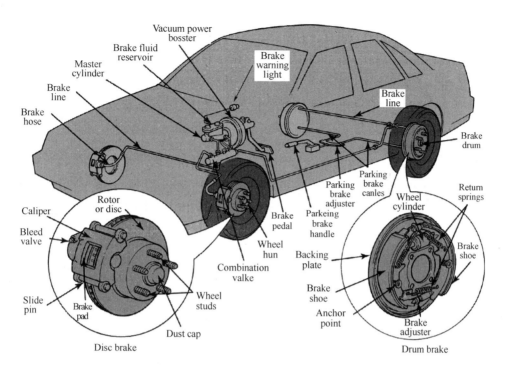

Figure 22-2　Typical vehicle brake system showing all typical components

Friction materials 摩擦材料

Brake shoes and pads are constructed in a similar manner. The pad or shoe is composed of a metal backing plate and a friction lining. The lining is either bonded (glued) to the metal, or riveted. Generally, riveted linings provide superior performance, but good quality bonded linings are perfectly adequate.

Friction materials will vary between manufacturers and type of pad and the material compound may be referred to as: asbestos, organic, semi-metallic, metallic. The difference between these compounds lies in the types and percentages of friction materials used, material binders and performance modifiers.

Generally speaking, organic and non-metallic asbestos compound brakes are quiet, easy on rotors and provide good feel. But this comes at the expense of high temperature operation, so they may not be your best choice for heavy duty use or mountain driving. In most cases, these linings will wear somewhat faster than metallic compound pads, so you will usually replace them more often. But, when using these pads, rotors tend to last longer.

Semi-metallic or metallic compound brake linings will vary in performance based on the metallic contents of the compound. Again, generally speaking, the higher the metallic content, the better the friction material will resist heat. This makes them more appropriate for heavy duty applications, but at the expense of braking performance before the pad reaches operating temperature. The first few applications on a cold morning may not give strong braking. Also, metallics and semi-metallics are more likely to squeal. In most cases, metallic compounds last longer than non-metallic pads, but they tend to cause more wear on the rotors. If you use metallic pads, expect to replace the rotors more often.

When deciding what type of brake lining is right for you, keep in mind that today's modern cars have brake materials which are matched to the expected vehicle's performance capabilities. Changing the material from OEM specification could adversely affect brake feel or responsiveness. Before changing the brake materials, talk to your dealer or parts supplier to help decide what is most appropriate for your application. Remember that heavy use applications such as towing, stop and go driving, driving down mountain roads, and racing may require a change to a higher performance material.

Some more exotic materials are also used in brake linings, among which are Kevlar and carbon compounds. These materials have the capability of extremely good performance for towing, mountain driving or racing. Wear characteristics can be similar to either the metallic or the non-metallic linings, depending on the product you buy. Most race applications tend to wear like metallic linings, while many of the street applications are more like the non-metallics.

[词汇]

master cylinder	主缸	bond	n.结合（物），黏结（剂）
hydraulic	水力的，液压的	glue	vt.胶合，粘贴，黏合
piston	n.活塞，柱塞，活塞	rivet	铆钉，铆接
reservoir	n.储器，油箱，积蓄	asbestos	n.石棉
dual	adj.双的，二重的，双重的	organic	adj.器官的，有机的，组织的，建制的
emergency	n.紧急		
drum	n.鼓，鼓轮，鼓筒	semi-metallic	半金属（性）的
caliper	n.卡钳	metallic	adj.金属（性）的
disc	n.轮盘，盘	binder	n.胶接剂，毡填料，黏合剂
brake shoe	n.闸瓦，制动蹄，制动块	modifier	n.改良剂，调节器，改性剂，改进剂
pad	n.衬垫，密封，垫		
rotor	n.转子，旋转器	OEM	原始设备制造商
check valve	n.回压阀，单流阀，止回阀	Kevlar	凯夫拉尔纤维（一种质地牢固重量轻的合成纤维）
wheel cylinder	轮缸		
lining	n.加衬里，内层，衬套		

[注释]

Caliper 制动钳：盘式制动器的制动钳，制动时钳上的制动块压向制动盘产生制动作用。

[问题]

1. What are the main components of the hydraulic system?
2. How does the hydraulic brake system work?
3. What kinds of material are used in brake linings?
4. What's the difference between disc brake and drum brake?

Lesson 23

Disc Brake
盘式制动器

Disc brakes are used on the front wheels of most cars and on all four wheels on many cars. A disc rotor is attached to the wheel hub and rotates with the tire and wheel. When the driver applies the brakes, hydraulic pressure from the master cylinder is used to push friction linings against the rotor to stop it.

In the disc brake rotor assembly, the rotor is usually made of cast iron. The hub may be manufactured as one piece with the rotor or in two parts. The rotor has a machined braking surface on each face. A splash shield, mounted to the steering knuckle, protects the rotor from road splash.

A rotor may be solid or ventilated. Ventilated designs have cooling fins cast between the braking surfaces. This construction considerably increases the cooling area of the rotor casting. Also, when the wheel is in motion, the rotation of these fan-type fins in the rotor provides increased air circulation and more efficient cooling of the brake. Disc brakes do not fade even after rapid, hard brake applications because of the rapid cooling of the rotor.

The hydraulic and friction components are housed in a caliper assembly. The caliper assembly straddles the outside diameter of the hub and rotor assembly. When the brakes are applied, the pressure of the pistons is exerted through the shoes in a 'clamping' action on the rotor. Because equal opposed hydraulic pressures are applied to both faces of the rotor throughout application, no distortion of the rotor occurs, regardless of the severity or duration of application. There are many variations of caliper designs, but they can all be grouped into two main categories: moving and stationary caliper. The caliper is fixed in one position on the stationary design. In the moving design, the caliper moves in relation to the rotor.

Most late-model cars use the moving caliper design. This design uses a single hydraulic piston and a caliper that can float or slide during application. Floating designs 'float' or move on pins or bolts. In sliding designs, the caliper slides sideways on machined surfaces. Both designs work in basically the same way.

In the single piston floating caliper, the single-piston caliper assembly is constructed from a single casting that contains one large piston bore in the inboard section of the casting. Inboard refers to the side of the casting nearest the center line of the car when the caliper is mounted. A fluid inlet hole and bleeder valve hole are machined into the inboard section of the caliper and connect directly to the piston bore.

The caliper cylinder bore contains a piston and seal. The seal has a rectangular cross section. It is located in a groove that is machined in the cylinder bore. The seal fits around the outside diameter of the piston and provides a hydraulic seal between the piston and the cylinder wall. The rectangular seal provides automatic adjustment of clearance between the rotor and shoe and linings following each application. When the brakes are applied, the caliper seal is deflected by the hydraulic pressure and its inside diameter rides with the piston within the limits of its retention in the cylinder groove. When hydraulic pressure is released, the seal relaxes and returns to its original rectangular shape, retracting the piston into the cylinder enough to provide proper running clearance. As brake linings wear, piston travel tends to exceed the limit of deflection of the seal; the piston therefore slides in the seal to the precise extent necessary to compensate for lining wear. (See Figure 23-1).

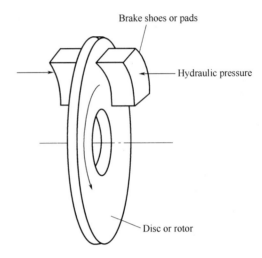

Figure 23-1 Hydraulic pressure forces brake pads against the rotor to stop the car

The top of the piston bore is machined to accept a sealing dust boot. The piston in many calipers is steel, precision ground, and nickel chrome plated, giving it a very hard and durable surface. Some manufacturers are using a plastic piston. This is much lighter than steel and provides for a much lighter brake system. The plastic piston insulates well and prevents heat from transferring to the brake fluid. Each caliper contains two shoe and lining assemblies. They are constructed of a stamped metal shoe with the lining riveted or bonded to the shoe and are mounted in the caliper on either side of the rotor. One shoe and lining assembly is called the inboard lining because it fits nearest to the center line of the car. The other is called the outboard shoe and lining assembly.

As already mentioned, the caliper is free to float on its two mounting pins or bolts. Teflon sleeves in the caliper allow it to move easily on the pins. During application of the brakes, the fluid pressure behind the piston increases. Pressure is exerted equally against the bottom of the piston and the bottom of the cylinder bore. The pressure applied to the piston is transmitted to the inboard shoe and lining, forcing the lining against the inboard rotor surface. The pressure applied to the bottom of the cylinder bore forces the caliper to move on the mounting bolts toward the inboard side, or toward the car. Because the caliper is one piece, this movement causes the outboard section of the caliper to apply pressure against the back of the outboard shoe and lining assembly, forcing the lining against the outboard rotor surface. As the line pressure builds up, the shoe and lining assemblies are pressed against the rotor surfaces with increased force, bringing the car to a stop.

The application and release of the brake pressure actually causes a very slight movement of the piston and caliper. Upon release of the braking effort, the piston and caliper merely relax into a released position. In the released position, the shoes do not retract very far from the rotor surfaces.

As the brake lining wears, the piston moves out of the caliper bore and the caliper repositions itself on the mounting bolts an equal distance toward the car. This way, the caliper assembly maintains the inboard and outboard shoe and lining in the same relationship with the rotor surface throughout the full length of the lining.

Sliding calipers are made to slide back and forth on the steering knuckle support to which it is mounted. There is a V shaped surface, sometimes called a rail, on the caliper that matches a similar surface on the steering knuckle support. These two mating surfaces allow the caliper to slide in and out. The internal components of the caliper are the same as those previously described.

The stationary or fixed caliper has a hydraulic piston on each side of the rotor. Larger calipers may have two pistons on each side of the rotor. The inboard and outboard brake shoes are pushed against the rotor by their own pistons. The caliper is anchored solidly and does not move. The seals around the pistons work just like those already described. The main disadvantage of the stationary caliper is that it has more hydraulic components. This means they are more expensive and have more parts to wear out.

[词汇]

rotor	n. 转动体，转子	duration	n. 持续，持久，持续时间
hub	n. 轮毂，中心体，毂	distortion	n. 扭曲，变形，曲解，失真
master cylinder	主缸	caliper	n. 制动钳
lining	n. 里衬，衬套，衬垫	inboard	adj. 内侧的
cast iron	n. 铸铁，锻铁	bleeder	n. 流出装置，泄放装置，放出阀
splash	n. 飞溅，溅射，喷雾		
shield	n. 遮护板，挡，屏	rectangular	adj. 矩形的，长方形的，成直角的
steering knuckle	转向节		
ventilate	vt. 使通风，给…装通风设备	boot	n. 防尘罩
fin	n. 散热片，鳍状物，稳定器叶片，稳定筋，稳流筋，翅	Teflon	n. 特氟隆，聚四氟乙烯
		sleeve	n. 套，套筒，套管
severity	n. 严重性	anchor	n. 支座，固定，吊钩，固定器

[注释]

Disc brake 盘式制动器：又称为碟式制动器，顾名思义是取其形状而得名。它由液压控制，主要零部件有制动盘、分泵、制动钳、油管等。制动盘用合金钢制造并固定在车轮上，随车轮转动。分泵固定在制动器的底板上固定不动。制动钳上的两个摩擦片分别装在制动盘的两侧。

[问题]

1. What are the main components of disc brakes?
2. How does the disc brake operate?
3. Please explain the construction of disc brakes.
4. What are the advantages of the floating caliper?

Lesson 24

Tires
轮胎

Tires are among the most important and least understood parts of the vehicle. Everything concerned with driving——starting, moving and stopping——involves the tires. Because of their importance to driving easefully and safety, learning the basics of tires will pay off in dollar savings and safe driving.

Common sense and good driving habits will afford maximum tire life. Fast starts, sudden stops and hard cornering are hard on tires and will shorten their useful life span. Make sure that you don't overload the vehicle or run with incorrect pressure in the tires. Both of these practices will increase tread wear.

For optimum tire life, keep the tires properly inflated, rotate them every six months or 6000 miles (9600 km), and have the wheel alignment checked periodically.

Inspect your tires frequently. Be especially careful to watch for bubbles in the tread or sidewall, deep cuts or under-inflation. Replace any tires with bubbles in the sidewall. If cuts are so deep that they penetrate to the cords, discard the tire. Any cut in the sidewall of a radial tire renders it unsafe. Also, look for uneven tread wear patterns that may indicate the front end is out of alignment, the tires are out of balance or are improperly inflated.

24.1 Tire construction 轮胎结构

Modern tires use a combination of materials to contain pressurized air. The foundation of the tire is the plies (layers of nylon, polyester, fiberglass or steel) just beneath the tread that provides flexibility and strength. Regardless of size, cost or brand, there are only three types of tires-bias, bias-belted, and radial, now the standard on all passenger vehicles (See Figure 24-1).

Bias tires, the old stand-by, are constructed with cords running across the tread (from bead-to-bead) at an angle about 35° to the tread centerline; alternate plies reverse direction. Crisscrossing adds strength to the tire sidewalls and tread. When properly inflated, these tires give a relatively soft, comfortable ride.

Bias-belted tires are similar, but additional belts of fiberglass or rayon encircle the tire under the tread. The belts stabilize the tread, holding it flatter against the road with less squirm (side movement). Belted tires offer a firmer ride, better traction, improved

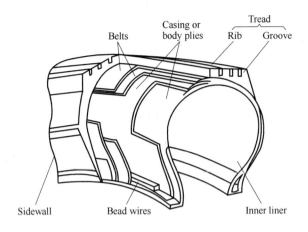

Figure 24-1 The main parts of a tire

puncture resistance and longer life than bias ply tires. Bias tires are now found mainly on antique vehicles to preserve their original appearance, and in some commercial applications.

Radial tires now rule the road as they are original equipment on virtually every passenger car and light truck. Radials are constructed with steel or fabric carcass plies crossing the tread at approximately a 90° angle, and two or more belts circle the tire under the tread. The sidewalls flex while the tread remains rigid, accounting for the characteristic sidewall bulge of a radial. The tread runs flatter on the road with a better grip and the inherently harsher ride is offset by superior handling and mileage.

24.2 Tire technology 轮胎技术

Since 1985, when the 27.5 mpg CAFE (Corporate Average Fuel Economy) standards took effect, there were a lot of changes in tires. Tires are very important in meeting the CAFE standards because they are responsible for 20% of a vehicle's total drag. The reduced rolling resistance of radial tires has made them the standard design. However, even with all the recent tire developments, it has to be a compromise. A tire that handles well sacrifices tread wear; a soft-riding tire sacrifices traction; a tire that reduces rolling resistance and delivers improved fuel economy sacrifices braking stability.

Tire selection

For maximum satisfaction, tires should be used in sets of four. Mixing of different types (radial, bias-belted, fiberglass belted) must be avoided. In most cases, the vehicle manufacturer has designated a type of tire on which the vehicle will perform best. Your first choice when replacing tires should be to use the same type of tire that the manufacturer recommends.

When radial tires are used, tire sizes and wheel diameters should be selected to maintain ground clearance and tire load capacity equivalent to the original specified tire. Radial tires should always be used in sets of four.

24.3　Understanding tire sizes 了解轮胎尺寸

The P-Metric system is now used as the measurement standard for passenger car tires. The first number in the P-Metric system is the width of the tire in millimeters, measured from sidewall to sidewall. To convert to inches, divide by 25.4 In the example above, the width is 185mm or 7.28 inches.

The second number is the aspect ratio. This is a ratio of sidewall height to width. In the example above, the tire is 7.28 inches wide, multiply that by the aspect ratio to find the height of one sidewall. In this case, $185 \times 0.60 = 111$mm or 7.28 inches $\times 0.6 = 4.36$ inches.

The last number is the diameter of the wheel in inches.

To figure the outside diameter of a tire, take the sidewall height and multiply by two, (remember that the diameter is made up of two sidewalls, the one above the wheel, and the one below the wheel) and add the diameter of the wheel to get your answer.

Example… 185/60R14 85H or 185/60HR14

185mm $\times 0.60 = 111$mm $\times 2 = 222$mm + 355.6mm (14 inches) = 577.6mm or 22.74 inches

24.4　Tire types 轮胎类型

Original Equipment (OE) tires are usually a compromise. The vehicle designer needs to blend handling, noise, ride, and wear to create a "perfect tire" for the average driver. Most people find that their needs may be biased more toward handling or ride than the average driver. When replacing OE tires it is recommended, and in some municipalities required, that the replacement tires are of OE specifications or better. Tires are known by many names and styles. Each type has a slightly different function, as well as different capabilities:

Max/Exotic performance tires are usually technically advanced, combining expensive materials and precision lightweight construction techniques to provide superior handling in wet or dry conditions and have extremely high speed capabilities (Z rated or higher).

Ultra high performance tires are the top level of tires that are available in a wide range of sizes. They are low profile tires designed to give high speed capabilities and quick steering response with outstanding cornering in wet or dry conditions (V or Z speed rating).

High performance tires are a slight upgrade from OE tires in terms of handling. They offer nearly the handling of the ultra high performance tires, but at a significantly lower price (H or lower speed rating).

Ultra high performance and high performance all season tires are derived and usually based on the ultra high/high performance non-all season tire. They are altered in tread pattern to gain in snow traction and the rubber compound is changed to be pliable over a wider temperature range. The snow capabilities of this type of tire is minimal, but is usually enough to get through an inch or two of snow (H to Z speed ratings).

Touring tires combine the appearance and responsive handling of a performance tire with more of a smooth ride quality and lower noise levels. this type of tire will, typically wear longer than a performance tire (S to V speed ratings).

All season (or mud + snow) tires are aimed mainly at domestic sedans, these tires offer very long tread wear, plush ride, and predictable handling.

Snow tires are specially constructed to grip snowy surfaces. The rubber is specially formulated to stay pliable in the cold and provide better traction on ice. The interlocking tread pattern of the snow tire allows it to bite the snow for additional stop-and-go traction.

Competition tires are the highest performing street legal tire you can purchase. These are special purpose tires that feature a very shallow tread pattern, stiff construction, and high grip tread compounds. Usually these tires are very prone to hydroplaning, and offer practically no tread wear.

[词汇]

span	n.跨度,跨距,范围	polyester	n.聚酯
inflate	vt.使膨胀,使得意,使(通货)膨胀,使充气	fiberglass	n.玻璃纤维,玻璃丝
		bead	n.胎圈
rotate	v.旋转,轮换	squirm	n.& vt.轮胎蠕动
wheel alignment	车轮定位	flexibility	n.弹性,适应性,机动性,挠性
bubble	v.& n.气泡,起泡,泡,水泡	bias	n.斜交
sidewall	n.侧壁(侧墙,轮胎侧壁)	rayon	n.人造丝
cut	n.切口	encircle	vt.环绕,围绕,包围,绕…行一周
inflation	n.充气,膨胀		
cord	n.帘布轮胎	carcass	n.胎体,外胎身行
discard	vt.丢弃,抛弃	flex	n.弯曲,挠曲,花线
unsafe	adj.不安全的,危险的,不安稳的	traction	n.牵引,牵引力
		compromise	n.妥协,折衷
uneven	adj.不平坦的,不平均的,不均匀的,奇数的	exotic	adj.外来的,外国的
		lightweight	adj.轻的(重量轻的,标准重以下的)
tread	n.轮胎花纹,轮胎胎面		
ply	n.层片,层,股	pliable	adj.易曲折的,柔软的,圆滑的,柔韧的
layer	n.层		
nylon	n.尼龙		

[注释]

1. bead 胎圈:胎圈是轮胎的一部分,它是轮胎牢固地安装在轮辋上。胎圈由钢丝圈、帘布层包边和胎圈包布组成。

2. Sedan 轿车:美国人常用这一词来指家用四门汽车。封闭式车身,固定式刚性结构车顶,有2~3排座位,4个侧门,或增加一后门。

[问题]

1. Please describe tire construction.
2. What's the radial tire?
3. How do you select tires?
4. What kinds of tires are there in the automobile?

Chapter 3　Automotive Electric Equipments
汽车电器

Lesson 25

Ignition System
点火系统

There are many different types of ignition systems. Most of these systems can be placed into one of three distinct groups: the conventional breaker point type ignition systems (in use since the early 1900s); the electronic ignition systems (popular since the mid 70s); and the distributorless ignition system (introduced in the mid 80s).

The automotive ignition system has two basic functions: it must control the spark and timing of the spark plug firing to match varying engine requirements, and it must increase battery voltage to a point where it will overcome the resistance offered by the spark plug gap and fire the plug.

How does the ignition system work 点火系统如何工作

An automotive ignition system is divided into two electrical circuits——the primary and secondary circuits. The primary circuit carries low voltage. This circuit operates only on battery current and is controlled by the breaker points and the ignition switch. The secondary circuit consists of the secondary windings in the coil, the high tension lead between the distributor and the coil (commonly called the coil wire) on external coil distributors, the distributor cap, the distributor rotor, the spark plug leads and the spark plugs.

The distributor is the controlling element of the system. It switches the primary current on and off and distributes the current to the proper spark plug each time a spark is needed. The distributor is a stationary housing surrounding a rotating shaft. The shaft is driven at one-half engine speed by the engine's camshaft through the distributor drive gears. A cam near the top of the distributor shaft has one lobe for each cylinder of the engine. The cam operates the contact points, which are mounted on a plate within the distributor housing.

A rotor is attached to the top of the distributor shaft. When the distributor cap is in place, a spring-loaded piece of metal in the center of the cap makes contact with a metal strip on top of the rotor. The outer end of the rotor passes very close to the contacts connected to the spark plug leads around the outside of the distributor cap.

The coil is the heart of the ignition system. Essentially, it is nothing more than a transformer which takes the relatively low voltage (12 volts) available from the battery and increases it to a point where it will fire the spark plug as much as 40000 volts. The term "coil" is perhaps a misnomer since there are actually two coils of wire wound about an iron core. These coils are insulated from each other and the whole assembly is enclosed in an oil-filled case. The primary coil, which consists of relatively few turns of heavy wire, is connected to the two primary terminals located on top of the coil. The secondary coil consists of many turns of fine wire. It is connected to the high-tension connection on top of the coil (the tower into which the coil wire from the distributor is plugged). (See Figure 25-1).

Under normal operating conditions, power from the battery is fed through a resistor or resistance wire to the primary circuit of the coil and is then grounded through the ignition points in the distributor (the points are closed). Energizing the coil primary circuit with battery voltage produces current flow through the primary windings, which induces a

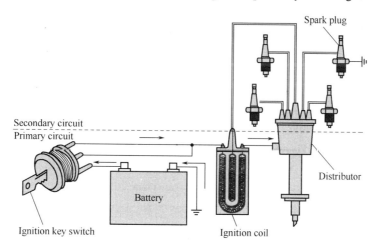

Figure 25-1 Major components of the ignition system

very large, intense magnetic field. This magnetic field remains as long as current flows and the points remain closed.

As the distributor cam rotates, the points are pushed apart, breaking the primary circuit and stopping the flow of current. Interrupting the flow of primary current causes the magnetic field to collapse. Just as current flowing through a wire produces a magnetic field, moving a magnetic field across a wire will produce a current. As the magnetic field collapses, its lines of force cross the secondary windings, inducing a current in them. Since there are many more turns of wire in the secondary windings, the voltage from the primary windings is magnified considerably up to 40000 volts.

The voltage from the coil secondary windings flows through the coil high-tension lead to the center of the distributor cap, where it is distributed by the rotor to one of the outer terminals in the cap. From there, it flows through the spark plug lead to the spark plug. This process occurs in a split second and is repeated every time the points open and close, which is up to 1500 times a minute in a 4-cylinder engine at idle.

To prevent the high voltage from burning the points, a condenser is installed in the circuit. It absorbs some of the force of the surge of electrical current that occurs during the collapse of the magnetic field. The condenser consists of several layers of aluminum foil separated by insulation. These layers of foil are capable of storing electricity, making the condenser an electrical surge tank.

Voltages just after the points open may reach 250 volts because of the amount of energy stored in the primary windings and the subsequent magnetic field. A condenser which is defective or improperly grounded will not absorb the shock from the fast-moving stream of electricity when the points open and the current can force its way across the point gap, causing pitting and burning.

[词汇]

ignition	n.点火，点燃	housing	n.壳体，罩壳
breaker	n.断电器	lobe	n.凸角
distributorless	无分电器的	cam	n.凸轮
timing	n.适时，时间选择，定时，调速	contact point	n.触点
spark plug	n.火花塞	rotor	n.转子
gap	n.间隙，间隔	transformer	n.变压器
primary	adj.初级的，原来的，根源的	misnomer	n.误称
secondary	adj.次级的，副的，次等的	iron core	铁芯
winding	n.绕，缠，绕组，线圈	turn	n.圈，匝，转动
tension	n.张力，拉力，电压	resistor	n.电阻器
lead	n.导线，导程	resistance	n.电阻
distributor	n.分配器，配电盘	terminal	n.端子，接头，端点
coil	n.线圈	tower	n.塔，柱，杆
element	n.元件，部件，零件	idle	n.怠速，空转
stationary	adj.不动的	condenser	n.冷凝器，电容器

foil	*vt.* 衬托，阻止，挡开，挫败，贴箔于	defective	*adj.* 有故障的，有毛病的，有缺点的
surge	*n.* 浪涌，电涌	ground	*vt.* 使⋯接地

[注释]

  Ignition system　点火系统：将蓄电池的低压电转变成高压电，并按发动机不同情况的要求，适时地产生足够能量的电火花，点燃各缸混合气。

[问题]

1. What are the main types of the ignition system?
2. What's the function of the ignition system?
3. Please list the main components of the ignition system。
4. What's the purpose of the ignition coil?

Lesson 26

Starting System
启动系统

The internal combustion engine must be rotated before it will run under its own power. The starting system is a combination of mechanical and electrical parts that work together to start the engine. The starting system is designed to change the electrical energy, which is being stored in the battery, into mechanical energy. To accomplish this conversion, a starter or cranking motor is used. The starting system includes the following components: (See Figure 26-1).

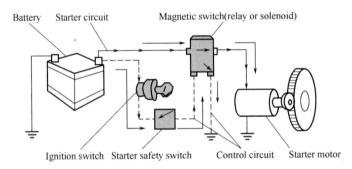

Figure 26-1 Major components of the starting system

1. Battery
2. Cable and wires
3. Ignition switch
4. Starter solenoid or relay
5. Starter motor
6. Starter drive and flywheel ring gear
7. Starting safety switch

The starting system functions to crank the engine fast enough to allow the engine to start. The starting system and ignition system must work together for good engine starting. The mechanic must understand the operation of the starting system because malfunction of one of the system's components could prevent the engine from starting.

When the driver turns the key switch to START, current flows from the battery through the key switch to the solenoid. The solenoid allows battery current to flow directly from the battery to the starter motor, which in turn cranks the engine.

The automotive battery serves as an energy 'bank'. It receives energy from the vehicle's charging system and stores it until needed. Then it provides this energy to the many vehicle electrical systems on demand. The battery converts electrical energy into chemical energy during charging. It then converts it back into electricity during discharging.

The key switch, or ignition switch, controls the ignition circuit. It also controls the starting system and the power for the instruments and vehicle accessories. Most are steering wheel lock-type switches, which are mounted on the steering column.

The starter motor, or starter, is a compact but very powerful direct-current electric motor designed to crank the engine fast enough for it to start. It rotates a small gear called a pinion. A starter drive assembly connects the small pinion gear to the end of the starter motor. The pinion gear meshes with the ring gear on the engine's flywheel. When the driver turns the key switch, the starter motor drives the pinion gear, which drives the flywheel and cranks the engine.

The gear reduction ratio between the starter motor and the engine must be high enough to provide enough torque to turn the engine over at cranking speed. There are approximately 15 to 20 teeth on the flywheel ring gear for every tooth on the drive pinion gear. This means the armature will rotate approximately 15 to 20 times for every engine revolution. In order to turn the engine over at 100 rpm, the armature must rotate at 1500 to 2000 rpm.

If the pinion gear remained meshed with the flywheel ring gear at engine speeds above 1000 rpm, the armature would be spun at very high speeds. These speeds would damage the armature and the commutator. To avoid this, the starter drive assembly is designed to disengage the pinion gear from the ring gear as soon as the engine begins to operate.

The solenoid is a magnetic switch mounted on top of the starter motor. It has two important functions: it controls the electrical circuit between the battery and starter motor and it shifts the pinion gear in and out of mesh with the ring gear.

All cars equipped with automatic transmissions, and most with manual transmissions, have a device to prevent the engine from being started in gear. Without this device, the car would lunge forward or backward if mistakenly started in gear, possibly causing an accident. This device is a neutral safety switch in the starting system circuit. It is mechanically opened when the transmission shift lever is moved to any position other than NEUTRAL or PARK.

A starter drive includes a pinion gear set that meshes with the flywheel ring gear on the engine's crankshaft. To prevent damage to the pinion gear or the ring gear, the pinion gear must mesh with the ring gear before the starter motor rotates. To help assure smooth engagement, the end of the pinion gear is tapered. Also, the action of the armature must always be from the motor to the engine. The engine must not be allowed to spin the armature. The ratio of the number of teeth on the ring gear and the starter drive pinion gear is usually between 15 : 1 and 20 : 1. This means the starter motor is rotating 15 to 20 times faster than the engine. Normal cranking speed for the engine is about 200 rpm. If the starter drive had a ratio of 18 : 1, the starter would be rotating at a speed of 3600 rpm. If the engine started and was accelerated to 2000 rpm, the starter speed would increase to 36000 rpm. This would destroy the starter motor if it was not disengaged from the engine.

[词汇]

starting system	启动系统	discharging	n.放电
internal combustion engine	内燃机	instrument	n.仪器，仪表，器具
conversion	n.变换，转化	accessory	n.附件，零件
cranking motor	启动机	steering wheel	转向盘
battery	n.蓄电池	steering column	转向柱
cable	n.电缆，海底电报，缆，索	compact	adj.紧凑的，紧密的，简洁的
ignition switch	点火开关	pinion	n.小齿轮
solenoid	n.电磁线圈，螺线管线圈	reduction ratio	减速比
		armature	n.电枢，衔铁
relay	n.继电器	commutator	n.整流器，换向器
starter motor	启动机	disengage	vt.放开，解开，解除，分离，使分离
drive	n.传动，驱动，传动装置	automatic transmission	自动变速器
malfunction	n.故障	neutral	n.空挡
charging	n.充电，充气，进气	crankshaft	n.曲轴

[问题]

1. What are the main components of the starting system?
2. Please describe the working process of the starting system.
3. What's the function of the starter?
4. Why is the neutral safety switch used?

Lesson 27

Charging System
充电系统

27.1 The Basics 基础

The automotive storage battery is not capable of supplying the demands of the electrical system for an extended period of time. Every vehicle must be equipped with a means of replacing the current being drawn from the battery. A charging system is used to restore the electrical power to the battery that was used during engine starting. In addition, the charging system must be able to react quickly to high load demands required of the electrical system. It is the vehicle's charging system that generates the current to operate all of the electrical accessories while the engine is running. (See Figure 27-1).

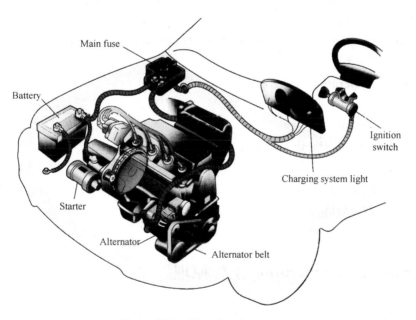

Figure 27-1 The charging system

The purpose of the charging system is to provide the electrical energy needed to charge the battery and to power all the electrical components and systems on the automobile. When the engine is not running, the battery provides this electrical energy. When the engine is running, the charging system takes over. The alternator is the heart of the charging system. It is an alternating-current generator mounted on the engine, which is driven by a belt from the crankshaft. The alternator develops alternating current, which is changed into direct current. Alternating current changes from positive (+) to negative (−) in a regular cycle. Direct current does not change from positive (+) to negative (−). Only direct current can be used to charge a battery.

A voltage regulator, either inside or outside the alternator, senses the electrical needs of the vehicle and adjusts the output of the alternator accordingly. An indicator light on the instrument panel allows the driver to observe whether the system is operating properly. The battery is connected electrically to the alternator, so that either one may supply the electrical needs, and so that the alternator can charge the battery.

Two basic types of charging systems have been used. The first was a DC generator, which was discontinued in the 1960s. Since that time the AC alternator has been the predominant charging device. The DC generator and the AC alternator both use similar operating principles.

As the battery drain continues, and engine speed increases, the charging system is able to produce more voltage than the battery can deliver. When this occurs, the electrons from the charging device are able to flow in a reverse direction through the battery's positive terminal. The charging device is now supplying the electrical system's load requirements; the reserve electrons build up and recharge the battery.

If there is an increase in the electrical demand and a drop in the charging system's output equal to the voltage of the battery, the battery and charging system work together to supply the required current.

The entire charging system consists of the following components:

1. Battery
2. AC or DC generator
3. Drive belt
4. Voltage regulator
5. Charge indicator (lamp or gauge)
6. Ignition switch
7. Cables and wiring harness
8. Starter relay (some systems)
9. Fusible link (some systems)

27.2　Principle of Operation　工作原理

All charging systems use the principle of electromagnetic induction to generate electrical power. Electromagnetic principle states that a voltage will be produced if motion between a conductor and a magnetic field occurs. The amount of voltage produced is affected by:

The speed at which the conductor passes through the magnetic field.

The strength of the magnetic field.

The number of conductors passing through the magnetic field.

When the conductor is parallel with the magnetic field, the conductor is not cut by any flux lines. At this point in the revolution there is zero voltage and current being produced.

As the conductor is rotated 90 degrees, the magnetic field is at a right angle to the conductor. At this point in the revolution the maximum number of flux lines cut the conductor at the north pole. With the maximum amount of flux lines cutting the conductor, voltage and current are at maximum positive values.

When the conductor is rotated an additional 90 degrees, the conductor returns to being parallel with the magnetic field. Once again no flux lines cut the conductor, and voltage and current drop to zero.

An additional 90-degree revolution of the conductor results in the magnetic field being reversed at the top conductor. At this point in the revolution, the maximum number of flux lines cuts the conductor at the south pole. Voltage and current are now at maximum negative values.

When the conductor completes one full revolution, it returns to a parallel position with the magnetic field. Voltage and current return to zero. The sinc wave is determined by the angle between the magnetic field and the conductor. It is based on the trigonometry sine function of angles. The sine wave shown plots the voltage generated during one revolution.

It is the function of the drive belt to turn the conductor. Drive belt tension should be checked periodically to assure proper charging system operation. A loose belt can inhibit charging system efficiency, and a belt that is too tight can cause early bearing failure.

27.3 DC Generators 直流发电机

The DC generator is similar to the DC starter motor used to crank the engine. The housing contains two field coils that create a magnetic field. Output voltage is generated in the wire loops of the armature as it rotates inside the magnetic field. This current is sent to the battery through the brushes.

The components must be polarized whenever a replacement DC generator or voltage regulator is installed. To polarize an externally grounded field circuit (A-type field circuit), use a jumper wire and connect between the BAT terminal and the ARM terminal of the voltage regulator. Make this jumper connection for just an instant. Do not hold the jumper wire on the terminals. For an internally grounded field circuit (B-type), jump the F terminal and the BAT terminal.

[词汇]

charging system	充电系统	negative	adj.负的，负片，阴性的
accessory	n.附件，零件	voltage regulator	电压调节器
alternator	n.交流发电机	indicator light	指示灯
positive	adj.正的，阳的，阳极	instrument panel	仪表盘

discontinue	v.停止，中止	conductor	n.导体
predominant	adj.卓越的，主要的，突出的	flux	n.磁通量
electron	n.电子	sine wave	正弦波
starter	n.启动机	tension	n.绷紧，电压，拉力
fusible	adj.可熔的	DC generator	直流发电机
electromagnetic	adj.电磁的	housing	n.壳体，罩壳
induction	n.感应	jumper wire	跨接线

[问题]

1. What's the purpose of the charging system?
2. What are the main components of the charging system?
3. How does the charging system operate?
4. What's the difference between the DC generator and AC alternator?

Lesson 28

Battery
电池

28.1 Introduction 简介

Everything electrical in a vehicle is supplied current from the battery. The battery is one of the most important parts of a vehicle because it is the heart or foundation of the electrical system. The primary purpose of an automotive battery is to provide a source of electrical power for starting and for electrical demands that exceed alternator output.

The battery also acts as a stabilizer to the voltage for the entire electrical system. The battery is a voltage stabilizer because it acts as a reservoir where large amounts of current (amperes) can be removed quickly during starting and replaced gradually by the alternator during charging.

The battery must be in good (serviceable) condition before the charging system and the cranking system can be tested. For example, if a battery is discharged, the cranking circuit (starter motor) could test as being defective because the battery voltage might drop below specifications.

The charging circuit could also test as being defective because of a weak or discharged battery. It is important to test the vehicle battery before further testing of the cranking or charging system.

28.2 Battery construction 电池结构

28.2.1 Case

Most automotive battery cases (container or covers) are constructed of polypropylene, a thin (approximately 0.08 in., or 2 mm, thick), strong, and lightweight plastic. In contrast, containers for industrial batteries and some truck batteries are constructed of a hard, thick rubber material.

Inside the case are six cells (for a 12 volt battery). See Figure 28-1. Each cell has positive and negative plates. Built into the bottom of many batteries are ribs that support the lead-alloy plates and provide a space for sediment to settle, called the sediment chamber. This space prevents spent active material from causing a short circuit between the plates at the bottom of the battery.

A maintenance-free battery uses little water during normal service because of the alloy material used to construct the battery plate grids. Maintenance-free batteries are also called low-water-loss batteries.

28.2.2 Grids

Each positive and negative plate in a battery is constructed on a framework, or grid, made primarily of lead. Lead is a soft material and must be strengthened for use in an automotive battery grid. Adding antimony or calcium to the pure lead adds strength to the lead grids.

Battery grids hold the active material and provide the electrical pathways for the current created in the plate.

Maintenance-free batteries use calcium instead of antimony, because 0.2% calcium has the same strength as 6% antimony. A typical lead-calcium grid uses only 0.09% to 0.12% calcium. Using low amounts of calcium instead of higher amounts of antimony reduces gassing. Gassing is the release of hydrogen and oxygen from the battery that occurs during charging and results in water usage.

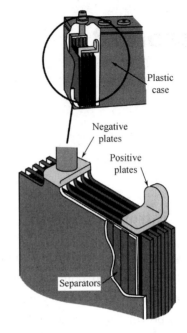

Figure 28-1 Batteries are constructed of plates grouped into cells and installed in a plastic case

Low-maintenance batteries use a low percentage of antimony (about 2% to 3%), or use antimony only in the positive grids and calcium for the negative grids. The percentages that make up the alloy of the plate grids constitute the major difference between standard and maintenance-free batteries. The chemical reactions that occur inside each battery are identical regardless of the type of material used to construct the grid plates.

28.2.3 Posituve plates

The positive plates have lead dioxide (peroxides), in paste form placed onto the grid framework. This process is called pasting. This active material can react with the sulfuric acid of the battery and is dark brown in color.

28.2.4 Negative plates

The negative plates are pasted to the grid with a pure porous lead, called sponge lead, and are gray in color.

28.2.5 Separators

The positive and the negative plates must be installed alternately next to each other without touching. Nonconducting separators are used, which allow room for the reaction of the acid with both plate materials, yet insulate the plates to prevent shorts. These separators are porous (with many small holes) and have ribs facing the positive plate. Separators can be made from resin-coated paper, porous rubber, fiberglass, or expanded plastic. Many batteries use envelope-type separators that encase the entire plate and help prevent any material that may shed from the plates from causing a short circuit between plates at the bottom of the battery.

28.2.6 Cells

Cells are constructed of positive and negative plates with insulating separators between each plate. Most batteries use one more negative plate than positive plate in each cell; however, many newer batteries use the same number of positive and negative plates. A cell is also called an element. Each cell is actually a 2.1 volt battery, regardless of the number of positive or negative plates used. The greater the number of plates used in each cell, the greater the amount of current that can be produced. Typical batteries contain four positive plates and five negative plates per cell. A 12 volt battery contains six cells connected in series, which produce 12.6 volts (6 × 2.1 = 12.6) and contain 54 plates (9 plates per cell × 6 cells). If the same 12 volt battery had five positive plates and six negative plates, for a total of 11 plates per cell (5 + 6), or 66 plates (11 plates × 6 cells), then it would have the same voltage, but the amount of current that the battery could produce would be increased. See Figure 28-2.

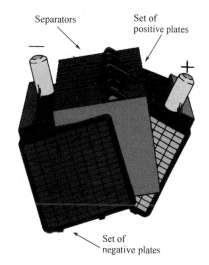

Figure 28-2 Two groups of plates are combined to form a battery element

The amperage capacity of a battery is determined by the amount of active plate material in the battery and the area of the plate material exposed to the electrolyte in the battery.

28.2.7 Partitions

Each cell is separated from the other cells by partitions, which are made of the same material as that used for the outside case of the battery. Electrical connections between cells are provided by lead connectors that loop over the top of the partition and connect the plates of the cells together. Many batteries connect the cells directly through the partition connectors, which provide the shortest path for the current and the lowest resistance.

28.2.8 Electrolyte

Electrolyte is the term used to describe the acid solution in a battery. The electrolyte used in automotive batteries is a solution (liquid combination) of 36% sulfuric acid and 64% water. This electrolyte is used for both lead-antimony and lead calcium (maintenance-free) batteries. The chemical symbol for this sulfuric acid solution is H_2SO_4.

H_2 = Symbol for hydrogen (the subscript 2 means that there are two atoms of hydrogen)

S = Symbol for sulfur

O_4 = Symbol for oxygen (the subscript 4 indicates that there are four atoms of oxygen)

Electrolyte is sold premixed in the proper proportion and is factory installed or added to the battery when the battery is sold. Additional electrolyte must never be added to any battery after the original electrolyte fill. It is normal for some water (H₂O) in the form of hydrogen and oxygen gases to escape during charging as a result of the chemical reactions. The escape of gases from a battery during charging or discharging is called gassing. Only pure distilled water should be added to a battery. If distilled water is not available, clean drinking water can be used.

28.3 How a battery works 电池工作原理

28.3.1 Principle involved

The principle of how a battery works is based on a scientific principle discovered years ago that states:

When two dissimilar metals are placed in an acid, electrons flow between the metals if a circuit is connected between them.

This can be demonstrated by pushing a steel nail and a piece of solid copper wire into a lemon. Connect a voltmeter to the ends of the copper wire and nail, and voltage will be displayed. A fully charged lead-acid battery has a positive plate of lead dioxide (peroxide) and a negative plate of lead surrounded by a sulfuric acid solution (electrolyte). The difference in potential (voltage) between lead peroxide and lead in acid is approximately 2.1 volts.

28.3.2 During discharging

The positive plate lead dioxide (PbO_2) combines with the SO_4, forming $PbSO_4$ from the electrolyte and releases its O_2 into the electrolyte, forming H_2O. The negative plate also combines with the SO_4 from the electrolyte and becomes lead sulfate ($PbSO_4$). See Figure 28-3.

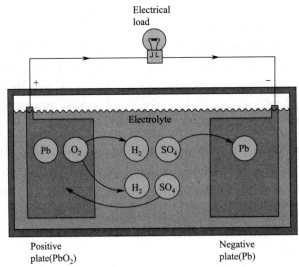

Figure 28-3 Chemical reaction for a lead-acid battery that is fully charged being discharged by the attached electrical load

28.3.3 Fully discharged state

When the battery is fully discharged, both the positive and the negative plates are Pb-SO_4 (lead sulfate) and the electrolyte has become water (H_2O). As the battery is being discharged, the plates and electrolyte approach the completely discharged state. There is also the danger of freezing when a battery is discharged, because the electrolyte is mostly water.

CAUTION: Never charge or jump start a frozen battery because the hydrogen gas can get trapped in the ice and ignite if a spark is caused during the charging process. The result can be an explosion.

28.3.4 During charging

During charging, the sulfate from the acid leaves both the positive and the negative plates and returns to the electrolyte, where it becomes normal-strength sulfuric acid solution. The positive plate returns to lead dioxide (PbO_2), the negative plate is again pure lead (Pb), and the electrolyte becomes H_2SO_4. See figure 28-4.

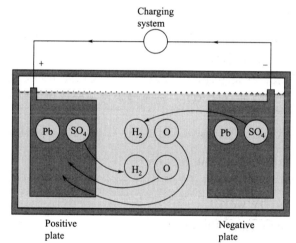

Figure 28-4 Chemical reaction for a lead-acid battery that is fully discharged being charged by the attached generator

[词汇]

stabilizer	n.稳定装置；稳定器；稳定剂	antimony	n.锑（符号 Sb）
reservoir	n.蓄水池；贮液器；储藏；蓄积	calcium	n.钙
charging	充电	pathway	n.路，道；途径，路径
serviceable	adj.有用的，可供使用的；耐用的	dioxide	n.二氧化物
		peroxide	n.过氧化氢；过氧化物
cranking	n.摇动；起动	porous	adj.多孔渗水的；能渗透的；有气孔的
polypropylene	n.[高分子]聚丙烯		
lead-alloy	铅合金	nonconducting	adj.不导电的
maintenance-free	免维护的	separator	n.分离器，分离装置；防胀器
framework	n.框架，骨架；结构，构架	rib	vt.装肋于，给…装肋材
grid	n.格栅，栅架	envelope	n.信封，封皮；壳层，外壳

cell	n. 单格电池	sulfuric acid	硫酸
amperage	n. 安培数，电流强度	subscript	n. 下标；脚注
partition	n. 划分，分开；分割；隔离物；隔墙	dissimilar	adj. 不同的
		copper	n. 铜
electrolyte	n. 电解液，电解质；电解	lemon	n. 柠檬
sulfuric	adj. 硫的		

[注释]

1. Battery 电池：构造主要有正（负）极板、隔板、电解液、槽壳、连接条和极桩等组成。

2. Maintenance-free battery 免维护蓄电池：顾名思义最大的特点就是"免维护"。和铅酸蓄电池比它的电解液的消耗量非常小，在使用寿命内基本不需要补充蒸馏水。

3. Positive plate，negative plate 正极板、负极板：均由栅架和活性物质组成。蓄电池充、放电的化学反应主要是依靠极板上的活性物质与电解液进行的。

4. Grid 栅架：其作用是固结活性物质。栅架一般由铅锑合金铸成，具有良好的导电性、耐蚀性和一定的机械强度。

5. Separator 隔板：插放在正、负极板之间，以防止正、负极板互相接触造成短路。隔板应耐酸并具有多孔性，以利于电解液的渗透。

6. Electrolyte 电解液：在蓄电池的化学反应中，起到离子间导电的作用，并参与蓄电池的化学反应。电解液由纯硫酸（H_2SO_4）与蒸馏水按一定比例配制而成。

[问题]

1. What's the construction of the battery?
2. What's the cell?
3. How does the battery work?
4. What are the functions of the grid?

Lesson 29

Antilock Brake System
防抱死制动系统

If the brakes are applied too hard when driving on slippery road surfaces, they may lock up or stop the wheel. The wheel then loses frictional contact with the road and skids and the vehicle is no longer under control. Experienced drivers know that the way to prevent lock-up is to pump the brake pedal up and down rapidly.

Many late-model cars are now equipped with an antilock brake system (ABS). The antilock brake system does the same thing as an experienced driver. It senses that a wheel is about to lock-up or skid and it rapidly interrupts the braking pressure to the brake system at that wheel. (See Figure 29-1).

The brains behind the antilock brake system is the computer, which monitors system operation at all times. It processes information from the wheel sensors and determines wheel speed. From this information, the electronic controller can determine whether one wheel is turning slower than the other wheels.

The computer gets its information on wheel speeds from wheel sensors located on each wheel. Each sensor assembly consists of a magnetic pickup sensor and a toothed sensor ring. The front sensor rings are attached to the back side of the rotor assembly. The rear

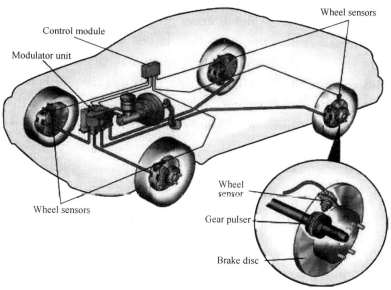

Figure 29-1 Antilock brake system

sensor rings are attached to the axle shaft. The pickup assemblies are bolted to brackets at each wheel.

The wheel sensors are essentially magnetic pickup assemblies. Each pickup assembly consists of a permanent magnet with a coil of wire wound around it. The sensor is positioned extremely close to the sensor ring, which rotates as the wheel turns. As the teeth pass the pickup assembly, the signal is induced in the coil by electromagnetic induction as the magnetic field goes from strong to weak and back to strong. This signal change is used by the computer to determine wheel speed.

The antilock brake system uses a hydraulic control unit in place of the standard master cylinder. The hydraulic control unit consists of a master cylinder, a vacuum or hydraulic booster, electric pump, accumulator, a solenoid valve body assembly, and pressure control and warning switches.

The electric pump is a high pressure pump designed to run at frequent intervals for short periods of time. The pump fills the hydraulic accumulator and supplies high pressure brake fluid to the brake system.

The accumulator is a nitrogen gas-filled assembly used to store and supply pressure to the brake system. The accumulator is attached to the pump housing. The top chamber of the accumulator is filled with nitrogen gas. The bottom chamber contains brake fluid, which is supplied from the hydraulic electric pump. A diaphragm is used to separate the two chambers.

CAUTION: Do not disassemble any accumulator. The nitrogen gas contained in the accumulator is pressurized to 1200 psi (8274 kPa). Antilock brakes use extremely high pressure, so always follow service manual procedures when working on one of these systems.

During operation, the electric pump supplies brake fluid to the lower chamber of the accumulator, and the diaphragm moves upward, compressing the nitrogen gas in the upper chamber. The nitrogen gas, which is under pressure in the top chamber, then pushes down on the diaphragm, causing the brake fluid in the bottom chamber to be maintained at a very high pressure. During normal braking conditions (no antilock control), the accumulator supplies pressurized brake fluid to the booster and the rear brakes. During antilock braking conditions, the accumulator also supplies pressurized brake fluid to the front brakes. The accumulator can provide pressure required for a number of stops if the electric pump should fail.

The solenoid valve assembly is a set of electrically operated solenoid switching valves. The main solenoid valve opens a connection between the boost pressure chamber of the brake power booster and the internal master cylinder reservoir and closes the flow to the reservoir during antilock control. This provides a continuous supply of high pressure brake fluid during antilock control to replace the fluid being allowed back to the reservoir. When antilock control stops, the main valve closes and the return to the reservoir is reopened. By closing the main valve, accumulator pressure is removed from the front brake circuits within the master cylinder. (See Figure 29-2).

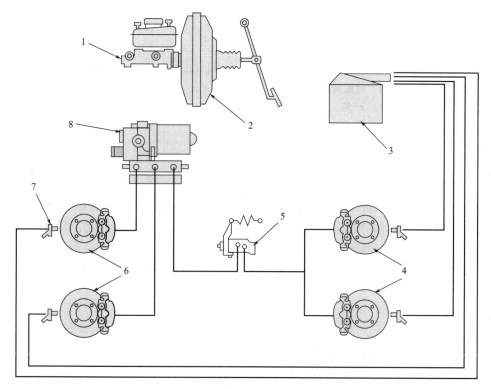

Figure 29-2 Anti-lock braking system (ABS) layout: 1, master cylinder; 2, brake servo or booster; 3, electronic control unit; 4, rear disc brakes; 5, load apportioning valve (if used); 6, front disc brakes; 7, wheel speed sensor; 8, hydraulic modulator

A set of smaller solenoid valves is located in a solenoid valve body. The valve body contains three pairs of electrically operated solenoid valves: a pair for each of the front brakes and a pair that controls both back brakes together. Each pair contains a normally open inlet solenoid valve and a normally closed outlet solenoid valve. During normal braking conditions (no antilock control), brake pressure is supplied to the brakes through the inlet solenoid valves upon brake application.

The computer determines the rotation speed of each wheel. If it senses a possible wheel lock-up, it goes into the antilock function and then applies voltage to the appropriate solenoid valves. When the system goes into antilock control, the computer will open and close the appropriate inlet and outlet solenoid valves, which control the operation of any of the brakes on any of the four wheels and prevent wheel lock-up. When the system is in antilock brake operation, the brake pedal will pulsate at an extremely fast rate. Pressure control and warning switches warn the driver of any malfunction in the system.

[词汇]

lock-up	锁住	pickup	n.拾波,检取
antilock brake system	防抱死制动系统	toothed	adj.有齿的
skid	vt.汽车侧滑,滑动,打滑	ring	n.齿圈
		controller	n.控制器

electromagnetic induction	电磁感应	malfunction	n. 不正常工作，故障状态，故障，误动作，失灵
booster	n. 增压器		
accumulator	n. 蓄电池，积储器，蓄压器	disassemble	vt. 解开，分解
solenoid valve body assembly	电磁阀体总成	pressurize	vt. 增压，密封，使…加压
nitrogen	n. 氮		
chamber	n. 室，房间，议院，	pulsate	vi. 搏动，跳动，有规律地跳动
diaphragm	n. 薄膜，膜片		

[注释]

　　Antilock brake system（ABS） 防抱死制动系统：根据行驶中的轮胎与路面间的摩擦对各车轮给予不同的最佳的制动力，通常采用控制车轮的制动液压的方法。其基本功能是可感知制动轮每一瞬间的运动状态，并根据其运动状态相应地调节制动力的大小，避免出现车轮的抱死现象，可使汽车在制动时维持方向稳定性和缩短制动距离，有效地提高行车的安全性。

[问题]

1. What's the function of antilock brake system?
2. How does the antilock brake system work?
3. How many parts are there in antilock brake system?
4. What's the role of solenoid valves?

Lesson 30

Air-Conditioning System
空调系统

An automotive air-conditioning system is a closed pressurized system. It consists of compressor, condenser, receiver/dryer or accumulator, expansion valve or orifice tube, and an evaporator. In a basic air-conditioning system, the heat is absorbed and transferred in the following steps. (See Figure 30-1).

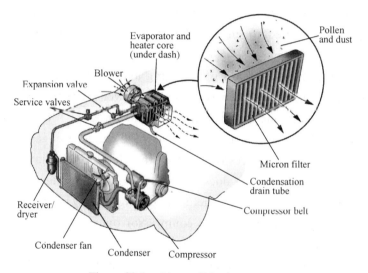

Figure 30-1 Air conditioning system

Refrigerant leaves the compressor as a high-pressure, high-temperature vapor.

By removing heat via the condenser, the vapor becomes a high-pressure, lower-temperature liquid.

Moisture and contaminants are removed by the receiver/dryer, where the cleaned refrigerant is stored until it is needed.

The expansion valve converts the high-pressure liquid changes into a low-pressure liquid by controlling its flow into the evaporator.

Heat is absorbed from the air inside the passenger compartment by the low-pressure, low-temperature refrigerant, causing the liquid to vaporize.

The refrigerant returns to the compressor as a low-pressure, higher-temperature vapor.

To understand the operation of the five major components, remember that an air-conditioning system is divided into two sides: the high side and the low side. High side refers to the side of the system that is under high pressure and high temperature. Low side refers to the low-pressure, low-temperature side of the system.

30.1 The Compressor 压缩机

The compressor is the heart of the automotive air-conditioning system. It separates the high-pressure and low pressure sides of the system. The primary purpose of the unit is to draw the low-pressure vapor from the evaporator and compress this vapor into high-temperature, high-pressure vapor. This action results in the refrigerant having a higher temperature than surrounding air, and enables the condenser to condense the vapor back to a liquid. The secondary purpose of the compressor is to circulate or pump the refrigerant through the condenser under the different pressures required for proper operation. The compressor is located in the engine compartment. Although there are numerous types of compressors in use today, they are usually one of two types.

Every compressor is equipped with an electromagnetic clutch as part of the compressor pulley assembly. It is designed to engage the pulley to the compressor shaft when the clutch coil is energized. The purpose of the clutch is to transmit power from the engine to the compressor and to provide a means of engaging and disengaging the refrigeration system from engine operation. The clutch is driven by power from the engine's crankshaft, which is transmitted through one or more belts (a few use gears) to the pulley, which is in operation whenever the engine is running. When the clutch is engaged, power is transmitted from the pulley to the compressor shaft by the clutch drive plate. When the clutch is not engaged, the compressor shaft does not rotate, and the pulley freewheels.

The clutch is engaged by a magnetic field and disengaged by springs when the magnetic field is broken. When the controls call for compressor operation, the electrical circuit to the clutch is completed, the magnetic clutch is energized, and the clutch engages the compressor. When the electrical circuit is opened, the clutch disengages the compressor.

Two types of electromagnetic clutches have been in use for many years. Early-model air-conditioning systems used a rotating coil clutch. The magnetic coil, which engages or disengages the compressor is mounted within the pulley and rotates with it. Electrical connections for the clutch operation are made through a stationary brush assembly and rotating slip rings, which are part of the field coil assembly. This older rotating coil clutch, now in limited use, has been largely replaced by the stationary coil clutch.

With the stationary coil, wear has been measurably reduced, efficiency increased, and serviceability made much easier. The clutch coil does not rotate. When the driver first energizes the air-conditioning system from the passenger compartment dashboard, the pulley assembly is magnetically drawn to the stationary coil on the compressor body, thus engaging the clutch and activating the air-conditioning system. Depending on the system, the magnetic clutch is usually thermostatically controlled to cycle the operation of the compressor (depending on system temperature or pressure). In some system designs, the clutch might operate continually when the system is turned on. With stationary coil design, service is not usually necessary except for an occasional check on the electrical connections.

30.2　Condenser 冷凝器

The condenser consists of a refrigerant coil tube mounted in a series of thin cooling fins to provide maximum heat transfer in a minimum amount of space. The condenser is normally mounted just in front of the vehicle's radiator. It receives the full flow of air from the movement of the vehicle.

The purpose of the condenser is to condense or liquefy the high-pressure hot vapor coming from the compressor. To do so, it must give up its heat. The condenser receives very hot, high-pressure refrigerant vapor from the compressor through its discharge hose. The refrigerant vapor enters the inlet at the top of the condenser and as the hot vapor passes down through the condenser coils, air (following its natural tendencies) moves from the hot refrigerant into the cooler air as it flows across the condenser coils and fins. This process causes a large quantity of heat to transferred to the outside air and the refrigerant to change from a high-pressure hot vapor to a high-pressure warm liquid. This high-pressure warm liquid flows from the outlet at the bottom of the condenser through a line to the receiver/dryer.

In an air-conditioning system, which is operating under an average heat load, the condenser has a combination of hot refrigerant vapor in the upper two-thirds of its coils. The lower third of the coils contains the warm liquid refrigerant, which has condensed. This high-pressure, liquid refrigerant flows from the condenser and on toward the evaporator. In effect, the condenser is a true heat exchange.

30.3　Evaporator 蒸发器

The evaporator, like the condenser, consists of a refrigerant coil mounted in a series of thin cooling fins. It provides a maximum amount of heat transfer in a minimum amount of space. The evaporator is usually located beneath the dashboard or instrument panel. Upon receiving the low-pressure, low-temperature liquid refrigerant from the thermostatic expansion valve or orifice tube in the form of an atomized (or droplet) spray, the evaporator serves as a boiler or vaporizer. This regulated flow of refrigerant boils immediately. Heat from the core surface is lost to the boiling and vaporizing refrigerant, which is cooler than the core, thereby cooling the core. The air passing over the evaporator loses its heat to the cooler surface of the core, thereby cooling the air inside the car. As the process of heat loss from air to the evaporator core surface is taking place, any moisture (humidity) in the air condenses on the outside of the evaporator core and is drained off as water. A drain tube in the bottom of the evaporator housing leads the water outside the vehicle.

This dehumidification of the air is an added feature of the air-conditioning system that adds to passenger comfort. It can also be used as a means of controlling fogging of the vehicle windows. Under certain conditions, however, too much moisture can accumulate on the evaporator coils. An example would be when humidity is extremely high and the maximum cooling mode is selected. The evaporator temperature might become so low that moisture would freeze on the evaporator coils before it can drain off.

Through the metering, or controlling, action of the thermostatic expansion valve or orifice tube, greater or lesser amounts of refrigerant are provided in the evaporator to adequately cool the car under all heat load conditions. If too much refrigerant is allowed to enter, the evaporator floods. This results in poor cooling due to the higher pressure (and temperature) of the refrigerant. The refrigerant can neither boil away rapidly nor vaporize. On the other hand, if too little refrigerant is metered, the evaporator starves. Poor cooling again results because the refrigerant boils away or vaporizes too quickly before passing through the evaporator.

The temperature of the refrigerant vapor at the evaporator outlet will be approximately 4 to 16 degrees Fahrenheit higher than the temperature of the liquid refrigerant at the evaporator inlet. This temperature differential is the superheat that ensures that the vapor will not contain any droplets of liquid refrigerant that would be harmful to the compressor.

[词汇]

air-conditioning system	空调系统	drive plate	拨盘，带动盘，驱动圆盘
pressurize	vt.增压，密封，使……加压	serviceability	n.可维修性，可用性
		dashboard	n.汽车等的仪表板，马车等前部的挡泥板
compressor	n.压缩机		
condenser	n.冷凝器，电容器	instrument panel	仪表板
receiver	n.接收器，容器	thermostatic	adj.温度调节装置的
dryer	n.干燥机，干燥器，烘缸	atomize	vt.使分裂为原子，将……喷成雾状
accumulator	n.蓄电池，蓄压器，能量积存装置		
		droplet	n.小滴，微滴
expansion	n.膨胀	boiler	n.锅炉，蒸发器，热水器
orifice	n.量孔，小洞		
evaporator	n.蒸发器，脱水器	vaporizer	n.蒸发器
refrigerant	n.制冷剂	humidity	n.湿度
contaminant	n.致污物，污染物	drain	v.排泄，排出，排水
pulley	n.滑轮，滑车，皮带轮	dehumidification	n.去湿，干燥，湿度降低

[注释]

Air-conditioning system 空调系统：发动机驱动压缩机压缩可蒸发的制冷剂，此过程伴随有温度升高，然后制冷剂流入冷凝器中，经冷却后复原为液态。将压缩机传给制冷剂的热量送到系统外，制冷剂经膨胀阀喷射到蒸发器中再行蒸发，需要的蒸发热从外部空气中吸收。进入空气的湿度过高时，在冷凝器中凝结成水，从而使空气干燥。

[问题]

1. What are the main components of the air conditioning system?
2. What's the main purpose of the compressor?
3. When does the clutch engage?
4. How does the evaporator operate?

Lesson 31

Electric Car
电动汽车

An electric car is a car powered by an electric motor rather than a gasoline engine. From the outside, you would probably have no idea that a car is electric. In most cases, converting a gasoline-powered car creates electric cars, and in that case it is impossible to tell. When you drive an electric car, often the only thing that clues you in to its true nature is the fact that it is nearly silent. Under the hood, there are a lot of differences between gasoline and electric cars:

The gasoline engine is replaced by an electric motor.

The electric motor gets its power from a controller.

The controller gets its power from an array of rechargeable batteries.

31.1 The Controller 控制器

A simple DC controller connected to the batteries and the DC motor. If the driver floors the accelerator pedal, the controller delivers the full 96 volts from the batteries to the motor. If the driver take his/her foot off the accelerator, the controller delivers zero volts to the motor. For any setting in between, the controller "chops" the 96 volts thousands of times per second to create an average voltage somewhere between 0 and 96 volts. The controller takes power from the batteries and delivers it to the motor. The accelerator pedal hooks to a pair of potentiometers (variable resistors), and these potentiometers provide the signal that tells the controller how much power it is supposed to deliver. The controller can deliver zero power (when the car is stopped), full power (when the driver floors the accelerator pedal), or any power level in between.

The controller normally dominates the scene when you open the hood, as you can see here: In this car, the controller takes in 300 volts DC from the battery pack. It converts it into a maximum of 240 volts AC, three-phase, to send to the motor. It does this by using very large transistors that rapidly turn the batteries' voltage on and off to create a sine wave. When you push on the gas pedal, a cable from the pedal connects to these two potentiometers.

The signal from the potentiometers tells the controller how much power to deliver to the electric car's motor. There are two potentiometers for safety's sake (Figure32-1).

The controller reads both potentiometers and makes sure that their signals are equal. If they are not, then the controller does not operate. This arrangement guards against a situation where a potentiometer fails in the full-on position.

The controller's job in a DC electric car is easy to understand. Let's assume that the battery pack contains 12 12-volt batteries, wired in series to create 144 volts. The controller takes in 144 volts DC, and delivers it to the motor in a controlled way. The very simplest DC controller would be a big on/off switch wired to the accelerator pedal. When you push the pedal, it would turn the switch on, and when you take your foot off the pedal, it would turn it off. As the driver, you would have to push and release the accelerator to pulse the motor on and off to maintain a given speed. (See Figure 31-1).

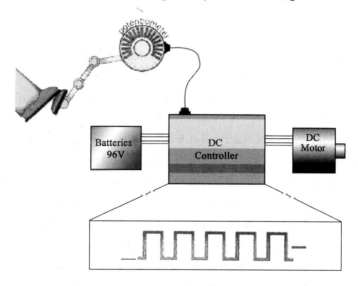

Figure 31-1 The operation of electric car

Obviously, that sort of on/off approach would work but it would be a pain to drive, so the controller does the pulsing for you. The controller reads the setting of the accelerator pedal from the potentiometers and regulates the power accordingly. Let's say that you have the accelerator pushed halfway down. The controller reads that setting from the potentiometer and rapidly switches the power to the motor on and off so that it is on half the time and off half the time. If you have the accelerator pedal 25 percent of the way down, the controller pulses the power so it is on 25 percent of the time and off 75 percent of the time.

31.2 The Motor 电机

Electric cars can use AC or DC motors: If the motor is a DC motor, then it may run on anything from 96 to 192 volts. Many of the DC motors used in electric cars come from the electric forklift industry. If it is an AC motor, then it probably is a three-phase AC motor running at 240 volts AC with a 300 volt battery pack. DC installations tend to be simpler and less expensive. A typical motor will be in the 20000-watt to 30000-watt range. A typical controller will be in the 40000-watt to 60000-watt range (for example, a 96-volt controller will deliver a maximum of 400 or 600 amps). DC motors have the nice feature that you can overdrive them (up to a factor of 10-to-1) for short periods of time. That is, a 20000-watt motor will accept 100000 watts for a short period of time and deliver 5 times its rated horsepower. This is great for short bursts of acceleration. The only limitation is heat build-up in the motor. Too much overdriving and the motor heats up to the point where it self-destructs.

31.3　The Batteries 电池

Right now, the weak link in any electric car is the batteries. There are at least six significant problems with current lead-acid battery technology:

They are heavy (a typical lead-acid battery pack weighs 1000 pounds or more).

They are bulky (the car we are examining here has 50 lead-acid batteries, each measuring roughly 6″× 8″ by6″).

They have a limited capacity (a typical lead-acid battery pack might hold 12 to 15 kilowatt-hours of electricity, giving a car a range of only 50 miles or so).

They are slow to charge (typical recharge times for a lead-acid pack range between four to 10 hours for full charge, depending on the battery technology and the charger).

They have a short life (three to four years, perhaps 200 full charge/discharge cycles).

They are expensive (perhaps \$2000 for the battery pack shown in the sample car).

You can replace lead-acid batteries with NiMH batteries. The range of the car will double and the batteries will last 10 years (thousands of charge/discharge cycles), but the cost of the batteries today is 10 to 15 times greater than lead-acid. In other words, an NiMH battery pack will cost \$20000 to \$30000 (today) instead of \$2000. Prices for advanced batteries fall as they become mainstream, so over the next several years it is likely that NiMH and lithium-ion battery packs will become competitive with lead-acid battery prices. Electric cars will have significantly better range at that point.

31.4　The Charging System 充电系统

Any electric car that uses batteries needs a charging system to recharge the batteries. The charging system has two goals:

To pump electricity into the batteries as quickly as the batteries will allow.

To monitor the batteries and avoid damaging them during the charging process.

The most sophisticated charging systems monitor battery voltage, current flow and battery temperature to minimize charging time. The charger sends as much current as it can without raising battery temperature too much. Less sophisticated chargers might monitor voltage or amperage only and make certain assumptions about average battery characteristics. A charger like this might apply maximum current to the batteries up through 80 percent of their capacity, and then cut the current back to some preset level for the final 20 percent to avoid overheating the batteries.

[词汇]

hood	n. 发动机罩	overdriving	n. 超速传动
array	n. 排列，编队，军队，衣服，大批	lead-acid battery	铅酸电池
		halfway	adj. 中途的，部分的，不彻底的
rechargeable	adj. 可再充电的		
accelerator pedal	油门踏板	pack	n. 一群；一组；一堆
chop	vt. 剁碎，砍，（风浪）突变	bulky	adj. 庞大的，体积大的，笨重的
hook	v. 钩住，沉迷，上瘾		
potentiometer	n. 电位计，分压计	charger	n. 充电器
dominate	v. 支配，占优势	assumption	n. 假定；设想；假说
three-phase	三相	capacity	n. 容量，容积；负载量；电容量
forklift	n. 叉车	preset	vt. 事先调整
amp	n. 安培	lithium-ion	n. 锂离子
amperage	n. 电流量，电流强度	overheating	n. 过热
self-destruct	v. 自毁	rated	adj. 定价的，额定的
guard	vi. 提[预]防	burst	v. 爆裂，炸破，急于，爆发
full-on	n. 全开		

[注释]

Electric car 电动汽车：目前人们所说的电动汽车多是指纯电动汽车，即是一种采用单一蓄电池作为储能动力源的汽车。它利用蓄电池作为储能动力源，通过电池向电机提供电能，驱动电动机运转，从而推动汽车前进。从外形上看，电动汽车与日常见到的汽车并没有什么区别，区别主要在于动力源及其驱动系统。

[问题]

1. What are the main components of the electric car?
2. What are the advantages of the electric car?
3. What's the function of the DC controller?

Lesson 32

Hybrid Electric Vehicles
混合动力汽车

A hybrid vehicle is one that uses two different methods to propel the vehicle. A hybrid electric vehicle, abbreviated HEV uses both an internal combustion engine and an electric motor to propel the vehicle. Most hybrid vehicles use a high-voltage battery pack and a combination electric motor and generator to help or assist a gasoline engine. The internal combustion engine (ICE) used in a hybrid vehicle can be either gasoline or diesel, although only gasoline-powered engines are currently used in hybrid vehicles. An electric motor is used to help propel the vehicle, and in some designs, is capable of propelling the vehicle alone without having to start the internal combustion engine.

32.1 Classifications of hybrid electric vehicles 混合动力汽车分类

32.1.1 Series hybrid

The types of hybrid electric vehicles include series, parallel, and series-parallel designs. In a series-hybrid design, sole propulsion is by a battery-powered electric motor, but the electric energy for the batteries comes from another on-board energy source, such as an internal combustion engine. In this design, the engine turns a generator and the generator can either charge the batteries or power an electric motor that drives the transmission. The internal combustion engine never powers the vehicle directly. See Figure 32-1 and Figure 32-2.

The engine is only operated to keep the batteries charged. Therefore, the vehicle could be moving with or without the internal combustion engine running. Series-hybrid vehicles also use regeneration braking to help keep the batteries charged. The Chevrolet VOLT is an example of a series-hybrid design.

The engine is designed to just keep the batteries charged, and therefore, is designed to operate

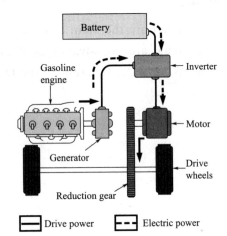

Figure 32-1 A drawing of the power flow in a typical series-hybrid vehicle.

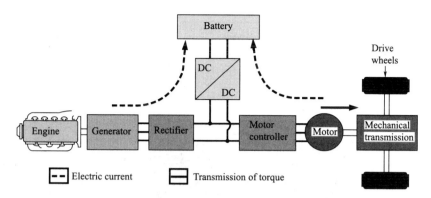

Figure 32-2 This diagram shows the components included in a typical series-hybrid design. The solid-line arrow indicates the transmission of torque to the drive wheels. The dotted-line arrows indicate the flow of electrical current.

at its most efficient speed and load. An advantage of a series-hybrid design is that no transmission, clutch, or torque converter is needed.

A disadvantage of a series-hybrid design is the added weight of the internal combustion engine to what is basically an electric vehicle. The engine is actually a heavy on-board battery charger. Also, the electric motor and battery capacity have to be large enough to power the vehicle under all operating conditions, including climbing hills.

All power needed for heating and cooling must also come from the batteries so using the air conditioning in hot weather and the heater in cold weather reduces the range that the vehicle can travel on battery power alone.

32.1.2 Parallel hybrid

In a parallel-hybrid design, multiple propulsion sources can be combined, or one of the energy sources alone can drive the vehicle. In this design, the battery and engine are both connected to the transmission.

The vehicle using a parallel-hybrid design can be powered by the internal combustion engine alone, by the electric motor alone (full hybrids only), or by a combination of engine and electric motor propulsion. In most cases, the electric motor is used to assist the internal combustion engine. One of the advantages of using a parallel hybrid design is that by using an electric motor or motors to assist the internal combustion engine, the engine itself can be smaller than would normally be needed. See Figure 32-3 and Figure 32-4.

NOTE: A parallel-hybrid design could include additional batteries to allow for plug-in capability, which could extend the distance the vehicle can travel using battery power alone.

One disadvantage of a parallel-hybrid design is that complex software is needed to seamlessly blend electric and ICE power. Another concern about the parallel-hybrid design is that it had to be engineered to provide proper heating and air-conditioning system operation when the ICE stops at idle.

32.1.3 Series-parallel hybrid

The Toyota and Ford hybrids are classified as series-parallel hybrids because they can

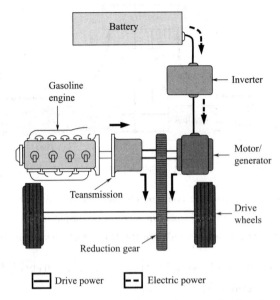

Figure 32-3 The power flow in a typical parallel-hybrid vehicle

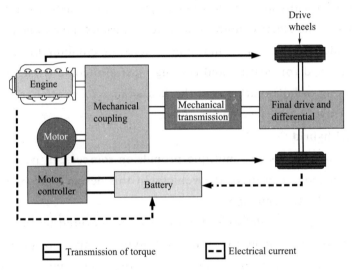

Figure 32-4 Diagram showing the components involved in a typical parallel-hybrid vehicle. The solid-line arrows indicate the transmission of torque to the drive wheels, and the dotted-line arrows indicate the flow of electrical current.

operate using electric motor power alone or with the assist of the ICE. Series-parallel hybrids combine the functions of both a series and a parallel design.

The internal combustion engine may be operating even though the vehicle is stopped if the electronic controller has detected that the batteries need to be charged. See Figure32-5.

NOTE: The internal combustion engine may or may not start when the driver starts the vehicle depending on the temperature of the engine and other conditions. This can be confusing to some who are driving a hybrid electric vehicle for the first time and sense that the engine did not start when they tried to start the engine.

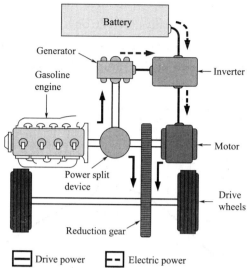

Figure 32-5　A series-parallel hybrid design allows the vehicle to operate in electric motor mode only or in combination with the internal combustion engine.

32.2　Belt alternator starter systems　带式交流发电机兼启动机系统

The belt system, commonly called the belt alternator starter (BAS), is the least expensive system that can be used and still claim that the vehicle is a hybrid. For many buyers, cost is a major concern and the BAS system allows certain hybrid features without the cost associated with an entire redesign of the engine and powertrain. Consumers will be able to upgrade from conventional models to BAS hybrids at a reasonable cost and will get slightly better fuel economy.

The BAS concept is to replace the belt-driven alternator with an electric motor that serves as a generator and a motor. When the engine is running the motor, acting as a generator, it will charge a separate 36-volt battery (42-volt charging voltage). When the engine needs to be started again after the engine has been stopped at idle to save fuel (idle stop), the BAS motor is used to crank the engine by taking electrical power from the 36-volt battery pack and applies its torque via the accessory belt, and cranks the engine instead of using the starter motor.

NOTE: A BAS system uses a conventional starter motor for starting the ICE the first time, and only uses the high voltage motor-generator to start the ICE when leaving idle stop mode.

The motor-generator is larger than a standard starter motor so more torque can be generated in the cranking mode, also referred to as the motoring mode. The fast rotation of the BAS allows for quicker starts of the engine, and makes the start/stop operation possible. Having the engine shut off when the vehicle is at a stop saves fuel. Of course, the stopping of the engine does create a sense that the engine has stalled, which is a common concern to drivers unfamiliar with the operation of hybrid vehicles.

A typical BAS system will achieve a 8% to 15% increase in fuel economy, mostly affecting the city mileage with little, if any, effect on the highway mileage. On extremely small vehicles, the belt alternator starter might nudge a vehicle into the mild hybrid category. The BAS system is the type used in the Saturn VUE hybrid SUV. See Figure 32-6 and Figure 32-7.

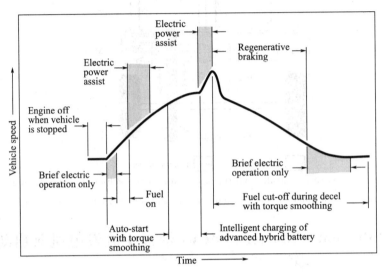

Figure 32-6　This chart shows what is occurring during various driving conditions in a BAS-type hybrid

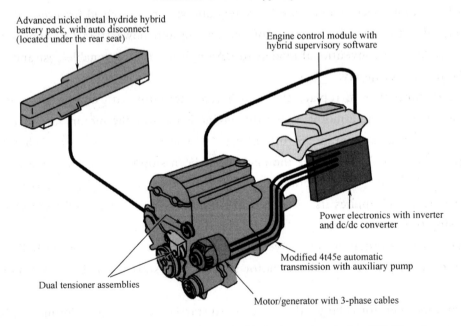

Figure 32-7　The components of a typical belt alternator-starter (BAS) system

[词汇]

hybrid vehicle	混合动力汽车	pack	n. 一群；包裹；（纸牌的）一副；一组
propel	vt. 驱动		

generator	n. 发电机	dotted-line	点划线
series	n. 串联	plug-in	插入式
parallel	n. 并联	powertrain	n. 传动系
series-parallel	串并联	idle stop	怠速停机
propulsion	n. 推进；推进力	motoring mode	电机驱动模式
solid-line	实线	nudge	vt. （用肘）轻推；推进

[注释]

1. Series Hybrid 串联式混合动力系统：一般由内燃机直接带动发电机发电，产生的电能通过控制单元传到电池，再由电池传输给电机转化为动能，最后通过变速机构来驱动汽车。

2. Parallel Hybrid 并联式混合动力系统：有两套驱动系统：传统的内燃机系统和电机驱动系统。两个系统既可以同时协调工作，也可以各自单独工作驱动汽车。这种系统适用于多种不同的行驶工况，尤其适用于复杂的路况。

3. Series-parallel Hybrid 混联式混合动力系统：特点在于内燃机系统和电机驱动系统各有一套机械变速机构，两套机构或通过齿轮系，或采用行星轮式结构结合在一起，从而综合调节内燃机与电动机之间的转速关系。

4. Belt Alternator Starter（BAS）带式交流发电机兼启动机：它通过皮带与发动机曲轴连接，只要发动机转它就转，既可利用发动机的转动给电池充电，也可反过来以电池的电力为发动机辅助出力。

[问题]

1. What's the hybrid vehicle?
2. How are the hybrid vehicles classified?
3. What are the advantages of the series hybrid?
4. How does the belt alternator starter system work?

Lesson 33

Fuel Cell Car
燃料电池汽车

33.1 What is a Fuel Cell? 什么是燃料电池

If you want to be technical about it, a fuel cell is an electrochemical energy conversion device. A fuel cell converts the chemicals hydrogen and oxygen into water, and in the process it produces electricity.

The other electrochemical device that we are all familiar with is the battery. A battery has all of its chemicals stored inside, and it converts those chemicals into electricity too. This means that a battery eventually "goes dead" and you either throw it away or recharge it.

With a fuel cell, chemicals constantly flow into the cell so it never goes dead—as long as there is a flow of chemicals into the cell, the electricity flows out of the cell. Most fuel cells in use today use hydrogen and oxygen as the chemicals.

The fuel cell will compete with many other types of energy conversion devices, including the gas turbine in your city's power plant, the gasoline engine in your car and the battery in your laptop. Combustion engines like the turbine and the gasoline engine burn fuels and use the pressure created by the expansion of the gases to do mechanical work. Batteries converted chemical energy back into electrical energy when needed. Fuel cells should do both tasks more efficiently.

A fuel cell provides a DC (direct current) voltage that can be used to power motors, lights or any number of electrical appliances.

There are several different types of fuel cells, each using a different chemistry. Fuel cells are usually classified by the type of electrolyte they use. Some types of fuel cells work well for use in stationary power generation plants. Others may be useful for small portable applications or for powering cars.

The proton exchange membrane fuel cell (PEMFC) is one of the most promising technologies. This is the type of fuel cell that will end up powering cars, buses and maybe even your house. Let's take a look at how they work...

33.2 Proton Exchange Membrane 质子交换膜

The proton exchange membrane fuel cell (PEMFC) uses one of the simplest reactions

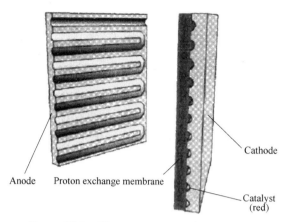

Figure 33-1 The components of a PEM fuel cell

of any fuel cell. First, let's take a look at what's in a PEM fuel cell:

In Figure 33-1 you can see there are four basic elements of a PEMFC:

1. The anode, the negative post of the fuel cell, has several jobs. It conducts the electrons that are freed from the hydrogen molecules so that they can be used in an external circuit. It has channels etched into it that disperse the hydrogen gas equally over the surface of the catalyst.

2. The cathode, the positive post of the fuel cell, has channels etched into it that distribute the oxygen to the surface of the catalyst. It also conducts the electrons back from the external circuit to the catalyst, where they can recombine with the hydrogen ions and oxygen to form water.

3. The electrolyte is the proton exchange membrane. This specially treated material, which looks something like ordinary kitchen plastic wrap, only conducts positively charged ions. The membrane blocks electrons.

4. The catalyst is a special material that facilitates the reaction of oxygen and hydrogen. It is usually made of platinum powder very thinly coated onto carbon paper or cloth. The catalyst is rough and porous so that the maximum surface area of the platinum can be exposed to the hydrogen or oxygen. The platinum-coated side of the catalyst faces the PEM.

The pressurized hydrogen gas (H_2) enters the fuel cell on the anode side. This gas is forced through the catalyst by the pressure. When an H_2 molecule comes in contact with the platinum on the catalyst, it splits into two H^+ ions and two electrons (e^-). The electrons are conducted through the anode, where they make their way through the external circuit (doing useful work such as turning a motor) and return to the cathode side of the fuel cell.

Meanwhile, on the cathode side of the fuel cell, oxygen gas (O_2) is being forced through the catalyst, where it forms two oxygen atoms. Each of these atoms has a strong negative charge. This negative charge attracts the two H^+ ions through the membrane, where they combine with an oxygen atom and two of the electrons from the external circuit to form a water molecule (H$_2$O).

This reaction in a single fuel cell produces only about 0.7 volts. To get this voltage up to a reasonable level, many separate fuel cells must be combined to form a fuel-cell stack.

PEMFCs operate at a fairly low temperature (about 176 degrees Fahrenheit, 80 degrees Celsius), which means they warm up quickly and don't require expensive containment structures. Constant improvements in the engineering and materials used in these cells have increased the power density to a level where a device about the size of a small piece of luggage can power a car.

33.3 Efficiency of Fuel Cells 燃料电池效率

Pollution reduction is one of the primary goals of the fuel cell. By comparing a fuel-cell-powered car to a gasoline-engine-powered car and a battery-powered car, you can see how fuel cells might improve the efficiency of cars today.

Since all three types of cars have many of the same components (tires, transmissions, etc.), we'll ignore that part of the car and compare efficiencies up to the point where mechanical power is generated. Let's start with the fuel-cell car (All of these efficiencies are approximations, but they should be close enough to make a rough comparison.).

33.4 Fuel-Cell-Powered Electric Car 燃料电池动力汽车

If the fuel cell is powered with pure hydrogen, it has the potential to be up to 80-percent efficient. That is, it converts 80 percent of the energy content of the hydrogen into electrical energy. But hydrogen is difficult to store in a car. When we add a reformer to convert methanol to hydrogen, the overall efficiency drops to about 30 to 40 percent.

We still need to convert the electrical energy into mechanical work. This is accomplished by the electric motor and inverter. A reasonable number for the efficiency of the motor/inverter is about 80 percent. So we have 30- to 40-percent efficiency at converting methanol to electricity, and 80-percent efficiency converting electricity to mechanical power. That gives an overall efficiency of about 24 to 32 percent.

[词汇]

fuel cell	燃料电池	anode	n.阳极,正极
electrochemical	adj.电化学的	electron	n.电子
gas turbine	汽轮机	molecule	n.分子
power plant	发电厂	catalyst	n.催化剂
laptop	n.便携式电脑	cathode	n.阴极,负极
electrical appliance	电器	etched	adj.被侵蚀的,被蚀刻的
electrolyte	n.电解,电解液	wrap	vt.包;裹;卷
proton	n.质子	ion	n.离子
membrane	n.(薄)膜,隔膜	platinum	n.铂(元素符号Pt);白金

porous	*adj.* 多孔的；有气孔的	methanol	*n.* 甲醇，木醇
reformer	*n.* 重整器	inverter	*n.* 逆变器

[注释]

1. Fuel cell　燃料电池：燃料电池是一种将氢和氧的化学能通过电极反应直接转换成电能的装置。这种装置的最大特点是反应过程不涉及燃烧，因此其能量转换效率不受"卡诺循环"的限制，其能量转换率高达60%～80%，实际使用效率则是普通内燃机的2～3倍。另外，它还具有燃料多样化、排气干净、噪声低、对环境污染小、可靠性及维修性好等优点。

氢氧燃料电池装置从本质上说是水电解的"逆"装置。电解水过程中，通过外加电源将水电解，产生氢和氧；而在燃料电池中，则是氢和氧通过电化学反应生成水，并释放出电能。按电解质划分，燃料电池大致上可分为五类：碱性燃料电池（AFC）、磷酸型燃料电池（PAFC）、固体氧化物燃料电池（SOFC）、熔融碳酸盐燃料电池（MCFC）和质子交换膜燃料电池（PEMFC）。

2. Proton Exchange Membrane　质子交换膜：燃料电池中隔离氢气和氧气的介电膜。只允许氢质子穿过介电膜到达吸附在阴极板上氧的附近，这样只剩下电子留在PEM氢的一侧。

[问题]

1. What's a fuel cell?
2. What are the kinds of the fuel cell?
3. What are the main components of a PEMFC?

Lesson 34

Electric Power Steering (EPS)
电动助力转向

34.1 Purpose of the System 系统的作用

With a conventional power assisted (hydraulic) steering system, a belt driven pump provides pressure to the control valve which is integral in the power steering rack. When the steering shaft is turned, the control valve provides pressure to assist (decrease effort) in turning the steering gear.

On some BMW vehicles, this control pressure is reduced by increasing vehicle speed via an electronically controlled bleed off valve (Servotronic). However, hydraulic power assisted steering systems utilize a reservoir, hydraulic fluid, pump, hoses/lines, cooler, hydraulic valve/steering rack, Servotronic valve. Electric Power Steering (EPS) is used for the first time by BMW in the E85. It provides the typical BMW power assisted steering characteristics and 'feel'. The EPS is a very direct, sporty steering element with a change-over between normal and 'Sport' mode by the Dynamic Driving Control (Sport) button.

The EPS differs from the conventional hydraulic power assisted steering system by utilizing electrical/electronic components to provide power assisted steering while retaining a complete mechanical connection. The EPS is a 'dry system', the hydraulic components and oil are not required.

The programmed EPS control functions are influenced by vehicle speed and provide additional benefits regarding steering tuning, absorption adjustments and active steering return characteristics.

34.2 System Components 系统组成

The EPS system is divided into 3 component groups:
Upper steering column assembly
Steering gear with rack
Lower steering spindle

34.3 Upper Steering Column Assembly 上转向柱总成

The upper steering column mechanical section starts at the steering wheel and ends at the connection to the lower steering spindle. The upper steering column is secured by 4 bolts to a bracket which is welded to the instrument panel support frame. In addition, the support frame bracket is secured by 4 bolts to the body.

The electrical section pertains to the EPS servo unit which consists of the EPS Control Module and the electric motor. The remaining upper steering column section contains the steering lock with ignition switch and the steering column adjustment mechanism (manual tilt and telescopic).

34.4　Servo Unit　伺服装置

The servo unit provides active steering-effort assistance as required by steering force and vehicle conditions (Figure 34-1). The servo unit is located on the upper steering column and is protected in the passenger compartment, it consists of:

Electric motor

Worm gear

Control unit

Internal sensors for electric motor speed, steering torque, temperature and voltage.

Coil-spring cassette for the internal steering torque sensor.

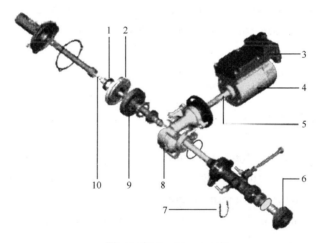

Figure 34-1　Servo unit

1—Magnet wheel; 2—Steering torque sensor; 3—EPS control module; 4—Electric motor; 5—Worm gear shaft; 6—Steering angle sensor; 7—Shipping/service steering locking pin; 8—EPS housing; 9—Driven gear; 10—Torsion bar

34.5　Lower Steering Spindle　下转向轴

The lower steering spindle connects the upper steering column to the steering gear. It runs in the engine compartment from the bulkhead through two universal joints to the steering gear. The lower steering spindle is encased in a plastic sleeve for corrosion protection. The sleeve is made from high temperature resistant plastic. The two parts of the lower steering spindle interslide in a ball-bearing mounting.

The ball-bearing mounting is necessary for:

Self adjusting length.

Equalization during steering wheel height adjustment.

Telescopic collapsing in event of a crash.

34.6 Steering Gear 转向器

The steering gear is a purely mechanical rack and pinion system. The steering deflection forces are counteracted by a damped thrust member, which is integrated in the steering gear.

This thrust member has an integral damper element in addition to the tension spring. In the event of rapid steering movements, the rack is not influenced by high deflection forces. Without a damped thrust member, the rack would cause noises when returning at high speed.

34.7 Principle of Operation 工作原理

EPS controls servo assistance for steering. In addition to the measuring the driver's steering torque, the EPS Control Module also monitors further inputs such as:

Vehicle speed

Dynamic Driving Control (Sport) button

Steering angle velocity

Internal system temperature

Steering angle

The EPS calculates an assistance set point. The electric motor is activated via the integrated power electronics and the torque is transmitted through the worm gear to the driven gear (attached to the steering column output shaft).

The Servotronic function (vehicle speed dependent steering assistance) is also integrated. The corresponding assistance and damping characteristics are stored in the EPS Control Module. The required assistance torque is gradually increased when the engine is started and reduced (with a delay) when the engine is switched off.

34.8 Steering Torque Measurement 转向力矩的测量

The driver's steering torque is measured by a steering torque sensor integrated in the servo unit. The function is based on the magnetoresistive principle, these sensors are currently used in BMWs include wheel speed sensors and Valvetronic position sensors. The magnetoresistive elements resistance changes as a function of the magnetic field acting on them. The input shaft of the upper steering spindle is connected by a torsion bar to the output shaft. A magnet wheel is mounted on the input shaft. The magnetoresistive element is mounted on the output shaft.

The magnetic field lines are deflected by the magnet wheel as a result of the rotation of the input shaft with respect to the output shaft (slight twist due to the resistance from the tires on the road, steering gear, etc.). This deflection generates a resistance change (in one of the resistors) causing a voltage change in the evaluation electronics. Two output signals (different voltage values) are generated which are constantly monitored for plausibility by the EPS Control Module. Based on this voltage change, the EPS calculates the extent of the driver's steering torque. The leads for signal transmission, power supply and ground run in a coil spring cassette mounted on the pinion shaft. The coil spring cassette is located in the worm gear housing.

[词汇]

steering	n. 转向	worm gear	n. 蜗轮
rack	n. 齿条	coil-spring	螺旋弹簧
bleed	vi. 渗气	cassette	n. 盒子，盒式磁带
reservoir	n. 储油缸	engine compartment	发动机室
cooler	n. 冷却器；冷却装置	bulkhead	n. 舱壁，隔板；隔墙
servotronic	adj. 电控伺服的	universal joint	万向节
sporty	adj. 运动型的	steering gear	转向器
dynamic driving control	动态驾驶控制	encase	vt. 装入，包住，围
tuning	n. 调整	ball-bearing	n. 球轴承
spindle	n. 主轴	mounting	n. 支架
bracket	n. 支架	equalization	n. 均等，平等化，同等化
weld	vt. 焊接		
instrument panel	仪表板	deflection	n. 偏转
pertain	vi. 属于；关于	counteract	vt. 抵消，中和，阻碍
module	n. 组件[模块]	activate	vt. 刺激，使活动
tilt	vi. 倾斜[侧]，斜置，歪斜	damping	n. 阻尼；减幅，衰减
		magnetoresistive	adj. 磁阻的
telescopic	adj. 伸缩的	evaluation	n. 评定[价，估]，测[鉴，推]定
servo unit	伺服机构，伺服装置		

[注释]

Electric Power Steering (EPS) 电动助力转向：该系统由电动机直接提供转向助力，省去了液压动力转向系统所必需的动力转向油泵、软管、液压油、传送带和装于发动机上的皮带轮，既节省能量，又保护了环境。

[问题]

1. What are the main components of EPS?
2. How does the ESP work?
3. What's the function of the servo unit?

Lesson 35

Vehicle Networks
车辆网络

35.1 Need for network 网络需求

Since the 1990s, vehicles have used modules to control the operation of most electrical components. A typical vehicle will have 10 or more modules and they communicate with each other over data lines or hard wiring, depending on the application.

Most modules are connected together in a network because of the following advantages.

• A decreased number of wires are needed, thereby saving weight and cost, as well as helping with installation at the factory and decreased complexity, making servicing easier.

• Common sensor data can be shared with those modules that may need the information, such as vehicle speed, outside air temperature, and engine coolant temperature. See Figure 35-1.

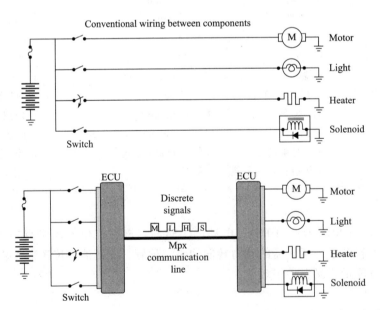

Figure 35-1 Module communications makes controlling multiple electrical devices and accessories easier by utilizing simple low-current switches to signal another module, which does the actual switching of the current to the device.

35.2 Modules and nodes 模块与节点

Each module, also called a node, must communicate to other modules. For example, if the driver depresses the window-down switch, the power window switch sends a window-down message to the body control module. The body control module then sends the request to the driver's side window module. This module is responsible for actually performing the task by supplying power and ground to the window lift motor in the current polarity to cause the window to go down. The module also contains a circuit that monitors the current flow through the motor and will stop and/or reverse the window motor if an obstruction causes the window motor to draw more than the normal amount of current.

35.3 Types of communication 通信的类型

The types of communications include the following:

• Differential. In the differential form of module communication, a difference in voltage is applied to two wires, which are twisted to help reduce electromagnetic interference (EMI). These transfer wires are called a twisted pair.

• Parallel. In the parallel type of module communication, the send and receive signals are on different wires.

• Serial data. The serial data is data transmitted over one wire by a series of rapidly changing voltage signals pulsed from low to high or from high to low.

• Multiplexing. The process of multiplexing involves the sending of multiple signals of information at the same time over a signal wire and then separating the signals at the receiving end.

This system of intercommunication of computers or processors is referred to as a network. See Figure 35-2.

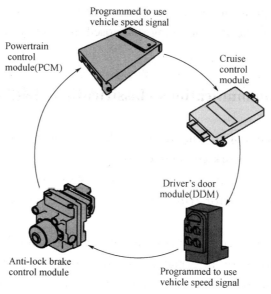

Figure 35-2 A network allows all modules to communicate with other modules

By connecting the computers together on a communications network, they can easily share information back and forth. This multiplexing has the following advantages.

- Elimination of redundant sensors and dedicated wiring for these multiple sensors.
- Reduction of the number of wires, connectors, and circuits.
- Addition of more features and option content to new vehicles.
- Weight reduction due to fewer components, wires, and connectors, thereby increasing fuel economy.
- Changeable features with software upgrades versus component replacement.

35.4 Module communications configuration 模块通信结构

The three most common types of networks used on vehicles include:

1. Ring link networks. In a ring-type network, all modules are connected to each other by a serial data line (in a line) until all are connected in a ring.

2. Star link networks. In a star link network, a serial data line attaches to each module and then each is connected to a central point. This central point is called a splice pack, abbreviated SP such as in "SP 306." The splice pack uses a bar to splice all of the serial lines together. Some GM vehicles use two or more splice packs to tie the modules together. When more than one splice pack is used, a serial data line connects one splice pack to the others. In most applications, the BUS bar used in each splice pack can be removed. When the BUS bar is removed, a special tool (J 42236) can be installed in place of the removed BUS bar. Using this tool, the serial data line for each module can be isolated and tested for a possible problem. Using the special tool at the splice pack makes diagnosing this type of network easier than many others.

3. Ring/star hybrid. In a ring/star network, the modules are connected using both types of network configurations. Check service information (SI) for details on how this network is connected on the vehicle being diagnosed and always follow the recommended diagnostic steps.

35.5 Network communications classifications 网络通信分类

The Society of Automotive Engineers (SAE) standards include the following three categories of in-vehicle network communications.

CLASS A: Low-speed networks, meaning less than 10,000 bits per second (bps, or 10 Kbs), are generally used for trip computers, entertainment, and other convenience features.

CLASS B: Medium-speed networks, meaning 10,000 to 125,000 bps (10 to 125 Kbs), are generally used for information transfer among modules, such as instrument clusters, temperature sensor data, and other general uses.

CLASS C: High-speed networks, meaning 125,000 to 1,000,000 bps, are generally

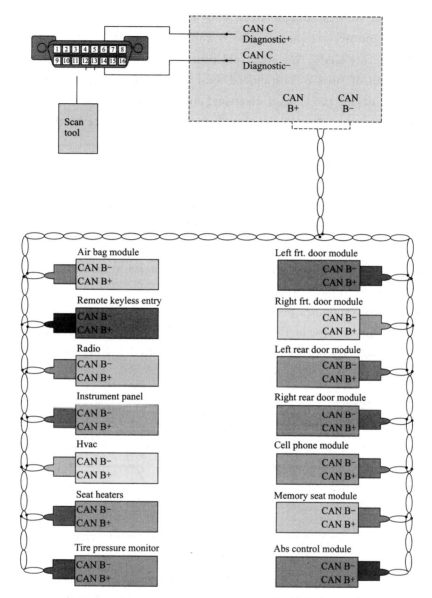

Figure 35-3 A typical BUS system showing module CAN communications and twisted pairs of wire.

used for real-time powertrain and vehicle dynamic control. High-speed BUS communication systems now use a controller area network (CAN). See Figure 35-3.

A BUS is a term used to describe a communications network. Therefore, there are connections to the BUS and BUS communications, both of which refer to digital messages being transmitted among electronic modules or computers.

35.6　Controller area network 控制器区域网

Robert Bosch Corporation developed the CAN protocol, which was called CAN 1.2, in 1993. The CAN protocol was approved by the Environmental Protection Agency (EPA) for 2003 and newer vehicle diagnostics, and a legal requirement for all vehicles by 2008. The CAN diagnostic systems use pins 6 and 14 in the standard 16 pin OBD-II (J-1962) connector. Before CAN, the scan tool protocol had been manufacturer specific.

A protocol is set of rules or a standard used between computers or electronic control modules. Protocols include the type of electrical connectors, voltage levels, and frequency of the transmitted messages. Protocols, therefore, include both the hardware and software needed to communicate between modules.

The CAN protocol offers the following features:

• Faster than other BUS communication protocols.

• Cost effective because it is an easier system than others to use.

• Less effected by electromagnetic interference (Data is transferred on two wires that are twisted together, called twisted pair, to help reduce EMI interference.)

• Message based rather than address based which makes it easier to expand.

• No wakeup needed because it is a two-wire system.

• Supports up to 15 modules plus a scan tool.

• Uses a 120 ohm resistor at the ends of each pair to reduce electrical noise.

• Applies 2.5 volts on both wires: H (high) goes to 3.5 volts when active; L (low) goes to 1.5 volts when active. See Figure 35-4.

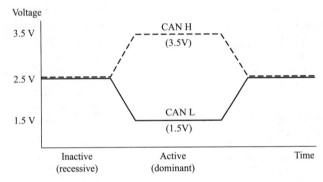

Figure 35-4　CAN uses a differential type of module communication where the voltage on one wire is the equal but opposite voltage on the other wire. When no communication is occurring, both wires have 2.5 volts applied. When communication is occurring, CAN H (high) goes up 1 volt to 3.5 volts and CAN L (low) goes down 1 volt to 1.5 volts.

[词汇]

module	n. 模块；组件	multiplexing	n. 多路传输，多路复用；多重发讯
node	n. 节点		
obstruction	n. 障碍；阻碍；妨碍	Intercommunication	n. 双向（或多向）通信；连通
differential	n. 差分，差动		
electromagnetic interference (EMI)	电磁干扰	redundant	adj. 冗余的
		dedicated	adj. 专用的
parallel data	并行数据	changeable	adj. 可变的
serial data	串行数据	ring link network	环状网络

star link network	星状网络	Environmental Protection Agency (EPA)	美国环境保护署
splice	n. 拼接；接合	diagnostics	n. 诊断
pack	n. 包装；一群；背包；包裹；一副	OBD-Ⅱ the Second On-Board Diagnostics	第二代车载自诊断
abbreviate	vt. 使简短；缩简；缩略；使用缩写词	BUS	n. 总线
service information (SI)	业务信息	twist	vt. 扭成一束；搓
Society of Automotive Engineers (SAE)	美国汽车工程师学会	wakeup	醒来；叫醒
instrument cluster	仪表盘	scan tool	扫描工具

[注释]

1. Protocol 协议：计算机通信网是由许多具有信息交换和处理能力的节点互连而成的。要使整个网络有条不紊地工作，就要求每个节点必须遵守一些事先约定好的有关数据格式及时序等的规则。这些为实现网络数据交换而建立的规则、约定或标准就称为网络协议。协议是通信双方为了实现通信而设计的约定或通话规则。

2. Controller Area Network 控制器区域网路（简称 CAN 或 CANbus）：是一种通信协定，其特点是允许网路上的设备直接互相通信，网路上不需要主机（Host）控制通信。

[问题]

1. Why the network is needed in vehicle?
2. Please describe the types of communications。
3. What is the meaning of the star link network?
4. How are the in-vehicle network communications classified?

Lesson 36

Air Bags
安全气囊

A typical supplemental inflatable restraint (SIR) or air bag system includes two important elements. The electrical system includes the impact sensors and the electronic control module. Its main functions are to conduct a system self-check to let the driver know that it is functioning properly, detect an impact, and to send a signal that inflates the air bag. The air bag module is located in the steering wheel. It contains the air bag and the ports that cause it to inflate. The knee diverter cushions the driver's knee from impact and helps prevent the driver from sliding under the air bag during a collision. It is located underneath the steering column and behind the steering column trim. (See Figure 36-1).

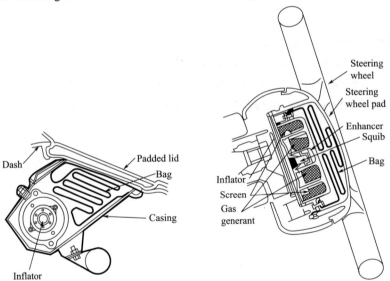

Figure 36-1 Two gas bag installations: *left*, in the dash for the front seat passenger and, *right*, in the steering wheel hub, for rhe driver.

In Figure 36-1, an electrically fired squib generates the heat to frie the pellets which generate the gas. As the bags inglate, they push away the padded trim panels beneath which they are housed.

36.1 Electrical System Components 电气系统部件

Diagnostic monitor assembly. The diagnostic monitor contains a microcomputer that monitors the electrical system components and connections. The monitor performs a self-check of the microcomputer internal circuits and energizes the system readiness indicator during prove out and whenever a fault occurs. System electrical faults can be detected and translated into coded indicator displays. If a certain fault occurs, the microcomputer disables the system by opening a thermal fuse built into the monitor. If a system fault exists and the indicator is malfunctioning, an audible tone signals the need for service. If certain faults occur, the system is disarmed by a firing circuit disarm device incorporated within the monitor or diagnostic module.

An air bag system backup power supply is included in the diagnostic monitor to provide air bag deployment power if the battery or battery cables are damaged in an accident before the crash sensors close. The power supply depletes its stored energy approximately one minute after the positive cable of the battery is disconnected.

WARNING: The backup power supply energy must be depleted before any air bag component service is performed. To deplete the backup power supply energy, disconnect the positive battery cable and wait one minute.

Sensors. The sensors detect impact and signal the air bag to inflate. At least two sensors must be activated for the air bag to inflate. There are usually five sensors: two at the radiator support, one at the right-hand fender apron, one at the left-hand fender apron, and one at the cowl in the passenger compartment. (A few systems use only two sensors——one in front of the radiator and another in the passenger compartment.) There is an interlock between the sensors, so that two or more must work together to trigger the system. Keep in mind that air bag systems are designed to deploy in case of frontal collisions only. While the design of individual systems varies, deployment generally occurs anywhere between 12 to 28 mph.

All the sensors use some type of inertia switching mechanism, which provides for the breakaway of a metal ball from its captive magnet. This function causes a signal to activate a portion of the deployment program set up in the control processor. The system is still capable of directly applying battery power to the squib or detonator. At least two sensors, one safing and one front crash sensor, must be activated to inflate the air bag.

An integrated version within this network includes a safing sensor, sometimes attached to the original crash sensor. This device confirms the attitude and magnitude of the frontal deceleration forces and will offer the microprocessor a second option before actual deployment. This is all it takes to complete the firing sequence, and the bag will deploy.

Wiring harness. The harness connects all system components into a complete unit. The wires carry the electricity, which signals the air bag to inflate. The harness also passes the signals during the self-diagnostic sequence.

Sir or air bag readiness light. This light lets the driver know the air bag system is working and ready to do its job. The readiness lamp lights briefly when the driver turns the key from off to run. A malfunction in the air bag system causes the light to stay on continuously or to flash, or the light might not come on at all. Some systems have a tone generator that sounds if there is a problem in the system or if the readiness light is not functioning.

36.2　Air Bag Module 气囊模块

The bag itself is composed of nylon and is sometimes coated internally with neoprene. All the air bag module components are packaged in a single container, which is mounted in the center of the steering wheel. This entire assembly must be services as one unit when repair of the air bag system is required. The air bag module is made up of the following components.

Igniter assembly. Inflation of the air bag is caused by an explosive release of gas. In order for the explosion to occur, a chemical reaction must be started. The igniter does this when it receives a signal from the air bag monitor. Actually, the igniter is a two-pin bridge device. When the electrical current is applied, it arcs across the two pins creating a zerconic potassium perchlorate (ZPP). This material ignites the propellant. Some newer-model seat bags now use solid propellant and argon. This gas has a stable structure, cools more quickly, and is inert as well as nontoxic. (See Figure 36-2).

Inflater module. This module contains the ZPP. Once it triggers the igniter, the

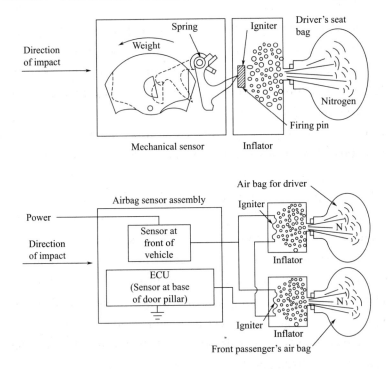

Figure 36-2　*Top*, mechanically actuated bag firing mechanism; *bottom*, electrichally actuated alternative. The latter has the advantages of greater compactness of the parts that may have to be accommodated in the steering wheel hub and the sensors and electronic control unit can be sited in the most appropriate positions

propellant charge is progressive burning sodium azide, which converts to nitrogen gas as it burns. It is the nitrogen gas that fills the air bag. Almost as soon as the bag is filled, the gas is cooled and vented, deflating the assembly as the collision energy is absorbed. The driver is cradled in the envelope of the supplemental restraint bag instead of being propelled forward to strike the steering wheel or be otherwise injured by follow-up inertia energy from seat belt restraint systems. In addition, a certain degree of facial protection against flying objects is obtained just when it is needed.

It is important to remember that the tandem action of at least one main sensor and a safing sensor will initiate safety restraint system activation. The micro-controller also provides failure data and trouble codes for use in servicing various aspects of most systems.

Mounting plate and retainer ring. These attach the air bag assembly to the inflator. They also keep the entire air bag module connected to the steering wheel.

Liner and steering wheel trim cover. The liner houses the air bag. The trim cover goes over the exterior of the steering wheel hub.

Passenger-side air bags are very similar in design to the driver's unit. The actual capacity of gas required to inflate the bag is much greater because the bag must span the extra distance between the occupant and the dashboard at the passenger seating location. The steering wheel and column make up this difference on the driver's side.

CAUTION: When the air bag is deployed, a great deal of heat is generated. While the heat is not harmful to passengers, it may damage or melt the clock spring electrical connector. When replacing a deployed air bag module, examine all of the electrical connections for signs of scorching or damage. If damage exists, it must be repaired.

[词汇]

supplemental	*adj.* 补充的,辅助的	indicator	*n.* 指示灯
inflatable	*adj.* 可充气的	disable	*v.* 使残废,使失去能力,丧失能力
restraint	*n.* 制约,抑制,限制	thermal	*adj.* 热的,热量的
air bag	安全气囊	audible	*adj.* 听得见的
impact	*n.* 冲击,碰撞,撞击	tone	*n.* 声音,音调,纯音
module	*n.* 模块	crash	*n.* 碰撞,摔毁,事故
self-check	自检	backup	*adj.* 备用的
steering wheel	方向盘	deplete	*vt.* 耗尽,使衰竭
knee	*n.* 膝,膝盖	radiator	*n.* 散热器
diverter	*n.* 分流器,转向器	support	*n.* 支座,支柱,支架
cushion	*n.* 垫子,软垫,衬垫	fender	*n.* 翼子板
column	*n.* 柱;支柱	apron	*n.* 车身围裙前的围板,挡泥板上的橡皮板
trim	*n.* 装饰		
diagnostic	*adj.* 诊断的	cowl	*n.* 罩
monitor	*n.* 监视器,监控器	interlock	*v.* 互锁
microcomputer	*n.* 微型计算机	deploy	*vt.* 展开,部署,使用
readiness	*n.* 准备状态,备用状态	captive	*adj.* 可捕获的,被吸引住的

magnet	n. 磁铁	potassium	n. 钾
portion	n. 一部分，一分	perchlorate	n. 高氯酸盐
deployment	n. 展开	propellant	n. 推进剂，发射药
attitude	n. 状态（体位，空间方位角，态度）	argon	n. 氩
magnitude	n. 大小，数量，巨大，广大，量级	nontoxic	adj. 无毒的
harness	n. 线束，导线，吊带	sodium	n. 钠
self-diagnostic	自诊断的	azide	n. 叠氮化物
generator	n. 发生器	cradle	n. 托架，吊架，吊盘
neoprene	n. 氯丁二烯橡胶	tandem	adj. 串联的，前后串列的
igniter	n. 点火剂，引爆装置	inflator	n. 充气机，空压机，增压泵
bridge	n. 电桥，桥接线，桥接条	trouble code	故障码
zerconic	adj. 锆的，含锆的		

[注释]

Air bag 安全气囊：安装在方向盘中间和助手席前面工具箱盖的上面，在车身遭到猛烈撞击时，它会在零点零几秒内爆发性充气并膨胀出来，阻挡你的头部和胸部。

[问题]

1. What are the main parts of the air bag?
2. What's the function of the wheel sensors?
3. How does the inflater work?
4. How can the electrical faults be detected in the air bag?

Lesson 37

Dual-clutch Transmission
双离合器变速器

Most people know that cars come with two basic transmission types: manuals, which require that the driver change gears by depressing a clutch pedal and using a stick shift, and automatics, which do all of the shifting work for drivers using clutches, a torque converter and sets of planetary gears. But there's also something in between that offers the best of both worlds --the dual-clutch transmission, also called the semi-automatic transmission, the "clutchless" manual transmission and the automated manual transmission.

In the world of racecars, semi-automatic transmissions have been a staple for years. But in the world of production vehicles, it's a relatively new technology --one that is being defined by a very specific design known as the dual-clutch, or direct-shift, gearbox.

This article will explore how a dual-clutch transmission works, how it compares to other types of transmissions and why some predict that it is the transmission of the future.

37.1 Hands-On or Hands-Off 结合或分离

A dual-clutch transmission offers the function of two manual gearboxes in one. To understand what this means, it's helpful to review how a conventional manual gearbox works. When a driver wants to change from one gear to another in a standard stick-shift car, he first presses down the clutch pedal. This operates a single clutch, which disconnects the engine from the gearbox and interrupts power flow to the transmission. Then the driver uses the stick shift to select a new gear, a process that involves moving a toothed collar from one gear wheel to another gear wheel of a different size. Devices called synchronizers match the gears before they are engaged to prevent grinding. Once the new gear is engaged, the driver releases the clutch pedal, which re-connects the engine to the gearbox and transmits power to the wheels.

So, in a conventional manual transmission, there is not a continuous flow of power from the engine to the wheels. Instead, power delivery changes from on to off to on during gearshift, causing a phenomenon known as "shift shock" or "torque interrupt." For an unskilled driver, this can result in passengers being thrown forward and back again as gears are changed.

A dual-clutch gearbox, by contrast, uses two clutches, but has no clutch pedal. Sophisticated electronics and hydraulics control the clutches, just as they do in a standard automatic transmission. In a DCT, however, the clutches operate independently. One clutch controls the odd gears (first, third, fifth and reverse), while the other controls the even gears (second, fourth and sixth). Using this arrangement, gears can be changed without interrupting the power flow from the engine to the transmission. (See Figure 37-1).

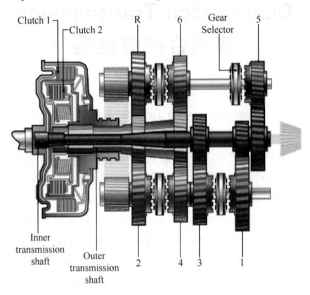

Figure 37-1 6-speed basic design

37.2 Dual-clutch Transmission Shafts 双离合轴

A two-part transmission shaft is at the heart of a DCT. Unlike a conventional manual gearbox, which houses all of its gears on a single input shaft, the DCT splits up odd and even gears on two input shafts. How is this possible? The outer shaft is hollowed out, making room for an inner shaft, which is nested inside. The outer hollow shaft feeds second and fourth gears, while the inner shaft feeds first, third and fifth.

The Figure 37-2 shows this arrangement for a typical five-speed DCT. Notice that one clutch controls second and fourth gears, while another, independent clutch controls first, third and fifth gears. That's the trick that allows lightning-fast gear changes and keeps power delivery constant. A standard manual transmission can't do this because it must use one clutch for all odd and even gears. .

37.3 Multi-plate Clutches 多片离合器

Because a dual-clutch transmission is similar to an automatic, you might think that it requires a torque converter, which is how an automatic transfers engine torque from the engine to the transmission. DCTs, however, don't require torque converters. Instead, DCTs currently on the market use wet multi-plate clutches. A "wet" clutch is one that

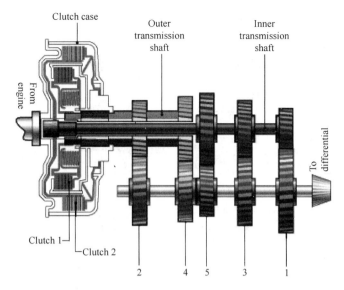

Figure 37-2　Basic arrangement

bathes the clutch components in lubricating fluid to reduce friction and limit the production of heat. Several manufacturers are developing DCTs that use dry clutches, like those usually associated with manual transmissions, but all production vehicles equipped with DCTs today use the wet version. Many motorcycles have single multi-plate clutches. (Scc Figure 37-3).

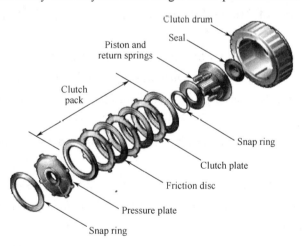

Figure 37-3　Basic multi-plate wet clutch design

　　Like torque converters, wet multi-plate clutches use hydraulic pressure to drive the gears. The fluid does its work inside the clutch piston, seen in the diagram above. When the clutch is engaged, hydraulic pressure inside the piston forces a set of coil springs part, which pushes a series of stacked clutch plates and friction discs against a fixed pressure plate. The friction discs have internal teeth that are sized and shaped to mesh with splines on the clutch drum. In turn, the drum is connected to the gearset that will receive the transfer force. Audi's dual-clutch transmission has both a small coil spring and a large diaphragm spring in its wet multi-plate clutches. (See Figure 37-4).

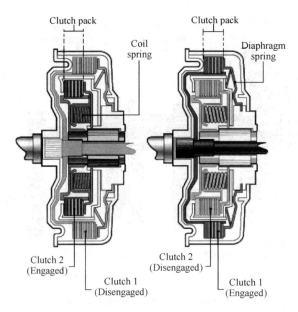

Figure 37-4　Basic dual wet clutch design

To disengage the clutch, fluid pressure inside the piston is reduced. This allows the piston springs to relax, which eases pressure on the clutch pack and pressure plate.

37.4　Pros and Cons of Dual-clutch Transmissions 双离合器变速器的优缺点

Hopefully it's becoming clear why the DCT is classified as an automated manual transmission. In principle, the DCT behaves just like a standard manual transmission: It's got input and auxiliary shafts to house gears, synchronizers and a clutch. What it doesn't have is a clutch pedal, because computers, solenoids and hydraulics do the actual shifting. Even without a clutch pedal, the driver can still "tell" the computer when to take action through paddles, buttons or a gearshift.

Driver experience, then, is just one of the many advantages of a DCT. With upshifts taking a mere 8 milliseconds, many feel that the DCT offers the most dynamic acceleration of any vehicle on the market. It certainly offers smooth acceleration by eliminating the shift shock that accompanies gearshifts in manual transmissions and even some automatics. Best of all, it affords drivers the luxury of choosing whether they prefer to control the shifting or let the computer do all of the work.

Perhaps the most compelling advantage of a DCT is improved fuel economy. Because power flow from the engine to the transmission is not interrupted, fuel efficiency increases dramatically. Some experts say that a six-speed DCT can deliver up to a 10 percent increase in relative fuel efficiency when compared to a conventional five-speed automatic.

Many car manufacturers are interested in DCT technology. However, some automakers are wary of the additional costs associated with modifying production lines to accommodate a new type of transmission. This could initially drive up the costs of cars outfitted with

DCTs, which might discourage cost-conscious consumers.

In addition, manufacturers are already investing heavily in alternate transmission technologies. One of the most notable is the continuously variable transmission, or CVT. A CVT is a type of automatic transmission that uses a moving pulley system and a belt or chain to infinitely adjust the gear ratio across a wide range. CVTs also reduce shift shock and increase fuel efficiency significantly. But CVTs can't handle the high torque demands of performance cars.

DCTs don't have such issues and are ideal for high-performance vehicles. In Europe, where manual transmissions are preferred because of their performance and fuel efficiency, some predict that DCTs will capture 25 percent of the market. Just one percent of cars produced in Western Europe will be fitted with a CVT by 2012.

[词汇]

planetary gear	行星齿轮	multi-plate clutch	多片离合器
clutchless	adj. 无离合的	stack	n. 堆；一大堆；存储栈
racecar	n. 赛车	clutch plate	离合器片
staple	n. 主要产品；主题，主要部分；主食	friction disc	摩擦盘
		drum	n. 毂
synchronizer	n. 同步器	gearset	n. 齿轮组
grinding	adj. 磨的；碾的；摩擦的	solenoid	n. 电磁线圈
odd gear	奇数齿轮	hydraulics	n. 液压装置
even gear	偶数齿轮	paddle	n. 扁板，类似铁铲的工具；洗衣板
lightning-fast	adj. 快如闪电的		
torque converter	变矩器		

[注释]

1. Dual-clutch transmission 双离合变速器：DCT 是两个传统手动变速箱的集合体（分别为奇数和偶数挡），拥有两个离合器，两根输入轴，但仅有一根输出轴。离合器的分离与接合，以及挡位切换都在电脑的掌控下通过液压机构进行控制，因此也能提供手动换挡模式。

2. Continuously variable transmission 无级变速器：它的变速比不是间断的点，而是一系列连续的值，譬如可以从 3.455 一直变化到 0.85。CVT 结构比传统变速器简单，体积更小，它既没有手动变速器的众多齿轮副，也没有自动变速器复杂的行星齿轮组，它主要靠主、从动轮和金属带来实现速比的无级变化。

[问题]

1. What are the main components of the dual-clutch transmission?
2. How does the dual-clutch transmission work?
3. How are the automotive transmissions classified?
4. What are the advantages of the dual-clutch transmission?

Lesson 38

Automotive Communication Technology
汽车通信技术

The automotive system is nowadays a complex distributed system with various demands of networking capabilities. Most automakers share common subcontractors, and in a modern automotive application more and more applications developed by different subcontractors needs the possibility of interaction. One automotive application consists of one or several Electronic Control Units (ECUs). In an automotive system consisting of several automotive applications more than 70 ECUs might need to distribute more than 2500 signals. This makes the automotive system complicated in terms of networking. To manage this complexity the automotive industry has these last years set up several big consortiums in order to agree on a common scalable electric architecture (e.g., AUTOSAR) and a common scalable communication system (e.g., FlexRay) to support the automotive systems of tomorrow.

In the near future hydraulic automotive systems, such as steering and braking, will be replaced by communication networks (wires). The former is offered by subcontractors today, and the latter has been shown to work in several prototype cars. These new steer-by-wire and brake-by-wire solutions are commonly called X-by-Wire (XBW) systems.

The requirements of an automotive communication network come from the applications it has to support. Major automotive applications that involve networking and the usage of field buses are XBW, chassis systems, powertrain systems and infotainment or multimedia. Looking at XBW systems, the two most important requirements are dependability and fault-containment. However, for chassis systems determinism is more important whereas high bandwidth is needed in powertrain systems. Multimedia devices require high bandwidth and plug-n-play capabilities.

Today several different field buses are used to address these various communication demands. A big issue that the automotive system producers deal with is that too many field bus technologies exist today. To interconnect these systems there is a need for high bandwidth together with flexibility and determinism. It is desirable to move from using too many technologies to fewer more general. To reduce the complexity evolving in a modern automotive system it would be good to commit on a set of networking protocols that can be used in most of the applications typically found in an automotive system.

38.1 Technologies used today 现在的技术

Some of the more common field bus technologies interconnecting ECUs today are the

Controller Area Network (CAN), the Local Interconnect Network (LIN), byteflight and the Media Oriented Systems Transport (MOST).

CAN - The Controller Area Network (CAN) was initiated in 1981 and developed by Bosch. In 1994 it became an ISO standard and today it is the most widely used vehicular network. CAN transmits message frames in an event-triggered fashion. Frames can be transmitted at speeds of up to 1 Mbps, although 500Kbps is the more common choice for, e.g., engine control, ABS systems and cruise control. Speeds of less than 125 Kbps are used for comfort electronics (e.g., seat and window control).

LIN - The Local Interconnect Network (LIN) is a time-triggered master-slave field bus. With LIN, message frames are sent at speeds of 20 Kbps. The physical medium is a single wire. LIN is an open standard (standardised in 2000) inexpensive network that is used in automotive systems to control devices such as seat control, light sensors and climate control. LIN is often used together with CAN, as LIN complements CAN being much cheaper and simpler still providing the communications required for many automotive applications.

byteflight - In 1996 BMW started to develop byteflight, which is a Flexible Time Division Multiple Access (FTDMA) network typically using a star topology (although bus and cluster topologies are possible as well). Messages are sent in frames at 10 Mbps, using a minislotting concept. The physical medium used is plastic optical fiber. One of the strengths of the byteflight protocol is its support for event-triggered message transmission, although both static and dynamic message frame transmissions are possible.

byteflight guarantees deterministic (constant) latencies for a bounded number of high priority real-time messages. Moreover, it is possible to send non-real-time messages in a prioritised manner thanks to the Minislotting mechanism. Clock synchronization is provided by a dedicated master node, achieving clocks synchronized with a precision in the order of 100ns. Any byteflight node can be configured as the master node. It is possible to avoid babbling idiots using a star coupler.

Typical applications supported by byteflight are, for example, airbag systems and sear-belt tensioners, as they feature fast response-time requirements and short mission times. MOST - To support communications for multimedia application, MOST, or Media Oriented Systems Transport is commonly used. MOST was initiated in 1997 and supports both time-triggered and event-triggered traffic with predictable frame transmission at speeds of 25 Mbps. Moreover, MOST will be available with speeds of 150 Mbps in the near future. MOST is using plastic optical fiber as communication medium.

Typical applications where MOST is used are, for example, the interconnection of telematics and infotainment, such as video displays, GPS navigation systems, active speakers and digital radios. MOST was the first networking technology that was approved by DVD-CCA to carry protected digital video streams.

38.2 Technologies for tomorrow 未来技术

XBW systems need fault-tolerant communication with deterministic message transmissions and low jitter. This is traditionally solved using Time Division Multiple Access (TDMA) protocols due to their deterministic nature.

Three of the more common TDMA-based field buses for automotive applications are TT-CAN, TTP and FlexRay. However, as we will see, they differ in their bandwidth and fault-tolerant capabilities.

TT-CAN - TT-CAN, or Time-Triggered CAN, is a time-triggered session layer on top of CAN. This provides a hybrid TDMA on top of Carrier Sense Multiple Access (CSMA) allowing for both time-triggered and event triggered traffic. TT-CAN is standardised by ISO and intended for XBW systems, although it does not provide the same level of fault-tolerance as the other two XBW candidates, i.e., TTP and FlexRay (presented below).

TTP - TTP/C (TTP), or the Time-Triggered Protocol, is part of the Time-Triggered Architecture (TTA) by TTTech. The first TTP communication controller was released in 1998. TTP is a pure time-triggered TDMA protocol. Using TTP, frames are sent at speeds of 5-25 Mbps depending on the physical medium. Research is going on to reach speeds of 1 Gbps using an Ethernet based star architecture. TTP uses both twisted pair and optical bus medium.

FlexRay - In 1998 BMW and Daimler-Chrysler analysed the current available automotive networks (e.g., CAN, TTP, MOST and byteflight) and found out that none of those technologies would ful_l future needs of next generation automotive systems, especially when the automotive industry will take the next step towards XBW. Office-oriented communication protocols can not be used either, since they are not automotive qualified in terms of operating temperatures and electromagnetic requirements.

As a response to this, the FlexRay consortium was formed with the goal to develop a new protocol, called FlexRay. This new protocol should be the solution for the introduction of XBW systems as well as the replacement of some of field buses currently used, thus reducing the total number of in-car networks.

FlexRay is expected to be the de-facto communication standard for high-speed automotive control applications interconnecting ECUs in future automotive systems. A special area of interest will be high-speed safety-critical automotive systems such as XBW and advanced powertrain applications.

FlexRay provides both time-triggered and event triggered message transmission. The event-triggered message transmission is done in the same way as in byteflight using minislotting. Messages are sent in frames using either single or dual channels (the latter for redundancy or doubling the bandwidth) at 10 Mbps and there are no limitations to increase this speed due to protocol mechanisms. At the physical layer, both electrical and optical solutions are adopted. Using FlexRay, the ECUs are interconnected using either a passive bus topology, the way most ECUs are connected today, or an active (multiple) star topology.

FlexRay complements CAN and LIN being suitable for both powertrain systems (high bandwidth and event triggered traffic) and XBW systems (dependability and fault-containment).

[词汇]

subcontractor	n.转包商，次承包者	priority	n.优先，重点；优先权
steer-by-wire	线控转向	synchronization	n.同步，同期
brake-by-wire	线控制动	master node	主节点
field bus	n.现场总线	babbling	adj.胡说的
powertrain	n.传动系	idiot	n.白痴；[口]傻子；极蠢的人
infotainment	n.信息与娱乐	predictable	adj.可预言[报]的
dependability	n.可靠性，强度	telematics	n.信息通信业务，远程信息处理
plug-n-play	n.即插即用	jitter	vt.抖动
flexibility	n.机动性，适应性，灵活性	deterministic	adj.确定的，决定论的；定数论的
vehicular	adj.车辆的		
event-triggered	事件触发	Ethernet	n.以太网
master-slave	主从	consortium	n.共同体
protocol	n.协议，规程，规约	redundancy	n.冗余
latency	n.潜伏期，潜伏状态		

[注释]

1. AUTOSAR（Automotive Open System Architecture）　汽车开放系统架构。
2. FlexRay　一种网络协议标准。
3. Controller Area Network（CAN）　控制器局域网协议。
4. Time-Triggered CAN　事件触发的 CAN。
5. Local Interconnect Network（LIN）　局部连接网络。
6. byteflight　一种网络协议名称。
7. Media Oriented Systems Transport（MOST）　媒体系统传输协议。
8. Carrier Sense Multiple Access（CSMA）　载波侦听多路访问方式。
9. Flexible Time Division Multiple Access（FTDMA）　可变的分时多路访问方式。

[问题]

1. What are the kinds of the automotive communication network?
2. Where is LIN used?
3. What are the advantage of FlexRay?

Lesson 39

Intelligent Vehicle Applications
智能车辆的应用

The field of intelligent vehicles is rapidly growing worldwide, both in the diversity of applications and in increasing interest from the automobile, truck, public transportation, industrial, and military sectors. IV systems offer the potential to significantly enhance safety and operational efficiency.

39.1 Intelligent vehicle application areas 智能车辆应用领域

We can readily segment IV application areas into systems that:
advise or warn the driver (collision warning),
partially control the vehicle, either for steady-state driver assistance or as an emergency intervention to avoid a collision (collision avoidance), or
fully control the vehicle (vehicle automation).
Collision-warning systems include functions such as forward-collision warning, blind-spot warning, lane-departure warning, lane-change or merge warning, intersection collision warning, pedestrian detection and warning, rear-impact warning, and rollover warning for heavy vehicles. A special category of collision warning is driver monitoring, to detect and warn of drowsiness or other impairments that prevent the driver from safely operating the vehicle. If the driver does not adequately respond to warnings, collision-avoidance systems might take control of the steering, brakes, or throttle to maneuver the vehicle back to a safe state. Driver-assistance systems include functions such as adaptive cruise control, lane keeping, precision docking, and precise maneuvering.

Vehicle-automation systems include low speed automation, autonomous driving, and close-headway platooning (which provides increased roadway throughput), and electronic vehicle guidance in segregated areas such as busways and freight terminals. These systems can be autonomous, with all instrumentation and intelligence on the vehicle, or cooperative, where assistance comes from the roadway, other vehicles, or both. Roadway assistance typically takes the form of passive reference markers in the infrastructure. Vehicle-vehicle cooperation lets vehicles operate in closer proximity for increased efficiency, usually by transmitting key vehicle parameters and intentions to following vehicles. The general philosophy is that autonomous systems will work on all roadways in all situations at a useful performance level and take advantage of cooperative elements, as available, to augment and enhance system performance.

39.2 Automobiles 汽车

Passenger car applications could provide a substantial benefit by alleviating the hundreds of thousands of deaths and injuries that occur annually worldwide from highway accidents. However, because of the need to minimize false alarms and maximize reliability for this consumer market, the introduction of automobile systems is proceeding slowly, although steadily.

1. Collision warning. The CW systems listed earlier have been extensively prototyped and tested. Night vision are now available on some automobiles, and Mitsubishi and Nissan have announced the near-term availability of CW packages. Forward-collision warning and lane-departure warning should become available in the next few years. The Japanese Smartway concept will implement user services such as lane keeping, intersection collision avoidance, pedestrian avoidance, and headway keeping. A model-deployment project should be operational by 2003, with nationwide implementation in 2015.

European Commission funding is also supporting research in longitudinal and lateral collision warning. The US Intelligent Vehicle Initiative (IVI) program is establishing a partnership with key automotive manufacturers to perform precompetitive research in human factors (driver workload), high-accuracy digital map databases, and the development of metrics and testing methodologies for collision-warning and collision-avoidance products.

2. Driver assistance and collision avoidance. The high-profile driver-assistance product is adaptive cruise control, available in Europe and Japan and soon to be introduced in the US. ACC senses slower vehicles ahead and adjusts speed to establish a safe following distance, resuming the desired speed when the road ahead is clear. Current ACC systems are geared for highway speeds; the next-generation systems (now in testing) will also support stop-and-go congested conditions. In 1999, Mitsubishi introduced its new Driver Support System in Japan, which supplements ACC with lane-departure warning and side and rear monitoring through machine vision.

Honda, Nissan, and Toyota have developed several safety subsystems in the joint Advanced Safety Vehicle project, including lane positioning, headway control, automatic braking, obstacle warning, drowsiness warning, and nighttime pedestrian warning. Publicly funded research in Europe is focusing on driver monitoring, road-condition sensing, vision enhancement, heading control (intelligent steering control to optimize a vehicle's trajectory), and sensor fusion. The US Department of Transportation (DOT) has begun a five-year, \$35-million project with General Motors to develop and test preproduction rear-end collision-avoidance systems.

3. Automated operation. Fully automated vehicle operation offers safe travel, more efficient traffic flows, and driver convenience. This capability has been prototyped and demonstrated extensively during the '90s, establishing technical feasibility. Current research focuses on refining system approaches. Fully functional automated cars, developed by the University of Korea, the Mechanical Engineering Laboratory in Japan, the University of Pavia (Italy), Ohio State University, and the University of California, among others, are being tested and refined.

39.3 Special vehicles 专用车辆

Current research in this area focuses on snow removal for highway maintenance, automation of repetitive vehicle movements in industrial complexes, and autonomous vehicles for military operations.

California and Minnesota are testing systems that provide lane-edge indications to snowplow drivers attempting to clear roads in low or zero-visibility conditions resulting from high winds or blizzards. To provide lane tracking, the systems either apply magnetic referencing to the highway, indicating each lane's position, or use highly accurate digital maps and precise GPS positioning on board the snowplow. In each case, the driver remains in control of the steering, using a display indicating the lane edge to accurately guide the snowplow. The IVI program has awarded an operational test to the Minnesota DOT to provide expanded testing of these techniques.

39.4 Industrial automation 工业自动化

At seaports, shuttling of transport containers is typically done by "yard tractors," which take on containers at shipside and transport them several hundred meters away to a storage area. The Port of Rotterdam has automated this highly repetitive operation with FROG transponder technology. Other ports worldwide are considering implementing such a system.

Additionally, large industrial complexes might have substantial freight movements between on-site facilities, which are typically served by trucks. In the Combi-Road system, developed in the Netherlands, unmanned tractors operating on dedicated path carry freight back and forth between such points. The system uses magnetic lateral referencing, along with an array of optical beacons to detect obstacles. Implementation is now under discussion for an industrial site in the southern part of the Netherlands, and the Dutch government is considering this approach for transporting freight out of the Port of Rotterdam and distributing it throughout the country via special lanes constructed alongside the public highways.

39.5 Military operations 军事领域

The US Department of Defense seeks to deploy unmanned vehicles for hazardous military scout missions. Demo Ⅲ, the current, third-generation program, calls for highly capable vehicles operating cooperatively both on-road and off-road. Requirements for on-road operations create an overlap with ITS, and useful spin-offs to the automobile and truck industries are expected. The vehicles must operate both singly and in convoys on highways at up to 65 kilometers per hour, and off-road at up to 32 kmph. The Demo Ⅲ sensor suite includes a forward-looking 77-GHz FMCW (Frequency Modulated Continuous Wave) radar, stereo machine vision (separate color, monochrome, and infrared cameras) with gaze control, ladar (laser radar), 2-GHz foliage penetrating radar, and rear-vision cameras.

Initial on-road operations are planned for demonstration in late 2000, with full capability achieved at the program's conclusion in 2001.

Autonomous scout vehicles are also under development in Germany. The Primus program uses substantial machine vision capabilities, with a two-axis platform for gaze control of a color camera. This program has achieved 50 kmph on-road and 10 kmph offroad operations, with ladar sensing for obstacle detection.

[词汇]

diversity	n.多样（性），参差，变化	reference	n.标识，标志
military	adj.军用的，军事的；战争的	marker	n.标识，标志
segment	n.段，片，部分，节，部门	infrastructure	n.基础，基础结构
steady-state	稳态，定态	proximity	n.接[邻，附，临]近
collision	n.（车、船）碰[互]撞	intention	n.意图；意向；打算；目的
intervention	n.干涉，妨碍	philosophy	n.哲理，原理
blind-spot	n.盲点	prototype	n.样机[品]
lane-departure	离开车道	smartway	n.智能公路
lane-change	变换车道	deployment	n.调度，使用
merge	vt.合并；混入	high-profile	n.鲜明的姿态
pedestrian	n.行人	supplement	vt.补充，增补
rollover	n.倾翻	trajectory	n.轨道，轨迹
drowsiness	n.睡意	fusion	n.融合
impairment	n.损害，损伤	preproduction	n.试验性生产，试制
maneuver	vt.操纵	snowplow	n.雪犁，扫雪车
docking	n.码头；停泊处	seaport	n.海港，港口
headway	n.（前后两车间的）车间时距	shipside	n.码头的靠船一侧
platooning	n.排队	container	n.集装箱
throughput	n.通道通过量，通道吞吐量	shuttling	n.短程来回运输（线，工具）
segregate	vt.分开	Rotterdam	n.鹿特丹（荷兰港市）
busway	n.公共汽车专用道	transponder	n.无线电发射机应答器
freight	n.货运	unmanned	adj.无人驾驶[操纵]的
terminal	n.终点站，总站，航空集散站	tractor	n.拖拉机；牵引车
instrumentation	n.仪器；仪表	beacon	n.烽火；信号；指向标
roadway	n.车道，道路；路基；路面	scout	vt.观察；侦察；搜索

overlap	*n.* 重复，部分一致；交搭；重叠		大小 [稳定性]
spin-off	*n.* 创造新的事物而不影响原物的	monochrome	*adj.* 单色的

[注释]

1. Intelligent vehicle　智能车辆：是电子计算机等最新科技成果与现代汽车工业相结合的产物。通常具有自动驾驶、自动变速、甚至具有自动识别道路的功能。

2. Collision avoidance　避撞。为将事故防患于未然，通过车辆及道路的各种传感器掌握道路、周围车辆的状况等驾驶环境信息，通过车载机、道路信息提供装置等实时地提供给驾驶员，并进行危险警告，最终实现自动驾驶。

[问题]

1. Where are the intelligent vehicles used?
2. What's the meaning of the collision avoidance?
3. What is the application area of the intelligent vehicle in military operation?

Chapter 4　Engine Troubleshooting and Repair
发动机故障诊断与修理

Lesson 40

Overheating: Causes and Cures
发动机过热：原因和措施

  Internal combustion engines run on heat. Chemical energy in the fuel is transformed into thermal energy when the fuel burns, which produces mechanical energy to push the pistons, spin the crankshaft and drive the vehicle down the road.

  As efficient as today's engines are, they still waste a LOT of the heat energy they produce. The average gasoline engine is only about 22 to 28% efficient. That means over two-thirds of the heat produced by each gallon of fuel either goes out the tailpipe or is soaked up by the engine itself. Diesels squeeze a little more bang out of each buck's worth of fuel with efficiently ratings of 32 to 38%, but even that leaves a lot of waste heat that must be managed and carried away by the cooling system.

  Ironically, the hotter an engine runs the more efficient it becomes. But there's a limit because aluminum pistons and heads can only get so hot before they start to soften and melt. The same goes for cast iron. Engineers have been tinkering with exotic ceramic materials and metallic-ceramic alloys in an attempt to build high temperature, super efficient engines. They've realized some significant gains but ceramics are still too expensive for everyday applications.

40.1　The Normal working Temperature of Engines 发动机正常工作温度

Most engines today are designed to operate within a "normal" temperature range of about 195 to 220 degrees F. A relatively constant operating temperature is absolutely essential for proper emissions control, good fuel economy and performance.

A 50/50 mixture of water and ethylene glycol antifreeze in the cooling system will boil at 225 degrees if the cap is open. But as long as the system is sealed and holds pressure, a radiator cap rated at 15 psi will increase the boiling temperature of a 50/50 coolant blend up to 265 degrees F. If the concentration of antifreeze to water is upped to 70/30 (the maximum recommended), the boiling temperature under 15 psi of pressure goes up to 276 degrees.

So does this mean a cooling system with a maximum concentration of antifreeze in the coolant (70%) can run as hot as 276°F without boiling over? Theoretically yes——but realistically no. The clearances in most of today's engines are much, much closer than those in engines built in the 1970s and early 1980s. Piston-to-cylinder clearances are much tighter to reduce blowby for lower emissions. Valve stem-to-guide clearances also are closer to reduce oil consumption and emissions, too. Plus, many engines today have aluminum heads with overhead cams. Such engines don't handle higher than normal temperatures well, and are very vulnerable to heat damage if the engine gets too hot.

Anytime temperatures climb beyond the normal range, the engine is running in the danger zone.

40.2　Consequences of Overheating 过热的后果

If the engine overheats, the first thing that will happen is a gasoline engine will start to detonate. The engine will ping and start to lose power under load as the combination of heat and pressure exceed the octane rating of the fuel. If the detonation problem persists, the hammer-like blows may damage the rings, pistons or rod bearings.

Overheating can also cause preignition. Hot spots develop inside the combustion chamber that become a source of ignition for the fuel. The erratic combustion can cause detonation as well as engine run-on in older vehicles with carburetors. Hot spots can also be very damaging and burn holes right through the top of pistons.

Another consequence of overheating may be a blown head gasket. Heat makes aluminum swell almost three times faster than cast iron. The resulting stress can distort the head and make it swell in areas that are hottest like those between exhaust valves in adjoining cylinders, and areas that have restricted coolant flow like the narrow area that separates the cylinders. The typical aluminum head swells most in the middle, which can crush the head gasket if the head gets hot enough. This will cause a loss of torque in the gasket allowing coolant and combustion leaks to occur when the head cools.

Overheating is also a common cause of OHC cam seizure and breakage.

Wait, there's more. If the coolant gets hot enough to boil, it may cause old hoses or an age-weakened radiator to burst under the increased pressure. Pistons may swell up and scuff or seize in their bores, causing serious engine damage. Exhaust valve stems may stick or scuff in their guides. This, in turn, may cause valves to hang open which can damage pistons, valves and other valvetrain components. And if coolant gets into the crankcase, you can kiss the bearings and bottom end of the engine goodbye.

A HOT warning lamp should never be ignored. Though a few high tech cars like Cadillacs with the Northstar engine can disable cylinders to "air-cool" the engine and keep it running at reduced power in the event of coolant loss, most engines will suffer serious damage if they overheat. So advise your customers to stop driving at the first sign of overheating. Turn the engine off, let it cool down and try to find and fix the cause before risking further travel.

40.3　Causes of Overheating 过热的原因

Overheating can be caused by anything that decreases the cooling system's ability to absorb, transport and dissipate heat: A low coolant level, loss of coolant (through internal or external leaks), poor heat conductivity inside the engine because of accumulated deposits in the water jackets, a defective thermostat that doesn't open, poor airflow through the radiator, a slipping fan clutch, an inoperative electric cooling fan, a collapsed lower radiator hose, an eroded or loose water pump impeller, or even a defective radiator cap.

One of nature's basic laws says that heat always flows from an area of higher temperature to an area of lesser temperature, never the other way around. The only way to cool hot metal, therefore, is to keep it in constant contact with a cooler liquid. And the only way to do that is to keep the coolant in constant circulation. As soon as the circulation stops, either because of a problem with the water pump, thermostat or loss of coolant, temperatures begin to rise and the engine starts to overheat.

The coolant also has to get rid of the heat it soaks up while passing through the block and head (s). So the radiator must be capable of doing its job, which requires the help of an efficient cooling fan at slow speeds.

Finally, the thermostat must be doing its job to keep the engine's average temperature within the normal range. If the thermostat fails to open, it will effectively block the flow of coolant and the engine will overheat.

40.4　What to Check 检查什么

Thermostat——Severe overheating can often damage a good thermostat. If the engine has overheated because of another problem, therefore, the thermostat should be tested or replaced before the engine is returned to service.

One way to check the thermostat is to start the engine and feel the upper radiator hose (or use an infrared noncontact thermometer to read its temperature). The hose should not feel uncomfortably hot until the engine has warmed-up and the thermostat opens. If the hose does not get hot, it means the thermostat is not opening.

Another way to test the thermostat is to remove it and dip it into a pan of boiling water (it should open). The exact opening temperature can be checked by using a thermometer.

If the thermostat needs to be replaced, install one with the same temperature rating as the original. Most cars and light trucks since 1971 require thermostats with 192 or 195 degree ratings. Using a cooler thermostat (160 or 180) in an attempt to "cure" a tendency to overheat can increase fuel and oil consumption, ring wear and emissions. On newer vehicles with computerized engine controls, the wrong thermostat can prevent the computer system from going into closed loop resulting in major performance and emission problems if the engine fails to reach its normal operating temperature.

Cooling system leaks——Loss of coolant because of a leak is probably the most common cause of overheating. Possible leak points include hoses, the radiator, heater core, water pump, thermostat housing, head gasket, freeze plugs, automatic transmission oil cooler, cylinder head (s) and block.

Make a careful visual inspection of the entire cooling system, and then pressure test the cooling system and radiator cap. A pressure test will reveal internal leaks such as seepage past the head gasket as well as cracks in the head or block. A leak-free system should hold pressure for at least a minute or more.

It's important to pressure test the radiator cap, too, because a weak cap (or one with too low a pressure rating for the application) will lower the coolant's boiling point and can allow coolant to escape from the radiator.

Fan——With mechanical fans, most overheating problems are caused by a faulty fan clutch——though a missing fan shroud can reduce the fan's cooling effectiveness by as much as 50% (depending on the fan's distance from the radiator) which may be enough to cause the engine to overheat in hot weather or when working hard.

Defective fan clutches are a common and often overlooked cause of overheating. The shear characteristics of the clutch fluid gradually deteriorates over time, with an average loss in drive efficiency of about 200 rpm per year. Eventually slippage reaches the point where effective cooling is no longer possible and overheating results. (On average, the life of a fan clutch is about the same as a water pump. If one needs to be replaced, the other usually does too.)

If the fan clutch shows signs of fluid leakage (oily streaks radiating outward from the hub of the clutch), spins freely with little or no resistance when the engine is off, or wobbles when the fan is pushed in or out, it needs to be replaced.

With an electric cooling fan, check to see that the fan cycles on when the engine gets hot and when the air conditioner is on. If the fan fails to come on, check the fan motor wiring connections, relay and temperature sensor. Try jumping the fan directly to the battery. If it runs, the problem is in the wiring, relay or sensor. If it fails to run, the fan motor is bad and needs to be replaced.

Water pump——Any wobble in the pump shaft or seepage would call for replacement. In some instances, a pump can cause an engine to overheat if the impeller vanes are badly eroded due to corrosion or if the impeller has come loose from the shaft. The wrong pump may also cause an engine to overheat. Some engines with serpentine drive belts require a special water pump that turns in the opposite direction of those used on the same engine with ordinary V-belts.

Belts & hoses——Check belt tension and condition. A loose belt that slips may prevent the water pump from circulating coolant fast enough and/or the fan from turning fast for proper cooling.

The condition of the hoses should also be checked. Recommend new hoses if the old ones are over 5 years old.

Sometimes a lower radiator hose will collapse under vacuum at high speed and restrict the flow of coolant from the radiator into the engine. This can happen if the reinforcing spring inside the hose is missing or damaged.

Radiator   The most common problems radiators fall prey to are clogging (both internal and external) and leaks. Dirt, bugs and debris can block air flow through the core and reduce the radiator's ability to dissipate heat. Internal corrosion and an accumulation of deposits can likewise inhibit coolant circulation and reduce cooling. A good way to find clogs is to use an infrared thermometer to "scan" the surface of the radiator for cold spots. If clogged, the radiator should be removed for cleaning or replaced. Backflushing the cooling system and/or using chemical cleaners can remove rust and hard water scale, but may do little to open up a clogged radiator.

When refilling the cooling system, be sure you get it completely full. Air pockets in the head (s), heater core and below the thermostat can interfere with proper coolant circulation and cooling. If the cooling system has no bleeder valves to vent air, you may have to temporarily loosen a heater hose to get all the air out of the system.

Excessive exhaust backpressure. A clogged catalytic converter is usually the culprit here, but don't overlook the possibility of a crushed pipe or a collapsed double wall pipe. Check intake vacuum at idle. If it reads low and continues to drop, inspect the exhaust system.

Retarded or overadvanced ignition timing (may also contribute to detonation & preignition).

Overheated incoming air. On older vehicles with a carburetor or throttle body injection, check the operation of the heated air intake system on the air cleaner. If the temperature control valve is stuck so only heated air from around the exhaust manifold is drawn into the air cleaner, it may contribute to detonation and/or overheating. Also check the heat riser valve for manifold heat on older V6 and V8 engines. If stuck shut, it may be overheating the intake manifold.

Dragging brakes. A caliper that's sticking or a parking brake that isn't releasing may be making the engine work too hard.

Overworking the engine. The cooling systems in many passenger cars today are marginal and have little excess capacity to handle extra heat generated by towing or high speed mountain driving in hot weather.

[词汇]

gallon	n. 加仑	adjoining	adj. 邻接的，隔壁的
tailpipe	n. 尾管	seizure	n. 卡住，扣押，咬住
buck	n. 美元	breakage	n. 破裂，划
tinker	vi. 做焊锅匠，笨拙的修补	impeller	n. 叶轮
ethylene	n. 乙烯	thermometer	n. 温度计
glycol	n. 乙二醇	deteriorate	v. (使) 恶化
concentration	n. 浓度，浓缩	wobble	vi. 摇晃，摇摆，游移不定，抖动
detonate	n. 爆燃，爆破	seepage	n. 渗出，渗流，渗漏
preignition	n. 早燃	serpentine	adj. 蛇形的
consequence	n. 结果	backflush	n. 回洗，反冲洗
gasket	n. 衬垫，垫圈	bleeder	n. 流出装置，泄放装置，放出阀
swell	v. (使) 膨胀，增大	backpressure	n. 反压力（背压，吸入压力）

[注释]

Tailpipe 尾管：排气系统最后段的管子，装在消音器后方并延伸到车辆的尾部。

[问题]

1. What consequences can be created by engine overheating?
2. What are the main reasons of engine overheating?
3. How do we check the thermostat?
4. How do we check the radiator?

Lesson 41

Diesel Diagnostics
柴油机诊断

Diesel engines are real misers when it comes to sipping fuel. They're also known for their pulling power and rugged durability. That's why diesels continue to be a popular option in many pickup trucks today. But diesels are also known for their idle clatter, black smoke and cold-weather starting woes.

When temperatures drop, several things happen that can make a diesel hard to start. First, the oil in the crankcase thickens. At the same time, battery output drops, reducing the number of amps available to crank the engine. The 15W-40 multi-viscosity motor oil, a popular warm weather choice with many diesel owners these days, may become too thick when temperatures go below freezing or plunge to zero or below. Straight 30-or 40-weight oils would definitely be too thick. The increased drag created by the cold oil can reduce cranking speed to the point where the engine may not generate enough cranking compression and/or fuel pressure to light the fire.

One of the first things you should check when diagnosing a "hard to start" complaint, therefore, is the dipstick. If the oil is thick and globby, it may not be the correct viscosity for winter driving. Ask the customer what kind of oil he's been using and when it was last changed. Switching to a lighter oil such as a 10W-30 (never anything lighter in a conventional oil!) may be all that's needed to improve cold cranking. For really cold weather, you might recommend a CG-4 rated synthetic motor oil.

The next thing that needs to be checked is minimum cranking speed. The rpm needed to light the fire will vary according to the application, but General Motors says its 6.2L and 6.5L diesels with Stanadyne rotary injection pumps need at least 100 rpm when cold, and 180 rpm when hot.

If the engine isn't cranking fast enough, check battery charge and condition, as well as the cable connections and the starter's amp draw. Problems in any of these areas can make any engine hard to start. If the battery is low, recharge it and check the output of the charging system, too.

41.1 Glow Plugs 预热塞

If slow cranking isn't the problem, perhaps there's something wrong with the glow plug system. Most passenger car and light truck diesels have glow plugs to assist cold starts. The glow plugs are powered by a relay and timer that routes voltage to the plugs for the prescribed number of seconds. When the timer runs out, the relay is supposed to turn off the voltage. But relays sometimes stick and continue to feed voltage to the glow plugs causing them to burn out.

One or two bad glow plugs on a V8 engine might not cause a noticeable starting problem during warm weather, but it can when temperatures drop.

Glow plugs can be checked by measuring their resistance or continuity. Excessive resistance or a lack of continuity would tell you the plug is bad.

If one or more glow plugs have burned out, are heavily coated with carbon or are not receiving their usual dose of start-up voltage, the engine will become progressively harder to start as temperatures drop, and will idle roughly and produce white smoke in the exhaust for several minutes once it finally starts. If all the glow plugs are burned on the end, you'd better check the injection timing because it is probably overadvanced.

To see if the glow plug module is providing power to the glow plugs, use a voltmeter to check each plug for the specified voltage when the ignition key is turned on. No voltage? Check the glow plug control module connections, ground and wiring harness. The glow plugs themselves can be checked by measuring their resistance. Replace any plugs that read out of specifications.

Hard starting can sometimes be caused by a glow plug module that fails to turn the glow plugs on or doesn't keep the plugs on long enough when the weather is cold. On GM 6.2/6.5L diesels, there have been reports of heat from a still-warm engine causing the 125-degree inhibit switch inside the controller to shut off making the engine hard to restart. The cure here is to relocate the control module away from the engine. On Ford 7.3L diesels, the control module can cut off early if there are two or more bad glow plugs. We have also heard of control modules that do not keep the glow plugs on long enough for easy cold weather starting. The on-time is sufficient for warm weather, but not cold weather.

41.2 Fuel Problems 燃油问题

Unlike gasoline, diesel oil is adversely affected by cold temperatures. Diesel is made of heavier hydrocarbons that turn to wax when temperatures drop. The "cloud point" or point at which wax starts to form for ordinary summer-grade No. 2 diesel fuel can range from 10 to 40 degrees. If the fuel tank contains summer grade fuel and temperatures drop, wax crystals can form in the water/fuel separator, causing a blockage.

The cure here is to pull the vehicle into a warm garage so it can thaw out, replace the water/fuel separator as needed, then add an approved "fuel conditioner" additive to the tank (some manufacturers do not approve any additives or prohibit the use of specific ingredients such as alcohol that are found in some additives), or drain the tank and refill it with No. 1 diesel fuel. To prevent the same thing from happening again, you might recommend the installation of an aftermarket fuel heater.

Water in the fuel is another problem that can cause starting and performance problems. Condensation that forms during cold weather is the primary source of contamination. Water that gets into the fuel tank usually settles to the bottom because water and oil don't mix. The water is sucked into the fuel line and goes to the filter or water/fuel separator (if the vehicle has one). Here it can freeze, causing a blockage that stops the flow of fuel to the engine. So if the filter or separator is iced up, the fuel tank needs to be drained to get rid of the water.

41.3 Fuel Contamination 燃油污染

Another difference with diesel fuel is that it tastes good to certain microbes, especially if there's water in the tank. Certain bacteria can actually thrive inside a diesel fuel tank, forming slime, acids and other creepy stuff that can gum up fuel lines, filters, injection pumps and injectors. Infected fuel often has a "rotten egg" odor, and leaves a black or green coating on the inside of fuel system components. The growth rate of most organisms increases with warmer temperatures, but some can thrive down to freezing temperatures.

To get rid of a bug infestation, the fuel tank needs to be drained and cleaned. A biocide approved for this type of use should also be used to kill the organisms and to prevent their reappearance. The cleaning process should be followed by a fresh tank of fuel treated with a preventative dose of biocide. If the fuel lines and injection pump have also been contaminated, they will also have to be cleaned.

41.4 Fuel Delivery Problems 供油问题

To start and run properly, injector timing has to be accurate. A quick visual inspection will tell you if the timing marks are lined up. Refer to the vehicle manufacturer's timing procedure if you suspect timing is off or the pump has been replaced recently. On newer diesels with electronic injection pumps or direct injection, you'll need a scan tool to make any changes.

Air in the fuel can also be a cause of hard starting or a no start condition. Air can make the engine die after it starts, and make restarting difficult. Air can enter the system through any break in the fuel line or via a bleedback condition.

To determine if air is the problem, install a clear return hose on the return side of the injection pump. Crank the engine and observe the line. Air bubbles in the fuel would tell you air is entering the inlet side of the pump. The injection pump itself is usually not the source of the air leak, so check the fuel lines and pump.

A worn or clogged pump can also make an engine hard to start. If the condition has been getting steadily worse accompanied by a loss of power, and the engine has a lot of miles on it (more than 75000), the underlying cause may be a pump that needs to be replaced.

Before condemning the pump, though, check the fuel filters. Clogged filters can cause fuel restrictions that prevent the pump from doing its job properly. The primary water separator/fuel filter usually needs to be changed about every 30000 to 40000 miles, and the secondary filter about every 20000 to 30000 miles. Newer fuel systems with a single filter usually require service about once a year. If the filter has been neglected, chances are it may be restricted or plugged.

41.5　Won't Start　不能启动

A diesel engine that cranks normally but won't start regardless of the outside temperature either has low compression or a fuel delivery problem. If compression is okay, check the fuel gauge (out of fuel?). Then check the fuel filters and lines for obstructions.

If the injection pump isn't pushing fuel through the lines to the injectors, it may have a faulty solenoid. Listen for a "click" inside the pump when the ignition switch is turned on. No click means the solenoid and/or pump need to be replaced. If it clicks but there's no fuel coming through the injector lines (and the filter and lines are not obstructed), the pump is probably bad and needs to be replaced.

41.6　Injector Problems　喷油器问题

Diesel injectors can suffer from the same kinds of ailments as gasoline injectors, including varnish deposits, clogging, wear and leakage. Today's low sulfur diesel fuels are more likely to leave varnish and gum deposits on injectors, and also provide less lubrication so you might recommend an additive to keep things flowing smoothly.

Diesel injectors operate at much higher pressures than gasoline injectors. Over time, their opening pressure can drop. Up to 300 psi is considered acceptable but more than 300 psi means the injectors should be replaced or reset back to their original operating specs. You'll need some type of pop tester to check the opening pressure of the injectors if you suspect this kind of problem.

Dirty injectors will lean out the air/fuel mixture, causing a loss of power, rough idle and sometimes white smoke in the exhaust. Leaky injectors will richen the air/fuel mixture and cause black smoke.

There are a couple of ways to find a bad injector on a diesel engine. One is to use a digital pyrometer to check the operating temperature of each cylinder. A temperature reading that's lower than the rest would indicate a weak cylinder. If compression is okay, the problem is restricted fuel delivery. Another quick check is to use an ohmmeter that reads tenths of ohms to measure the resistance of the glow plugs while the engine is running. The resistance of the plug goes up with temperature, so if one or two cylinders read low, you've found the problem. For example, if a glow plug normally reads 1.8 to 3.4 ohms on a hot, running engine, a reading of 1.2 to 1.3 ohms on a glow plug would tell you that cylinder isn't producing any heat.

41.7　Troubleshooting Black Smoke 诊断黑烟问题

Black smoke is usually a signal that there's too much fuel, not enough air or injector pump timing is off. One of the most common causes of this condition is an air inlet restriction. The cause may be a dirty air filter, a collapsed intake hose or even an exhaust restriction. Diesels are unthrottled so there is no intake vacuum to measure.

41.8　Troubleshooting White Smoke 诊断白烟问题

White smoke usually occurs when there is not enough heat to burn the fuel. The unburned fuel particles go out the tailpipe and typically produce a rich fuel smell. It's not unusual to see white smoke in the exhaust during cold weather until the engine warms up.

As mentioned earlier, bad glow plugs or a faulty glow plug control module can cause white smoke on engine start up. Low engine cranking speed may also produce white smoke.

If white smoke is still visible after the engine has warmed up, the engine may have one or more bad injectors, retarded injection timing or a worn injection pump. Low compression can also be a source of white smoke. Air in the fuel system can also cause white smoke.

41.9　Stalling Problems 失速问题

If a diesel stalls when decelerating, it may indicate a lubrication problem in the injector pump. The first thing that should be checked is the idle speed. If low, it could prevent the pump governor from recovering quickly enough during deceleration to prevent the engine from stalling.

Water in the fuel can also cause stalling by making the metering valve or plungers inside the pump stick. Use of a lubricating additive may help cure this condition. If an additive doesn't help, the pump may have to be cleaned or replaced.

[词汇]

pickup	n. 小吨位运货汽车	blockage	n. 封堵，堵塞，障碍
clatter	n. 咔嗒，哗啦声，嘈杂的谈笑声	condensation	n. 浓缩
woe	n. 悲哀	microbe	n. 微生物，细菌
dipstick	n. 量油尺，量杆，测深尺	slime	n. 黏液
golw	n. 发热	creepy	adj. 爬行的，悚然的

gum	vt. 上胶，分泌树胶质，发黏，锉深齿	stall	n. 失速，脱流停车，抛锚汽车停车场
infestation	n. 出现（骚扰，蔓延）	bubble	n. 泡，气泡，起泡
biocide	n. 除污底毒剂，杀生物剂	ailment	n. 小毛病，疾病
reappearance	n. 再现	gum	n. 胶，胶黏，树胶
condemn	vt. 决定废弃，宣告不适用，宣告没收	acceptable	adj. 可接受的，合意的
pyrometer	n. 高温计	tailpipe	n. 排气管，尾喷管

[注释]

  Dicscl cngine 柴油机：柴油机采用压缩空气的办法提高空气温度，使空气温度超过柴油的自燃测试，这时再喷入柴油、柴油喷雾和空气混合的同时自己点火燃烧。德国人狄塞尔想出了这个办法并取得了专利权，所以柴油机又叫狄塞尔发动机。

[问题]

1. How to check starting difficulty of the diesel engines?
2. Please describe the process of checking glow plugs.
3. What kinds of troubles are there in diesel injectors?
4. Why does the diesel engine create black smoke?

Lesson 42

Engine Rebuilding Tips
发动机修理要点

Back in the 1970s and 1980s, the average life cycle of an engine was about five would develop an oil consumption problem and begin to experience other signs of wear (loss of compression, loss of power, increased emissions, lower oil pressure, internal noise, etc.). Carburetors were partly to blame for the wear because rich fuel mixtures wash the lubricating oil off the cylinder walls and dilute the oil in the crankcase. These older engines were also built much "looser" (wider tolerances) than most of today's engines, which also increased blowby. Consequently, the rings, bearings and valve guides all experienced accelerated wear.

Today, the situation is much different. The average service life of a 1990s vintage engine is about 10 to 12 years! Fuel injection has all but eliminated the fuel wash down problem, and much tighter tolerances have greatly reduced blowby and oil dilution in the crankcase. So fewer engines are being rebuilt today as a result.

Improvements in engine technology have extended engine life and reduced the need for engine service. Even so, the current "technology trough" will eventually pass and the numbers of engines being replaced and rebuilt will once again rise. The number of five-to 10-year-old light trucks on the road, for example, has jumped from 18 million in 1985 to nearly 60 million today. Many of these will need engine work before long.

42.1 Engine Rebuilding 发动机修理

Rebuilding an engine can cost less than replacing it. Assuming the original engine is rebuildable (wear is not excessive and there is no serious damage), and the amount of machine work required to restore it is minimal, you may realize 20% to 50% or more savings doing a rebuild versus replacing the engine. Most of the savings comes from the labor you put into tearing down the engine and then reassembling it after any necessary machine work has been done.

The tools required to rebuild an engine are minimal: normal hand tools, some feeler gauges, a torque wrench, a ring expander and ring compressor. Any machine work that's needed can be farmed out to a local machine shop.

If the cylinders are worn, they'll have to be bored or honed to accept oversize pistons and rings. If not, you can run a glaze breaker down the bores and do the work yourself. If you don't have valve and seat refacing equipment, you'll have to send that out, too. Worn guides can be reamed out, replaced or relined in-house with a few special tools. But jobs such as head resurfacing, line boring, crank refinishing, etc. will have to be farmed out. Find a reputable local machine shop that you can use for this type of work.

Another reason for doing your own engine work is to control the quality of parts and work that goes into the engine. This is something you can't control when you buy an engine from an outside source. It may be top quality, or it may not. But you don't want to find out "the hard way." The truth is, some remanufacturers reuse a much higher percentage of parts than others do, obviously for cost savings purposes.

You can also save by buying the parts you need in an engine kit rather than individually. A kit gives you everything you need in one box and reduces the chance of mismatching parts. The parts in a kit usually include bearings, rings, pistons, timing chain and gear set, valve seals, gaskets, oil pump, camshaft, lifters and other miscellaneous parts.

You can usually get OEM or better quality parts in most kits, which may be better than the parts found in some remanufactured engines.

One aftermarket supplier of engine kits now offers a 100000 warranty (including labor) on all of the parts in its premium engine kits-which is a better deal than you'll find on almost any replacement engine, new or remanufactured.

42.2 Crankshaft Bearings 曲轴轴承

New bearings are almost always a must when rebuilding an engine. When you remove the old bearings, inspect them for unusual wear or damage such as scoring, wiping, dirt or debris embedded in the surface of the bearings, pitting or flaking. Anything other than normal wear may indicate an underlying problem that needs to be corrected before the new bearings are installed.

Dirt contamination often causes premature bearing failure. The underlying cause may have been a missing air filter, air leaks into the crankcase (missing oil filler cap, PCV valve, etc.), or not changing the oil and filter often enough.

If the engine has a "spun" bearing, it's likely the bearings were starved for oil-possibly as a result of a failed or badly worn oil pump, an obstruction in the oil pump's pickup screen, or too low an oil level in the crankcase (leaky gaskets or seals).

Excessive heat can be another cause of bearing failure. Bearings are primarily cooled by oil flow between the bearing and journal. Anything that disrupts or reduces the flow of oil not only raises bearing temperatures but also increases the risk of scoring or wiping the bearing. Conditions that can reduce oil flow and cause the bearings to run hot include a worn oil pump, restricted oil pickup screen, internal oil leaks, a low oil level in the crankcase, aerated oil (oil level too high), fuel-diluted oil from excessive blowby or coolant-contaminated oil from internal coolant leaks.

Misalignment is another condition that may indicate the need for additional work. If the center main bearings are worn more than the ones toward either end of the crankshaft, the crankshaft may be bent or the main bores may be out of alignment. The straightness of the crank can be checked by placing it on V-blocks, positioning a dial indicator on the center journal and watching the indicator as the crank is turned one complete revolution. If runout exceeds limits, the crank must be straightened or replaced.

Main bore alignment can be checked by inserting a bar about .001 inch smaller in diameter than the main bores through the block with the main caps installed and torqued. If the bar doesn't turn easily, the block needs to be align bored. Alignment can also be checked with a straight edge and feeler gauge. A deviation of more than .0015″ in any bore calls for align boring. Line boring must also be done if a main cap is replaced.

The concentricity of the main bores is also important, and should usually be within .0015″. If not, reboring will be necessary to install bearings with oversized outside diameters.

Connecting rods with elongated big end bores can cause similar problems. If the rod bearings show a diagonal or uneven wear pattern, it usually means the rod is twisted. Rods with elongated crank journal bores or twist must be reconditioned or replaced.

Uneven bearing wear may also be seen if the crankshaft journals are not true. To check the roundness of the crank journals, measure each journal's diameter at either bottom or top dead center and again at 90 degrees either way. Rod journals typically experience the most wear at top dead center.

Comparing diameters at the two different positions should reveal any out-of-roundness if it exists. Though the traditional rule of thumb says up to .001″ of journal variation is acceptable, many of today's import engines can't tolerate more than .0002″ to .0005″ of out-of-roundness (always refer to the specs).

To check for taper wear on the crankshaft journals (one end worn more than the other), barrel wear (ends worn more than the center) or hourglass wear (center worn more than the ends), measure the journal diameter at the center and both ends. Again, the generally accepted limit for taper wear has usually been up to .001″, but nowadays it ranges from .0003″ to .0005″ for journals 2″ or larger in diameter.

The journal diameter itself should be within .001″ of its original dimensions, or within .001″ of standard regrind dimensions for proper oil clearances with a replacement bearing. If a journal has been previously reground, there's usually a machinist's mark stamped by the journal. A 10, 20 or 30 would indicate the crank has already been ground to undersize, and that further regrinding may be out of the question depending on how badly the crank is worn.

When you're ready to install new bearings, make sure you have the correct size (standard size for a standard crank, or oversized bearings for an undersize crank), that you've checked the installed bearing clearances, that the bearings are prelubed to protect them against a dry start, that the oil holes and tangs on the bearings are all properly located, and that the rod and main cap bolts are torqued to specifications.

Another component that should also be replaced along with the bearings is the oil pump. Oil pumps wear with age, and may cause a loss of oil pressure that can be very damaging to the bearings.

42.3　Piston Rings 活塞环

Low compression and oil burning are usually a sign of worn rings and/or cylinders. Replacing the piston rings can restore compression if the cylinders do not exceed service specifications. But if the cylinders are worn or damaged, reboring the cylinders to oversize will be necessary to restore proper clearances and compression.

Replacement rings come in various materials and sizes. Most compression rings are cast iron, though many import engines have steel rings. Rings may be plain faced, chrome-plated, inlaid with molybdenum ("moly") or nitrided for added durability. Replacement rings should generally be the same types as the original.

Ring sizes can be confusing because ring thickness and width may change from one model year to the next. You may have to refer to the VIN number to determine the correct rings for the engine. Oversize rings and pistons of the corresponding size will obviously be needed if the cylinders need to be bored or honed to oversize.

Some shops "plateau" the cylinders after honing. This can be done various ways, but one way to do this yourself is to give each cylinder a few strokes with a flexible brush-type "Flex-Hone" in a drill. This helps remove surface debris and knocks the sharp peaks off the ridges left in the bores by honing.

Cylinders must always be cleaned before new rings and pistons are installed. This means scrubbing the bores with warm soapy water and a brush to remove all traces of honing residue and metal.

Always use a ring expander to install new rings on pistons, and a ring compressor to install the piston assemblies in the block. Cylinder walls must also be lubed to protect the rings and pistons against scuffing when the engine is first started.

42.4　Camshaft 凸轮轴

Camshaft wear in high mileage engines is a common problem, so inspect the cam carefully to see if it is worn or bent. If the engine needs a new cam, you can install a stock replacement cam or a performance cam. Performance cams provide increased lift and duration for more power. If you opt for a hotter cam, be sure to follow the camshaft supplier's application recommendations for lift and duration. A common mistake is "overcamming" a street engine. Too much lift and duration will move the engine's power curve too far up the rpm scale, and may require other extensive modifications such as larger valves, stiffer valve springs, performance manifolds and modifications to the carburetor or fuel injection system to optimize performance.

When a cam is being replaced, new lifters and valve springs should also be installed. Reusing old lifters with a new cam can damage the cam lobes.

Roller lifters can generally be reused, but not on a camshaft designed for flat bottom (actually slightly convex) lifters (and vice versa).

In addition to a new cam, the engine may also need a new timing belt or chain and gear set. The recommended replacement interval for timing belts on most older engines (those made before 1993) is 60000 miles. The replacement interval for many newer belts has been increased to 100000 miles. Timing chains have no specified replacement interval, but do stretch with age. This has an adverse effect on valve timing as well as ignition timing, so the chain and gears should be replaced if wear exceeds specifications.

42.5 Valve Work 气门修理工作

The valve components that may have to be replaced will depend on the age and condition of the engine. New exhaust valves are often needed because they run much hotter than intake valves and often "burn" or fail because of erosion and heat cracking. Exhaust valves also stretch with age, which increases the danger of valve breakage. For this reason, you might want to replace all the exhaust valves with new ones regardless of their condition.

Intake valves can generally be reused unless bent or worn. Replacement is required if stem wear exceeds specifications.

If guides are worn, which they usually are, the engine can suck a lot of oil. Evidence of this is usually heavy black carbon deposits on the backs of the intake valves and heavy carbon deposits on the pistons and in the combustion chambers. Minor guide wear can be reduced somewhat by knurling. If integral guides are worn, they may be drilled out to accept thin wall bronze or cast iron guide liners, or reamed to oversize (which requires new valves with oversize stems). Worn guides in aluminum heads can also be lined, or reamed to oversize or pressed out and replaced with new guides.

Unless valve seats are cracked or badly worn, they can usually be reconditioned by cutting or grinding. Damaged or badly worn seats in aluminum heads will have to be replaced. Bad seats in cast iron heads can sometimes be repaired by machining out the old seat to accept an insert.

42.6 Head Gaskets 气缸垫

The number one mistake to avoid when replacing a blown head gasket is to simply install a new gasket without checking or repairing anything else. In many instances, a blown gasket is not the real problem but a symptom of some other underlying condition such as a hot spot, overheating or detonation. If the underlying problem is not identified and corrected, the new gasket will likely suffer the same fate as its predecessor.

Always inspect the cylinder head for cracks or other problems when it is removed, especially if the engine overheated. Aluminum overhead cam heads are much more likely to warp and crack than cast iron heads when an engine gets too hot. If an OHC won't turn once the followers have been removed, the head is probably warped and will have to be straightened and/or align bored.

Cracks are not always visible to the naked eye. Porosity leaks in aluminum heads may not show up unless the cooling system is under pressure. To minimize the risk of a repeat gasket failure, cast iron heads should be Magnafluxed (magnetic crack detection) to check for cracks. Penetrating dye will reveal cracks in aluminum. Pressure testing is also an excellent method of detecting internal cracks and porosity leaks in both cast iron and aluminum.

The cylinder head and block should also be checked for flatness before the new head gasket is installed. Flatness specs vary depending on the application, but on most pushrod engines with cast iron heads, up to .003″ (0.076 mm) out-of-flat lengthwise in V6 heads, .004″ (0.102 mm) in four cylinder or V8 heads, and .006″ (0.152 mm) in straight six cylinder heads is considered acceptable. Most aluminum heads, on the other hand, should have no more than .002″ (0.05 mm) out-of-flat in any direction.

Aluminum OHC heads should be checked for flatness in two places: across the face of the head with a straight edge, and down the OHC cam bores with a straightedge or bar.

If an OHC aluminum head requires resurfacing, the amount of metal that can be safely removed is usually quite limited. If a head has been resurfaced and the installed height is too short, cam timing can be adversely affected. Too much compression may also create detonation problems. To compensate, a copper or steel shim may be used with the head gasket to raise the head and restore proper head height (if available). Otherwise, the head may have to be replaced.

Surface finish is also very important. As a rule, most push rod engines with cast iron heads can handle a surface finish of anything between 54 to 113 microinches RA (60 to 125 RMS). But many aluminum OHC heads require a smoother finish to seal properly. Many late model Japanese engines have "multi-layered steel" (MLS) head gaskets that require a very smooth finish of 7 to 15 RA! Such heads should not be resurfaced unless the head is warped or the surface is damaged.

Finally, if the engine has torque-to-yield (TTY) head bolts, replace them. Reusing TTY bolts is risky because you have no way of knowing how far they're been stretched. Also, make sure you have the latest head bolt torque specs. Vehicle manufacturers often revise their original head bolt torque specs to correct problems that have arisen in the field. The new specs can be found in technical service bulletins (TSBs) from the manufacturers.

[词汇]

tolerance *n.* 公差   carburetor *n.* 化油器，汽化器

crankcase	n. 曲轴箱	hone	v. 细磨
vintage	adj. 旧式的，古典的，最好的	reface	vt. 光面（重修表面，更换摩擦片）
blowby	n. 窜漏（指气缸和活塞之间运动时流体的渗漏）	ream	vt. 扩展，铰大，榨取，铰除，刮
		guide	n. 导管
profitable	n. 有利的，有益的，有用的	reline	vt. 换衬里，重新划线
minimal	adj. 最小的，最小限度的	crank	n. 曲柄，弯轴
feeler gauge	测隙规，触杆规，厚薄规	profitability	n. 收益性，利益率
wrench	n. 扳手	kit	n. 成套工具，用具箱，整套零件
oversize	adj. 加大尺寸	premature	adj. 过早的（早熟的）

[注释]

OEM Original Equipment Manufacturer 原［初］始设备制造厂家

[问题]

1. What kinds of tools are required in order to rebuild an engine?
2. How do you check crankshaft bearings?
3. How do you check camshafts?
4. What should we check when installing head gaskets?

Chapter 5　Chassis Troubleshooting and Repair
底盘故障诊断与修理

Lesson 43

A Guide to Four-Wheel Alignment
四轮定位指南

Today four-wheel alignment is almost mandatory for all front-wheel drive vehicles as well as rear-wheel drive vehicles with independent rear suspensions. It's also recommended for rear-wheel drive cars and trucks too, especially SUVs with oversized tires and knee-high ride heights.

So how exactly do you do a four-wheel alignment? Mechanical alignment equipment such as measuring sticks and camber bubble gauges can be used on the rear wheels as well as the ones up front to check toe and camber. Likewise, backing a vehicle onto a two-wheel alignment rack after checking the front wheels can be used to check rear toe and camber. But both of these approaches fall short of a true four-wheel alignment because neither method establishes a link between the front and rear wheels or takes into account the affect rear toe and camber have on front wheel geometry, steering and handling.

The rear wheels can be perfectly parallel to one another with zero total toe, but if the axle is cocked slightly in the chassis it will create a thrust angle resulting in rear axle steer. The vehicle won't steer straight or track straight, causing off-center steering and increased toe wear on the front tires. The front tires wear in this case because the built-in geometry of the steering arms causes the front tires to toe-out slightly anytime the wheels are steered even if it is only a little bit to one side or the other. The severity of the effect will depend on how far out of alignment the rear axle is with respect to the chassis. The greater the thrust angle, the greater the effect, the further off from center the steering will be, and the greater the toe wear on the front tires.

Factory specs for thrust angle vary, and some manufacturers do not provide thrust angle service specs. Generally speaking, the thrust angle should be no more than two-tenths of a degree. Ideally it should be zero. An angle that exceeds specifications can create steering and tracking problems.

43.1 Thrust Angle Alignment 推力角定位

One way to cope with a thrust angle is to do a "thrust angle" alignment. By using the rear wheels as a reference point for the front wheels, the toe setting for each front wheel (individual toe) can be aligned to the rear thrust angle (total rear toe, actually) rather than the vehicle centerline to compensate for rear axle misalignment.

This approach allows the steering wheel to be recentered and minimizes toe wear, but it does not correct rear wheel or axle misalignment. It also does not take into account rear camber, which may also be out of specification and causing its own tire wear or steering problems (cross-camber at the rear wheels can create a steering pull, too). But on RWD vehicles as well as some FWD applications where there are no factory adjustments for rear axle alignment or rear toe, a thrust angle alignment is better than just doing the front wheels and letting it go.

43.2 All Four 四轮定位

Four-wheel alignment (also called "total" wheel alignment) aligns all four wheels so they're parallel to each other, parallel to the vehicle's centerline, perpendicular to the road surface and within factory specifications for camber, caster and toe. When that is achieved, a vehicle should track straight, have a centered steering wheel, handle properly, provide maximum tread life and minimal rolling resistance. This requires alignment equipment that can compute the geometry of all four wheels with respect to each other and vehicle centerline. From this, the angles can be compared to one another as well as specifications to determine what, if any, corrections are needed.

Four-wheel alignment equipment is more sophisticated than simple two-wheel alignment equipment or simple mechanical systems, so it costs more ? which is a drawback if you're only doing a small number of alignments. On the other hand, upgrading your equipment might open the doors of opportunity and allow to you handle a higher volume of work more profitably.

43.3　The Job Itself 自身的工作

The first step is the prealignment inspection to check for worn or damaged steering and suspension components. This should be nothing new to anyone who has been doing two-wheel alignments, but well summarize to help jog your memory. Start by checking the tires (condition, tread wear, inflation pressure and sizes), then measure ride height front and rear on both sides. Check the steering and suspension for looseness as well as worn or damaged parts. This includes the steering couplings, steering gear, steering linkage, ball joints, control arm bushings, struts, shocks, rear suspension and wheel bearings. Any parts that do not meet manufacturer specifications must be replaced before proceeding with the alignment because worn and damaged parts cannot hold proper alignment.

Next comes the setup of the alignment equipment itself. The type of equipment your shop has will determine what procedure you follow, but most four-wheel aligners have four alignment sensor heads (one for each wheel), some type of computerized display and a drive-on rack with turning plates for the front wheels, slip plates for the back wheels, and a hydraulic jack to raise the suspension.

After you're pulled the vehicle on the rack, checked the tires, measured ride height and performed the prealignment inspection of the steering and suspension, the suspension needs to be "settled" to get accurate alignment readings. This is done by making sure the wheels are positioned on the turning plates and slip plates, and that the locking pins have been removed from the plates so they are free to move. The plates allow the wheels to move sideways as the suspension moves up and down. This allows the suspension to seek its normal ride height after you bounce the front and rear of the vehicle several times.

The use of rear slip plates is not required with rear-wheel drive vehicles that have solid axle housings, but they should be used with any vehicle (FWD or RWD) that has an independent rear suspension.

Once the vehicle is in position and is ready to be aligned, install each of the sensor heads on the wheels following the equipment manufacturer's directions, then compensate the heads to eliminate wheel runout.

Enter the vehicle year, make and model information into the aligner computer. If the equipment has a database of alignment specs, it will automatically compare the reference specs against the actual readings to let you know if the wheels are in or out of range. If your aligner does not have a database of specifications, refer to an alignment specification guide or a service manual. Most specs list a minimum (MIN), preferred (PREF) and maximum (MAX) reading for caster, camber, front and rear toe. A turning angle (toe-out on turns) specification along with an SAI specification in degrees will also be listed for most (but not all) vehicles.

Preferred specifications are exactly what the name implies. These are the settings that should be used when aligning most vehicles because they keep wheel geometry working within the normal design range of the steering and suspension.

The minimum and maximum numbers define the range of "acceptable" settings allowed by the vehicle manufacturer, and should be used primarily as a guide when checking initial alignment readings. The minimum and maximum caster and camber readings generally allow up to a degree of leeway either way from the preferred setting. Toe settings may allow from 1/16 to 1/4 inch of variance depending on the application.

Any alignment reading that falls outside the accepted range is out of tolerance and calls for realigning the wheels. If a reading is right on the border, you have to make a judgment call. As long as the vehicle is experiencing no problems, the alignment setting is probably OK as is. But in some cases, a reading that falls at or near the minimum or maximum may not be "good enough" for some applications or customers, and may require realigning the wheels to the preferred settings to optimize tire wear, steering and handling performance or to correct an existing problem.

If corrections are needed, the following sequence can be used (or one recommended by the vehicle manufacturer or alignment equipment supplier):

1. Rear camber
2. Rear toe
3. Caster/camber one side front
4. Caster/camber other side front
5. Front toe

Rear camber is usually set first because the tilt of the rear wheels not only alters rear ride height (which in turn can affect the front caster reading), it also affects rear toe. Rear toe must then be set before front toe because it establishes tracking as well as the thrust line. If a thrust angle alignment is being performed on a RWD vehicle where rear toe cannot be changed without straightening the frame, rear toe becomes the reference point for aligning front toe.

Next comes front camber and caster, which must be adjusted prior to setting front toe because of their effect on toe. Finally, toe is set with the steering wheel and linkage centered, which is necessary to equalize the steering linkage on both sides for center steering. If this is not done, the steering may be off-center and/or the wheels may not toe-out evenly when turning, creating a tire wear problem.

[词汇]

alignment	n.定位	bubble	n.泡，气泡
mandatory	adj.命令的，强制的，托管的	toe	n.车轮的前端，轮胎缘距
SUV	运动型实用车	gauge	n.规，计，表
oversize	n.超径，尺寸过大	rack	n.齿条，架，导轨
stick	n.棒，杆，条	cock	vt.使耸立，使竖起，堆成锥形
camber	n.外倾，前轮外倾	specs	n.规格

caster	n. 后倾，主销后倾	misalignment	n. 未对准，不重合，不一致
prealignment	n. 预先对准	perpendicular	adj. 垂直的，正交的
jog sb.'s memory	唤起某人的记忆	tread	n. 轮胎面，鞋底
toe-out	后束	profitably	adv. 有利地，有益地
geometry	n. 几何形状，几何图，几何参数	coupling	n. 联轴节，偶合，偶联
chassis	n. 底盘	bushing	n. 衬套，镶套

[注释]

1. Camber 前轮外倾：车轮中心平面也不是垂直于地面的，而是向外倾斜一个角度，称为车轮外倾角。因为假如空车时车轮正好垂直于地面，满载时，车桥则因受压而变形，中间下沉，两端上翘，车轮便随之变为内倾，这样将加速轮胎的磨损。另外，内倾的车轮从两端向内挤压轮毂上的轴承，加重了它的负荷，降低了使用寿命。因此在安装车轮时要预先使车轮有一定的外倾，这也使其与拱行路面相适应。

2. SUV 运动型实用车：美国人对皮卡、吉普等车型的称呼。不论车辆是否有无改装，只要可开去游玩娱乐的汽车，可载越野摩托车的小卡车等都可称运动型实用车。

[问题]

1. How does the thrust angle affect the vehicle?
2. What's four-wheel alignment?
3. What kinds of jobs need to do during the prealignment?
4. Please explain the procedure of four-wheel alignment.

Chapter 6 Automotive Electrical Equipment Troubleshooting and Repair
汽车电器故障诊断与修理

Lesson 44

Toyota Fuel Injection System
丰田燃油喷射系统

Toyota's multi-port fuel injection system, based on Bosch L-Jetronic technology, has been used since the early 1980s on its family of engines. The system has evolved over the years, earning a reputation for being relatively trouble-free. Even so, older high-mileage cars and trucks can develop problems that are common to all fuel injection systems: Pumps wear out; regulators fail; injectors become dirty or worn; cold start injectors can leak; and intake systems can become restricted due to accumulated carbon and fuel varnish. So if you're encountered a Toyota with fuel-related driveability problems, here are some pointers on how the system works and tips on how to diagnose and repair those applications.

44.1 Measuring Air Flow 测量空气流量

To regulate the air/fuel mixture, the engine computer needs to know how much air is being sucked into the engine. On the older Toyota EFI systems, air flow is measured mechanically with a flap-style air flow meter. A flap inside the meter rotates when incoming air pushes against it. Connected to the flap is an arm that rubs across a resistor grid (potentiometer). This changes the air flow meter's output voltage in proportion to air flow.

The greater the air flow, the higher the resistance created by the potentiometer. So the meter's output voltage drops as air flow increases.

Over time, the potentiometer's contacts inside the air flow meter can wear, causing erratic or inconsistent readings. Shorts or opens in the circuitry will also disrupt the voltage signal, depriving the engine computer of this vital bit of information. The result can be poor cold driveability, hesitation or poor performance.

The TCCS (Toyota Computer Control System) should set a code 2, 31 or 32 if the air flow meter signal is missing or out of range, but it may not always detect an intermittent problem. To find this kind of fault, an oscilloscope can help you analyze the air flow meter's output voltage as a waveform. If you don't see a nice linear change in the output voltage as the flap moves from idle to wide open throttle, it means the potentiometer is skipping and the air flow meter needs to be replaced.

Another way to check the operation of the air flow meter as well as the entire feedback circuit through the computer is to use a scope to compare injector dwell (on time) to the air flow signal. If you have a good air flow signal but injector dwell fails to increase as air flow goes up, there's a control problem in the computer.

The flap-type air flow meters should also be inspected by pushing the flap with your finger. There should be no binding when the flap is pushed open, and spring pressure should return it to its closed position. A buildup of varnish or dirt may cause binding, so be sure to inspect the air filter if you find any dirt in the unit.

A temperature sensor located in the intake plumbing is used to measure air temperature so the computer can calculate how much air is actually entering the engine. Cold air is denser than warm air, and requires a slightly richer fuel mixture. The air temperature sensor changes resistance, so if the signal goes flat or disappears, it also can upset the air/fuel mixture and cause driveability problems. Codes that would indicate a fault in the air temperature sensor circuit include 8, 23 and 24. You can use an ohmmeter to check the sensor's output. If the reading is out of specifications or fails to change as the temperature increases, the sensor is bad and needs to be replaced.

Starting in the mid-1990s, Toyota introduced a second-generation air flow sensor that combines the functions of the air flow meter and air temperature sensor into one unit. The new mass air flow sensor uses a hot wire to measure air mass rather than volume and has no moving parts. A reference voltage is applied to a thin wire inside the sensor that heats it to about 100°C hotter than ambient air temperature. As air flows through the sensor and past the hot wire, it carries away heat and cools the wire. The electrical control circuit for the wire is designed to maintain a constant temperature differential, so the amount of extra voltage that's required to offset the cooling effect and keep the wire hot tells the control box how much air is entering the engine.

With both the early and late-style air flow sensors, vacuum leaks can cause driveability problems by allowing unmetered air to enter the engine. Air leaks around the throttle body, injector O-rings, intake manifold gaskets or vacuum hose connections can cause the air/

fuel ratio to go lean. So if you find a code 25 (lean air/fuel ratio), start looking for leaks.

Finding an air leak can be a time-consuming exercise in patience. One method is to use a propane bottle and hose to check out suspicious areas. When propane vapor is siphoned in through a leak, the idle will smooth out and the rpm will change. Another trick is to turn off the engine and lightly pressurize (no more than 5 psi) the intake manifold with shop air. Then use a hand bottle to spray soapy water at possible leak points. Bubbles would indicate a leak. Another technique is to use a device that fills the intake manifold with smoke to reveal leaks.

Another often-overlooked cause of air leakage is the EGR valve. If the valve sticks open, it will act much like a vacuum leak, causing a lean misfire at idle and hesitation problems.

44.2 The Fuel Circuit 油路

Fuel flows from a tank-mounted pump through the fuel line to an in-line filter usually located in the engine compartment. It then goes to a common fuel rail (which Toyota calls the "fuel delivery pipe") on the engine to supply the injectors. The fuel injectors plug into the rail and are removed as an assembly with the rail. On V6 applications, there's a separate rail for each cylinder bank. Unfortunately, Toyota doesn't include a test valve on the fuel rail for checking fuel pressure. To perform a pressure check, you have to disconnect the cold start injector fuel fitting and attach a pressure gauge.

The pressure regulator is mounted on the end of the fuel rail, and maintains pressure at a constant level as engine load and intake vacuum change. A vacuum hose connects the regulator to the intake manifold so the diaphragm inside can react to changes in intake vacuum. A bypass valve inside the regulator routes excess fuel through a return line back to the fuel tank.

System operating pressure varies depending on the application, but typically ranges from 30 to 37 psi with the vacuum hose connected to the regulator, and 38 to 44 psi with the hose disconnected and plugged.

Note: If you're replacing a regulator on a turbocharged engine, make sure you get the correct replacement because the regulator on these applications is calibrated differently from those on non-turbo motors.

Also, don't confuse the pressure regulator with a little round plastic gizmo that may be mounted on the end of the fuel rail. This is a pulse damper that helps dampen noise and resonance caused by the pulsing of the injectors.

Starting in 1996, some Toyota EFI systems have a "returnless" design, in that the regulator is located in the fuel tank with the pump.

44.3 Pressure Problems 压力问题

If fuel pressure reads low, or the engine seems to starve for fuel under load, don't overlook the fuel pickup filter inside the fuel tank as a possible cause. In many instances, the system may flow enough fuel at idle to develop normal pressure, but run out of fuel at higher speeds or loads. Rust, dirt and scum inside the tank may be blocking the flow of fuel into the pump. Likewise, accumulated dirt and debris may be clogging the in-line filter.

Toyota says the best method for confirming a suspected fuel starvation problem is to road test the vehicle with a fuel pressure gauge safely installed on the engine. If the pressure reading drops when the engine is under load, it means the system isn't maintaining normal pressure. But is it the pump, filter or what?

You can rule out the pressure regulator if the system maintains normal pressure at idle, and the pressure rises when you disconnect the regulator's vacuum hose. No change in pressure would indicate a defective regulator or plugged vacuum line.

A good way to check out the pump, pickup filter and inline filter is to measure fuel delivery volume. Relieve system pressure, then disconnect the fuel supply line at the fuel filter or fuel rail, or disconnect the return hose from the rail. Place the open end of the fuel hose in a measuring cup or graduated cylinder. If you're disconnecting the return hose, you'll have to attach another piece of hose to the fuel rail and use that to route fuel into the container. With the engine off, use jumpers to bypass the pump relay. Energize the pump for 30 seconds and measure the volume of fuel delivered.

As a rule, a good pump should deliver about one quart of fuel in 30 seconds.

If a pump's output volume and/or pressure is low, the pump motor might be running slow due to internal wear. A typical fuel pump runs at 5000 to 6000 rpm and pulls about 3 to 6 amps. But as the armature brushes become worn and the brush springs weaken, increased resistance will reduce the pump's current draw and cause the motor to run slower and deliver less fuel.

The pump motor can be checked using an ohmmeter to measure the motor's internal resistance. As a rule, most good pumps should read 2 to 50 ohms. If the pump is open (reads infinity) or shows zero resistance (shorted), the motor is bad and the pump needs to be replaced.

Another way to check the operation of the pump while it is still inside the tank is to view the pump's current flow with an oscilloscope. Connect a milliamp current probe to the pump's voltage supply wire and start the engine. The waveform can reveal the condition of the motor's brushes and armature. A "good" waveform will generally seesaw back and forth with relative consistency and minimal variation between the highs and lows. A "bad" waveform will show large or irregular drops in the pattern, with large differences between the highs and lows. In other words, the greater the sawtooth in the pattern, the greater the wear in the pump.

Even if the pump motor is OK, fuel delivery problems can be caused by the pump's voltage supply. Low battery voltage, low system operating voltage, a poor ground connection or excessive resistance in the pump's wiring connectors or the relay can all have an adverse effect on the operating speed of the pump. The pump must have normal voltage to run at full speed, so always check the pump's wiring connectors and voltage supply when you encounter a pump with low pressure or volume output.

The pump's supply voltage should be within half a volt of normal battery voltage. If low, check the wiring connectors, relay and ground. A good connection should have less than 1/10 of a volt drop (ideally no voltage drop) across it. A voltage drop of more than 0.4 volts can create enough resistance to cause a problem.

44.4　Residual Pressure 残余压力

If an engine is hard to start when hot, fuel may be boiling in the rail because the system isn't holding residual pressure when the ignition is shut off. To prevent vapor lock and reduce the cranking time when restarting the engine, a check valve inside the fuel pump holds the pressure in the line. Toyota says pressure should remain above 21 psi for five minutes after the engine is turned off. If the system fails to hold pressure, either the check valve or pressure regulator is leaking, or an injector is leaking. Regulator leaks can be ruled out by pinching off the return line. Injector leaks can be checked by removing the fuel injector and rail assembly from the manifold and pressurizing the rail. No fuel drips? Then it's the pump check valve.

44.5　Injectors 喷油器

Four different types of injectors may be used in Toyota engines: Pintle-style, hole-type (cone valve and ball valve), high-resistance and low-resistance. Bosch pintle-style injectors are used on the older TCCS applications, while Nippondenso hole-type injectors are used on newer engines. The hole-type injectors spray fuel through holes drilled in a director plate at the injector tip. There are currently three different types including side-feed injectors used on the 3SGTE and 2TZ-FE engines.

The valve design of the older pintle-style injectors makes them more susceptible to deposit buildup than the hole-type injectors. So if you're diagnosing a lean fuel condition on a Toyota with pintlestyle injectors, the injector may need to be cleaned.

Low resistance injectors are found on older Toyotas up to about 1990, and measure 2 to 3 ohms at room temperature. They are used with an external resistor in a voltage-controlled driver circuit, or without an external resistor in a current-controlled driver circuit. High-resistance injectors (13.8 ohms) are used on the newer applications and do not require an external resistor.

When the ignition is turned on, voltage is supplied to the fuel injectors directly through the ignition circuit or through the EFI main relay, depending on the application. The driver circuits in the computer then provide a ground to complete the connection and energize the injectors.

Toyota says never to apply battery voltage directly to a low resistance injector to test it because doing so can overheat and damage the windings in the solenoid. Use a resistor wire to protect the injector.

If an engine is misfiring and has a dead cylinder, and you're already ruled out ignition misfire or loss of compression as possible causes, use a stethoscope to listen to the injector. A steady buzz would tell you the injector is working and that the driver circuit is OK. No buzzing means a wiring or control problem. Check for voltage at the injector terminal when the key is on. No voltage? Check the EFI relay, fuse and wiring circuit. If there is voltage, use a logic probe or oscilloscope to see if the computer driver circuit is grounding the injector. No on-off signal would indicate a wiring problem or bad computer.

Injector resistance can be measured directly with an ohmmeter. An open, short or out-of-specification reading would tell you the injector has failed and needs to be replaced.

If the injector is buzzing but the cylinder is running lean or misfiring, the problem is likely a buildup of fuel varnish in the injector orifice or valve. Cleaning is the solution here, either on or off the vehicle. On-car cleaning saves time and can often restore the injectors to like-new performance. Off-car cleaning means you have to pull the injectors, but it gives you the opportunity to examine their spray pattern. There should be no solid streamers of liquid fuel, only a cone-shaped mist. If cleaning fails to restore the pattern, it's time for a new injector.

44.6 Cold Start Injector 冷启动喷油器

Toyota uses a cold start injector on most applications to squirt extra fuel into the manifold when a cold engine is first started. The "on time" of the injector is controlled by a start injector time switch and the computer. The number of seconds the cold start injector is energized (typically 2 to 8 seconds) is limited by a heater circuit inside the timer, that has two coils. A bimetallic switch inside the timer is normally closed so, when the engine is started, current flows through the cold start injector solenoid and both heater coils inside the timer. Within a few seconds, the heater coils trip the bimetallic switch causing it to open and turn off the cold start injector.

If the timer fails, the cold start injector will never come on and the engine may be hard to start when cold. The circuit can be checked by using a voltmeter to test for voltage at the cold start injector when the ignition is turned on. You should also check the resistance across the injector's terminals to check for an open or shorted solenoid. A good cold injector should read 2 to 4 ohms.

[词汇]

flap	n. 可偏转的翼片	disrupt	v. 破坏，干扰，使…分裂，毁坏
potentiometer	n. 电位计，分压器	oscilloscope	n. 示波器
inconsistent	adj. 不一致的，不协调的，矛盾的	binding	n. 黏结，约束
reading	n. 读数	varnish	n. 漆

propane	n.丙烷	bimetallic	adj.双金属的
siphon	n.虹吸，虹吸管	returnless	adj.回不来的
gizmo	n.这个人，新玩意，小物件	scum	n.浮渣，泡沫，渣滓
damper	n.缓冲器，阻尼器	relieve	vt.减轻，解除，卸载
resonance	n.共振，谐振	graduated	adj.有刻度的
starvation	n.缺乏	rail	n.导管
sawtooth	n.锯齿，锐齿	ohmmeter	n.电阻计，欧姆计
pintle	n.枢轴（开口销，枢栓，扣钉）	oscilloscope	n.示波器
stethoscope	n.听诊器	seesaw	n.起伏
buzz	v.作嗡嗡声，嗡嗡作响，逼近	consistency	n.一致性，连贯性
squirt	v.喷出	variation	n.变化，变动，变量

[问题]

1. How is the air flow measured in cars?
2. How do you find air leaks?
3. Describe the configuration of the fuel circuit。
4. How do you check injectors?

Chapter 7　Automotive Maintenance
汽车保养

Lesson 45

Fall and Winter Service Checklist
秋季和冬季检查项目

It's that time of year again to start promoting seasonal service checks and winterizing services. So before cold weather hits, here are some service items that ought to be checked.

45.1　Tires 轮胎

Tires obviously play a very important role in safe driving because of their affect on traction, handling and braking. Worn tires can be dangerous to drive on because traction is reduced, and maximum traction is often required on wet and slick roads. Here are some things to look for when inspecting the tires:

Tread depth　If the tread is worn down to the wear bars, or minimum specifications, the tires need to be replaced.

Toe wear　A feathered wear pattern across the tread on the front tires or heavy shoulder wear usually indicates toe misalignment (toe in or out). Check alignment and realign as needed.

Camber wear　Also called edge wear, it shows up on the inside or outside shoulders of the tread. Wear on the inside edge of both tires may be due to negative camber or toe misalignment (too much toe-out). If only one tire shows edge wear, check for collapsed control arm bushings, a bent strut, mislocated strut tower, or a bent spindle. Wear on the outside shoulder of the tires can be caused by positive camber, toe misalignment (too much toe-in), or hard cornering (driving too fast).

Cupped ware Badly cupped tires tells you the tires are bouncing as they roll. The underlying cause here may be a wheel balance problem (check for missing weights or excessive runout), or worn shocks or struts.

Uneven wear This can occur if the tires are not rotated regularly (every 6000 miles or so).

Inflation pressure Refer to the owner's manual or vehicle decal for the recommended inflation pressure front and rear. Low tires may indicate a lack of maintenance or porosity leaks in alloy wheels.

45.2 Brakes 制动器

Good brakes are absolutely essential for safe driving year-round, especially on slick roads. Inspecting the following items will help assure your customer's brakes are up to the task:

Brake performance If possible, test drive the vehicle and check pedal feel, brake balance and stopping ability. If brakes pull, grab, make noise or the pedal pulsates, further diagnosis is needed.

Abs system Turn the ignition on to verify that the ABS warning light circuit works. The ABS light should come on for a few seconds, then go out. No light? Then you've found a bulb that needs replacing or a wiring problem. If the light remains on, further diagnosis will be required.

Brake pedal Apply the brakes and start the engine. Does the pedal drop slightly? It should if the vacuum booster is working (note: this does not happen with hydroboost brakes). How does the brake pedal feel? Is it firm? A soft or mushy-feeling pedal usually indicates air in the lines or leaks. A pedal that slowly sinks is a classic symptom of a worn master cylinder. Is the amount of pedal travel normal? A low pedal may indicate worn linings, the need for adjustment, defective or frozen drum brake adjusters or a low fluid level.

Brake lights Do the brake lights come on when you step on the pedal? No lights may indicate a defective or misadjusted brake light pedal switch or burned out bulbs in the taillights.

Parking brake Apply the parking brake. Does the pedal or handle work smoothly? Is it adjusted properly? Does the brake light on the instrument panel come on? No brake warning light may indicate a bad bulb or defective or misadjusted parking brake switch. Does the parking brake hold the vehicle? Put the transmission into gear with the parking brake applied. If it fails to hold the vehicle, it needs adjusting. Now release the parking brake. Failure to release fully means the linkage or cables need attention.

Brake fluid A low level may indicate a leak or worn linings. Discoloration indicates contamination and the need for a fluid change. The moisture content of the fluid can be measured with chemical test strips, an electronic fluid tester or a brake fluid refractometer. Recommend a fluid change if you find more than 2 to 3 percent moisture.

Brake linings Remove a front wheel and measure the thickness of the brake pads. If worn down to minimum specifications or if wear indicators are making contact with the rotor, new linings are needed. If the pads are still above specs, you might recommend replacing them anyway if they're near the end of their service life or if they're noisy.

Rotors Note the condition of the rotors. Deep scratches or grooves indicate a need for resurfacing. Measure runout and parallelism. If out of specs, resurfacing or replacement is needed. Are there discolored spots, heat cracks or warpage? These may also indicate a need for rotor resurfacing or replacement.

Calipers Note the condition of the calipers and caliper mounts, and inspect for fluid leaks. Uneven pad wear usually indicates a caliper is sticking. The cause may be corrosion on the caliper mounting guides or keyway.

Drums Pull a drum and inspect the drum surface, brake shoes, hardware and wheel cylinder. If the shoe linings are at or below minimum specifications, new shoes are needed. If the linings are still above minimum specs, but are getting thin, new shoes should be recommended to extend the life of the brakes. Check wheel cylinders for leaks. If leaking, they must be rebuilt or replaced. New shoes will also be required if the old ones have been contaminated with brake fluid or grease.

Brake lines & hoses Check the entire system for leaks, including the master cylinder, proportioning valve, steel brake lines and rubber hoses. Have a helper apply the brakes while you look underneath. Rubber hoses should not expand under pressure. Any hoses that are chaffed, cracked or swell under pressure need to be replaced. Leaks are potentially very dangerous because they may lead to brake failure. Leak repairs should never be postponed.

45.3 Suspension 悬架

BALL JOINTS-Loaded joints need to have the weight taken off of them before checking. If the joint doesn't have an internal wear indicator, use a dial indicator to measure joint movement. Always refer to the ball joint specifications for the vehicle.

TIE ROD ENDS No visible free play allowed. Worn tie rod ends can cause rapid toe wear and steering instability.

Inner tie rod sockets On rack & pinion steering equipped vehicles, check by pinching the rubber bellows. Feel for any looseness while the steering is rocked back and forth. The presence of fluid in the bellows would indicate internal fluid leaks. On a rack with hard plastic bellows, the inner sockets can be inspected by rocking the steering wheel back and forth while watching the tie rod for looseness, or by loosening the large end of the bellows and sliding it away from the housing for direct visual inspection.

Idler arms & pitman arms Check idler arms for wear by applying pressure and checking play with a dial indicator. Looseness here can also affect toe alignment and steering stability.

Steering gear Rock the steering wheel back and forth to check for wear and excessive play. On racks, check the rack mounts, too.

Control arm bushings Worn, collapsed or damaged bushings can affect camber and caster alignment. Don't forget to check the rear control arms, too.

Shocks & struts Check for leaks, indications of bottoming or other damage. The old "bounce test" is still a valid procedure for finding worn dampers. But a test drive will tell you more.

Ride Height Ride height should be checked front and rear at the specified locations, and compared side-to-side. If below the minimum specs or if off by more than half an inch side-to-side, the springs may need to be replaced.

45.4　Exhaust System 排气系统

Exhaust manifold (s) Is there any detectable exhaust noise when the engine is running? Are there any indications of leakage past the exhaust manifold gaskets (discolored streaks)? Are there any cracks in the exhaust manifold (s)? Are the manifold bolts tight?

Head pipe connection Leaks where the head pipe mates with the exhaust manifold are very common due to engine vibration and rocking (especially in FWD cars).

45.5　Battery & Charging System 蓄电池和充电系统

Battery charge Measure battery voltage with the engine and all accessories off. If the battery is less than 75 percent charged, it may indicate a charging problem or an aging battery. The average battery will usually last four to five years with proper care. But premature failure can occur as a result of chronic undercharging, overcharging, abuse or vibration. Plates become "sulfated" if the battery is run down and not fully recharged. Undercharging can result from infrequent or short trip driving, low alternator output, a defective regulator or corroded cables or wiring problems.

Battery condition Use a load tester or electronic tester to check the condition of the battery. If it does not recover quickly enough or fails to maintain a minimum voltage, it needs to be replaced.

Battery cables Are they clean and tight? If loose or corroded, clean and replace as needed. If the cables have been replaced, are they the proper gauge size? Undersized cables may not be able to carry enough amps for reliable cold weather starting. Also, check the engine ground straps. Loose or missing straps are a common cause of charging and cranking problems.

Charging voltage Start the engine and measure the charging voltage. If it does not meet specs, further diagnosis may be needed to isolate the cause.

Starter Start the engine. Does it crank normally? Slow cranking may indicate poor battery cable or ground connections.

[词汇]

winterize	vt.使…准备过冬（使…防冻，使…适合冬季使用）	underneath	adv.在下面
		dial indicator	n.千分表，标度盘式指示器
traction	n.牵引	free play	n.游隙，自由间隙
tread	n.轮胎花纹，轮胎胎面	tie rod	横拉杆
camber	n.外倾，前轮外倾	bellows	n.波纹管，波形膜
inflation	n.充气，通货膨胀	pitman arm	转向垂臂
pulsate	vi.搏动，跳动，有规律地跳动	detectable	adj.可检测的
booster	n.增压器	sulfate	v.以硫酸或硫酸盐处理，使变为硫酸盐
refractometer	n.折射仪，折射计		
runout	n.跳动，突破，溢流	corrode	v.使腐蚀，侵蚀
parallelism	n.平行度，二重性，类似	undersized	adj.较一般为小的，不够大的
warpage	n.翘曲	starter	n.启动器

[问题]

1. How do you check tires?
2. How many items are there for the brake inspection?
3. How do you check the exhaust system?
4. What kind of premature failure occurs to the battery?

附 录

附录 1 Automotive Acronyms 汽车缩写词

1.1 OBD2/SAE ACRONYMS 第二代车载诊断系统/(美国)汽车工程师学会缩写字

ABS	antilock brake system	防抱死制动系统
A/C	air conditioning	空调
AC	air cleaner	空气滤清器
AIR	secondary air injection	辅助空气喷射
A/T	automatic transmission or transaxle	自动变速器或变速驱动桥
B+	battery positive voltage	蓄电池正极电压
BARO	barometric pressure	大气压力
CAC	charge air cooler	进气冷却器
CFI	continuous fuel injection	连续燃油喷射
CL	closed loop	闭环
CKP	crankshaft position sensor	曲轴位置传感器
CKP REF	crankshaft reference	曲轴基准
CMP	camshaft position sensor	凸轮轴位置传感器
CMP REF	camshaft reference	凸轮轴基准
CPP	clutch pedal position	离合器踏板位置
CTP	closed throttle position	节气门关闭位置

DFCO	decel fuel cut-off mode	减速断油方式
DFI	direct fuel injection	直接燃油喷射
DLC	data link connector	数据链接连接器
DTC	diagnostic trouble code	诊断故障码
DTM	diagnostic test mode	诊断测试方式
EBCM	electronic brake control module	电子制动控制模块
EBTCM	electronic brake traction control module	电子制动牵引力控制模块
EC	engine control	发动机控制
ECM	engine control module	发动机控制模块
ECL	engine coolant level	发动机冷却液面
ECT	engine coolant temperature	发动机冷却液温度
EEPROM	electrically erasable programmable read only memory	电可擦除可编程只读存储器
EFE	early fuel evaporation	燃油早期汽化，进气管预热
EGR	exhaust gas recirculation	废气再循环
EGRT	EGR temperature	废气再循环温度
EI	electronic ignition	电子点火
EM	engine modification	发动机变型
EPROM	erasable programmable read only memory	可擦除可编程只读存储器
EVAP	evaporative emission system	蒸发排放系统
FC	fan control	风扇控制
FEEPROM	flash electrically erasable programmable read only memory	闪存电可擦除可编程只读存储器
FP	fuel pump	燃油泵
FPROM	flash erasable programmable read only memory	闪存可擦除可编程只读存储器
FT	fuel trim	燃油修正
FTP	federal test procedure	联邦试验程序
GCM	governor control module	调速器控制模块
GEN	generator	发电机
GND	ground	接地
HC	hydrocarbon	碳氢化合物
HVS	high voltage switch	高电压开关
HVAC	heating ventilation and air conditioning system	加热通风和空调系统
IA	intake air	进气
IAC	idle air control	怠速空气控制
IAT	intake air temperature	进气温度
IC	ignition control circuit	点火控制电路
ICM	ignition control module	点火控制模块
IFI	indirect fuel injection	间接燃油喷射

IFS	inertia fuel shutoff	惯性燃油关闭
I/M	inspection/maintenance	检查/保养
IPC	instrument panel cluster	仪表板组件
ISC	idle speed control	怠速控制
KOEC	key on, engine cranking	钥匙在 on 位置，发动机起动
KOEO	key on, engine off	钥匙在 on 位置，发动机不转
KOER	key on, engine running	钥匙在 on 位置，发动机运转
KS	knock sensor	爆震传感器
KSM	knock sensor module	爆震传感器模块
LT	long term fuel trim	长期燃油修正
MAF	mass airflow sensor	空气流量传感器
MAP	manifold absolute pressure sensor	歧管绝对压力传感器
MC	mixture control	混合气控制
MFI	multiport fuel injection	多点燃油喷射
MIL	malfunction indicator lamp	故障指示灯
MPH	miles per hour	每小时英里数
MST	manifold surface temperature	歧管表面温度
MVZ	manifold vacuum zone	歧管真空区
NVRAM	nonvolatile random access memory	非易失随机存储器
OBD	onboard diagnostics	车载诊断
OBD Ⅰ	onboard diagnostics generation one	第一代车载诊断
OBD Ⅱ	onboard diagnostics, second generation	第二代车载诊断
OC	oxidation catalyst	氧化催化剂
ODM	output device monitor	输出装置监控
OL	open loop	开环
PAIR	pulsed secondary air injection	脉冲式二次空气喷射
PCM	powertrain control module	传动系控制模块
PCV	positive crankcase ventilation	强制曲轴箱通风
PROM	program read only memory	可编程序只读存储器
PSA	pressure switch assembly	压力开关总成
PSP	power steering pressure	动力转向压力
RAM	random access memory	随机存取存储器
RM	relay module	继电器模块
ROM	read only memory	只读存储器
RPM	revolutions per minute	每分钟转速
SC	supercharger	机械增压器
SCB	supercharger bypass	增压器旁通
SDM	sensing diagnostic mode	传感诊断模块
SFI	sequential fuel injection	顺序燃油喷射
SRI	service reminder indicator	维护提示指示灯

SRT	system readiness test	系统状态测试
ST	short term fuel trim	短期燃油调整
TB	throttle body	节气门体
TBI	throttle body injection	节气门体喷射
TC	turbocharger	涡轮增压器
TCC	torque converter clutch	变矩器离合器
TP	throttle position	节气门位置
TPS	throttle position sensor	节气门位置传感器
TVV	thermal vacuum valve	热真空阀
TWC	three way catalyst	三元催化剂
TWC + OC	three way + oxidation catalytic converter	三元 + 氧化催化转换器
VAF	volume airflow	空气流量
VCM	vehicle control module	车辆控制模块
VR	voltage regulator	电压调节器
VS	vehicle sensor	车辆传感器
VSS	vehicle speed sensor	车速传感器
WOT	wide open throttle	节气门全开

1.2 EMISSIONS RELATED TERMINOLOGY 与排放有关术语

AAV	anti-afterburn valve (Mazda)	防（熄火后）继燃阀
AIS	air injection system (Chrysler)	二次空气喷射系统
CC	catalytic converter	催化转化器
CCP	controlled canister purge (GM)	控制式碳罐净化
CCV	canister control valve	碳罐控制阀
CEC	crankcase emission control system (Honda)	曲轴箱排放控制系统
CFC	chlor ofluorocarbons	氟里昂
CP	canister purge (GM)	碳罐净化
ECS	evaporation control system (Chrysler)	蒸发控制系统
EEC	evaporative emission controls (Ford)	蒸发排放控制
EECS	evaporative emissions control system (GM)	蒸发排放控制系统
EFE	early fuel evaporation system (GM)	燃油早期汽化系统
EGR-SV	EGR solenoid valve (Mazda)	EGR 电磁阀
EGRTV	EGR thermo valve (Chrysler)	EGR 热控阀
EVRV	electronic vacuum regulator valve for EGR (GM)	EGR 电子真空调节阀
HAIS	heated air intake system (Chrysler)	加热式进气系统
OC	oxidation converter (GM)	氧化转化器
PAFS	pulse air feeder system (Chrysler)	脉冲式供气系统

PAIR	pulsed secondary air injection system（GM） 脉冲式二次空气喷射阀
PVS	ported vacuum switch 孔式真空阀
TAC	thermostatic air cleaner（GM） 温度调节的空气滤清器
TVS	thermal vacuum switch 热真空开关
TVV	thermal vacuum valve（GM） 热真空阀

1.3 COMPUTERIZED ENGINE CONTROL SYSTEMS TERMINOLOGY 计算机化发动机控制系统术语

C3	computer command control system（GM） 计算机指令控制系统
C4	computer controlled catalytic converter system（GM） 计算机控制催化转化器系统
CAS	clean air system（chrysler）清洁空气系统
CCC	computer command control system(GM) 计算机指令控制系统
CVCC	compound vortex controlled combustion system（Honda） 复合涡流调整燃烧系统
ECCS	electronic concentrated control system（Nissan） 电子集中控制系统
EEC	electronic engine control（Ford） 电子发动机控制
ELB	electronic lean burn（Chrysler） 电子稀薄燃烧
MCU	microprocessor controlled unit（Ford） 微处理器控制单元
PGM-FI	programmed gas management fuel injection（Honda） 编程汽油控制燃油喷射
SCC	spark control computer（Chrysler） 点火控制计算机
TCCS	toyota computer controlled system 丰田计算机控制系统

1.4 SENSORS TERMINOLOGY 传感器术语

ACTS	air charge temperature sensor（Ford） 进气温度传感器
AFS	air flow sensor（Mitsubishi） 空气流量传感器
AFM	air flow meter 空气流量计
APS	absolute pressure sensor（GM） 绝对压力传感器
APS	atmospheric pressure sensor（Mazda） 大气压力传感器
ATS	air temperature sensor（Chrysler） 空气温度传感器
BARO	barometric pressure sensor（GM） 大气压力传感器
BMAP	barometric/manifold absolute pressure sensor（Ford） 大气/歧管绝对压力传感器
BP	backpressure sensor（Ford） 背压传感器
BPS	barometric pressure sensor（Ford & Nissan） 大气压力传感器

BPT	back-pressure transducer	背压传感器
CID	cylinder identification sensor（Ford）	气缸识别传感器
CMP	camshaft position sensor（GM）	凸轮轴位置传感器
CP	crankshaft position sensor（Ford）	曲轴位置传感器
CTS	charge temperature switch（Chrysler）	充气温度传感器
CTS	coolant temperature sensor（GM）	冷却液温度传感器
CTVS	choke thermal vacuum switch	阻风门热真空开关
ECT	engine coolant temperature（Ford & GM）	发动机冷却液温度
EGO	exhaust gas oxygen sensor（Ford）	排气氧传感器
EGRPS	EGR valve position sensor（Mazda）EGR	阀位置传感器
EOS	exhaust oxygen sensor	废气氧传感器
EPOS	EGR valve position sensor（Ford）EGR	阀位置传感器
EVP	EGR valve position sensor（Ford）EGR	阀位置传感器
FLS	fluid level sensor（GM）	液位传感器
HEGO	heated exhaust gas oxygen sensor	加热式排气氧传感器
IAT	inlet air temperature sensor（Ford）	进气温度传感器
IATS	intake air temperature sensor（Mazda）	进气温度传感器
KS	knock sensor	爆震传感器
MAF	mass airflow sensor	空气流量传感器
MAP	manifold absolute pressure	进气歧管绝对压力
MAT	manifold air temperature	进气歧管空气温度
MCT	manifold charge temperature（Ford）	进气歧管空气温度
OS	oxygen sensor	传感器
PIP	profile ignition pickup（Ford）	点火拾波器
SS	speed sensor（Honda）	速度传感器
TA	temperature air（Honda）	空气温度
TP	throttle position sensor（Ford）	节气门位置传感器
TPP	throttle position potentiometer	节气门位置电位计
TPS	throttle position sensor	节气门位置传感器
TPT	throttle position transducer（Chrysler）	节气门位置传感器
TVS	thermal vacuum switch（GM）	热真空开关
VAF	vane airflow sensor	翼板型空气流量传感器
VSS	vehicle speed sensor	车速传感器
WOT	wide open throttle switch（GM）	节气门全开开关
WSS	wheel speed sensor	轮速传感器

1.5　ELECTRONIC COMPONENTS TERMINOLOGY 电子元件术语

ALCL	assembly line communications link（GM）	装配线通讯链接

ALDL	assembly line data link (GM)	装配线数据链接
ASDM	airbag system diagnostic module (Chrysler)	气囊系统诊断模块
BCM	body control module (GM)	车身控制模块
CALPAK	calibration pack	校正卡
CECU	central electronic control unit (Nissan)	中央电控单元
CPU	central processing unit	中央处理器
DLC	data link connector	数据链接连接器 (GM)
EACV	electronic air control valve (Honda)	电子空气控制阀
EBM	electronic body module (GM)	电子车身模块
EBCM	electronic brake control module (GM)	电子制动控制模块
ECA	electronic control assembly	电控总成
ECM	electronic control module (GM)	电控制模块
ECU	electronic control unit (Ford, Honda & Toyota)	电控单元
EEPROM	electronically erasable programmable read only memory chip	电可擦可编程只读存储芯片
EPROM	erasable program mable read only memory chip	可擦可编程只读存储芯片
EI	electronic ignition (GM)	电子点火
IC	integrated circuit	集成电路
ICS	idle control solenoid (GM)	怠速控制电磁阀
ISC	idle speed control (GM)	怠速控制
LCD	liquid crystal display	液晶显示器
LED	light emitting diode	发光二极管
MIL	malfunction indicator lamp	故障指示灯
PCM	powertrain control module (supercedes ECM)	传动系控制模块
SES	service engine soon indicator (GM)	尽快维修发动机指示灯
TCC	torque converter clutch (GM)	变矩器离合器
VCC	viscous converter clutch (GM)	黏性变矩器离合器

1.6 ELECTRONIC IGNITIONS TERMINOLOGY 电子点火术语

BID	breakerless inductive discharge (AMC)	无断电器感应放电
CDI	capacitor discharge ignition (AMC)	电容放电点火
C3I	computer controlled coil ignition (GM)	计算机控制点火线圈点火
CSSA	cold start spark advance (Ford)	冷启动点火提前
DIS	distributorless ignition system (Ford)	无分电器点火系统
DIS	direct Ignition system (GM)	直接点火系统
EDIS	electronic distributorless ignition system (Ford)	电子无分电器点火系统

HEI	high energy ignition (GM)	高能点火
ITCS	ignition timing control system (Honda)	点火正时控制系统
SDI	saab direct ignition	绅宝直接点火
SSI	solid state ignition (Ford)	固态点火

1.7 SPARK CONTROL SYSTEMS AND DEVICES TERMINOLOGY 点火控制系统和装置术语

CCEV	coolant controlled engine vacuum switch (Chrysler)	冷却液控制的发动机真空开关
CSC	coolant spark control (Ford)	冷却液点火控制
CSSA	cold start spark advance (Ford)	冷启动点火提前
DRCV	distributor retard control valve	分电器延迟控制阀
DSSA	dual signal spark advance (Ford)	双信号点火提前
DVDV	distributor vacuum delay valve	分电器真空延迟控制阀
ESA	electronic spark advance (Chrysler)	电子点火提前
ESC	electronic spark control (GM)	电子点火控制
ESS	electronic spark selection (Cadillac)	电子点火选择
EST	electronic spark timing (GM)	电子点火正时
PVA	ported vacuum advance	孔式真空提前
PVS	ported vacuum switch	孔式真空开关
SAVM	spark advance vacuum modulator	点火提前真空调制器
SPOUT	spark output signal (Ford)	点火输出信号
TCS	transmission controlled spark (GM)	变速器控制点火
TIC	thermal ignition control (Chrysler)	热点火控制
TRS	transmission regulated spark (Ford)	变速器调整点火
VDV	vacuum delay valve	真空延迟阀

1.8 FUEL SYSTEM TERMINOLOGY 燃油系统术语

AIS	automatic idle speed motor (Chrysler)	自动怠速电机
ABSV	air bypass solenoid valve (Mazda)	空气旁通电磁阀
ASD	automatic shutdown relay (Chrysler)	自动关闭继电器
CANP	canister purge solenoid valve (Ford)	碳罐净化电磁阀
CCEI	coolant controlled idle enrichment (Chrysler)	冷却液控制怠速加浓
CER	cold enrichment rod (Ford)	冷态加浓杆
CIS	continuous injection system (Bosch)	连续喷射系统
CPI	central port injection (GM)	喷射

CVR	control vacuum regulator（Ford）	控制真空调节器
DEFI	digital electronic fuel injection（Cadillac）	数字电子燃油喷射
DFS	deceleration fuel shutoff（Ford）	减速断油
EFC	electronic fuel control	电子燃油控制
EFC	electronic feedback carburetor（Chrysler）	电子反馈式化油器
EFCA	electronic fuel control assembly（Ford）	电子燃油控制总成
EFI	electronic fuel injection	电子燃油喷射
FBC	feedback carburetor system（Ford & Mitsubishi）	反馈式化油器
FBCA	feedback carburetor actuator（Ford）	反馈式化油器执行器
FCA	fuel control assembly（Chrysler）	燃油控制总成
FCS	fuel control solenoid（Ford）	燃油控制总成
FDC	fuel deceleration valve（Ford）	燃油减速阀
FI	fuel injection	燃油喷射
IAC	idle air control（GM）	怠速空气控制
ISC	idle speed control（GM）	怠速控制
JAS	jet air system（Mitsubishi）	喷射空气系统
MCS	mixture control solenoid（GM）	混合气控制电磁阀
MFI	multiport fuel injection	多点燃油喷射
MPFI	multi point fuel injection	多点燃油喷射
MPI	multi port injection	多点喷射
PFI	port fuel injection（GM）	进气口燃油喷射
SFI	sequential fuel injection（GM）	顺序燃油喷射
SMPI	sequential multiport fuel injection（Chrysler）	顺序多点燃油喷射
TABPV	throttle air bypass valve（Ford）	节气门空气旁通阀
TBI	throttle body injection	节气门体喷射
TV	throttle valve	节气门阀

1.9 GENERAL 通用

AC	alternating current	交流电
A/F	air/fuel ratio	空燃比
A/T	automatic transmission	自动变速器
ATC	after top center	上止点后
ATDC	after top dead center	上止点后
ATF	automatic transmission fluid	自动变速箱油
AWD	all-wheel drive	全轮驱动
BAT	battery	蓄电池
BHP	brake horsepower	制动马力
Btu	British thermal units	英国热量单位

CC	cubic centimeters 立方厘米，毫升
cfm	cubic feet per minute 立方英尺/分
CID	cubic inch displacement 立方英寸工作容积
dB	decibels 分贝
DC	direct current 直流电
DOHC	dual overhead cams 双顶置式凸轮
DVOM	digital volt ohm meter 数字电压电阻表
EMI	electromagnetic interference 电磁干扰
FWD	front-wheel drive 前轮驱动
gal	gallon 加仑
GND	ground 接地
GPM	grams per mile 每英里克数
Hg	mercury 汞
hp	horsepower 马力
IGN	ignition 点火
ID	inside diameter 内径
I/P	instrument panel 仪表板
kHz	kilohertz 千赫兹
kPa	kilopascals 千帕斯卡
lb. ft.	pound feet 磅英尺
MPG	miles per gallon 英里/加仑
MPH	miles per hour 英里/时
OD	outside diameter 外径
OE	original equipment 原始设备
OEM	original equipment manufacture 原始设备制造商
OHC	overhead cam 顶置凸轮
P/B	power brakes 动力制动
P/N	part number 零件号
PPM	parts per million 百万分之几
PS	power steering 动力转向
PSI	pounds per square inch 每平方英寸磅数
pt.	pint 品脱
Qt.	quart 夸脱
RFI	radio frequency interference 射频干扰
RPM	revolutions per minute 每分钟转数
SOHC	single overhead cam 单顶置凸轮
TACH	tachometer 转速表
TDC	top dead center 上止点
VAC	volts alternating current 交流电压
VDC	volts direct current 直流电压

VIN	vehicle identification number	车辆识别号码
WOT	wide open throttle	节气门全开

1.10 MISCELLANEOUS 其他

ABS	antilock brake system	防抱死制动系统
API	American Petroleum Institute	美国石油学会
DOT	Department of Transportation	运输部
DRB	diagnostic readout box (Chrysler)	诊断读取盒
EPA	Environmental Protection Agency	美国环保署
ISO	International Standards Organization	国际标准化组织
NHTSA	National Highway Traffic Safety Administration	（美国）国家公路交通安全管理局
SAE	Society of Automotive Engineers	美国汽车工程师学会

附录2 Automotive Tech Terms 汽车技术术语

2.1 AIR CONDITIONING 空调

accumulator 存储器
freon 氟里昂
chlorofluorocarbons（CFC） 氯氟碳化合物
compressor 压缩机
compressor clutch 压缩机离合器
desiccant 干燥剂
evaporator 蒸发器
condenser 冷凝器
refrigerant 制冷剂
R-134a 制冷剂 R-134a
R-12 制冷剂 R-12
schrader valve 维修阀
orifice tube 量管
rotary compressor 转子压缩机
variable displacement compressor 可变排量压缩机

2.2 ALIGNMENT 定位

Ackerman steering 阿克曼转向
bump steer 颠簸转向
camber 外倾
caster 后倾
king pin inclination（KPI） 主销内倾
positive camber 正外倾
positive caster 正后倾
negative camber 负外倾
negative caster 负后倾
steering axis inclination（SAI） 主销内倾
toe 车轮的前端
toe-in 前束
toe-out 后束
total toe 总前束
thrust angle 推力角
wheelbase 轴距

2.3 BODY 车身

A pillar 前立柱
B pillar 中立柱
base coat 底漆
bonnet 发动机罩
C pillar 后立柱
datum plane 基准面
high strength steel（HSS） 高强度钢
inner quarter panel 后侧内围板

primer 底漆
primer/sealer 底漆/密封膏
rear panel 后围板
roof panel （车身）顶板
rustproofing 防锈

self-etching primer 自蚀刻底漆
scuttle panel 前围上盖板
sunroof 顶窗
undercoating 内涂层

2.4 BRAKES 制动

antilock brake system（ABS） 防抱死制动系统
anti-rattle springs/shims 防振弹簧/垫片
asbestos 石棉
asbestos linings 石棉衬片
backing plate 底板
bellmouth 锥形孔
bleeder hose 放气软管
bleeder screw 放气螺丝
bleeding the brakes 制动放气
brake balance 制动平衡
brake job 制动
brake fade 制动衰退
brake fluid 制动液
brake grease 制动润滑脂
brake hose 制动软管
brake lathe 制动器车床
brake lines 制动管路
brake linings 制动衬片
brake pedal switch 制动踏板开关
brake noise 制动噪声
brake pedal switch 制动
brake spoon 制动爪柄
brake warning light 制动警告灯
caliper 制动钳
caliper piston 制动钳活塞
coefficient of friction 摩擦系数
combination valve 组合阀
composite rotor 复合转子
discard thickness 报废厚度
disc brakes 盘式制动

drum 制动鼓
dual master cylinder 双主缸
dust boot 防尘罩
electronic brake control module（EBCM） 电子制动控制模块
emergency brake 应急制动
fixed calipers 固定钳
floating calipers 浮动钳
fluid reservoir 储液缸
gravity bleeding 自流放气
hold-down springs 压紧弹簧
hydraulic modulator assembly 液压调节总成
hydraulic pressure 液压压力
integral ABS 整体式防抱死制动系统
manual bleeding 手工放气
master cylinder 主缸
maximum drum diameter 最大制动鼓直径
metering valve 配压阀
minimum rotor thickness 最小转子厚度
nonintegral ABS 非整体式防抱死制动系统
pad 衬垫
parking brake 驻车制动
phenolic piston 苯酚活塞
power booster 增压器
power brakes 动力制动
pressure differential valve 压差阀
primary shoe 主制动蹄
proportioning valve 比例阀
rear wheel antilock brakes（RABS） 后轮防抱死制动
rear wheel antilock brake system（RWAL）

后轮防抱死制动系统
return springs　回位弹簧
riveted linings　铆接的衬片
rotor　转子
secondary shoe　副制动蹄
self-adjuster　自调整装置
semi-metallic linings　半金属衬片

shoes　制动蹄
stability control　稳定性控制
traction control　牵引力控制
vacuum booster　真空增压器
vented rotor　通风式转子
wheel cylinder　轮缸
wheel speed sensor　轮速传感器

2.5　CHARGING & STARTING SYSTEM 充电和启动系统

alternator　交流发电机
alternating current　交流电
battery　蓄电池
battery cables　蓄电池线
battery terminals　蓄电池接线柱
brushes　电刷
charging voltage　充电电压
cold cranking amps（CCA）　冷启动电流
cranking voltage　启动电压
diode　二极管
electrolyte　电解液

externally regulated　外部调节
field coil　磁场线圈
internally regulated　内部调节
regulator　调节器
solenoid　电磁线圈
starter　启动机
stator　定子
voltage drop　电压降
voltage regulator　电压调节器
warning light　警告灯

2.6　COOLING SYSTEM 冷却系统

antifreeze　防冻液
bypass hose　旁通管
coolant　冷却液
coolant reservoir　贮液罐
corrosion inhibitors　防腐剂
defrosters　除霜器
electric cooling fan　冷却电风扇
ethylene glycol（EG）　乙烯乙二醇
fan　风扇
fan clutch　风扇离合器
fan relay　风扇继电器
heater core　加热器
heater control valve　加热器

heater hose　加热器
hose　软管
heating ventilation & air conditioning（HVAC）　采暖、通风和空调
lower radiator hose　下散热器管
propylene glycol（PG）　丙烯乙二醇
radiator　散热器，水箱
radiator cap　散热器盖
serpentine belt　蛇形皮带
thermostat　节温器
upper radiator hose　上散热器管
V-belt　形皮带
water pump　水泵

2.7 DRIVELINE 传动系

all-wheel drive（AWD） 全轮驱动
automatic slip regulation（ASR） 自动滑转调整
automatic transmission 自动变速器
axle 轴
boots 防尘罩
cardan joint 万向节
center differential 中央差速器
clutch 离合器
clutch disk 离合器从动盘
differential 差速器
driveshaft 传动轴
four-wheel drive（4WD or 4×4） 四轮驱动
front-wheel drive（FWD） 前轮驱动
halfshafts 半轴
limited slip differential 防滑差速器
locking differential 锁止差速器
lockup torque converter 锁止式变矩器
manual transmission 手动变速器
pinion gear 小齿轮
pressure plate 压盘
ring gear 齿圈
torque converter 液力变矩器
torque converter clutch 变矩器离合器
traction control 牵引力控制
transfer case 分动箱
transaxle 变速驱动桥
transmission 变速器
wheel bearings 车轮轴承

2.8 ELECTRONICS 电子学

air temperature sensor 空气温度传感器
assembly line data link（ALDL） connector 装配线数据链接连接器
barometric pressure sensor 大气压力传感器
camshaft position sensor 凸轮轴位置传感器
check engine light 检查发动机灯
closed loop 闭环
computerized engine control 计算机化发动机控制
control module 控制模块
coolant temperature sensor 冷却液温度传感器
crankshaft angle sensor 曲轴传感器
electronic control module（ECM） 电子控制模块
EGR valve position sensor EGR 阀位置传感器
knock sensor 爆震传感器
light emitting diode（LED） 发光二极管
liquid crystal display（LCD） 液晶显示
manifold absolute pressure sensor（MAP） 歧管绝对压力传感器
mass airflow sensor 空气流量传感器
open loop 开环
oxygen sensor（O_2） 氧传感器
powertrain control module（PCM） 传力系控制模块
sensor 传感器
throttle position sensor（TPS） 节气门位置传感器
vane airflow sensor 翼板式空气流量传感器
vehicle speed sensor 车速传感器

2.9　ELECTRICAL SYSTEM 电气系统

alternating current（AC）　交流电
Amps　安培数
circuit breaker　断路器
continuity　导通
direct current（DC）　直流电
fuse　保险丝
fuse panel　熔断器板
fusible link　熔性连接
ground　接地
halogen headlights　卤素大灯
ignition switch　点火开关
incandescent lights　白炽灯
instrument panel　仪表板

integrated circuit（IC）　集成电路
light emitting diode（LED）　发光二极管
ohmmeter　电阻表
Ohms　欧姆
open　开路
parallel circuit　并联电路
series circuit　串联电路
short　短路
voltmeter　电压表
Volts　伏特
wiring connector　配线连接器
wiring harness　线束
wiring schematic　配线示意图

2.10　EMISSIONS CONTROL 排放控制

air pump　空气泵
air injection reaction（AIR）　二次空气喷射
canister purge control valve　活性炭净化控制阀
carbon monoxide（CO）　一氧化碳
carbon dioxide（CO_2）　二氧化碳
catalytic converter　催化转化器
catalyst　催化剂
charcoal canister　活性炭罐
diverter valve　分流阀
early fuel evaporation　早期燃油汽化
emissions testing　排放试验

exhaust gas recirculation（EGR）　废气再循环
heat riser　升温装置
hydrocarbons（HC）　碳氢化合物
oxides of nitrogen（NO_x）　氮氧化物
ported vacuum switch（PVS）　孔式真空开关
positive crankcase ventilation（PCV）　曲轴箱强制通风
three-way catalytic converter（TWC）　三元催化转换器
thermal vacuum switch（TVS）　热真空开关
thermal vacuum valve（TVV）　热真空阀
vacuum delay valve　真空延迟阀

2.11　ENGINE 发动机

align bore　定位镗缸
align hone　定位磨缸
balance　平衡

balance shaft　平衡轴
cam bearings　凸轮轴承
camshaft　凸轮轴

cam followers　凸轮随动件
combustion chamber　燃烧室
compression ratio　压缩比
compression rings　压缩环
connecting rod　连杆
cooling jackets　冷却水套
counterweights　平衡重
crankshaft　曲轴
cylinder　气缸
cylinder block　气缸体
cylinder sleeves　气缸套
cylinder boring　气缸缸径
cylinder head　气缸盖
cylinder honing　气缸搪磨
displacement　排量
dual overhead cam（DOHC）　双顶置凸轮轴
exhaust manifold　排气歧管
exhaust valve　排气门
flywheel　飞轮
gasket　气缸垫
harmonic balancer　谐振平衡器
head bolts　缸盖
head gasket　缸盖垫
horsepower　马力
hydraulic lifters　液压挺杆
inline cylinder block　直列气缸体
intake manifold　进气歧管
intake valve　进气门
journals　轴颈
lash adjusters　间隙调节器
lifters　挺杆
main bearings　主轴承
mechanical lifters　机械挺杆
oil cooler　机油冷却器
oil filter　机油滤清器
oil galleys　机油油道
oil pan　油底壳
oil pan gasket　油底壳垫
oil pressure　机油压力
oil pressure sending unit　机油压力传感器

oil plugs　机油塞
oil pump　机油泵
oil pump pickup　机油泵集滤器
oil ring　油环
overhead cam（OHC）　顶置式凸轮
overhead valve（OHV）　顶置式气门
piston　活塞
piston rings　活塞环
piston skirt　活塞裙部
pushrods　推杆
rear main oil seal　后主油封
revolutions per minute（RPM）　每分钟转数
ring end gap　活塞环端隙
rocker arms　摇臂
rod bearings　连杆轴承
roller lifters　滚子挺杆
tappets　挺杆
timing belt　正时皮带
timing chain　正时链条
timing chain cover　正时链条盖
timing chain cover gasket　正时链条盖垫片
timing gears　正时齿轮
torque　扭矩
valve　气门
valve cover gasket　气门罩垫
valve grinding　气门磨削
valve guide　气门导管
valve height　气门高度
valve interference　气门干涉
valve lash　气门间隙
valve overlap　气门重叠
valve spring　气门弹簧
valve spring keeper　气门弹簧锁块
valve spring retainer　气门弹簧锁块
valve stem　气门杆
valve stem seal　气门杆密封
valve timing　气门正时
valvetrain　气门组
variable valve timing　可变气门正时
wrist pin　活塞销

2.12 ENGINE PERFORMANCE & TROUBLESHSOOTING 发动机性能和诊断

backfire 回火
backpressure 背压
blowby 漏气
bold start 冷启动
compression test 压缩检测
detonation 爆震
diagnostic flow chart 诊断流程图
dieseling 柴油机化
fault codes 故障码
flash codes 闪码
fuel starvation 缺油
gas line freeze 汽油管结冻
hesitation 喘抖
idle mixture 怠速混合气
idle speed 怠速
ignition pattern 点火图型
ignition timing 点火正时
intake vacuum 进气真空
jump start 跨接线连接启动
misfire 缺火
oil consumption 机油消耗
overheating 过热
peak firing voltage 峰值点火电压
power balance test 功率平衡测试
raster pattern 光栅
secondary ignition pattern 次级点火图型
stalling 失速
trouble codes 故障码
tune-up 调整

2.13 EXHAUST SYSTEM 排气系统

catalytic converter 催化转化器
exhaust manifold 排气歧管
exhaust manifold gasket 排气歧管垫
exhaust pipe 排气管
heat shields 热防护层
muffler 消声器
pipe hanger 排气管吊架
resonator 谐振器
tailpipe 排气管

2.14 FUEL SYSTEM 燃油系统

accelerator pump 加速泵
air bleeds 放气
air/fuel ratio 空燃比
carburetor 化油器
choke 阻风门
electric fuel pump 电动燃油泵
electronic fuel injection (EFI) 电子燃油喷射
feedback carburetor 反馈式化油器
fuel bowl 燃油浮子室
fuel filter 燃油滤清器
fuel injector 喷油器
fuel inlet needle valve 燃油进油针阀
fuel jets 燃油量孔

fuel pressure regulator 油压调节器
fuel pump 燃油泵
fuel rail 蓄油管
fuel sending unit 燃油传感器
float 浮子
idle air control (IAC) motor 怠速空气控制电机
idle jets 怠速喷嘴
intercooler 中间冷却器
lean mixture 稀混合气
main jets 主喷嘴
mass airflow EFI system 空气流量式电子燃油喷射系统
mechanical fuel pump 机械油泵
multiport fuel injection (MPI or MFI) 多点燃油喷射
port fuel injection (PFI) 进气口燃油喷射
rich mixture 浓混合气
supercharger 增压器
throttle 节气门
throttle body injection (TBI) 节气门体喷射
throttle kicker solenoid 节气门强制降挡电磁线圈
throttle linkage 节气门拉杆
throttle return spring 节气门回位弹簧
throttle stop 节气门挡块
turbocharger 涡轮增压器
waste gate 废气门

2.15 IGNITION SYSTEM 点火系统

ballast resistor 镇流电阻
breaker plate 断电盘
breaker points 断电触点
centrifugal advance 离心提前
coil-on-plug ignition 点火线圈和火花塞一体的点火
direct ignition system 直接点火系统
distributor 分电器
distributorless ignition system (DIS) 无分电器式点火系统
electrode 电极
electronic ignition 电子点火
electronic spark timing (EST) 电子点火正时
high energy ignition (HEI) 高能点火
ignition cables 点火导线
ignition coil 点火线圈
ignition module 点火模块
ignition pickup 点火传感器
ignition switch 点火开关
primary ignition circuit 初级点火电路
primary voltage 初级电压
radio frequency interference (RFI) 射频干扰
rotor 转子
secondary ignition circuit 次级点火电路
secondary voltage 次级电压
spark advance 点火提前
spark gap 火花间隙
spark plug 火花塞
spark retard 火花延迟
timing advance 正时提前
vacuum advance 真空提前

2.16 LUBRICANTS 润滑剂

automatic transmission fluid (ATF) 自动变速箱用油
gear lube 齿轮润滑剂
motor oil 机油

synthetic grease　合成润滑脂
synthetic oil　合成机油
viscosity　黏度
wheel bearing grease　车轮轴承润滑脂

2.17　SAFETY 安全

air bags　气囊
crash sensors　撞击传感器
crush zone　挤压区
energy absorbers　吸能装置
passive restraint system　被动限制系统
seat belts　安全带
seat belt retractors　安全带收缩器
supplemental inflation restraint（SIR）　辅助膨胀约束
supplemental restraint system（SRS）　辅助约束系统

2.18　STEERING，SUSPENSION & CHASSIS 转向，悬架和底盘

air springs　空气弹簧
air assist shocks　空气辅助减震器
ball joint　球铰接头
bias ply tire　斜交轮胎
body control module（BCM）　车身控制模块
bushings　衬套
coil springs　螺旋弹簧
control arm　控制臂
electronic ride control　电子行驶控制
four wheel steering（4WS）　四轮转向
gas pressurized shocks　气压式减震器
hub nut　轮毂螺帽
inflation pressure　充气压力
idler arm　空转臂
leaf springs　钢板弹簧
parallelogram steering　转向平行四边形
MacPherson struts　麦佛逊柱
monotube shocks　单管式减震器
oversteer　过度转向
pitman arm　转向垂臂
power steering　动力转向
rack & pinion steering　齿轮齿条式转向
radial tire　子午线轮胎
rebound　回弹
recirculating ball steering　循环球转向
spindle　心轴
struts　立柱
sway bar　横向稳定杆
temporary spare tire　临时备用胎
tie rod　横拉杆
tie rod end　横拉杆末端
tires　轮胎
torsion bar　扭力杆
understeer　转向不足
valve stems　阀杆
variable rate power steering　可变速度动力转向
variable rate springs　可变速比弹簧
wheel balancing　车轮平衡
wheel offset　车轮偏置距
wheel weights　车轮重量

2.19 TOOLS & EQUIPMENT 工具和设备

air compressor 空气压缩机
arc welder 电弧焊机
battery charger 蓄电池充电器
battery load tester 蓄电池负荷测试仪
brake spoon 制动爪柄
breakout box 接线盒
chassis dynamometer 底盘测功器
dial indicator 千分表
diagnostic computer 诊断计算机
digital storage oscilloscope (DSO) 数字储存示波仪
digital volt/ohm meter (DVOM) 数字电压/电阻表
dynamometer 测功机
engine dynamometer 发动机测功机
exhaust analyzer 废气分析仪
flaring tool 扩口工具
ignition scope 点火示波器
impact wrench 气动扳手
MIG welder (metal inert gas) 金属惰性气体焊接机
ohmmeter 电阻表
oscilloscope 示波器
oxy/acetylene welder 氧/乙炔焊接机
pinout box 管脚引出线盒
pipe bender 弯管机
pipe expander 扩管机
plasma cutter 等离子切割机
ratchet wrench 棘轮扳手
scan tool 扫描工具
test light 测试灯
TIG welder (tungsten inert gas) 钨惰性气体焊接机
timing light 正时灯
torque wrench 扭矩扳手
vacuum gauge 真空表
voltmeter 电压表

2.20 MISC. 其他

CAFE (corporate average fuel economy) 全体平均燃油经济性
cetane 十六烷
MPG (mils per gallon) 每加仑汽油可行驶英里数
octane 辛烷
OSHA (occupation health & safety administration) 职业安全和健康署
PM (preventive maintenance) 预防保养
rebuilt parts 修复件
remanufactured parts 修复件
SUV Sport Utility Vehicle 运动型多用途车
TDC (top dead center) 上死点
VIN (vehicle identification number) 车辆识别号码
warranty 保修

参 考 文 献
REFERENCES

1. James D. Halderman. Automotive Technology. Prentice Hall; 4th edition, 2012
2. David A. Crolla. Automotive Engineering Powertrain, Chassis System and Vehicle Body. Butterworth-Heinemann. 2009
3. Naunheimer, Harald. Automotive Transmissions-Fundamentals, Selection, Design and Aplication. Springer Verlag. 2010
4. T. K. GARRETT. The Motor Vehicle. Thirteenth Edition Butterworth-Hcincnmann. 2001
5. Julian Happian Smith. An Introduction to Modern Vehicle Design. Butterworth-Hcincnmann. 2002
6. http://auto.howstuffworks.com
7. http://www.icarumba.

前　言

党的二十大提出：全面推进乡村振兴。乡村旅游是实现乡村振兴的重要途径之一。

目前乡村旅游在发展过程中存在着诸多问题，旅游发展规划先行，乡村旅游发展急需从方法和实践方面获得支持，以推动乡村旅游的可持续发展。

目前将乡村旅游规划方法和案例实践相结合的著作还为数不多，编著者在高校多年一直从事旅游规划的教学科研工作，也主持了多项关于乡村旅游规划实践的横向课题，此次就从镇域和村域层面选取较为典型的蒋集镇和布金山景区所在的小王村进行实践案例剖析。"麻雀虽小，五脏俱全"，希望通过两个典型实践案例的剖析，总结出普适性的实现乡村旅游可持续发展的规律，为乡要旅游规划教学科研和实践方面提供借鉴参考。

本书将多年来的规划教学、规划科研和规划实践相结合，对于乡村旅游的可持续发展具有一定参考价值。在框架内容方面，本书分为两大部分，第一部分是方法篇——乡村旅游规划，主要对乡村旅游发展和乡村旅游规划的相关内容进行论述总结。其中，乡村旅游发展主要从乡村旅游发展背景、乡村旅游概念内涵与特征、乡村旅游发展历程与发展模式、我国乡村旅游存在问题与发展趋势、乡村旅游经营模式选择等方面进行论述；乡村旅游规划主要从乡村旅游规划概念、乡村旅游规划理论支撑与规划依据、乡村旅游规划原则和研究进展、乡村旅游规划技术路线与规划内容、乡村旅游规划过程中的社区参与和产品开发规划、乡村旅游设施与生态环境保护规划等方面进行论述。第二部分是实践篇——乡村旅游规划案例，选取典型镇域的蒋集镇和典型村域的小王村进行案例解析。

由于编著者能力有限，本书难免出现不足之处，还望读者不吝指正！

编著者
2023 年 12 月于泰山学院

目 录

方法篇 乡村旅游规划

第一章 绪论 … 3

一、乡村振兴战略 … 3
二、乡村旅游是乡村振兴的重要途径之一 … 3
三、乡村旅游将升级为国内旅游基础工程 … 4
四、乡村旅游需求日益增长 … 4

第二章 乡村旅游概念及发展状况 … 5

第一节 乡村旅游发展背景 … 5
一、乡村旅游发展政策背景 … 5
二、乡村旅游发展市场背景 … 8
第二节 乡村旅游概念与特征 … 9
一、乡村旅游的概念 … 9
二、乡村旅游特征 … 10
第三节 乡村旅游的发展历程与发展模式 … 11
一、乡村旅游的发展历程 … 11
二、乡村旅游发展模式 … 12
第四节 我国乡村旅游需要改进的方面与发展趋势 … 14
一、我国乡村旅游需要改进的方面 … 14
二、乡村旅游的发展趋势 … 15
第五节 乡村旅游经营管理模式 … 16
一、"农户+农户"模式 … 17
二、"公司+农户"模式 … 17
三、"公司+社区+农户"模式 … 18
四、公司制模式 … 18
五、股份制模式 … 18

六、"政府+公司+农户"模式 19
七、"个体+农庄"模式 19
八、"村委会+旅游合作社+投资商(引进外来旅游开发商)"模式 19
九、"整体租赁+制度保障"模式 19
十、"公司+村委会+农户"模式 20

第三章 乡村旅游规划的概念与内容　21

第一节　乡村旅游规划概念 21
一、旅游规划概念与类型 21
二、乡村旅游规划的含义 22

第二节　乡村旅游规划的理论支撑与规划依据 23
一、乡村旅游规划的理论支撑 23
二、乡村旅游规划依据 28

第三节　乡村旅游规划原则与研究进展 31
一、乡村旅游规划原则 31
二、乡村旅游规划研究进展 34

第四节　乡村旅游规划的技术路线与核心内容 38
一、乡村旅游规划技术路线 38
二、乡村旅游规划的核心内容 40

第五节　乡村旅游规划过程中的社区参与和产品开发规划 43
一、乡村旅游规划过程中的社区参与 43
二、乡村旅游产品开发规划 45

第六节　乡村旅游设施与生态环境保护规划 48
一、乡村旅游设施规划 48
二、乡村旅游生态环境保护规划 51

实践篇　乡村旅游规划案例

第四章　山东宁阳蒋集镇旅游发展总体规划　55

第一节　规划总论 55
一、规划性质 55
二、规划范围 55
三、规划原则 55
四、指导思想 56
五、规划分期 56

第二节　规划综合分析 57

一、上位规划分析 ·· 57
　　　二、区域旅游发展格局分析 ······································ 59
　　　三、发展条件分析 ·· 59
　　　四、旅游资源分析 ·· 60
　　　五、旅游市场分析 ·· 65
　　　六、旅游发展 SWOT 分析 ······································· 66
　第三节　规划战略定位 ·· 69
　　　一、规划发展战略 ·· 69
　　　二、规划发展定位 ·· 71
　第四节　空间布局规划 ·· 73
　　　一、空间结构规划 ·· 73
　　　二、项目体系规划 ·· 74
　　　三、项目规划布点 ·· 74
　第五节　分区项目规划 ·· 76
　　　一、友邦田园（齐鲁彩山研学旅游小镇）研学核心组团 ······· 76
　　　二、南部彩山森林康体养生组团 ································ 77
　　　三、南部历史感悟与滨湖休闲组团 ····························· 79
　　　四、中部智慧农业与工业观光研学组团 ······················· 80
　　　五、西北黄恩彤文化研学体验组团 ····························· 81
　　　六、北部汶河白鹭湿地研学游憩组团 ·························· 82
　　　七、北部三农文化研学组团 ····································· 86
　第六节　道路交通与配套服务设施规划 ······························· 89
　　　一、道路交通系统规划 ··· 89
　　　二、旅游线路系统规划 ··· 91
　　　三、配套服务设施规划 ··· 93
　第七节　旅游产业要素规划 ··· 94
　　　一、旅游住宿规划 ·· 94
　　　二、旅游餐饮规划 ·· 95
　　　三、文化娱乐规划 ·· 97
　　　四、旅游商品规划 ·· 98
　第八节　环境保护与安全系统规划 ····································· 100
　　　一、旅游资源保护规划 ··· 100
　　　二、生态环境保护规划 ··· 101
　　　三、旅游安全系统规划 ··· 102
　第九节　市场营销规划与规划分期 ····································· 103
　　　一、市场营销规划 ·· 103
　　　二、运营模式 ·· 106
　　　三、规划分期 ·· 106

四、近期行动计划 …… 108

第五章　山东肥城小王村布金山景区旅游总体规划　109

第一节　规划总论 …… 109
第二节　发展条件分析 …… 109
　　一、上位规划分析 …… 109
　　二、区位条件分析 …… 110
　　三、资源本底分析 …… 110
　　四、市场条件分析 …… 114
　　五、旅游发展 SWOT 分析 …… 115
第三节　旅游发展战略与定位 …… 117
　　一、旅游发展思路 …… 117
　　二、旅游发展战略 …… 117
　　三、旅游发展定位 …… 117
第四节　旅游发展布局与分区 …… 118
　　一、旅游发展功能分区 …… 118
　　二、旅游发展项目体系 …… 119
　　三、旅游发展分区规划 …… 120
第五节　旅游专项系统规划 …… 126
　　一、道路交通系统规划 …… 126
　　二、旅游服务设施规划 …… 127
　　三、环卫设施系统规划 …… 128
　　四、旅游解说系统规划 …… 129
第六节　运营体系规划与效益分析 …… 130
　　一、运营模式 …… 130
　　二、营销体系 …… 130
　　三、规划分期 …… 133
　　四、效益分析 …… 134

参考文献　135

方法篇
乡村旅游规划

第一章 绪论

一、乡村振兴战略

乡村振兴战略是习近平总书记2017年在党的十九大报告中提出的战略。实施乡村振兴战略，是党的十九大作出的重大决策部署，是决胜全面建成小康社会、全面建设社会主义现代化国家的重大历史任务，是新时代"三农"工作的总抓手。习近平总书记在参加十三届全国人大一次会议山东代表团审议时，全面阐述了乡村振兴战略，就推动乡村产业振兴、人才振兴、文化振兴、生态振兴、组织振兴作出重要指示，要求山东充分发挥农业大省优势，打造乡村振兴的齐鲁样板。

2017年党的十九大提出实施乡村振兴战略，2018年中央一号文件公布全面部署实施乡村振兴战略。文件指出了"我国发展不平衡不充分问题在乡村最为突出""实施乡村振兴战略，是解决人民日益增长的美好生活需要和不平衡不充分的发展之间矛盾的必然要求，是实现'两个一百年'奋斗目标的必然要求，是实现全体人民共同富裕的必然要求"。

为贯彻落实党的十九大、中央经济工作会议、中央农村工作会议精神和政府工作报告要求，科学有序推动乡村产业、人才、文化、生态和组织振兴，中共中央、国务院编制印发了《乡村振兴战略规划（2018—2022年）》。到2022年，乡村振兴的制度框架和政策体系初步健全。到2035年，乡村振兴取得决定性进展，农业农村现代化基本实现。到2050年，乡村全面振兴，农业强、农村美、农民富全面实现。

二、乡村旅游是乡村振兴的重要途径之一

党的十九大报告中首次提出实施乡村振兴战略，成为我国新时代"三农"工作的总抓手，同时围绕乡村振兴提出了"产业兴旺、生态宜居、乡风文明、治理有效、生活富裕"的总要求。乡村振兴目标的实现需要有关联性强、城乡统筹发展、持续增长的产业作为支撑。而乡村旅游作为连接城市和乡村的纽带和重要的旅游业态，在推动社会资源和文明成果在城乡之间的共享以及财富重新分配、促进农村经济发展、解决农村人口就业、保护农村生态环境、最终实现共同富裕等方面作用显著，成为乡村振兴的重要引擎。

三、乡村旅游将升级为国内旅游基础工程

乡村旅游业因可实现城乡需求与供给的有效对接、城乡统筹协调发展，增强农村经济的可持续发展能力，成为我国旅游发展中的重要组成部分。2009年，住房和城乡建设部和国家旅游局开展全国特色景观旅游名镇（村）示范工作；2010年，农业部和国家旅游局共同推进休闲农业与乡村旅游发展合作等。

休闲农业与乡村旅游连接农民与市民、城市与乡村、产地和销地，是贯穿农村一、二、三产业，融合生产、生活和生态功能，紧密连结农业、农产品加工业、服务业的新型产业形态和新型消费业态，是发展现代农业与促进旅游产业转型升级的重要载体。

四、乡村旅游需求日益增长

近年来，随着我国社会经济的不断发展和带薪休假制度的推行，人们的可支配收入和闲暇时间不断增加，人们参与休闲旅游的能力和愿望大大提高，促进了我国旅游业的迅速崛起，旅游产品也呈现出多元化的发展趋势。在游客出游半径缩减时，乡村旅游由于决策时间短、易抵达而得到快速发展。乡村旅游的发展，满足了返璞归真、回归自然、放松身心的旅游需求，深得城市游客的喜爱。

第二章
乡村旅游概念及发展状况

第一节 乡村旅游发展背景

一、乡村旅游发展政策背景

(一) 国家层面政策背景

1. "两山"理论

"两山"理论:"我们过去讲,既要绿水青山,又要金山银山。其实,绿水青山就是金山银山。"

2005年8月15日,时任浙江省委书记的习近平在安吉县余村考察时,首次提出"绿水青山就是金山银山"的重要理念。

(1) 十九大报告开启生态文明建设新时代

继"生态文明建设"写入十八大党章后,大量明晰、可操作的生态环境保护细节,首次出现在十九大报告中。"美丽中国"一词,在十九大报告中三次出现。

十九大报告中提出:"建设生态文明是中华民族永续发展的千年大计。必须树立和践行绿水青山就是金山银山的理念,坚持节约资源和保护环境的基本国策,像对待生命一样对待生态环境,统筹山水林田湖草系统治理,实行最严格的生态环境保护制度,形成绿色发展方式和生活方式,坚定走生产发展、生活富裕、生态良好的文明发展道路,建设美丽中国,为人民创造良好生产生活环境,为全球生态安全作出贡献。"

(2) 绿水青山就是金山银山

"我们既要绿水青山,也要金山银山。宁要绿水青山,不要金山银山,而且绿水青山就是金山银山。"

要按照绿色发展理念,树立大局观、长远观、整体观,坚持保护优先,坚持节约资源和保护环境的基本国策,把生态文明建设融入经济建设、政治建设、文化建设、社会建设各方面和全过程,建设美丽中国,努力开创社会主义生态文明新时代。

2. 大力发展全域旅游,大力发展"旅游+""+旅游"

全域旅游是指在一定区域内,以旅游业为优势产业,通过对区域内经济社会资源尤其是旅游资源、相关产业、生态环境、公共服务、体制机制、政策法规、文明素质等进行全方位、系统化的优化提升,实现区域资源有机整合、产业融合发展、社会共建共享,以旅游业带动和促进经济社会协调发展的一种新的区域协调发展理念和模式。

在全域旅游中,各行业积极融入其中,各部门齐抓共管,全体居民参与,充分利用目的地全部的吸引物要素,为前来旅游的游客提供全过程、全时空的体验产品,从而全面地满足游客的全方位体验需求。

3. 《国务院关于促进旅游业改革发展的若干意见》推动旅游业转型升级

2014年8月21日,《国务院关于促进旅游业改革发展的若干意见》正式发布,这是继《国务院关于加快发展旅游业的意见》、《国民旅游休闲纲要(2013—2020年)》和《中华人民共和国旅游法》颁布实施以来,党中央、国务院对旅游业改革发展做出的又一重大部署。该文件为促进旅游业持续健康发展提出了整体政策安排,对实现两大战略目标具有重要意义。该文件提出,抓紧研究新形势下中央财政支持旅游业发展的相关政策,做好国家旅游宣传推广、规划编制、人才培养和旅游公共服务体系建设。

① 旅游业发展的新空间。积极发展休闲度假旅游,大力发展乡村旅游,创新文化旅游产品,积极开展研学旅行,大力发展老年旅游,扩大旅游购物消费,以业态丰富的产品满足日益增长的消费需求。

② 乡村旅游发展的新思路。推动乡村旅游与新型城镇化有机结合,合理利用民族村寨、古村古镇,发展有历史记忆、地域特色、民族特点的旅游小镇,建设一批特色景观旅游名镇名村。

③ 旅游业发展的新政策。切实落实职工带薪休假制度;加强旅游基础设施建设;加大财政金融扶持;优化土地利用政策;加强人才队伍建设。

4. "田园综合体"必将成为乡村振兴的主旋律

2017年2月5日,"田园综合体"作为乡村新型产业发展的亮点措施被写进中央一号文件。文件提出:支持有条件的乡村建设以农民合作社为主要载体、让农民充分参与和受益,集循环农业、创意农业、农事体验于一体的田园综合体,通过农业综合开发、农村综合改革转移支付等渠道开展试点示范。

田园综合体是集现代农业、休闲旅游、田园社区于一体的乡村综合发展模式,目的是通过旅游助力农业发展,促进三产融合,是一种可持续性模式。

5. "美丽乡村"建设全面展开,奠定了乡村旅游的基础

为全面贯彻落实党的十八大精神,响应"美丽中国"建设目标,2013年中央一号文件第一次提出了要建设"美丽乡村"的奋斗目标,进一步加强农村生态建设、环境保护和综合整治工作。农业部也把建设美丽乡村、改善农村生态环境作为2013年农业农村经济重点工作之一。"美丽乡村"建设的全面展开,为乡村旅游的开展奠定了坚实的基础。党的二十大提出建设宜居宜业和美乡村。从建设社会主义新农村,到建设美丽乡村,再到建设和美乡村,既是乡村建设的"版本升级",更是乡村发展的"美丽蜕变"。

6. 供给侧结构性改革,提升经济增长的质量和数量

供给侧结构性改革,就是用增量改革促存量调整,在增加投资过程中优化投资结构、产业结构开源疏流,在经济可持续高速增长的基础上实现经济可持续发展与人民生活水平不断提高；就是优化产权结构，国进民进、政府宏观调控与民间活力相互促进；就是优化投融资结构，促进资源整合，实现资源优化配置与优化再生；就是优化产业结构、提高产业质量，优化产品结构、提升产品质量；就是优化分配结构，实现公平分配，使消费成为生产力；就是优化流通结构，节省交易成本，提高有效经济总量；就是优化消费结构，实现消费品不断升级，不断提高人民生活品质，实现创新-协调-绿色-开放-共享的发展。

2016年1月26日中央财经领导小组第十二次会议，习近平总书记强调，供给侧结构性改革的根本目的是提高社会生产力水平，落实好以人民为中心的发展思想。2017年10月18日，习近平总书记在十九大报告中指出，深化供给侧结构性改革。

（二）山东层面政策背景

1. 全力打造乡村振兴齐鲁样板

山东省委、省政府深入贯彻落实习近平总书记对新时代山东工作的总要求，聚焦"两个走在前列、一个全面开创新局面"目标定位，坚定不移走中国特色社会主义乡村振兴道路，把标准化理念贯穿乡村振兴全过程，全力打造乡村振兴齐鲁样板，绘就多样化的"齐鲁风情画"，形成具有山东特色的现代版"富春山居图"。

2. 提升旅游产业的品质，大力发展优质旅游

党的十九大报告指出，我国经济已由高速增长阶段转向高质量发展阶段，正处在转变发展方式、优化经济结构、转换增长动力的攻关期，建设现代化经济体系是跨越关口的迫切要求和我国发展的战略目标。大力发展优质旅游，要大幅度提升旅游产业的品质。之前旅游发展解决的是"有没有"的问题，现在要解决"不满意"问题。发展优质旅游，第一，要继续打造核心吸引物，打造具备文化象征的标志物、发展城市综合体和乡村旅游综合体，设计具有标志性的大型节庆活动等；第二，要发展丰富的业态，以充分满足游客的要求；第三，要大力推行"标准化"，制定并落实餐饮、住宿安全和卫生的标准，加大查处的力度，聘请社会成员、媒体明察暗访，并多部门联合执法检查，大力量落实"标准化"，将标准化覆盖全部的旅游产业、旅游行业。

3. 新旧动能转换助推经济转型升级

2017年5月，国家旅游局正式批复山东省为国家全域旅游示范省创建单位。省政府编制了《山东省全域旅游发展总体规划（2018—2025年）》，将发展全域旅游列入了新旧动能转换十大工程。山东新旧动能转换综合试验区是党的十九大后获批的首个区域性国家发展战略，也是我国第一个以新旧动能转换为主题的区域发展战略。山东新旧动能转换综合试验区位于山东省全境，包括济南、青岛、烟台三大核心城市，14个设区市的国家和省级经济技术开发区、高新技术产业开发区以及海关特殊监管区域，形成"三核引领、多点突破、融合互动"的新旧动能转换总体布局。

以泰安市为例，全市布局人工智能、生命健康、信息技术等未来产业，壮大高端装备制造、文化旅游体育、新能源等新兴产业，改造建材、化工、纺织等传统产业，打造彰显泰山魅力的国际著名旅游目的地城市和智能绿色低碳发展示范区。

4. 山东省政府出台加快乡村旅游发展的重要政策

山东省政府相继召开不同方面、不同层次、不同形式的重要会议，专题研究乡村旅游工作。山东省出台了《关于提升旅游业综合竞争力加快建成旅游强省的意见》，把发展乡村旅游摆上重要位置，主要指标年均增长20%以上，有关乡村旅游的内容占了四分之一的篇幅，足见山东蓄势发展乡村旅游的决心。

二、乡村旅游发展市场背景

1. 中国进入休闲时代，休闲旅游成为一种生活方式

2018年，我国人均GDP达到了1万美元，中国休闲旅游时代已经到来，休闲旅游成为民众主要的旅游形式，更成为一种新的生活方式。因此，匹配市场需求，供给侧必须实现从单一观光旅游向复合型休闲旅游的转型，形成观光、休闲、度假、康体、文化体验等多元休闲产业链。

2. 节假日短途休闲度假需求持续增长

随着城镇居民收入的不断增加，旅游消费能力也不断提升，加之居民充裕的闲暇时间，使人们拥有了越来越多可自由支配的短假期，于是近郊游逐步发展起来。节假日到近郊区休闲度假，远离城市的喧嚣，在田园环境中放松身心，感悟生活，成为一种生活方式。与此同时，随着游客需求的多元化，游客对旅游产品的质量要求也不断提高，生态化、个性化、特色化、主体化、非标准化的休闲产品将成为市场需求的热点。乡村旅游、滨水休闲、运动休闲、研学科普、文化体验、康养度假等主题休闲产品成为城市周边休闲度假旅游目的地发展的重要方向。

3. 研学旅游市场大有可为

研学旅游正处在大有可为的发展机遇期，研学与其他业态融合将成为未来的发展重点。

（1）研学的政策背景

2016年11月，教育部、国家发展和改革委员会等11部门联合印发《关于推进中小学生研学旅行的意见》，随后教育部发布《中小学综合实践活动课程指导纲要》，研学旅行纳入小学、初中、高中阶段的必修课。"研学＋旅行"有益补充了学校和家庭的教育，是实施素质教育的重要载体。

（2）研学旅行在国内方兴未艾

教育部等11部门推出《关于推进中小学研学旅行的意见》之后，研学旅行迎来了爆发式的增长。学校每学年组织安排1~2次研学旅行活动，每学年合计安排研学旅行活动：小学3~4天、初中4~6天、高中6~8天。随着研学旅行被纳入教学计划，研学旅行逐渐成为刚需，未来3~5年研学旅行市场需求会迅速提升。

国内游学即将进入4.0时代,未来5~10年将达到千亿的规模,教育旅游产业发展潜力巨大。

4. 养生养老市场值得关注

城市居民普遍开始关注养生,身体和心灵的双重养生越来越受到追捧,养生市场需求庞大,亟待满足。超过90%的游客愿意体验养生游,并注重"修身养性及生活方式体验"。

截至2018年底,全国60岁及以上老年人口23086万人,占总人口的16.7%,其中65岁及以上人口15003万人,占总人口的10.8%。预计到2030年,我国老年人口消费规模将达到8.6万亿元。

5. 济南省会城市群经济圈客源充足,市民出游率高

济南省会城市群经济基础良好,2020年省会城市群地区生产总值超过3.5万亿元,年均增长9%左右;城市功能明显强化,区域"一小时生活圈"更趋完善。济南省会城市群消费客群为旅游提供了充足的客源和良好的市场保障。因此,济南省会城市群市民是重要的旅游目标市场,市民的"富裕程度"等将直接影响城郊乡村旅游的发展层次、规模和质量。

第二节 乡村旅游概念与特征

一、乡村旅游的概念

乡村旅游是与都市旅游相对应的旅游形式,指以各种类型的乡村为背景,以乡村田园风光、乡村生活和乡村文化为旅游吸引物,以农业和农村特色资源为基础开发旅游产品,吸引游客前来观光游览、休闲度假、考察学习、参与体验的旅游活动。

由于世界各国对"乡村"概念的解释不同,目前对乡村旅游概念的界定尚未统一。

对于乡村旅游的概念,较典型的定义是英国Gannon以及Bramwe和Lane分别做出的。前者认为乡村旅游是指农民或乡村居民出于经济目的,为吸引旅游者前来旅游而提供的广泛的活动、服务和令人愉快事物的统称。后者认为乡村旅游不仅是基于农业的旅游活动,而是一个多层面的旅游活动,它除了包括基于农业的假日旅游外,还包括特殊兴趣的自然旅游、生态旅游,如步行、登山和骑马等旅游活动,探险、运动和健康旅游活动,打猎和钓鱼旅游活动,教育性旅游活动,文化与传统旅游活动,以及一些区域的民俗旅游活动。

近年来国内的研究中,学者们已经总结出更准确的定义。何景明和李立华对国内外诸多概念、定义进行详细分析后,认为狭义的乡村旅游是指在乡村地区,以具有乡村性的自然和人文客体为旅游吸引物的旅游活动。唐代剑和池静通过系统梳理,从乡村旅游发生的场所、凭借的资源,乡村旅游的特点,乡村旅游的本质特征(乡村性),乡村旅游与其他几个重要概念的关系入手,认为乡村旅游是一种凭借城市周边以及比较偏远地带的自然资源和人文资源,面向城市居民开发的集参与性、娱乐性、享受性、科技性于一体的休闲旅游产品,它的本质特性是乡土性。

刘德谦通过对乡村旅游、农业旅游和民俗旅游几个概念的辨析,认为乡村旅游的核心内容应该是乡村风情(乡村的风土人情);乡村旅游就是以乡村地域及农事相关的风土、风物、风俗、风景组合而成的乡村风情为吸引物,吸引旅游者前往休息、观光、体验及学习等的旅游活动。

二、乡村旅游特征

(1) 乡土性

乡村旅游地区古朴的村庄、原始的劳作形态、真实的民风民俗、土生的农副产品形成了"古、始、真、土"的特质,具有城镇无可比拟的贴近自然的优势,为游客回归自然、感受乡土创造了优越条件。

(2) 多元性

中国的乡村旅游资源大多以自然风貌、劳作形态、农家生活和传统习俗为主,这些资源受到季节、气候等多重元素的影响,呈现出地域的差异性和多样性,为多元化乡村旅游产品打造奠定了基础。

(3) 参与体验性

乡村旅游能够吸引旅游者的特色之处就在于所开展的各类体验性旅游项目,包括劳作、垂钓、划船、喂养、采摘、加工等参与性活动,这些活动往往是农村日常生活的一部分。通过丰富的体验活动,游客能更好地融入乡村旅游的全过程,对农家的生活状态、乡土民情有更深入的了解。

(4) 文化性

乡村的各种民俗节庆、工艺美术、民间建筑、民间文艺、婚俗禁忌、趣事传说等具有深厚的文化底蕴,是乡村旅游产品核心部分,对于城镇游客而言,具有强大的文化吸引力。

(5) 可持续性

乡村旅游的可持续性主要体现在农业和旅游的融合发展,农业丰富旅游活动内容,旅游向农业产业延伸和服务,推进农业转型升级。此外,乡村旅游着重关注旅游者体验、社区居民利益和乡村发展进步,实现乡村社区和乡村旅游的可持续发展。

(6) 经济性

乡村旅游资源大都依赖现有的农业资源、民俗资源等,且经营主体大部分是农民,不需要大量投资就可获得可观的经济收益。

第三节 乡村旅游的发展历程与发展模式

一、乡村旅游的发展历程

(一) 国外乡村旅游发展历程

国外乡村旅游萌芽于19世纪中叶的欧洲,但真正意义上的大众化的乡村旅游则起源于20世纪60年代的西班牙。由于工业化与城镇化的加快,城市居民开始向往和追求乡村宁静的田园生活和美好的自然环境,在市场需求的推动下,西班牙政府将废弃的古城堡改造成为农舍,并把规模较大的农庄也列入供游客旅游参观的区域,接待乡村观光的旅游者,乡村旅游应运而生。但在这个时期,乡村旅游者的人数较少,还没有真正意义上的为旅游者专门服务的乡村旅游设施,乡村旅游处于初级发展阶段。在20世纪70年代,由于铁路等交通设施的快速发展,城市与乡村地区的通达性得到改善,旅游者的可进入性增强,这促使了乡村旅游在许多国家广泛开展,并显示出极强的生命力和发展潜力。在20世纪80年代,全球绿色运动的掀起,推动了乡村旅游的快速发展,并使之成为发达国家现代旅游者的重要选择之一。在20世纪90年代,乡村旅游已成为生态旅游的一个重要组成部分,在世界旅游组织大力推动和鼓励下,乡村旅游开始由发达国家向发展中国家扩展,成为振兴地方经济的重要手段。

总体而言,乡村旅游在各国的发展虽然在时间、内容和形式上不尽相同,但其发展背景都十分相似,主要有两方面的原因。第一,城市化和现代化的推进,使人们产生了回归自然的心理需求;第二,工业的高速发展,使农业和农村地区逐渐被边缘化。

在这种状况下,各国政府为提高农民收入、拓宽农业功能、改善农村面貌,面对城市居民的乡村旅游需求,实施一系列的推动农业、农村发展的有力措施。

(二) 国内乡村旅游发展历程

1. 初创阶段 (自发阶段)

此阶段为20世纪80年代中后期至1994年,这一阶段为农家乐兴起的阶段。1986年,成都"徐家大院"的诞生标志着"农家乐"旅游模式拉开了乡村旅游的序幕。

2. 全面发展阶段

此阶段为1995—2001年。乡村假日经济蓬勃兴起。1995年"中国民俗风情游"旅游主题与"中国:56个民族的家"宣传口号带游客深入少数民族风情区;1998年"中国华夏城乡游"旅游主题与"现代城乡,多彩生活"宣传口号吸引大批旅游者来到乡村旅游。

3. 纵深发展阶段

此阶段为 2002—2006 年。2002 年，我国颁布了《全国农业旅游示范点、工业旅游示范点检查标准（试行）》，标志着我国乡村旅游开始走向规范化、品质化。2006 年旅游主题为"中国乡村游"，将乡村旅游的角色提到了更突出的位置，"新农村、新旅游、新体验、新时尚"全面推动乡村旅游提升发展。

4. 可持续发展阶段

此阶段为 2007 年至今。2007 年，"中国和谐城乡游"和"魅力乡村、活力城市、和谐中国"的提出推动了农村风貌整体提升。同年，国家旅游局和农业部联合发布了《关于大力推进全国乡村旅游发展的通知》，进一步推动乡村旅游发展。2008 年，《中共中央关于推进农村改革发展若干重大问题的决定》使乡村旅游的经营模式更加科学化。2009 年，《关于加快发展旅游业的意见》提出乡村旅游富民工程。2013 年，《关于加快发展现代农业进一步增强农村发展活力的若干意见》的发布和《国民休闲纲要》的出台对乡村旅游的发展提供了有力的政策支撑。

二、乡村旅游发展模式

（一）国外乡村旅游发展模式

根据乡村旅游开发项目、游客的旅游动机来划分，将国外乡村旅游划分为三种主要类型，观光型乡村旅游、休闲型乡村旅游、文化型乡村旅游。

（1）观光型乡村旅游

以乡村绿色景观和田园风光及独特的农业生产过程为核心吸引物，以参观特色农场、品尝农产品等为主要活动。观光型乡村旅游又细分为传统型乡村旅游和科技型乡村旅游，其中传统型乡村旅游以特色农产品生产过程为主要卖点，典型代表为澳大利亚葡萄酒旅游、法国村庄旅游、韩国观光农园。科技型乡村旅游以现代高科技手段建立的小型农、林、牧生产基地为主要卖点，典型代表为新加坡农业科技公园、美国基因农场等。

（2）休闲型乡村旅游

休闲型乡村旅游主要满足旅游者的健康、娱乐、放松、享受等高层次需求，在产品特色上更加突出休闲度假主题，产品表现形式更加强调创新、互动以及知识性。休闲型乡村旅游又分为休闲娱乐型乡村旅游、康体疗养型乡村旅游、自我发展型乡村旅游。休闲娱乐型乡村旅游主要特点是娱乐性强、互动参与性大、表现形式新颖，典型代表为日本都市农场"务农"旅游、意大利"生态教育农业园"、美国采摘水果度假活动、美国西部的牧场务农旅游等。康体疗养型乡村旅游主要凸显产品的医疗保健功能，开发诸如体检、按摩、理疗等与健康相关的乡村度假项目，典型代表为古巴医疗旅游、日本温泉旅游、法国森林旅游、西班牙海滨旅游等。自我发展型乡村旅游主要提供轻松环境，通过团队合作交流、自主探索学习等方式，学习新知识，兼有娱乐和教育培训意义，典型代表为日本观鸟旅游、美国农场学校等。

(3) 文化型乡村旅游

以乡村民俗、乡村民族风情以及传统民族文化为主题，典型代表为匈牙利乡村文化旅游、西班牙城堡游等文化旅游线路。

从各国乡村旅游成长的协调机制划分，主要有政府推动型、市场驱动型和混合成长型三种。

(1) 政府推动型乡村旅游

把乡村旅游作为公益事业来发展，把社会效益放在经济效益之上，政府主导，参与规划、经营、管理与推销等活动。典型代表为爱尔兰和葡萄牙等国。

(2) 市场驱动型乡村旅游

由市场自动调节乡村旅游经济的成长和变动趋势。在自然生态保护方面政府往往进行规制和干预。各种民间团体、行业协会等非政府组织能起到行业自律和保护行业利益的作用。典型代表为美国佐治亚州。

(3) 混合成长型乡村旅游

初期政府主导干预作用较强，在资金、宣传、基础设施建设、培训、规划甚至管理方面普遍干预扶持。后期政府职能弱化，主要起监管的职能。主导力量方面把政府的干预机制与市场经济结合起来。典型代表为法国。

(二) 我国乡村旅游的发展模式

按照乡村旅游点依托的条件和分布的地区，乡村旅游可以分为三种类型：都市依托型、景区依托型和特色村寨型。

(1) 都市依托型乡村旅游

主要分布在大都市郊区及郊县，交通便利，依托都市客源市场，回头率高，一般为周末市场，以城市景观反差较大的乡村自然风光和高科技农园为特色，为城市居民提供餐饮、休闲等服务，满足周末休闲度假需求为主要功能，典型代表为四川农家乐、北京民俗村。

(2) 景区依托型乡村旅游

主要分布在大型景区周边乡村，依托周边大型景区的游客量和便利的交通发展。以乡村民俗文化和原生态乡村生活为吸引物，以民俗和农业特色鲜明的餐饮和娱乐活动为主，是大型景区的辅助旅游产品。典型代表为四川九寨沟周边乡村。

(3) 特色村寨型乡村旅游

主要分布在乡村风貌保存完整的偏远地区，依托极具特色的民俗文化或较大规模的特色景观资源，强调景观和文化的原始性，以民居观光、民俗体验等旅游项目为主。游客来源范围较广，停留时间较长。典型代表为桂林龙胜梯田、福建土楼等。

我国目前乡村旅游提供的产品主要有：观光型乡村旅游、休闲型乡村旅游、乡村民俗游、康乐型乡村旅游、参与型乡村旅游、研修求知型乡村旅游。观光型乡村旅游以乡村绿色景观和田园风光为吸引物；休闲型乡村旅游以乡村自然景观和生产生活方式、科技型的农场或渔场等为吸引物；乡村民俗游以乡村地区民俗文化、民族文化及乡土文化为吸引物；康乐型乡村旅游以乡村良好的自然环境和生活方式等所具有的康体、健身功能为吸引物；参与型乡村旅游以参与务农劳作为主的体验农家劳作生活为吸引物；研修求知型乡村旅游以通过参加农场作业、农村社区活动，获得农业生产相关知识和对自我意志和人格的塑造为吸引物。

第四节 我国乡村旅游需要改进的方面与发展趋势

一、我国乡村旅游需要改进的方面

乡村旅游对农村经济发展、环境改善和文化保护都发挥了一定的积极促进作用。但也存在乡村旅游产品初级化、景观类型单一、缺乏经济效益等问题。因此，如何保护性地开发乡村旅游，完善乡村旅游产品体系，增加乡村旅游景观的地方特色，防治环境污染是今后必须解决的问题。

整体上看，我国乡村旅游还应在以下几方面改进：

（1）改变产品开发粗放现状

与国外乡村旅游发展现状相比较，目前我国乡村旅游的整体开发仍处于低水平阶段，旅游产品开发粗放、方向不明确。主要表现在：①各种乡村资源未能充分有效利用，开发深度不够，许多乡村旅游产品只是在原有生产基础上稍加改动和表层开发，缺乏创新设计和深度加工；②乡村旅游产品雷同，体现在农家庭院的建筑样式、园林风格、室内陈设、菜肴品种、娱乐项目等都比较趋同，缺乏个性化特征。

（2）提高经营管理水平

受乡村土地相对分散、小规模经营、从业人员文化水平偏低等因素的制约，我国乡村旅游的总体经营管理水平不高，发展规模小、个体经营占主体、产业经济结构不健全、经济贡献较低。

乡村旅游经营管理水平低下，主要表现在：①乡村旅游管理人员管理经验不足，乡村旅游发展理念观念不新，对于乡村旅游的发展缺乏全局和长远考虑；②乡村旅游经营管理人员相对较少，从业人员缺乏系统有效的培训。

（3）加强整体规划

一些地区乡村旅游开发盲目性很大，由于没有进行顶层规划设计与建筑风貌控制，乡村旅游景区地域上分布较广，组织线路的难度较大，乡村旅游与传统旅游景点之间也缺乏有机联系，不能差异化联动发展。

（4）基础设施及环境建设有待完善

大部分乡村基础设施底子薄，公共服务配套供给不足。同时，乡村旅游存在

"散、小、弱"的发展问题,导致乡村旅游餐饮、住宿、文化、娱乐等配套层次低,甚至不健全,难以满足游客多样化、品质化的旅游消费需求。

有些乡村旅游区缺少必要的消防设施和医疗设施,厨房、厕所的卫生条件与预期标准相差甚远。

(5) 丰富产品体系,强化品牌影响

诸多乡村旅游停留在"吃农家饭、干农家活、住农家房"的开发阶段,缺乏特色产品创新。目前,大多数乡村旅游同质化严重,缺乏对于民间民俗文化和自身资源禀赋的挖掘,缺少市场开拓意识。

在品牌推广方面,我国乡村旅游发展中缺乏品牌意识、乡村旅游整体形象不佳、品牌缺乏个性;在市场营销方面,营销手段落后,销售渠道、促销方式相对单一。

未能有效利用新媒体进行推广营销,也没有包装形成自身的品牌,旅游产品与活动单一,降低了产品的吸引力和游客的重游率。

(6) 补充策划管理人才

乡村旅游项目往往是农户或乡村自己策划、规划、设计、运营,缺乏专业化策划、规划、设计、运营、招商、推广营销、投融资团队。

对整个乡村资源缺乏挖掘和包装,营销策略陈旧。同时,乡村旅游从业人员专业水平不够,未经过系统的培训,从业人员专业素质和服务质量较差。

(7) 资源整合、加强产业融合

我国乡村旅游正处于快速发展期,乡村旅游产业呈现高速增长。但在乡村旅游产品供给方面,高质量乡村旅游产品仍然稀少。目前田园综合体、现代农业庄园、农家乐、生态农庄、古镇村落等项目众多,但是精品标杆型项目缺乏,以观光为主,一站式休闲度假项目缺乏。同时,乡村旅游与其他相关产业资源整合融合力度较小,与现代农业、教育、文化、康养等产业融合度不够,产业链条较短。

二、乡村旅游的发展趋势

(1) 乡村旅游向精品化、个性化、产业化发展

在消费升级和产业升级趋势的推动下,未来乡村旅游向精品化、个性化、产业化方向发展。围绕着"乡村旅游+"为核心,形成涵盖现代农业、康养地产等多产业要素的产业生态圈,产业链不断向上下游延伸。同时乡村旅游业态和产品不断丰富和创新,如乡村市集、现代农业庄园、现代农场等。

(2) 共享经济、智慧旅游助力乡村旅游新发展

共享经济可有效盘活乡村闲置资源,提升旅游者乡村旅游体验,为乡村经济增长注入新的动力。目前发展较为成熟的共享经济模式是"共享农庄"模式,"共享农庄"是将农村闲置的住房进行个性化设计改造,在线上对外出租。据报道,北京已有众多农庄加入"共享农庄"。

在智慧旅游助力乡村旅游新发展方面，依托大数据、云计算、互联网、人工智能等新兴技术，使乡村旅游景区管理智能化、精细化，有效解决目前乡村旅游服务水平低、信息不对称等发展难点，为游客带来更加智能、便捷的旅游体验。

（3）乡村旅游产品多样化

北京都市圈、长三角、珠三角等经济发达地区，以及成都、西安等西部城市，乡村旅游产品日渐多元化。乡村旅游产品的多元化一方面基于大众化且多元化的乡村旅游市场需求；另一方面，乡村旅游经营业主在产品和经营模式等方面的不断创新也是乡村旅游产品多元化的重要推动力。例如，在北京郊区已经初步形成了"乡村民宿""采摘篱园""生态渔村""养生山吧""休闲农庄""休闲庄园"等新兴业态。在日趋激烈的乡村旅游竞争格局下，产品多样化的趋势将势必延续并强化。

（4）营销渠道多元化，新媒体营销成为新趋势

产品多样化的同时，乡村旅游的营销渠道日趋多元化，随着乡村旅游市场的进一步多元化和细化，营销渠道的创新与多元化已成为必然的趋势和要求，新媒体营销成本小、受众多、效力高，因此新媒体推广营销成为新趋势。

（5）融资渠道多样化

在乡村振兴战略政策的导引下，越来越多的投资主体进入乡村地区，融资渠道不断拓展。从投资主体看，目前主要有政府、投资商和当地居民；从融资渠道来看，有政府财政转移支付、权益融资（土地流转）、社会集资（专业合作社）、投资商投资、贴息贷款、小额贷款等。乡村旅游的发展及其转型升级都离不开资金的支持。因此，融资渠道多样化趋势还将进一步强化，也需要不断地创新投融资模式，拓展融资渠道，如成立乡村旅游产业发展基金，乡村旅游股权投资银行，乡村旅游融资担保公司等，为参与乡村旅游发展的企业和村民提供融资贷款、风险评估等服务，打通乡村旅游发展的投融资瓶颈。

第五节　乡村旅游经营管理模式

根据现代服务业与国内外成功先例，采取"政府＋区域运营商＋开发商＋农民"即（G＋1＋X＋Z）的开发模式，走"政府支持、农民主体、企业参与"的科学发展道路。

关于（G＋1＋X＋Z）的说明：G指地方政府；1指区域运营商；X指次级开发商；Z指广大农民。

① 政府支持是前提。在乡村旅游发展的新形势下，政府应大力支持以农业休闲、乡村接待为核心的发展之路，在整体发展规划、区域环境优化、基础设施建设、招商优惠政策、社会新农村建设方面发挥重要的支持作用。

② 企业参与是关键。很多乡村旅游项目的投资比较大，需要企业参与，因此需要一个区域运营商和次级的项目投资开发商共同推进乡村旅游的整体开发。

③ 农民主体是根本。第一，要充分让农民参与到休闲农业、旅游服务产业与民俗文化创意产业的发展中来，从前期的项目建设到后期的运营，都要优先考虑让当地农民参与，拓宽其就业渠道，切实增加其收入来源。第二，要结合社会主义新农村建设，鼓励并协助农民创新有机农产品的开发，服务于创意农业项目的开发，实现农业产业结构的升级，保证其可持续发展。

近些年，乡村旅游发展迅速，成为趋势亮点。随着乡村旅游的逐渐转型、提质升级，经营管理模式愈来愈发挥着独特而显著的作用。

乡村旅游经营管理的模式是根据旅游资源和客源市场来确定的，不同的资源禀赋和地域客源市场，经营管理的模式也不一样。模式是否科学合理，决定着旅游资源与客源市场的结合度，直接影响着乡村旅游可持续发展。

一、"农户＋农户"模式

这是乡村旅游初期阶段的经营模式。在远离市场的乡村，农民对企业介入乡村旅游开发普遍有一定的顾虑，甚至还有抵触情绪，多数农户不愿把有限的资金或土地交给公司来经营，生怕有什么闪失使其"陷"进去，他们更相信那些"示范户"。在这些山村里，通常是"示范户"首先开发乡村旅游获得了成功，在他们的示范带动下，农户们纷纷加入旅游接待的行列，并从中学习经验和技术，在短暂的磨合下，形成"农户＋农户"的乡村旅游开发模式。这种模式通常投入较少，接待量有限，但乡村文化保留得最真实，游客花费少还能体验到最真的本地习俗和文化。但受管理水平和资金投入的影响，通常旅游的带动效应有限。在当前乡村旅游竞争加剧的情况下，这种模式具有短平快优势。

二、"公司＋农户"模式

这一模式通过吸纳当地农民参与乡村旅游的经营与管理，在开发浓厚的乡村旅游资源时，充分利用农户闲置的资产、富余的劳动力、丰富的农事活动，开展旅游活动。同时，通过引进旅游公司的管理，对接待服务进行规范，避免因不良竞争而损害游客的利益。山东的竹泉村乡村旅游的开发与管理，便是典型。其特色在于公司或投资商，充分听取农户的意见和看法，广泛地吸引农户参与到经营与管理中。

这一模式中有些需要注意的问题。第一，公司或投资商与农户的合作是建立在一定的经济基础上的，受投资商实力影响较大；第二，农户的知识层次、素质、服务意识等还有待于进一步提高；第三，在内部经营管理中，如何进行游客的分流与分配，是能否顺利实施的关键之一。但这样模式往往依赖公司实力，同时农民分配利益有限。

三、"公司＋社区＋农户"模式

这一模式应是"公司＋农户"模式的延伸。社区（如村委会）搭起桥梁，公司先与当地社区进行合作，再通过社区组织农户参与乡村旅游。公司一般不与农户直接合作，所接触的是社区，但农户接待服务、参与旅游开发则要经过公司的专业培训。公司制定相关的规定，以规范农户的行为，保证接待服务水平，保障公司、农户和游客的利益。此模式通过社区链接，便于公司与农户协调、沟通，有利于克服公司与农户因利益分配产生的矛盾。同时，社区还可对公司起到一定的监督作用，保证乡村旅游正规、有序发展。

四、公司制模式

这一模式的特点是发展进入快、起点层次高、开发有规模，如果思路对头、经营科学，乡村旅游开发会迅速走上有序化发展的道路。

公司制模式比较适合乡村旅游初期，随着农民的关注与参与，这种利益主体是公司的模式，将难以适应未来乡村旅游发展的趋势。农民作为乡村旅游参与主体，其积极性是不容忽视的，而采用公司制模式，农民很难从旅游收入中获得应有的利益，受益的仅是靠提升农产品附加值获得。

乡村旅游生财之源是公共资源，应是农民的公共资源，但在使用这种模式时，最大受益的是旅游公司，当地农民很难得到相应利益，并且还要承担旅游开发所带来的各种负面影响。这种资源与利益的失衡，极易引起农民的不满。

五、股份制模式

这一模式主要通过合作的形式合理开发旅游资源，按照各自的股份获得相应的收益。根据旅游资源的产权，可以界定为国家产权、乡村集体产权、村民小组产权和农户个人产权四种产权主体，在开发上可采取国家、集体和农户个体合作的方式进行，这样把旅游资源、特殊技术、劳动量转化成股本，收效一般按股份分红与按劳分红相结合。对于乡村旅游生态环境保护与恢复、旅游设施的建设与维护以及乡村旅游扩大再生产等公益机制的运行，企业可通过公益金的形式投入完成。

这种模式有利于乡村旅游上规模、上档次。特别是通过股份形式，扩大了乡村集体和农民的经营份额，有利于实现农民参与的深层次转变，从而引导居民自觉参与他们赖以生存的生态资源的保护。

这种模式需要优化股权，明确产权，进行跨地区跨资产的联合，降低风险，让当地农户代表成为合法股东参与企业经营管理，合理划分各自红利，使农户得到应有的股权。把社区居民的责（任）、权（利）、利（益）有机结合起来，以保证乡村旅游的良性发展。典型案例如乌镇、西递宏村等。

六、"政府＋公司＋农户"模式

从目前一些地区乡村旅游发展现状来看，这一模式实质是政府引导下的"企业＋农户"模式。在乡村旅游开发中，由县、乡各级政府和旅游主管部门按市场需求和全县旅游总体规划，确定开发地点、内容和时间，发动当地村民动手实施开发，开发过程中政府和旅游部门进行必要的指导和引导。由当地村民或村民与外来投资者一起承建乡村旅游开发有限责任公司，旅游经营管理按企业运作，利润由村民（乡村旅游资源所有者）和外来投资者按一定比例分成，除此以外，村民们还可以通过为游客提供住宿、餐饮等服务而获取收益。该模式减少了政府对旅游开发的投入，使当地居民真正得到了实惠，减少了旅游管理部门的管理难度，因而是一种切实可行的乡村旅游经营模式。

七、"个体＋农庄"模式

"个体＋农庄"模式是从规模农业个体户发展起来的，以"旅游个体户"的形式出现，通过对自己经营的农牧果场进行改造和旅游项目建设，使之成为一个完整意义的旅游景区，能完成旅游接待和服务工作。通过个体农庄的发展，吸纳附近闲散劳动力，通过手工艺、表演、服务、生产等形式加入服务业中，形成以点带面的发展模式。

八、"村委会＋旅游合作社＋投资商（引进外来旅游开发商）"模式

以村庄为单位，以村委会作为牵头人，整合各村的土地、林果、农产品等资源，成立乡村旅游合作社。旅游合作社是以农民自愿入社为前提组织起来的专业合作组织作为法人组织，以其为实体与外来投资商（旅游开发公司）进行合作。农民以土地、林果、农产品及其他资源、财产作为股本入股，按年度分红，且具有在旅游公司优先就业的权利。

九、"整体租赁＋制度保障"模式

在当地旅游局的指导下，村庄与有实力的旅游企业签订旅游开发合同，合作开发本村乡村旅游，是一种以合作社形式为基础的土地流转经营模式。企业与当地政府达成协议，政府授权企业对当地旅游资源进行投资和开发，实施独家经营。政府主要通过强化景区建设项目的审批管理来实施对旅游资源和环境的保护。农户通过获取补偿金、从事庭院服务和在景区工作获得收入。村委会对企业的经营活动进行监督，协调

农户与企业之间的关系，成立由农户代表、村委代表和企业代表组成的评估团，负责对乡村资源进行评估定价，从制度上保证各利益相关主体获得持久公平的收益权。

十、"公司＋村委会＋农户"模式

公司一般不与农户直接合作，而是通过当地村委会组织农户参与。在农民将土地承包经营权进行流转并与村委会签订协议的基础上，企业实现农民土地的集中使用，使农民共享成果，共担风险。公司负责资金与技术以及培训等。村委会负责将农户的闲散资金与设备收集与整合，组织农户参与乡村旅游，起到公司和农户之间协调作用，同时对公司起到监督作用。但该模式往往存在利益分配矛盾、农户参与性不强等问题。

第三章
乡村旅游规划的概念与内容

第一节 乡村旅游规划概念

一、旅游规划概念与类型

(1) 旅游规划概念

"规划"一词本身具有"谋划""筹划""全面的长远的发展计划"的含义。旅游规划至今没有公认的定义,美国旅游规划学者冈恩(Gunn,1979)曾指出:"规划作为对未来的预测,处理可预见的事件,是唯一能使旅游业获得好处的方法。"因此,可以说,旅游规划是旅游业发展的纲领和蓝图,是促进旅游业健康发展的重要条件。

(2) 旅游规划类型

旅游规划的类型划分有多种形式。美国知名旅游专家、前世界旅游组织(UNWTO)首席顾问爱德华·因斯克普(Edward Inskeep)把旅游规划划分为国家旅游规划、区域旅游规划、亚区域旅游规划、亚区旅游规划、开发区土地利用规划、设施用地规划、设施设计。世界旅游组织把旅游规划分为四个层次:全国和区域规划;社区、度假和开发区规划;景点规划;建筑、景观和工程设计。

王兴斌认为,旅游规划基本分为两类:旅游发展规划与旅游开发建设规划。旅游发展规划是区域旅游产业或旅游经济发展规划,可分为一国、一省、一市、一县/区、一乡/镇或跨行政区域的规划,其主要内容是确定旅游业在该区域内的产业地位、发展目标、发展阶段、总体形象、资源品位、市场定位、总体布局、主导产品、旅游基础和服务设施建设、发展旅游业的战略措施和保障体系。旅游开发建设规划则包括旅游区规划设计、旅游点和旅游设施的建筑设计、旅游产品或线路规划等。

根据《旅游规划通则》,旅游规划分为两个层次:旅游发展规划和旅游区规划。旅游发展规划是根据旅游业的历史、现状和市场要素的变化所制定的目标体系,以及为实现目标体系在特定的发展条件下对旅游发展的要素所做的安排。旅游区规划是指为了保护、开发、利用和经营管理旅游区,使其发挥多种功能和作用而进行的各项旅游要素的统筹部署和具体安排。

乡村旅游规划是旅游规划的一种特殊类型,因此,乡村旅游规划的划分,也可参照《旅游规划通则》的标准,划分为两个层次:乡村旅游发展规划和乡村旅游区规划。本书的研究重点将偏向于乡村旅游区的开发规划层面。

二、乡村旅游规划的含义

乡村旅游规划涉及乡村地区经济、资源、社会和环境等诸多因素，其基本任务是充分展现乡村旅游的内涵，实现乡村旅游开发的生态、社会和经济价值，并推动乡村的可持续发展。因此，乡村旅游规划便成为乡村旅游研究的重点。

王云才采用定性与定量相结合，以及景观科学理论等研究方法，全面系统地介绍了乡村旅游设计研究的背景、意义、现状及发展趋势，以及乡村景观评价、乡村旅游规划设计的技术、乡村景观意象与景观旅游规划设计、乡村可持续发展等问题。杨旭提出了发展乡村旅游的选址标准：比较优越的地理位置、优美的自然生态环境、农业生物优势或独特地方文化、典型的"生态、立体"农业。匡林认为全国乡村旅游开发应该按照"小项目、多功能、广收益"的特点，布点成网，形成两个市场、两套产品。何景明以西部地区发展乡村旅游的典型——成都为例，提出乡村旅游开发应注重规划、加强科技含量、进行产品差异化设计和整合营销、推进软硬环境建设等对策和建议。胡巍详细分析了乡村旅游开发中的旅游资源评价各个环节及其对乡村旅游规划的重要意义。

国内对乡村旅游规划与设计的研究主要是借鉴区域旅游规划的一般流程、选择一定的研究区域，进行案例研究。较多地停留在定性分析和一般归纳总结水平上，缺乏高质量的理论抽象。

基于乡村旅游的发展以及开发中的实践经验，国内专家学者对乡村旅游也进行了大量的实证研究工作。陈传康、骆静珊等在《安宁旅游开发规划》中规划了安宁"农家乐"旅游。马勇、舒伯阳等做了《武汉市蔡甸南湖旅游度假区开发总体规划》，其中有"南湖观光农业园项目策划"。王云才、郭焕成在《略论大都市郊区游憩地的配置——以北京市为例》中以北京郊区为例，研究都市郊区游憩地配置的内在规律。杨晓云在《乡村体验旅游开发初步研究》一文中，运用体验经济的新理念对丽江城郊乡村体验旅游进行了规划开发探讨等。这些文章或著作结合实例对乡村度假地的开发规划做了案例分析。

乡村旅游规划，就是根据某一乡村地区的旅游发展规律和具体市场特点而制定目标，以及为实现这一目标而进行的各项旅游要素的统筹部署和具体安排。

乡村旅游作为一种特殊的旅游形式，其规划应该顺其自然、顺应潮流，做到既能持续地吸引游客，又能使乡村地区在保持原来生活方式的基础上逐步发展，并能使当地居民从该项活动中获得效益。现阶段，我国的乡村旅游规划正处在起步阶段，具体内容还侧重于开发性研究与编制工作。

在理解乡村旅游规划的含义时，需要注意以下几点：

① 乡村旅游规划不仅是一项技术过程，而且也是一项决策过程；它不仅是一种科学规划，而且也是一种实用可行的规划，二者必须同时兼顾，才能规避"纸上画画，墙上挂挂"。

② 乡村旅游规划不仅是一种政府行为，而且也是一种社会行为，还是一种经济行为，不仅要求政府参与，而且规划工作还一定要有未来经营管理人员参与，并与当地群众、投资方相结合，避免规划的"技术失灵"。为此，应建立"开放式"规划体系，允许多重决策权（政府、专家、企业、群众）的协调参与；此外，为了更好地服务社会，还应建立一种机制，使规划师有能力在各部门的决策者之间进行协调，最终产生一个好规划。

③ 乡村旅游规划不是静态的和物质形态的蓝图式描述，而是一个过程，一个不断反馈、调整的动态过程，规划文本仅仅是这个过程的一个初始阶段，即目标的确定和指导性意见。面对未来的种种不确定性，乡村旅游规划必须采取弹性思想和方法。它同时也应该是一个全程规划的概念，应包含全产业链服务的思想在内。

第二节　乡村旅游规划的理论支撑与规划依据

一、乡村旅游规划的理论支撑

（1）旅游规划三元论

刘滨谊认为，旅游规划追求的基本核心和最终目标是为旅游者创造时间与空间的差异、文化与历史的新奇、生理与心理的满足，其中均蕴含着三个层面不同的需求：其一，旅游活动以及与之相关的文化历史与艺术层面，包括潜在于旅游环境中的历史文化、风土民情、风俗习惯等与人们精神生活息息相关的文明，即关于人们行为活动以及与之相应的经营运作的规划需求；其二，景观时空层面，基于景观空间布局的规划，包括区域、总体、景区、景点的时间与空间上的布局、设计，即关于景观时空布局的规划需求；其三，环境、生态、资源层面，包括土地利用、地形、水体、动植物、气候、光照等人文与自然资源在内的调查、分析、评估、规划、保护，即生态环境大地景观的规划需求。这些构成了旅游规划需求的三元。与需求对应，现代旅游规划的内容同样包含三元：以"旅游"为核心的群体行为心理规划和项目经营；以"景观"规划为核心的优美的旅游景观环境形象创造；以"生态"为核心的旅游环境生态保护。

（2）生态美学理论

景观中的美学原理是生态学和美学的有机结合，实际上是从生态学的方向研究美学问题，将生态学的重要观点吸收到美学之中，从而形成美学理论形态。景观生态美学从广义上来说包括人与自然、社会及人自身的生态审美关系，是一种符合生态规律的当代存在论美学。

在人居环境创作中，生态美学强调了自然生态之美；它同时强调人类在遵循生态规律和美的法则前提下，运用科学技术手段改造自然，创作人工生态美，带给人们的不仅仅是一时的视觉震撼，而是可持续发展利用。人工与自然的互惠共生，使城乡景观建设与生态系统特性各有所得，相得益彰，浑然一体，这就造就了人工和生态景观的和谐之美。

中国古代的天人合一观念开启了我们质朴无华的自然审美观，包含了丰富的景观美学思想。如我国园林艺术多追求的是"天人合一"的美学境界。

人类社会进入20世纪90年代，以个人心理感受为主要诉求的体验理论（experience）逐渐兴起，并逐渐渗透在观光休闲活动规划设计中。运用自己的视觉、听觉、味觉以及触觉，形成个人整体心理感受，已成为观光休闲体验活动设计的最高准则。人类向往自然，乡村旅游为人们提供了一个适当的体验机会。

（3）可持续发展理论

可持续发展作为世界性发展战略，给全球人类的生存提供了指导性的发展模式。根据1987年世界环境与发展委员会在题为《我们共同的未来》的报告中提出的思想，可持续发展指的是既能满足当代人的需要，又不对后代人满足其需要的能力构成危害的发展，基于此提出了可持续发展的内涵，即经济可持续、生态可持续和社会可持续三方面。

乡村旅游的可持续发展是一种生态合理、经济可行、社会适宜的旅游活动，是一种高效低耗、无公害的旅游活动。它在推动旅游业向前发展的同时，可以维持乡村旅游资源的合理、永续利用，保护和改善乡村生态平衡。乡村旅游的可持续发展还能带动农村经济的发展，增加农民收入，为今后农村经济的持续增长增加新的动力。改变传统的发展观念、杜绝短期行为，是实施乡村旅游可持续发展的根本保证。所以，在推进乡村旅游可持续发展的过程中，必须综合考虑乡村旅游在乡村生态、乡村社会文化、乡村经济三方面的具体实施环节。

在规划哲学理念上，可持续发展已经成为全世界的共识。可持续旅游开发可以满足经济、社会和文化的需求，在强调为当前的游客和东道主提供旅游和发展机会的同时，保留并强化后人享有同样的机会。可持续开发同时还包括与复杂的社会、经济和环境有关的切实有效的政策。对于可持续旅游开发，世界旅游组织提出过八条原则，可以概括为区域整体性、生态性、可持续、公平、充分的信息与沟通、地方公众主导、规划分析优先、良好的规划监测。在规划理念上，可持续旅游开发强调文化的完整性和生态过程，强调对自然和文化生态的保护和延续。

在乡村旅游规划中，更应该倡导可持续发展思想，因为乡村环境和乡村文化本身的脆弱性特征，要求在可持续发展原则的指导下，有效开展乡村旅游规划工作，以便对乡村资源进行科学开发、培育性开发，从而保障乡村旅游的持续性健康发展。

（4）系统理论

系统理论认为，系统是处于一定的相互关系并与环境发生关系的各组成部分的总体，它具有以下特征：

① 整体性。系统是由各组成部分构成的，但整体大于各个孤立部分之和，这是系统的核心特征。

② 有机关联性。系统内部诸因素之间以及系统与环境之间具有有机关联性。系统与外部环境之间的有机联系，使得系统具有开放性，系统内部诸因素之间的有机联系，使系统具有功能性，并且与系统的开放性一起保证系统的整体性。

③ 系统的动态性。动态性强调的是时间上的变化，一方面内部的结构是随时间而变化的；另一方面开放系统每时每刻都从整体状态演变为各个独立的状态，使系统调节得到加强。

乡村旅游规划动态发展的思想主要表现在目标和内容的动态演进。乡村旅游规划是一种控制和管理系统，随着系统内资源、市场、区域和乡村条件的变化，乡村旅游规划发展的目标和规划的内容也应做相应的调整。乡村旅游规划的弹性随着时间的推移而增大，其中近期规划要求具有稳定性和可行性，而远期规划则更需要体现动态发展的思想。

④ 有序性。系统是从无序向有序发展和演化的，这标志着系统组织性的增长。

⑤ 预决性。系统的发展方向不但取决于实际的状态，而且取决于对未来的预测，二者的统一就是预决性。

乡村旅游规划必须适应未来市场可能发生的变化，必须考虑社会发展趋势和都市消费时尚的整体变迁。乡村旅游的脆弱性在于其性质的确定性。如何进行乡村旅游资源的深度开发，以引导旅游消费走向，是乡村旅游规划不容忽视的问题。在现实基础上的前瞻，是以对市场容量和消费动态的科学分析作为保障的。据此，乡村旅游产品的设计要具有一定的超前性，以满足未来市场变化的需要，以适应未来的消费时尚。

乡村旅游规划不是一项独立的工作，它与乡村旅游地经济发展的各个方面有着千丝万缕的联系，如旅游规划专家组与本地旅游业界和学术界的关系、乡村旅游区各利益相关者之间的关系等。任何一个方面的关系处理不当都不利于乡村旅游规划的制定和实施。因此，乡村旅游规划是以系统化的观点进行编制，规划编制的每个过程和各个部分都进行了有机的协调和控制，以便共同完成乡村旅游规划的总体目标。

（5）闲暇游憩理论

现代休闲是一种生活常态，人们在这段时间内按照自己的意愿所从事的各种活动都称作休闲活动。休闲所注重的是人们对时间的使用、安排，以及由此而引起的对人们自我发展和完善的影响，从社会发展的过程来看，只是人们具体消费休闲时间的一种样式、一种手段。我们所熟知的休息、游憩、娱乐、运动、旅游等活动都毫无例外地从属于休闲的范畴。著名经济学家凯恩斯预言，人类将面临一个真正的永久的问题是："如何度过闲暇"。未来学家托夫勒在《第四次浪潮》中预言，未来社会的闲暇与旅游将成为"第五次浪潮"。

游憩，英文为 recreation，从词源上讲，来自拉丁语的 cecreatio，意思为更新、恢复。

游憩的本意是轻松、平静、自愿产生的活动，用于恢复体力和精力。

闲暇游憩理论，被公认为属于生活行为理论范畴。其实际研究内容十分广泛，主要内容至少有：闲暇历史与发展、闲暇与生理和心理、环境与闲暇行为、闲暇与休闲产业、休闲价值与社会发展五大方面。在闲暇与游憩理论研究领域，目前已经形成的基本理论命题至少有如下七个：

① 闲暇史是与人类伴生的历史，并且具有美好的发展趋势；
② 闲暇与游憩是维持人类生理、心理健康的充分必要条件；
③ 具游憩潜力的事物是一种资源；
④ 闲暇是一种前景广阔的现代产业；
⑤ 闲暇是人类的基本权利，是社会发展的重要方面，需要政府介入；
⑥ 闲暇类型具有地域、文化和发展阶段的差异；
⑦ 闲暇与可持续发展具有较密切的相关性。

（6）RMP 理论

① RMP 理论的提出。我国学者吴必虎首先提出了 RMP（R——resource，资源；M——market，市场；P——product，产品）模式，用来指导区域旅游开发规划。R 性分析是指旅游资源的评价和将旅游资源转化为产品，随着我国旅游业的发展，旅游业已经成为"高投入、高风险、高产出"的产业了，要在资源的利用上加大力气，形成规模化、特色化、品位化的产品；M 性分析是指产品需求弹性和旅游者动机，旅游产品本身是弹性很大的消费品，在消费层次上、在目的地选择上都是如此，根据对中国旅游者的分析，在当前和今后相当长的一段时间里，旅游者对旅游产品的选择仍然集中在中短途观光和城市周边的近程休闲；P 性分析是指产品创新，通过外部环境、规划设计、产品的组合开发等措施，打造重点特色产品，吸引更多的游客。

② RMP 理论和乡村旅游开发。资源-市场-产品是三位一体的，资源是打造产品的重要前提和基础，市场是将资源转化成产品的重要途径，产品是实现资源市场价值的重要载体。具体来说，乡村旅游开发中应该注重这样几个问题：

a. 资源调查和评价。资源调查和评价是旅游规划和开发的重要环节，旅游资源调查是对旅游资源进行考察、勘察、测量、分析、整理的一个综合过程，通过它可以了解旅游资源的现状，掌握旅游资源的利用状况和一些相关的数据，寻找开发利用潜力；可以供旅游主管部门和规划部门制定旅游规划和旅游宣传；可以建立旅游资源的档案资料，进行旅游资源的管理，可以促进旅游资源的保护；可以供旅游资源研究使用。

b. 市场导向。乡村旅游的开发是一个经济过程，就市场经济而言，开发与规划的最终目的是使旅游产品进入市场，所以要紧紧把握市场的脉搏，否则，即使旅游资源品质再高，其价值也无法实现，从而难以实现最佳旅游效益。乡村旅游的市场导向主要考虑两个问题：一是旅游业的发展趋势，从旅游业发展来看，人们越来越向往到充满"自然"和"怀旧"的偏僻地方进行旅游，可见乡村旅游的发展符合世界以及我国旅游业发展的总体方向和未来，具有广阔的发展空间。二是旅游者行为特征，尤其是游客的文化行为特征。不同文化层次、不同年龄阶段的游客，旅游需求不一样。必须重视这些差异，设计不同的乡村旅游产品。

c. 产品设计。资源的特色、市场的定位最终要通过产品来实现，好的产品可以提升资源的价值，满足和创造市场需求，获得良好的经济效益，坏的产品会降低资源的特色和品位，遭到市场的淘汰。

（7）利益相关者理论

利益相关者（stakeholder）概念源于"stake"一词，stake包含利益（interests）和主张（claims）的含义，既指某种利益或份额，同时也指对某种权利的主张（法律权利和道德权利）。1963年斯坦福研究所（Stanford Research Institute）首次使用了利益相关者理论这一术语。弗里曼把利益相关者定义为任何可以影响组织目标的或被该目标影响的群体或个人。由于旅游中涉及的各个组织或群体来自不同行业和部门，这些组织或群体各有其目标和利益指向，且往往是相互冲突、难以协调和动态变化的；新兴旅游目的地不断出现，旅游目的地间竞争日益加剧，成功整合旅游中各参与方的分散力量和资源无疑可以形成协同效应，增强旅游目的地的竞争力等，使得利益相关者理论很快在旅游研究中得到响应。世界旅游组织1999年制定的《全球旅游伦理规范》采用了"利益相关者"这一概念。旅游理论研究中还衍生出了"旅游利益相关者（tourism stakeholder）"术语。索特（Sautter）和莱森（Leisen）指出了旅游业的利益相关者。旅游目的地作为乡村旅游业运行和开展的载体，根据乡村旅游业发展过程中的多种关联要素，其利益相关者主要包括投资者、旅游者、当地政府、社区、竞争者等。以上这些利益相关者对乡村旅游目的地发展有着强有力的影响作用：它们既希望通过旅游目的地的开发来获取利益，但它们的利益点又不尽相同，且在某种程度上存在一定的冲突。

我国目前乡村旅游中存在着土地利用与旅游开发、旅游发展与环境保护、旅游者趣味变化与旅游产品同质化、乡村性与旅游城市化、当地居民与外来投资主体利益的矛盾。因此在乡村旅游规划中，应根据利益相关者理论，在规划的各个程序中，提高乡村旅游各利益相关者的参与程度，明确其利益和主张，重视旅游项目对目的地的社会、经济、环境等诸方面的影响，协调利益主体之间的关系，减少冲突，走旅游可持续发展的道路。

特别需要指出的是，乡村旅游中旅游资源包括当地民居和村落的整体环境，它们是居民赖以生存的生活环境，绝大多数属于居民的私有财产；同时旅游的本质在于文化，而文化的载体是人，乡村居民及其真实生活是乡村旅游发展的原动力。因此村民在乡村旅游中处于极为重要的位置，他们对旅游发展所持的态度及参与程度直接影响到旅游地发展的方向和进度，在规划中应该制定完善的参与机制贯穿于规划的全过程，切实保障村民利益。

社区参与是体现社区因素和居民意志的有效机制，在乡村旅游规划中实施社区参与能够协调社区居民与当地政府、开发商、旅游者等之间的关系，实现各方的利益诉求，也有助于规划设计与当地环境、社区和文化协调一致的产品，从而有利于实现旅游业的可持续发展。

为了实现乡村旅游的可持续发展，社区参与应在以下几个方面得到加强。

① 旅游规划的制定。社区参与规划的制定，一方面有利于培养居民的东道主意识，另一方面可增强乡村旅游规划的可操作性。

② 乡村环境的保护。旅游地资源和环境保护对社区居民具有更为重要的意义，通过参与环境的保护来敦促旅游企业在开发和经营活动中减少对环境的破坏，有利于形成良好的保护环境的社会氛围，加强对乡村传统文化的维护，这样有利于强化乡村居民的文化认同感和社会认同感，减少社会张力，促进社区文化的整合。

（8）旅游地生命周期理论

旅游地生命周期理论的起源，最早可追溯到《英格兰岛屿与海滨疗养胜地的成长》一文。但一般认为，旅游地生命周期理论最早由克里斯特勒在研究欧洲的旅游发展时提出。到目前为止，被学者们公认并广泛应用的旅游地生命周期理论是由加拿大学者巴特勒提出的。巴特勒在《旅游地生命周期概述》一文中，借用产品生命周期模式来描述旅游地的演进过程。他提出的旅游地的演化要经过探查阶段、参与阶段、发展阶段、巩固阶段、停滞阶段、衰退或复苏阶段。然而，旅游地生命周期的经典理论，对于所有旅游地均给定一个模式并且在时间尺度上是不确定的，因而导致了所有的目的地均可套用，且对于预测或分析的指导价值显得不足，同时在机制上更多的是一种外部市场原因的演绎，而对于目的地内部机制对生命周期的影响及生命周期的调整问题讨论尚少。

（9）旅游容量理论

旅游容量又称为旅游承载力，是对生态学中环境容量的概念借鉴产生的，它是指某一旅游地在一定时间、一定空间范围内，所能容纳的游客数量。合理开发和组织旅游活动，让旅游业走可持续发展的道路，需要合理规划旅游容量。乡村旅游地与风景名胜区、文化遗产地、主题公园等一般的旅游地不同，是乡村居民生产、生活的空间，在旅游容量的规划上，涉及的因素更多。因此，乡村旅游容量是指在维持乡村旅游地可持续发展和保证旅游活动吸引力的前提下，所能接受的旅游活动量。乡村旅游容量包括旅游心理容量，旅游资源容量，旅游生态容量，旅游地域容量，旅游经济发展容量。乡村旅游容量概念体系的提出为乡村旅游地的开发与管理提供了一个量化标准，为旅游地的可持续发展设置了一道警戒线，在乡村旅游规划过程中，容量是客观存在的，合理规划容量是必不可少的。

二、乡村旅游规划依据

（1）法律法规

《中华人民共和国旅游法》（2018年）；

《中华人民共和国城乡规划法》（2008年）；

《中华人民共和国环境保护法》（2014年4月24日修订通过，自2015年1月1日起施行）；

《中华人民共和国土地管理法》（2004年）；

《中华人民共和国水土保持法》（1991年）；

《中华人民共和国水污染防治法》（2017年6月27日修正，2018年1月1日起施行）；

《中华人民共和国大气污染防治法》（2018年10月26日修正）；

《中华人民共和国环境影响评价法》（2018年12月29日修正）；

《中华人民共和国森林法》（1998年）；

《中华人民共和国文物保护法》（2013年）；

《中华人民共和国农业法》（2012年）；

《中华人民共和国野生动物保护法》（2004年）；

《基本农田保护条例》（2017年）；

《中华人民共和国野生植物保护管理条例》（1997年）；

《中华人民共和国风景名胜区管理条例》（2006年）；

《村庄和集镇规划建设管理条例》（1993年）；

《旅游发展规划管理办法》（2000年）；

《旅游度假区等级管理办法》（2015年）；

《旅游安全管理办法》（2016年）；

《山东省旅游条例》（2016年）；

《山东省风景名胜区条例》（2017年）；

《山东省森林和野生动物类自然保护区管理办法》（2018年修订版）。

（2）行业标准与规范

《旅游规划通则》（GB/T 18971—2003）；

《旅游资源分类、调查与评价》（GB/T 18972—2017）；

《旅游区（点）质量等级的划分与评定》（GB/T 17775—2003）；

《风景名胜区总体规划标准》（GB/T 50298—2018）；

《旅游厕所质量要求与评定》（GB/T 18973—2022）；

《土地利用现状分类》（GB/T 21010—2017）；

《美丽乡村建设指南》（GB/T 32000—2015）；

《国家级森林公园总体规划规范》（LY/T 2005—2012）；

《旅游强乡镇评定标准》（DB37/T 1082）；

《山东省好客人家农家乐等级划分评定》（DB37/T 1671）；

《乡村旅游服务规范》（DB37/T 2180）；

《精品采摘园旅游服务规范与评定》（DB37/T 2328）。

（3）相关政策文件

《旅游发展规划管理办法》（国家旅游局令第12号）；

《关于进一步促进旅游投资和消费的若干意见》（国务院，2015年）；

《关于支持旅游业发展用地政策的意见》（国土资源部，2015年）；

《关于积极开发农业多种功能大力促进休闲农业发展的通知》（农业部，2015年）；

《关于进一步加强文物工作的指导意见》（国务院，2016年）；

《关于促进自驾车房车旅游发展的若干意见（征求意见稿）》（国家旅游局，2016年）；

《关于实施旅游休闲重大工程的通知》（国家发展和改革委员会、国家旅游局，2016年）；

《关于大力发展休闲农业的指导意见》（农业部，2016年）；

《关于加快美丽特色小（城）镇建设的指导意见》（国家发展和改革委员会，2016年）；

《关于推进中小学生研学旅行的意见》（教育部，2016年）；

《关于大力发展体育旅游的指导意见》（国家旅游局，2016年）；

《2017全国旅游工作会议工作报告》（国家旅游局，2017年）；

《关于促进健康旅游发展的指导意见》（国家卫生和计划生育委员会，2017年）；

《关于开展田园综合体建设试点工作的通知》（财政部，2017年）；

《山东省2017年政府工作报告》（山东省人民政府，2017年）；

《山东省乡村旅游提档升级工作方案》（山东省人民政府，2017年）；

《关于加快推进省级涉农资金统筹整合的实施意见（试行）》；

《关于开展农村宅基地"三权分置"试点促进乡村振兴的实施意见》；

《国家农村产业融合发展示范园认定管理办法（试行）》；

《山东省乡村振兴战略规划（2018—2022年）》；

《山东省推动乡村组织振兴工作方案》；

《山东省推动乡村生态振兴工作方案》；

《山东省推动乡村文化振兴工作方案》；

《山东省推动乡村人才振兴工作方案》；

《山东省推动乡村产业振兴工作方案》；

《关于发挥国土资源支撑保障作用促进乡村振兴的意见》（鲁国土资发〔2018〕8号）；

《中共山东省委、省人民政府关于贯彻落实中央决策部署实施乡村振兴战略的意见》；

《泰安市国民经济和社会发展第十三个五年规划纲要》；

《山东省住房和城乡建设厅关于组织申报山东省第一批美丽村居建设省级试点的通知》（鲁建村字〔2018〕43号）。

（4）技术规范

《城市用地分类及规划建设用地标准》（GB 50137—2011）；

《污水综合排放标准》（GB 8978—1996）；

《旅游业基础术语》（GB/T 16766—2017）；

《城市给水工程规划规范》（GB 50282—2016）；

《城市电力规划规范》（GB/T 50293—2014）；

《风景名胜区总体规划标准》（GB/T 50298—2018）；

《城市排水工程规划规范》（GB 50318—2017）；

《公共信息图形符号 第1部分：通用符号》（GB/T 10001.1—2012）。

第三节 乡村旅游规划原则与研究进展

一、乡村旅游规划原则

乡村旅游规划所要考虑的包括乡村的旅游市场需求、资源约束、社会宏观条件分析（主要是经济条件）等几个方面。由于"乡村"的特殊性，决定了其规划必须遵循以下一些基本原则。

（1）自然环保原则

在全球性生态化思潮的影响下，旅游规划作为一种技术产品，也应该具备生态化特征，强调对原生环境和本土意境的保护，承担起保护生态及文化多样性的重任。具体来说，在规划设计中，运用系统论和景观生态学的相关原理对旅游环境诸方面的生态平衡和协调发展予以保护，遵循的原则是利用程度最大化和可能造成的环境退化最小化。

自然环保原则是指乡村旅游规划设计要因地制宜，尽量保留自然特色，若无绝对必要就不改变原貌或增加建筑物。许多经营者以为乡村旅游就是普通的观光旅游，因而不顾原先遗存的自然资源和乡村特色，大兴土木，甚至变更土地用途，建园造景。这种做法既破坏了乡村原有的良好自然生态环境，浪费了宝贵的农业资源，又扭曲了发展乡村旅游的本质和目的。

（2）乡土特色原则

"特色就是生命"已成为旅游开发者的共识。有特色才有吸引力，才有竞争力。"人无我有，人有我优，人优我特"是旅游开发的成功之道。中国文化璀璨，综合资源丰富。同时，地球自然演化过程的差异性，使得每一处旅游资源往往具有景观上的独特性和不可替代性。所谓特色保护，就是在对该旅游资源的自然和文化景观内涵进行深度挖掘的基础上，对自然和文化诸要素内涵与特色的保护，避免在规划和开发过程中旅游资源自然和文化特色的丧失。乡土特色原则是指在设计构思上有别于城市公园绿化，体现野趣天成、返璞归真；在植物配置上注重适地适树，强调多样性和稳定性；所展示的也应该是当地的农耕文化和民俗文化。

（3）独特性原则

乡村具有不同类型，由于其不同的历史、文化、经济和社会发展而呈现出不同的特征，应该说都有一定的吸引力，但是我们必须在研究客源市场的基础上，选择具有独特吸引力的乡村进行旅游规划。以经济和社会的发展为划分依据，可以把乡村分为具有或保持一定时代特色（民居、饮食文化、服饰、耕作方式、节日、风俗习惯等）的乡村，越具有多种特色的乡村，就越有吸引力，应该寻找这样的乡村进行旅游规划。

（4）因地制宜原则

乡村地区的基础设施，如住房、道路交通系统、饮水供应系统、排水系统等，是乡村居民赖以生存的基础，而这些设施往往又具有地方独特性，在进行规划时，就要因地制宜，充分利用这些已有的基础设施。为适应城市旅游者的特殊需要，乡村地区还要建设必备的基础设施和其他旅游设施，在建设中，尽量符合或仿效当地的风格，并尽量使用当地的建筑材料。在规划建设时，应该结合本地的实际情况，包括资源、区位、市场、经济基础、投资环境与投资能力等，不能盲目地贪大求洋，更不能不顾本地的产业实际发展状况。

（5）利益均衡原则

乡村旅游作为新农村建设和乡村经济发展的一种模式，目的之一就在于提高目的地社区居民的生活质量，通过发展旅游为当地居民找到一条致富之路，这也是旅游业可持续发展的重要方面。发展旅游具有多种功能，如发展地方经济、提高当地居民的收入和生活质量、使开发商获得合理的利益回报、保护环境与资源等，因此，利益均衡是乡村旅游规划的重要原则之一。特别要关注当地社区居民和非人类利益相关者资源、环境等的利益，如果这些弱势群体的利益得不到充分的关注，既不利于规划的实施，也违背了发展旅游的初衷。只有遵循利益均衡原则，协调好社区居民与政府、投资人、旅游者之间的利益关系，才能使社区居民积极参与到当地的旅游开发与建设中，只有充分保护和进一步培育好规划区的环境，才能够使规划区旅游得到良性的持续发展。

在利益均衡原则指导下，乡村利益是需要被特别关注的一环。游客在乡村旅游中，可以参观游览乡村风景，也可以体验农民的日常生活，参与农民的田间劳动，但是这些活动都不能干扰当地村民的正常生活，要保证旅游规划顺应当地村民的生活方式。

（6）和谐生态原则

从美学的角度来看，在地球表面，土地格局、岩体、动植物之间存在着明显的和谐关系，形成了完整的统一体。大自然造就的景观特征的完整性越是统一、彻底、明显、强烈，对观察者的感官冲击就越大。而且，景观地段不同要素的和谐程度"不仅是获得快感的量度，也是美的量度"。因此自然景观和历史文化景观在设计时，要运用整体论的观点，保护和加强内在的景观质量，剔除不应该保留的要素，甚至是引进要素以加强自然特征，尽量地保持景区的原始性、完整性、统一性、和谐性。

乡村旅游是农业与旅游业结合的产物，要考虑经济效益，更要强调生态效益及社会效益。要用生态学原理来指导乡村旅游的建设，建立良性循环的生态系统，产生好的生态效益。生态性主要指两个方面：一方面是生态平衡；另一方面是生态美学，即从审美角度体现出生命、和谐和健康的特征。生命力主要体现在规划设计的旅游区应具有良好的生态循环再生能力。和谐则要求人工与自然互惠共生、相得益彰，即人工构筑物与生态环境形成一种和谐美。健康是指在争取人工与自然和谐的前提下，创造出无污染、无危害，使人生理、心理得到满足的健康旅游环境。

(7) 良性互动原则

良性互动原则主要是针对乡村旅游与人居环境之间的关系而言。众所周知，人居环境的改善，有利于发展旅游，发展旅游又能促进人居环境的改善。

乡村旅游区景观建设的好坏以人的需求为评价基础，在尊重自然的前提下，充分考虑人的活动需求和心理需求是建设乡村旅游区的出发点和归宿。人的需求，可以归纳为两类：其一是当地村每年居住、生产、生活的需求，其二是游客游憩活动的需求。

景观规划设计应该对以下几方面同时考虑，一方面是投资回报；另一方面是要最大限度满足游客游憩活动的舒适性；还要考虑乡村是村民最重要的聚居环境，村民兼有主人和游客的双重身份，乡村旅游区的景观建设，应该让村民为自己聚居环境的改善提议。

(8) 社区参与原则

乡村旅游能否可持续发展，关键在于当地人民是否能够真正认识自己文化的价值，能否成为当地文化的主动传承者和保护者。社区全面参与是乡村旅游发展的内在动力，也是衡量乡村旅游的重要标志和避免出现权力支配和利益分配不合理等现象的重要保证。因此，要遵循社区参与原则。

社区居民参与旅游发展应渗透到各个层面，从个别参与到群体参与、组织参与，逐步实现社区的全面参与。一方面，居民要参与旅游经济决策和实践、旅游规划和实施等；另一方面，居民不仅仅局限在谋求经济发展的层面，而且重视环境保护与社会传统文化的维护与继承的层面，参与旅游资源的管理、参与规划和决策的制定过程。乡村社区的参与要能在规划中反映居民的想法和对旅游的态度，从而达到发展乡村旅游的主要目的，即要有效地进行经济发展和资源保护；在社区内创造公平的利益分配体系；发展当地社区的服务者，增强他们保护资源的责任感，自觉地参与到旅游中来等。

(9) 创新原则

乡村旅游规划作为一个具体项目的策划，不同于一般区域旅游规划的平面展开，而是一类旅游产品系列中的具体项目设计，其创新性是实现效益的基础。但创新并不仅仅意味着规划者想象力的竞赛，而是开发深度的层次递进。一方面是旅游地文化的升华，转化为新的旅游产品；另一方面是旅游市场的拓展，适应更多层面的消费水平。从世界旅游发展过程看，旅游市场发育大体上经历如下阶段：贵族化旅游阶段、大众化旅游阶段和细分化旅游阶段。乡村旅游应属于细分化旅游阶段的专项旅游产品。当大多数乡村旅游经营者还以大众化旅游阶段的经营思维，在市场上推销重复的旅游产品，争夺重复的客源时，竞争的炽热化、恶性化就不可避免。因此，在现有旅游产品基础上进行有价值的变化，推出有特色的新产品，是旅游商家在竞争中立于不败之地的迫切需要。所以，创新是新的规划手段与规划思想的具体实践，是旅游产品和经营在现有层次上的深度开发。

二、乡村旅游规划研究进展

(1) 国外乡村旅游开发与规划研究进展

在乡村旅游开发与规划方面,国外仍以案例研究为主,内容包括乡村景观与土地利用、乡村文化多样性、旅游规划中的社会问题(诸如赌博、就业、女性问题等)、乡村环境与生态规划、保持乡村地区"原生性"和"乡村性"以及乡村社区参与旅游规划过程等。

佩吉在《现代旅游管理导论》一书中,总结了乡村旅游规划和管理过程中存在的问题,并提出乡村旅游发展的基本原则。L. Roberts 和 D. Hall 对西方乡村旅游规划项目类型进行了研究总结。

Giulio Senes 和 Alessandro Toccolini 以意大利乡村保护区 Parcodel Serio 为例,利用 UET 方法分析了可持续的土地利用规划。Barbel Tress 和 Gunther Tress 利用跨学科方法,研究了丹麦参与性乡村景观规划,认为景观规划师应与旅游规划专家、地方决策者和利益相关者通力合作进行乡村旅游规划。

Donald G. Reid 和 Heather Mair 则选取加拿大几个乡村旅游目的地,建立了一套乡村社区参与旅游规划的自我评估方法体系,通过该评估体系,以社区参与为中心的旅游规划能更好地实施。

(2) 国内乡村旅游开发与规划研究进展

我国是发展中国家,乡村旅游处于发展阶段,乡村旅游的经济收益及其影响成为研究界最感兴趣的焦点。

国内学者对乡村旅游开发与规划的研究主要涉及以下几方面内容:开发模式探讨,乡村旅游规划基础理论,乡村旅游规划建议,乡村旅游规划中社区参与,案例研究,乡村振兴视角研究等。

① 开发模式探讨方面。王宁以红色乡村旅游规划设计为研究对象,以定西市通渭县榜罗镇为例进行了规划设计实践研究,并将理论探索和实践应用相结合。在理论研究的基础上,提出"红色传承+情景体验+产业融合"的红色乡村旅游规划开发模式。薛美丽、薛威振、蔡帅军探讨红色文化旅游中特有的红色文化资源如何整合利用,希望改善千城一面的状况。以百色老革命根据地为例,依托百色红色文化、绣球文化、铜鼓文化等资源优势,推广"红色文化+旅游"构建乡村景观建设的新模式。马力、段然提出利用农村现有的产业、资源,引入营销的理念,形成"产业+旅游"的发展模式。以嵊州市贵门乡上乌山村为例,研究旅游发展战略及旅游产品定位问题,按照"产业+旅游"的模式,策划出对应的旅游项目。李晶、宋建军、王倩雯、马仲超通过对乡村旅游规划的理论研究、实地调查和市场分析,发现湖南省的乡村旅游普遍存在重游率低、旅游景点不突出、经营水平较低、旅游景点多而不精等问题。结合湖南新邵县长塘村的特点,明确了产业口碑与特色景观的重要性,提出了在尊重当地文化背景的前提下结合产业升级、乡村建设、园林休闲、人文呈现的乡村旅游模

式。王瑞综合分析了产业融合背景下乡村旅游的内涵及理论基础,以及产业发展与乡村旅游之间的相互关系,在产业融合驱动力因素的基础上,提出主动融合、互动融合、延伸融合三种融合模式。以望江县凉泉乡旅游发展规划作为案例,对望江县凉泉乡规划区进行产业现状分析,对发展成效和发展存在问题进行了分析,从凉泉乡旅游产业与农业、文化业、信息业融合等方面进行了规划研究。孙博根据统计学、市场营销学与地理学等分析乡村旅游区域规划的应用实例、盈利模式和环境因素,研究乡村旅游的发展模式与发展阶段。刘晨辰以环巢湖沿线乡村旅游发展为背景,通过对庐江县同大镇灵台村规划设计模式的深入研究,提出由旅游驿站延伸衔接美好乡村的联动新模式。唐建兵分析了成都乡村旅游规划存在的主要问题,将"反规划"理论引入成都乡村旅游规划中,初步建立起具有成都特色的乡村旅游"反规划"模式。

② 乡村旅游规划基础理论方面。韩云霞针对乡村旅游发展规划理论与实践实施进行初步探讨。肖剑锋针对国内当前乡村旅游规划中存在的问题,提出运用大市场营销理论逻辑框架进行科学规划的思路和要点:坚持以"人"为中心的发展战略,从政府有为的"讲政治"和市场有效的"公共关系"方面建立保障战略,并通过科学的营销战略满足游客需求和实现让"人"满意。李烨通过对国土空间规划编制要求的分析,提出新时期乡村旅游规划编制在理念、内容方面须进行重点把握及补充的诸多要点,并对其进行了详细探讨。何晶晶通过理论研究分析与技术思路的指导,在传统规划思想方法的基础上,从体验的三个层次出发,探讨体验式乡村旅游规划的内涵与方法,并对应分析体验式乡村旅游发展特征与提升效应。以苏州三山岛为案例,从乡村旅游资源价值萃取、市场需求等方面进行分析,确定苏州市三山岛体验式乡村旅游规划定位、目标以及体验提升策略。刘玮芳、徐洪武、方宇鹏从当下的旅游规划越来越重视环境保护和可持续发展的角度出发,运用反规划理论来探讨乡村旅游规划。陈文捷、段湘辉基于"反规划"视角对乡村旅游规划理论进行研究,侧重于关注乡村自然环境的保护和优先规划,分析了乡村旅游"反规划"的理念、过程、特征、原则、路径等,以促进乡村旅游的可持续发展。张立诚、蔡家瑞以四川宜宾市高县新寨村为实证案例,从轻旅游概念出发,通过对轻旅游短暂性、可重复性、特异性三种特点的分析,提出"一带三区"的规划方案。苏南将"慢旅游"理念融入乡村开发中,提出慢旅游理论下的乡村旅游开发概念,以"多元产业相结合、村民为主体、保护和延续地方文脉、游客深度体验、生态可持续性"为主要理念的慢旅游乡村开发设计的具体策略,并最终在云南省腾冲市荷花乡的开发设计实践中进一步研究。曾鸣针对规划者在制定乡村旅游规划时未充分考虑乡村的原真性,并将其作为乡村旅游的核心,从而导致出现乡村旅游区的城镇化景观泛滥,乡村特色不够突出,规划布局不合理等问题,从乡村旅游以及乡村旅游规划的相关理论出发,分析讨论了原真性视角下乡村旅游规划的思路、原则和方法,并总结出乡村旅游规划中应考虑到的原真性要素。唐代剑、池静认为,乡村旅游规划是根据乡村旅游发展规律和市场特点制定目标,以及为实现这一目标而进行的各项旅游要素的统筹部署和具体安排,现阶段乡村旅游规划侧重于开发性研究与编制,其核心应在选址、活动内容设置和游览组织设计三大块内容上。

王云才、刘滨谊运用景观规划学、景观地理学和景观生态学的综合观点，系统探讨了乡村景观、乡村景观规划的概念，乡村景观规划的原则和意义，并在此基础上进一步探讨了现阶段我国乡村景观规划的核心内容。熊凯将"意象"引入乡村旅游中，并分析了乡村意象的丰富内涵。

③ 乡村旅游规划建议方面。韩帅、陈曦分析了当前我国乡村旅游的基本情况，探讨了乡村在发展旅游方面存在的问题和不足之处，提出了优化乡村旅游发展路径的建议和策略。刘雨欣以吉林省集安市太王镇钱湾村为研究样本，系统梳理和分析基层乡村规划过程中取得的成就和存在的问题，并提出需要加大规划与风土人情匹配突显特色、乡村旅游规划定位要精准、空间结构布局要科学、规划调整与项目开发要聚焦市场等建议。李双英结合时代特征和乡村旅游发展规划存在问题，全方位、多角度探讨乡村未来的旅游规划策略，即完善基础设施建设，提高旅游产品的知名度，打造乡村旅游品牌，壮大人才队伍，保护当地文化。苏毅、祖振旗、宋子涵、刘玮、王笑笑以京郊密云金叵罗村为例进行实证研究，在分析现状自然疗愈资源条件的基础上，通过构建自然疗愈旅游路线，并从环境感知、实践体验、文化精神三个层面融合自然疗愈，实现乡村旅游建设规划探索。杨明、赵朝丛以重庆石柱县为例，以精准扶贫视角下的乡村旅游规划为主要研究内容，探索在精准扶贫背景下，对乡村的旅游资源进行合理的规划，以促进乡村经济社会发展活力，探索乡村旅游经济发展的长期可持续发展路径。张淑娟以溧阳市曹山乡村旅游项目为实证案例，论述了乡村旅游现状及发展策略，分析其在发展过程中存在的主要问题，提出以全域旅游、文旅结合、三产融合等策略推动乡村旅游规划，促进乡村旅游经济发展。李倩总结了目前国内农村旅游开发中的不足点，总结了多产业结合，以村民为主体，保护和延续地区的文化脉络，以及"生态持续性"等为主要理念的旅游村开发设计策略。朱鹏亮、邵秀英、翟泽华分析了我国乡村旅游点多、面广，在小尺度区域往往面临资源同质和产品同构的问题，以山西省左权县清漳河流域4个村的旅游扶贫规划为例，对整理出的181处旅游资源，采用德尔菲法进行评价与分析，探讨资源同质化背景下乡村旅游规划中的个性化资源挖掘、差异化形象定位与特色化旅游产品策划。尹振华提出在乡村旅游开发规划中，应注意农耕文化的灌输，提高文化品位；进行"亦农亦旅、农旅结合"的复合性开发；采取"做减法"的开发模式，减少对乡村环境的干扰和破坏；加强农耕文化与现代文化的"和谐相融"。李永文、王培雷认为，必须做好乡村旅游总体规划、专项规划和详细规划，避免无序开发、重复开发；突出地域特色、文化内涵，突出个性，审批立项时注意整体的多样性与个体的独特性。此外，陈文君探讨了我国现代乡村旅游深层次开发问题；周玲强、黄祖辉从可持续发展的角度提出了建议；郭焕成认为当前要在制定旅游总体规划的基础上，开展制定乡村旅游规划、农业旅游和民俗旅游规划。

④ 乡村旅游规划中社区参与方面。罗永常提出了民族村寨社区参与旅游开发的利益保障机制。郑群明、钟林生提出在乡村旅游开发、规划过程中，注重社区和居民参与的开发模式是最佳选择，应该引导乡村居民参与规划过程。宋章海、马顺卫倡导

社区参与乡村旅游发展的规划和开发决策，走乡村民主化道路。曹洪珍强调融入当地社会文化目标的旅游总体规划，提出社区居民参与乡村旅游的概念框架。

⑤ 案例研究方面。唐琦以平铺镇为例，对全域旅游视角下乡村旅游规划进行了研究。通过实地调研、资料收集等方法对平铺镇进行全面分析。结合平铺镇乡村旅游的发展诉求，以构建复合型乡村旅游目的地为目标，从优化乡村旅游空间布局、整合优势乡村旅游资源、促进产旅融合高质发展、完善旅游公共服务体系、建立多元协调管理机制出发，提出平铺镇乡村旅游五大规划策略。胡梦子、周嘉仪、蒋正容以湖州四联村旅游规划设计为例，分析乡村现有优势资源与不足，以田园综合体的设计理念，提出村落生产方式升级、生态环境重构、生活方式完善的设计思路，构建产业、自然与人和谐联动的共生环境，并据此提出湖州四联村的旅游规划方案。郭隽瑶、张妍以徐州市铜山区台上草莓小镇的实地调研为例，分析乡村旅游规划现状与优化路径，以更好地促进草莓小镇规划的完善与发展。刘玮、王婷、谭晓军以重庆市巫溪县乡村旅游总体规划为实证案例，运用区域协同发展理论，通过旅游产业类型引导、主题策划、重要项目节点实施、多元旅游开发模式应用对接旅游规划的核心路径，以期为景区依托型乡村旅游地规划方法提供借鉴。商丹妮以海南罗驿古村为实证案例，对海南地域文化背景下的乡村旅游规划进行了相关研究。郭培、周晓路、张川从江苏省常州市武进区乡村旅游规划的实例出发，通过分析武进区的地域发展特征，提出在城镇化水平较高、资源有限地区发展乡村旅游的规划思路；将旅游作为武进区乡村二次振兴的突破口，以全域整体优化提升为战略目标，以资源评估、体系设计、"适游性"引导为技术手段，形成适应武进区地方特征的乡村旅游发展路径。向然禹以武都镇黑宝彩谷田园综合体为例，探讨了乡村旅游中的田园综合体的开发原则，总体规划思路及产业发展策略。王红山针对河北省乡村旅游中普遍存在的"景观模式雷同""景观资源浪费""乡土特色缺失"等问题，以乡村景观为切入点，以河北省乡村旅游为依托，对河北省乡村旅游景观规划设计进行系统的研究，并提出景观空间规划中要着重做好景观斑块和景观廊道的规划，采用多种景观布局形式（带状式、单核式、双核式、多核式）相结合的方式，将各景观有序连接起来。刘斐借鉴精准扶贫理论与旅游扶贫模式相关研究，并与规划研究方法相结合，以福建省福清市一都镇为实证案例，提出旅游精准扶贫规划的设计重点，最终确定旅游精准扶贫的规划思路，主要包括精准识别体系构建与社区扶贫模式选择，进而在此基础上进行功能业态选择与项目空间规划；最后依据全域旅游思想，在全域景观塑造与精致空间生产战略引导下，进行功能布局与项目业态选择。

⑥ 乡村振兴视角研究方面。霍松涛从乡村振兴的视角探讨了乡村旅游产业规划问题。王晶晶、刘清泉、司端勇从乡村振兴的视角，对基于地方特色资源开发的乡村旅游规划进行了相关研究。洪占东、殷滋言以乡村振兴战略为背景，梳理合肥市三十岗乡的现状资源，调查三十岗乡旅游发展现状，总结三十岗乡发展过程中存在的问题，并提出三十岗乡乡村旅游规划建议。

⑦ 其他研究方面。石斌针对发展过程出现的问题，从规划与建筑两大角度出发，

基于社区营造理念，提出乡村旅游规划策略与营建导则，指明乡村旅游未来发展方向。刘琛结合相关理论以及对相关乡村旅游规划设计案例进行调研与分析，提出了基于研学旅行背景下的乡村旅游规划设计策略。最后运用实证研究法，以临武紫薇天下乡村旅游规划设计为例进行了实例研究。胡世伟通过高频度法和专家打分法相结合，对乡村旅游生态环境承载力测算的因子进行了相关研究。徐妍婷从当代体验旅游经济的视角对乡村旅游的规划思路进行分析。孙瑞桃、李庆雷基于现代乡村旅游发展出现的系列问题，从三生融合发展出发，在传统乡村旅游规划的基础上，以空间相互作用理论和空间规划等理论为指导，对三生共融型乡村旅游规划编制进行研究；以云南昆明的万溪冲为个案，探讨了三生共融型乡村旅游规划使生活、生产、生态空间既联系畅通又互不干扰的三生空间合理设计组织。卢珊珊研究了近年来不同规划编制单位编制的乡村旅游规划文本，并对其进行内容分析，以期厘清乡村旅游规划编制体系的基本框架，并提出对乡村旅游规划编制体系的建议。郑容以张家界"五号山谷"为例，从规划理念、规划设计以及规划的意义来分析乡村旅游规划在度假民居发展中的重要意义。徐彩球、金姝兰、黄建男、徐磊针对鄱阳湖流域矿产资源丰富，流域内矿产开发与环境保护之间的矛盾日益突出的问题，运用田野调查、农户访问以及计算机辅助GIS、RS等方法与技术，提出建设以国家矿山公园为导向，矿山旅游与"世界橙乡游""生态赣州游"相结合的乡村特色旅游。邱慧针对规划实践中社区处于边缘角色的问题，通过对社区参与乡村旅游规划的现状、影响因素、参与主体、参与形式和参与阶段进行了理论综合分析，提出乡村旅游规划的社区参与机制模型。选取郑州樱桃沟景区进行实证研究，从影响因素、社区参与主体、社区参与形式等角度对樱桃沟社区参与乡村旅游规划的机制模型进行优化。提出要注重当地居民诉求、让居民实实在在参与、从内部选取社区代表组织、让社区拥有一定筹码等条件，才能让当地社区成为真正的受益者。魏有广针对乡村地区的复杂性和利益主体的多元化特征，探讨了乡村旅游规划与乡村地区其他相关规划的协调关系，并在此基础上，初步构建了乡村旅游规划协调体系。

第四节 乡村旅游规划的技术路线与核心内容

一、乡村旅游规划技术路线

乡村旅游规划作为旅游规划的一种特殊类型，必须遵循旅游规划的一般原则与技术路线。规划技术路线是规划过程中所要遵循的一定逻辑关系，其中包含了规划的主要内容和制定规划的基本步骤。到现在为止，国内外还没有专门针对乡村旅游规划的技术路线，而针对一般的旅游规划技术路线，很多专家提出了众多方案，这些方案各具特色，但基本思路大体一致，这为乡村旅游规划技术路线的制定提供了参考。

乡村旅游规划共分五个阶段：规划准备和启动阶段、调查分析阶段、确定总体规划思路阶段、制定规划阶段、组织实施阶段。

(1) 第一阶段：规划准备和启动

规划的准备和启动工作主要包括：明确规划的基本范畴；明确规划的制定者和执行者；确定规划的参与者，组织规划工作组；设计公众参与的工作框架；建立规划过程的协调保障机制。这些是启动乡村旅游规划应该具备的基本条件。

召集不同领域的专家学者和管理人员组成一个工作小组，共同研究乡村旅游规划的经济、社会、环境、工程、建筑等问题。根据初步调查研究的具体情况，确定工作小组的人员，可以是市场与财务分析家、旅游行政管理者、乡村管理者、生态与环境专家、建筑师、地理学家、园林学家等。同时，吸收市民和村民参与，有利于使规划成为更切实可行的方案，而不仅仅是专家的"课题"。

(2) 第二阶段：调查分析

该阶段进行实地考察、市场调查，收集资料，这项工作非常重要。

这一阶段的工作包括：乡村旅游地总体现状分析，如乡村旅游地自然地理概况、社会经济发展总体状况、旅游业发展状况等；乡村旅游资源普查与评价，可以利用国家颁布的旅游资源分类与评价标准对乡村旅游资源进行科学、合理的分类，并做出定性和定量评价，将人们对乡村旅游资源的主观认识定量化，使其具有可比性；客源市场分析，通过调研客源市场，详细分析客源的市场结构，为市场定位、市场细分和市场营销推广打好基础；乡村旅游发展SWOT分析，在以上三个方面科学分析的基础上，对当地发展乡村旅游进行全面的综合考察，找出发展乡村旅游的优势、劣势、机遇和挑战，从而发挥优势，规避劣势。

(3) 第三阶段：确定总体规划思路

这一阶段的主要工作是：通过对以上乡村旅游发展的背景和现状进行系统分析，结合乡村的历史、社会、经济、文化、生态环境，综合确定乡村旅游发展的战略定位和发展思路。

(4) 第四阶段：制定规划

制定规划阶段是乡村旅游规划工作的主体部分，是构建乡村旅游规划内容体系的核心，主要工作就是根据前面的综合分析和战略定位，提出乡村旅游发展的具体措施，包括乡村旅游产业发展规划、乡村旅游的产品体系、乡村旅游的配套体系等。在具体的一个村庄内进行旅游规划时，需要考虑规划区域内社区居民或者当地农民的利益如何保障，通过科学的机制设计让居民或者农民更多地参与到未来的乡村开发中。

(5) 第五阶段：组织实施

依据乡村旅游规划的具体内容，并结合乡村地区实际发展现状，切实做好乡村旅游规划的具体实施工作。要根据经济、社会、环境效益情况，对规划实施的效果进行综合评估，并及时做好信息反馈，以便对规划内容进行适时的补充、调整和优化。

组织实施包括乡村旅游开发的时间周期，开发的模式，项目开发时序，项目如何进行融资，投资回收期以及相应的经济效益、社会效益、环境效益。

二、乡村旅游规划的核心内容

各地区在开展乡村旅游时,所处的地理区位、经济区位、交通区位、社会环境、乡村现状、资源禀赋各异,这就使乡村旅游规划的内容不能千篇一律,必须根据乡村旅游规划区的实际情况,对具体的规划内容进行适时的调整,或强化乡村旅游规划的内容体系中没有涉及的方面,或弱化其中的某些内容。总之,必须根据规划对象的具体情况因地制宜来确定规划的实际内容。然而,无论何种形式、何种范围的乡村旅游规划,其核心的规划内容是相似的与不可缺少的,在规划时必须有所体现。经过大量的理论研究和多项旅游规划实践的积累,笔者认为乡村旅游规划的核心内容应该包括以下九个方面。

(1) 乡村旅游总体现状分析

乡村旅游总体现状分析指对乡村旅游规划区所处的经济环境、社会环境、人文环境等多方面的综合考察,以及对当地旅游产业发展状况的全面把握,诸如自然条件、历史文脉、经济发展水平、交通状况、场地资源禀赋、土地性质、旅游产业发展现状(乡村民宿、乡村餐饮、配套服务设施状况、乡村旅游景点开发状况、交通设施发展状况、乡村旅游商品开发现状)等。通过分析这些内容,可以从宏观上了解当地发展乡村旅游的本底情况,对规划区的总体状况有全面和深刻的了解,为后续制定乡村旅游开发规划提供依据和支持。

(2) 乡村旅游资源普查及评价

乡村旅游资源普查是乡村旅游规划的基础性工作,乡村旅游资源普查是指对将要规划的乡村地区的旅游资源进行全面的考察和分析,同时搜集相关的各种文字、图片、视频等资料。在乡村旅游资源普查过程中,可以按照国家标准《旅游资源分类、调查与评价》对乡村旅游资源进行分类。但是,乡村旅游资源还有其特殊性,诸如乡村风貌、乡村景观、乡土物产、乡风民俗、乡村生活等,都是乡村地区所特有的。

乡村旅游资源评价是指在乡村旅游资源普查的基础上,对乡村旅游资源的分布、品质等级及未来开发潜力进行综合分析,从而为乡村旅游规划提供重要基础性依据。乡村旅游资源评价一般分为定性评价和定量评价两种。定量评价是对规划区的乡村旅游资源划分出具体的评价等级。定性评价是对当地的旅游资源状况进行总体的把握,通过与其他乡村旅游地的比较分析,确定出当地的特色资源和垄断性资源,将优势资源放大,从而确定当地需要树立的资源品牌。定性和定量评价两者结合起来,全面、客观地反映乡村规划区旅游资源的状况。

(3) 乡村旅游发展SWOT分析

SWOT分析法是目前通行的条件综合分析法,它通过对旅游规划区域面临的优势、劣势,以及外部环境的机遇和挑战的综合分析,来确定旅游业发展的战略措施,为决策制定提供依据。

乡村规划区域的优势和劣势包含区域经济条件、地方招商政策、资源禀赋状况、地理交通区位、产品特色、消费人群数量、品牌建设等。通过优劣势分析，可以客观认知自身，在发挥优势的同时，更要深入分析、研究自身的劣势与不足，以便在未来的发展中进行有效的规避。机遇和威胁是针对外部环境和竞争者而言的，诸如国家经济政策环境、旅游产业发展趋势、旅游产业政策调整、未来的竞争者、旅游需求变化、突发事件等，都是进行外部分析的基本内容。通过分析机遇，可以把握旅游产业发展新动向、新的市场机会，以便提前布局。通过分析威胁，可以规避市场风险，减少资源和资金的浪费。

（4）乡村旅游总体发展思路分析

乡村旅游发展的总体思路，就是对乡村旅游地总体状况进行 SWOT 综合分析，对乡村旅游资源进行考察及评价，从而对当地发展乡村旅游业进行战略定位，并确定当地发展乡村旅游的发展战略、发展目标。

第一，战略定位。对乡村旅游业进行战略定位，确定乡村旅游业在本地区经济发展和社会进步过程中的地位。战略定位是为下一步乡村旅游区发展提供战略方向和发展依据。第二，确定发展目标。乡村旅游发展目标可以划分为战略目标、社会与生态目标。战略目标可以细分为未来总体要达到的终极目标、近中期目标和远期目标。第三，确定产业发展的战略步骤。根据当地乡村旅游发展的总体目标进行拆分，对乡村旅游区进行分期发展规划，一般以时间为界限，分为近中远期战略任务。明确近期的战略任务以及具体的战术举措。

（5）乡村旅游分区开发规划

乡村旅游分区开发规划，是指根据乡村规划区内不同的自然条件、地理状况、人文条件、乡村旅游资源的特色，将资源要素相近、组成结构类似、发展方向一致的相关区域划分为一个主题性旅游区。乡村旅游分区开发规划一般包括以下内容：分区的地理范围，分区的基本概况，分区的发展定位，分区内重点开发项目等。其中，分区的发展定位包含了主题定位、特色定位和功能定位等内容。在乡村旅游分区开发规划中，需要遵循以下原则：①地缘特征原则。即空间范围的确定需要分析自然地理状况、人文环境特点、资源禀赋的差异性等要素，将地缘特征最相似的区域划为同一分区。②综合性原则。各分区之间的重点旅游产品应避免雷同，应各具特色，层次各异，又相互补充，避免同质化竞争，从而达到分区之间的差异化联动发展。同时，在同一分区内，也要进行功能的综合配置，形成一个内部相互组合协同的整体。③特色突出原则。特色是旅游业的基础核心，没有特色的乡村产品，就丧失竞争力和生存基础。分区开发规划应当充分考虑规划区内的特色旅游资源，在对资源赋存状况进行充分把握的基础上，进行分区划分。④主导因素原则。在任何一个乡村旅游资源区，乡村旅游资源的种类众多，识别其中的主导性资源，并以此为依托，抓住重点，把握主体性资源，并在此基础上才能有效进行规划设计。

（6）乡村旅游产品开发规划

乡村旅游产品开发规划是整个乡村旅游规划内容体系的核心，它是指根据不同的乡村旅游资源特色及资源禀赋状况，来规划设计不同类型、不同功能的乡村旅游产品，从而满足旅游者不同的旅游需求。在规划设计乡村旅游产品时，可以根据资源特色和市场需求，开发成观光型、体验型、休闲度假型、康体养生型、乡村节庆型等多种类型的乡村旅游产品。在乡村旅游产品开发过程中，还要综合考虑乡村旅游产品的线路规划组合问题。乡村旅游产品是一种具有鲜明乡村特色的旅游产品，从旅游产品组合理论上说，观光型、休闲型、娱乐型及节庆型的乡村旅游产品，一般应与周边地区其他具有差异性的旅游产品进行组合，从而形成区域整体化吸引力。因此，乡村旅游更应该与其他类型的旅游产品如风景名胜区、自然景区、历史文化景区等进行线路组合。此外，乡村旅游产品开发规划还涉及产品经营模式选择，通过选择合理的经营模式，可以更好地利用乡村旅游资源、调动利益相关者的积极性，使乡村旅游产品发挥最大作用。

（7）乡村旅游商品开发规划

乡村地区有着丰富的物产资源，诸多地方特产经过加工、包装后，就可以成为深受游客喜爱的旅游商品。乡村旅游商品的开发设计，就是依据市场需求，也就是旅游者的兴趣、爱好，开发设计不同类型、不同功能的旅游纪念品、旅游日用品、土特产品、特色食品等，丰富游客的乡村旅游体验。

乡村旅游商品种类繁多、功能各异，一般包括土特产品系列，诸如各地盛产的特色水果、海鲜、农作物等；旅游纪念品系列，如特色工艺品、乡村景点纪念品、民族风情纪念品等。

乡村旅游商品的开发设计应该坚持以下策略：

① 产品"包装"策略。乡村土特产品除旅游者自己使用外，往往也作为馈赠宾朋的礼品。因此，土特产品的包装就显得很重要，要简朴而不失艺术性，简单而不失巧妙构思。

② 产品创新策略。要用传统材料、传统工艺，融入创意元素，并结合新颖的故事题材来创新开发旅游商品，使之在保留原来商品的功能基础上，具有收藏、鉴赏、艺术价值。

③ 功能复合策略。在乡村旅游商品开发设计时，要尽可能把商品的实用性与纪念性、礼品性结合起来，使之既具有实用功能，又具有艺术观赏、收藏等功能，从而提高乡村旅游商品的附加值。

（8）乡村旅游市场营销规划

乡村旅游市场营销规划，是指在调查、分析本地乡村旅游市场现状的基础上，确定市场营销目标，从而进行乡村旅游形象设计，并规划设计针对性的市场营销方案。通过市场营销规划，可以巩固目标市场，拓展挖掘潜在的机会市场，增加市场辐射范围，树立起良好的乡村旅游形象，提高乡村旅游地的知名度和美誉度。

旅游区根据自身综合条件，确定一个或几个细分市场作为自己的目标市场。选择目标市场需要有一定的依据，一般要考虑以下几个方面：资源禀赋的价值大小，资源产品吸引力强弱，旅游区所要开发的旅游产品类型，周围区域的市场竞争程度等。在此基础上，再划分不同层次的目标市场。

旅游形象是旅游者对某一旅游地的总体认知和基本评价。旅游形象规划设计可以使当地政府和居民对本地的核心旅游资源、产品定位和发展目标有更清楚的认识，使旅游地在众多的同类产品中以鲜明的姿态出现在旅游者面前。在乡村旅游发展过程中，旅游形象规划设计发挥着越来越重要的作用。

市场营销规划涉及的内容很多，包括市场营销观念、市场营销战略、产品营销策略、销售渠道的建立、具体的促销策略、市场营销网络的构架等。其中，在市场营销观念方面，应该强化品牌意识，突出区域文化特色，注重社区服务的全面化、现代化。在市场促销方面，应合理运用各种广告宣传、公共关系等手段，加强联合促销的力度，如策划节庆活动促销、网络宣传促销等。

（9）乡村旅游支持保障体系建设

旅游业作为一种综合性很强的产业，需要协调各方面的关系，得到各个部门的支持，只有建立起完善的支持保障体系，实现各部门的协调、配合，才能促进旅游业的良性发展。

乡村旅游的发展也离不开各种支持保障体系的逐步完善。乡村旅游支持保障体系建设的内容包括管理与指导机构建设、乡村旅游经营管理工作、土地和税收政策支持、人力资源支持等。在管理与指导机构建设方面，可以成立各地乡村旅游指导机构专业委员会，在开发乡村旅游，特别是居民参与的旅游项目时，还要建立乡村旅游协会，作为行业自律组织。在乡村旅游标准化建设方面，应严格执行国家颁布的有关旅游行业的各种标准，建立市场准则和行为规范，实行对旅游企业的规范化管理，完善包括审批（年检、年审）、评比等内容的动态管理体系。

在政策支持方面，政府首先要发挥引导性作用，在基础设施建设、资金支持、土地供给、税收优惠政策制定上发挥积极作用。政府还应进行"引导性投资"，如通过产业引导基金、产业招商等。政府也要鼓励乡村居民的投资热情，积极引导他们参与旅游开发规划设计工作。在人力资源开发方面，要发挥政府的支持作用，在财力、师资等方面给予支持，帮助乡村地区培养、培训专业性人才，提高开发者、管理者对人力资源开发重要性的认识，逐步实行旅游从业人员持证上岗制度，实行先培训后上岗，制定优惠政策，吸引乡村旅游区以外的高层次人才到本地指导工作。

第五节　乡村旅游规划过程中的社区参与和产品开发规划

一、乡村旅游规划过程中的社区参与

社区是一个社会学概念，指聚居在一定空间的人群以一定的社会关系为基础所组成的社会生活共同体，是一种相对完整的社会实体。乡村旅游社区是指在乡村旅游资源地域范围内的常住居民，依赖乡村生产、乡村文化，在占有或利用乡村环境实体

（土地、村落、周围环境）的基础上形成的具有相同或相似的价值观和认知水平以及相对稳定的经济关系、政治关系和人际关系。

乡村旅游社区参与是指在乡村旅游发展中，社区群众通过各种方式和行为，全面而有效地参与到旅游活动中来，不仅参与旅游决策和规划，还参与旅游经济活动、旅游地环境保护、旅游地传统社会文化维护等多个方面。通过参与，使当地群众既能充分而公平地从旅游发展中获益，又能提高参与意识和参与能力使社区群众获得更多的自我发展机会，从而实现乡村旅游以及整个社区的可持续发展。

（1）社区居民参与规划及决策过程

在编制乡村旅游规划过程中，笔者询问社区居民有关旅游对社区居民的影响、社区居民对旅游的支持度等，发现旅游规划的社区参与性比较弱。是否开发旅游、旅游该怎么开发，基本上都是政府决策部门或者村委会商定。事实上，在乡村旅游规划过程中，需要确保社区居民拥有发言权和参与决策权，倾听居民对发展乡村旅游的看法。具体措施是，创造一个保证居民参与的咨询机制，充分反映居民的目标和社情民意，包括成立社区成员与旅游当局的联席会，定期开会商谈旅游发展相关问题；成立当地各阶层参加的旅游行业组织，使社区居民与其他利益主体之间实现沟通和协调。

社区居民作为乡村旅游发展中重要的利益相关者，必须对乡村旅游的发展与管理拥有决策权，让社区居民与政府和企业一道为乡村旅游的发展出谋划策，并提出意见。

社区居民参与具体决策内容包括：乡村旅游规划编制或对规划提出修改意见、决定乡村旅游发展的方向与管理模式、决定乡村旅游的经营方针及策略、决定乡村旅游发展利益分配机制等。具体参与决策的方法采用"居民-居民代表-决策层"模式。针对居民有权决策的每一事项召开相关居民大会，由居民分别发表意见，然后由他们民主选举居民代表，由居民代表收集整理居民所有的信息与意见，然后由他们作为代表参与到决策层的决策中，并适时地与居民进行沟通，成为他们的代言人与传话筒。这种双向沟通式的决策方式一方面反映了相关居民的意见，另一方面能灵活地适应决策过程中的变化因素。

（2）社区居民参与利益的分配过程

在乡村规划的实地调研过程中，参与旅游开发的社区居民或者当地农民很明显要积极得多，但他们对经济收入情况一般都有所保留。而没有参加旅游开发过程的居民则相对比较漠然，有的甚至对因为没有从中获益颇有微词。可见，经济收益驱动着社区居民对旅游开发的态度。社区居民参与利益分配，将有利于乡村旅游的可持续发展。

首先，要提供乡村居民参与乡村旅游、增加收益的机会，包括尽量给本地居民提供就业机会和商业机会。其次，旅游行政管理部门要在政策上和财政上给当地居民以扶持，包括制定保护居民从事旅游经营活动的法规条例；协助居民办理相关经营手续；规范其经营服务质量；为居民开展经营活动提供补助资金，协调金融机构提供低息贷款等。事实上，社区居民与政府、开发商的利益应该是互惠双向的。

利益分配是社区参与的最终目标，利益分配的实现效果直接影响社区参与的实现质量。目前，乡村旅游发展中由于社区参与的狭窄性，利益分配也存在很大的不公平性。社区居民参与所获利益包括经济利益、环境利益和社会文化利益，其中最让居民关心的始终是经济收益的分配，主要表现在直接经济收入、生活水平的提高等。

成立旅游社区行业组织，与社区居民共同制定利益分配方案，在制定过程中，要重点落实当地居民搬迁、占地、培训等方面的补偿，旅游收入分配，社区居民就业及福利改善等问题。大力协调社区居民通过资金投资、土地投资、技术投资等方式参与到乡村旅游发展中，包括餐饮设施的建设、管理，旅游产品的开发、销售等，增加居民的就业机会和商业机会；建立股份合作有限公司，将整个乡村旅游的投资额划分成等额股份，社区居民按投资大小享有股份的方式提高居民的控股权，具体运营模式可以是投资企业管理，也可外聘管理公司进行管理。

（3）社区居民参与教育和培训过程

对乡村旅游规划进行调研的时候发现，社区居民参与教育培训还比较薄弱。社区居民参与教育和培训，大致包括：一是接受旅游知识的教育，切实了解旅游业将会给自己的生活带来怎样的影响，以及如何正确看待旅游业；二是接受环境意识的教育，自觉树立环保观念；三是进行旅游服务技能和经营知识的培训；四是开展提高社区居民的旅游管理与规划能力的培训；五是介绍社区居民参与的条件、参与的过程、参与的政策、参与的收益等，提高社区居民参与旅游的积极性。从这个意义上说，居民参与教育培训与参与利益的分享是相辅相成的，目标上是一致的。相关的教育培训可由旅游行政管理部门或行业协会牵头实施。

（4）社区居民参与自然和文化保护

社区自然和文化环境的保护离不开居民的支持和参与。可采取的方法有：建立一定的渠道，居民反映对环境的要求，让居民参与旅游地环境政策的制定；监督和参与环境政策的实施，参与环境保护设备设施、机构的组织和运作；敦促旅游企业在开发和经营活动中减少对环境的破坏和污染，致力于形成良好的保护生态环境的社会氛围，同时对旅游者也形成良好的示范作用。在文化环境保护方面，以社区经济发展推动社区社会进步进程，努力改变旅游地社区文化的弱势地位；通过舆论、媒体等多种途径强化乡村居民的文化认同感和自豪感，并让其充分了解乡村旅游的发展对社区文化的影响和社会文化的未来发展方向；在青少年教育过程中，植入和加强社区传统文化内容，确保传统文化能够得到有效保留、传承和发扬。

二、乡村旅游产品开发规划

乡村旅游产品开发规划是指根据不同的乡村旅游资源特色及资源禀赋状况，来具体规划设计不同类型、不同功能的乡村旅游产品，从而更好地满足乡村旅游者的旅游需求，丰富他们的旅游内容。

1. 旅游资源产品化

乡村旅游资源是具有普遍性的潜在旅游产品，要将其转化为现实的旅游产品，需要在对乡村旅游资源进行客观综合评价的基础上，以市场需求为导向，进行乡村旅游资源的产品化开发。所谓旅游资源的产品化，它包含两个方面：一是旅游资源转化为产品，即旅游资源开发；二是旅游产品的重新组合，即旅游产品开发。要实现乡村旅游资源的产品化，必须做到以下两点：

（1）乡村资源产品化和乡村资源保护同步

国外乡村旅游开发过程中，往往由政府提供经济上的扶持，通过贷款、补贴和税收减免等措施帮助居民修缮历史悠久的老房子，将它们改造成为乡村旅游景点或是乡村旅游接待点。有些国家还成立了专门的机构，负责乡村地区旅游资源的保护和开发利用。乡村资源产品化和乡村资源保护同步，有效地解决了开发与保护的矛盾。

（2）注重乡村旅游产品的特色和组合

国外乡村旅游资源的开发过程中，十分注重产品的个性，比如法国的农场旅游。法国的农场划分为3大类型9个种类，其中美食品尝类包括了农场客栈、点心农场和农产品农场，休闲类包括了骑马农场、教学农场、探索农场和狩猎农场，住宿类包括暂住农场和露营农场，每一个农场都有自己的营业时间和营业范围，必须遵守一定的标准和规范。同为美食品尝类农场，农场客栈必须使用当地生产的农产品，使用当地的烹饪法，呈现出本地乡土美食的特色；点心农场一般在下午3~6点营业，只允许提供农场自产的点心，不能卖正餐；农产品农场要求主要原料必须以农场自己养殖的动植物为主，加工生产程序必须在农场内部进行。通过对乡村旅游资源的特色化挖掘和定位，更好地突出了产品的特色和个性，也指导了乡村旅游业开发的方向，避免了乡村旅游业开发的盲目性和无序状态。借鉴国外成功经验，国内开发乡村旅游也应该注重旅游产品的特色与组合，注重旅游产品的个性，充分实现旅游资源的产品化。

2. 旅游产品差异化

乡村旅游产品设计比较注重规划的可操作性和落地性，对具体旅游产品的特色和差异性有较高的要求。因此，乡村旅游规划必须要从乡村旅游产品差异化着手，提高规划的可操作性和实效性。

乡村旅游产品差异化分外部差异化和内部差异化。外部差异化是指不同区域（主要指民族差异和地域差异）的乡村旅游产品差异化，主要表现在自然环境、生态景观、价值取向、生活生产形态、民风民俗等方面。乡村旅游内部差异化是从空间尺度来说的，是指地域范围相对较小区域的乡村旅游产品差异化，一般是以区县域范围为单位。在该区域乡村中一般都有共同的生活生产方式和民风民俗。乡村旅游产品的内部差异化很大程度上取决于乡村自然环境和村庄历史文化渊源。

在资源产品化过程中，我们必须在对资源的正确评价和市场的客观分析基础上，进行特色化、个性化的产品规划设计。针对不同类型的乡村旅游资源，采取不同的资源产品化方式。

3. 旅游产品体验化

旅游体验是人类本能的需要，受到旅游动机和旅游场所的双重驱动，并随着旅游者的启程而展开，以旅游者返回居住地为终点。调查显示，随着游客消费心理的成熟，他们已不满足于"急行军"式的观光体验，期望近距离地、多方式地与旅游吸引物接触。在体验经济时代，由于人们对旅游产品需求量和品质的提升，旅游需求多样化，迫切要求在开发旅游产品时，要针对游客体验及个性诉求，进行有效的旅游产品供给。

通过主题化的设计，可以更好地形成产品的特色，满足游客的体验化需求。乡村旅游的体验化需要从两个方面考虑：

（1）旅游体验主题化

旅游体验需要有明确的主题，特色鲜明的主题是营造环境、营造气氛、增加游客吸引力的重要条件。目前，乡村旅游地普遍缺乏个性与特色，主要形式是采摘、农家乐。出现这种情况很大程度上是因为规划者、建设者、经营者缺乏鲜明独特主题的意识。主题的确定应根植于规划区域的资源禀赋，如所处的自然环境、民风民俗、乡土文化等，同时根据主要客源市场，即城市居民的需求，凸显个性、特色，与周边邻近地区的旅游产品进行差异化开发。规划选定主题，同时将游览观赏、农事参与、民俗体验、农家生活等活动内容进行主题化融入。

（2）旅游体验丰富化

对于城市居民而言，乡村旅游意味着离开城市的喧嚣、现代生活的压力，返璞归真，回归自然，到与城市存在差异的农村文化和环境中，寻求愉悦与放松。除了到农民家里体验田园生活之外，还需要有更多的选择和丰富的体验。因此乡村旅游开发必须加强乡村旅游体验产品的开发设计，为城市的旅游者提供丰富的产品和服务。同时要注重差异化体验场景的营造，遵循朴素、自然的基本原则，最大限度地突出和保持原汁原味的农家特色。

4. 旅游产品系列化

针对乡村旅游产品数量少，类型和功能单一，无法满足游客多种多样的旅游消费需求，造成游客停留短、当地居民收入少等问题，应该促进乡村旅游产品的系列化。着眼于紧密结合城市居民的观光休闲需求，在内容形式上要不断创新和多样化，形成产品系列。当前，国内外乡村旅游主要有高新技术农业观光园、花卉观光园、果蔬采摘园、茶园、农耕观光园、动物养殖园、特种蔬菜园、民俗观光村、民俗接待村、山村写生以及市民农园、共享农庄等多种形式，还可发展土特产品加工业、传统手工艺制作等。各乡村地区可根据自身的现实条件，选择若干项目进行开发，形成观光与参与相结合、动静相结合的产品开发组合系列，从而达到延长游客停留时间、增加当地居民收入、提高农产品附加值、提高旅游者满意度的目的。

第六节　乡村旅游设施与生态环境保护规划

一、乡村旅游设施规划

乡村旅游设施包括乡村旅游基础设施和乡村旅游服务设施。其中，乡村旅游基础设施包含交通设施、给排水设施、污水处理系统、电力通信系统等；乡村旅游服务设施包含乡村旅游住宿设施、商业与餐饮设施、游憩与娱乐设施、医疗救援设施。从广义上说，乡村旅游设施要满足旅游者的需求，从各个方面为旅游者提供服务；从形象上看，乡村旅游设施是乡村旅游区景观最重要的组成部分之一；从功能上讲，乡村旅游设施承载着各种旅游活动，是各种乡村旅游产品的载体。

1. 存在的主要矛盾

当前，我国乡村旅游设施规划中存在以下两方面的主要矛盾：

第一，旅游设施使用过程中居民与游客的矛盾。从设施的实际使用情况来看，许多乡村旅游设施不仅服务于游客，还同时服务于当地居民，如商店、道路、公共厕所、停车场等。到了旅游旺季，游客数量众多，乡村旅游设施就相对紧缺，经常造成居民生活的不便，也影响到了游客的游览质量。

第二，乡村旅游设施的配置与村庄用地的矛盾。在村庄规划中，建设用地一般是根据本村村民人口数量进行配置的。许多村庄规划时并未充分考虑到旅游人口的数量，服务设施用地面积偏小。旅游设施的选址也是一个非常重要的方面。若在乡村规划中没有考虑到旅游设施的规划，就需要在旅游规划中根据乡镇上位规划的设施布局和土地利用规划，重新进行考虑和协调。

2. 基础与服务协调配套

完善的乡村旅游基础设施可以保证乡村旅游进行科学有效的开发。因此，在开发规划时，需要对其进行全面而深入的研究和思考。在交通方面，应当对乡村旅游地及其周边的道路、出入口、停车场、游览步道、标识和导视等进行合理布局，使游客进得来、散得开、出得去。在给排水方面，需要保证给水的质量和安全，保证乡村旅游地的排水设施在暴雨时不会妨碍旅游者的通行，污水不会危及乡村的环境质量。在电力通信、供暖与空调、卫生设施等方面，也都应该相应配套，保证足够的容量。与此同时，乡村旅游开发还应当积极推动互联网的建设，如建设自己的旅游门户网站。另外，所有的基础设施之间应当统筹考虑、协调安排和弹性规划。

此外，还需要考虑旅游服务设施的完善和配套。在住宿方面，应当结合当地的社会经济和主要客源地客群结构及消费水平，尽量建设各种等级和形式的住宿设施，以满足不同人群的住宿需求。在商业与餐饮设施方面，应当尽量结合游客行为规律、人流量和公共空间进行布局，以方便旅客就近使用和集散。为了增加乡村旅游的乐趣，需要对一些游憩与娱乐设施进行艺术化的规划和设计，增强游客对乡村的记忆。此外，一些旅游辅助设施也不能忽略，如安全保障和行政组织设施等，对搞好乡村旅游也能起到至关重要的作用。当然，旅游服务设施之间及其与基础设施之间，也应当统筹考虑、协调安排和弹性规划。

3. 分散与集中有机结合

乡村旅游设施的空间布局主要有两种形式：一种是分散布置；另一种是集中布置。小型的接待设施如农家旅馆等，适宜结合农家住户分散布置到村落中。而商业娱乐设施宜适当集中，以形成游憩的氛围。从规划角度来看，商业服务设施都布置在主要道路的两边，而农家旅馆则分散布置在村落内。

以乡村旅游游客服务中心为例，一种是由政府旅游部门或旅游公司设置和管理的专业化的游客中心，主要功能有售票、购物、咨询、导游、展示、投诉、预订等。这种服务中心为减少对乡村旅游地的影响，并保证其功能和运营的相对独立性，一般位于与村落保持一定距离的独立建筑之中。但是一些乡村由于旅游地面积较大，交通流向较多而且比较复杂，为了满足服务和管理的需要，除了有旅游客服务中心集中行使管理职能外，还会有多个承担售票、购物、咨询、导游等功能的中小型服务点，它们一般散落在旅游地的各个交通出入口。

4. 单轨与双轨功能复合

所谓单轨，就是指乡村的旅游设施只为游客或只为当地村民服务。所谓双轨，就是指乡村的旅游设施既为游客服务又为当地村民服务。以乡村道路和其他基础设施为例，为了提高其使用效率，通常在规划时，既要考虑村民的出入交通问题，又要考虑游客的进出和集散问题。

规划更多考虑的应该是如何使更多的设施可以由居民与游客共用，实现主客共享，其使用方式上可以是部分使用、错时使用、错峰使用以及同时同地使用等。一些文化娱乐设施、休闲设施、餐饮设施等就可以比较多地共同使用。这样形成的基础和服务设施使用双轨制，既有利于当地居民的生产生活，又有利于游客的旅游活动。因此，为了增加设施的使用效率，营造舒适宜人、富有特色的村庄旅游环境与和谐的人居环境，规划时需要尽量对设施功能进行复合考虑。

5. 乡土与文脉完美融合

乡村旅游服务设施既是服务配套，同时也是乡村旅游的重要吸引物，因此，乡村旅游服务设施的设计在满足功能的同时，应该反映乡土文化，与当地的文脉相整合。

（1）乡村特色餐饮设施

餐饮设施建筑要具有乡土特色。引导居民发展特色旅游餐饮，包装形成"农家食坊"，为游客提供餐饮服务，将农业生产的有机食材与传统乡村饮食相结合，打造绿色美食体系，形成"乡村味道"农家食坊。

（2）乡村特色住宿设施

住宿设施应符合本地建筑风格，应与环境相协调。乡村旅游住宿设施是在乡村建设的适合城市居民旅游居住而又不失乡土特色的住宿设施。因此,一定要保持原汁原味的乡土建筑特色,与所在地的人文、地理、气候、民俗等相适应。要追求回归自然;讲究淳朴简洁,清新淡雅,赏心悦目,就地取材,其颜色的选择和建筑风格应与周围环境相协调、融洽、相映成趣。民居改造以风貌整治为主,除清洁能源的利用之外,加强庭院经济和景观环境的整治力度,为旅游接待服务提供良好的接待空间。客房内部采用乡土元素,以使游客居住在此,感受浓浓的乡土气息。

6. 技术与生态相互支撑

在旅游设施规划中需要在技术上引入生态的理念,使二者相互融合、相互支撑,以达到保护环境、节约资源、保持生态平衡、促进人与自然和谐相处的目标。

在乡村旅游设施规划中,技术与生态的相互支撑,主要表现在以下几个方面:

(1) 建筑功能生态化

从建筑功能生态化入手,突出旅游建筑与环境共生结构的设计,布局、采光、通风应当自然生态化。一方面,要重视建筑设施布局的生态化,根据建设场地气候、水文、地质地貌、植被以及周边景观环境特征,重视建筑设施在具体景观景点环境中的科学合理布局,充分利用和保持现有地形地貌特征,尽量减少和降低对景观环境的破坏,使建筑设施的体量、体型及整体构造与具体的景观环境和谐相处。另一方面,要重视建筑设施采光、通风的自然生态化设计,通过自然采光和自然通风结构设计,充分利用明媚的阳光和清新的空气,保持建筑设施与环境生态的自然交流,尽量减少能源损耗。

(2) 能源生态化

能源的生态化是乡村旅游区降低污染、保护生态环境的重要途径。能源生态化的重点是能源结构的调整及清洁能源的推广普及,如发展生态沼气等。

(3) 物质循环与再生

物质循环与再生是建立清洁景区的重要内容。建筑设施规划、设计、建设及运行中应充分考虑物质的循环利用,以减少物质的消耗,降低废弃物的产生量。节水技术应突出雨水收集利用、水循环利用。生态建材技术要突出当地石材、木材资源的利用,以及传统建材及建筑方式的挖掘利用。在各景区景点合理布局垃圾收集和处理站,普遍推行旅游垃圾袋装化收集和运出景区外集中进行无害化处理。

(4) 水生态化

水是乡村旅游景观中很重要的一个因素,景区建筑设施的设计应充分融入水生态化的理念,高度重视运用水生态设计技术,从供水、污水处理、水循环等各环节,通过生态化设计确保取水供水生态化、污水处理生态化以及水资源循环高效利用。

与乡村旅游结合得比较好的一个应用是人工湿地污水处理系统。人工湿地污水处理系统是投资低、能耗低、行之有效的处理与利用污水的系统工程,可作为污水二级处理的替代技术。它与常规污水处理系统的主要区别之一就是具有生物种群多样性的特点。

二、乡村旅游生态环境保护规划

旅游者乡村旅游的目的主要是享受大自然和娱乐休闲，从而达到身心放松的目的。因此好的环境对游客来说是极具吸引力的，它也是乡村得以持续发展的深层动力。生态环境保护规划就是从规划区现状出发，尊重自然规律，通过人们的主观努力，协调发展经济与环境之间的关系，以达到根据客观实际所规划的理想目标。它包括自然生态环境与社会生态环境保护。它的主要任务是：根据国家和地区的环境总体目标及旅游地的客观需要，针对旅游开发建设中可能出现的问题，对未来旅游和生态环境进行预测评估工作，并提出环境保护和整治的相关举措。

保护生态环境，促进乡村社会经济及其旅游事业的全面可持续发展，应当首先进行旅游开发的生态影响分析，然后分别从乡村旅游的旅游容量控制、制定生态环境保护措施这两个方面加以重点思考。

1. 旅游开发对生态的影响

乡村旅游业赖以生存和发展的根基，在于乡村的社会-自然-经济的复合生态系统。然而，在现实开发过程中，可能会由于在制定旅游业及相关行业发展政策时，未能充分考虑环境因素；或者由于旅游开发者和当地居民的急功近利行为，在开发、经营和管理中片面追求经济效益，结果造成负面影响，影响了乡村旅游业的可持续发展。旅游开发对生态的影响主要集中在：影响乡村生态质量、增加乡村生态环境负担、影响乡村生态文化等方面。

2. 乡村旅游的生态环保措施

为了实现乡村旅游生态规划的目标，需要采取一些有利于乡村生态环境保护的措施。

（1）把生态环境保护纳入法治轨道

严格执行环境保护和资源管理的法律、法规，严厉打击破坏生态环境的犯罪行为。加强生态环境保护的宣传教育，不断提高村民和游客的生态环境保护意识。重视生态环境保护的基础教育，积极搞好乡村公众教育。进一步加强监督，表扬先进典型，揭露违法行为，充分调动广大村民、游客参与乡村的生态环境保护。应当建立和完善生态环境保护责任制，实行严格的考核、奖罚制度。对于严格履行职责，在生态环境保护中做出重大贡献的单位和个人，应给予表彰、奖励。对于失职造成生态环境破坏的，应依照有关法律法规予以追究。

（2）实行保护和利用相结合的环保策略

乡村旅游资源是乡村发展旅游业的基础，旅游资源不加保护地被任意破坏，旅游业就成了无本之木，无源之水。保护旅游资源不受破坏，使其持续利用是发展旅游业的生命线，因此保护与利用是相互依存的，旅游业要发展必须注重生态发展。生态发展就是要求旅游资源的开发利用必须遵循生态规律，要受环境制约。从生态发展角度看,资源利用与保护相结合是关系生态系统的存在与发展的问题;从经济角度看,则是当前利益与长远利益相结合的问题。

(3) 制定全面有力的生态保育规划

乡村地区的田园生态环境是吸引旅游者的重要因素之一,是乡村旅游规划的重要组成部分,当然也是影响乡村规划的重要因素。所以,应充分考虑乡村地形、地貌特点,尽可能在不破坏建设规划场地原有的河流、山坡、树木等地理条件的同时,增加旅游功能方面的开发,从而创造出人工建筑与自然环境和谐一致,营造出富有当地特色的旅游生态环境。同时,还要调整由于不合理的开发经营和不规范的旅游行为而引起的生态负面影响,如生态多样性降低、土壤退化等。要加强对土壤、大气、水体等的保护和培育,使其朝着良性方向发展。

(4) 建立行之有效的生态环境保护监管体系

乡村的行政管理部门和个人应当各司其职,密切配合,共同推进旅游地的生态环境保护工作。要配合环保部门做好综合协调与监督,以加强自然资源开发的规划和管理,做好生态环境保护与恢复治理工作。要确定生态环境重点保护与监管的区域,结合本地实际,形成上下配套的生态环境保护与监管体系。

(5) 保障生态环境保护的科技支持能力

各乡村要把生态环境保护科学研究纳入本村的发展计划,鼓励科技创新,加强农村生态环境保护、生物多样性保护、生态恢复和水土保持等重点生态环境保护领域的技术开发和推广工作。在生态环境保护经费中,应确定一定比例的资金用于乡村生态环境保护的科学研究和技术推广,推动科研成果的转化,提高生态环境保护的科技含量和水平。要在旅游地建立早期预警制度,以加强生态环境恶化趋势的预测预报,做到未雨绸缪。

实践篇

乡村旅游规划案例

第四章
山东宁阳蒋集镇旅游发展总体规划

第一节 规划总论

一、规划性质

《山东宁阳蒋集镇旅游发展总体规划》为专项旅游规划,是围绕着山东宁阳蒋集镇经济、社会发展的总体战略部署,结合蒋集镇旅游业发展的现状,依据《山东省乡村旅游发展规划(2021—2025年)》制定的指导蒋集镇旅游发展的中长期战略规划。

二、规划范围

蒋集镇位于宁阳县中部,北依五岳之尊泰山,南临孔子故里曲阜,西与水泊梁山相望,距济南约100公里、泰安约40公里、曲阜约50公里、水泊梁山风景区约150公里。蒋集镇辖32个行政村,面积约65平方公里,耕地6.48万亩,2019年人口4.03万人。规划范围将综合考虑泰山曲阜等周边区域。

三、规划原则

1. 保护开发原则

良好的生态环境是旅游区生存和发展的根本,蒋集镇应将生态环境保护摆在重要的位置,应坚持"全生态"理念,在保护的前提下进行旅游开发,保护好优美的乡村自然风光,处理好生态保护与利用、防洪、建筑、交通等诸多关系。

2. 市场导向原则

要以未来市场需求为指引,根据市场的需求打造系列具有针对性的旅游产品和产业,增强蒋集镇旅游吸引力,做到自身发展与市场之间的互动。

3. 效益化原则

充分协调处理好蒋集镇环境效益、社会效益和经济效益的关系,协调处理好旅游发展与社会需求的关系,努力创造一个风景优美、设施完善、生态环境良好和旅游观光、人与自然协调发展的镇区。

4. 优化整合原则

对蒋集镇的旅游资源进行优化整合，农旅融合，联动发展，以打造友邦田园为核心，带动整个蒋集镇镇域旅游发展，同时联动泰山、曲阜等区域。

5. 转型升级原则

以"农旅为主、生态优先、三产融合"理念为引领，通过研学带动旅游发展，实现镇域经济的转型升级，从而带动经济社会的全面协调发展，实现蒋集镇乡村振兴和产业结构转型升级。

四、指导思想

根据蒋集镇"游学小镇、农旅蒋集、富美乡村"的发展定位，以"农旅为主、生态优先、三产融合"的理念不断推进乡村振兴。

要充分发挥蒋集镇在山水圣人线区位居中、成本洼地的优势，借助友邦田园和蒋集镇旅游产业集聚的雏形，打造旅游产业集群和研学高地，把蒋集镇打造为精品研学旅游特色小镇，伴随山水圣人旅游线走向全国、走向世界。最终带动农民共同富裕，进而实现预期的经济效益、社会效益和环境效益。

五、规划分期

本规划期限为2021—2035年，共15年。规划分为3期：

规划近期为2021—2025年，5年时间，蒋集旅游"培育成长期"。

规划中期为2026—2030年，5年时间，蒋集旅游"整合成熟期"。

规划远期为2031—2035年，5年时间，蒋集旅游"产业壮大期"。

1. 近期：2021—2025年为蒋集旅游"培育成长期"

进一步做大做强齐鲁彩山研学小镇，一方面挖掘和展示齐鲁文化；另一方面往彩山方向发展，重点开展乡村康养民宿和森林康养旅游，积极申报4A级旅游景区。同时联动白鹭生态保护区与张龙、郑龙等社会主义新农村的乡村旅游，大力开展宣传促销，开拓客源市场。完善基础设施和服务设施，建立健全保障体系；引导蒋集旅游"起好步、走好路"，取得良好的经济和社会效益，在宁阳旅游发展中发挥先行和示范作用。

2. 中期：2026—2030年为蒋集旅游"整合成熟期"

优化整合旅游资源和产品，培育重点项目和景区；完善乡村旅游营销体系，在巩固周边市场的基础上，积极开拓远程市场、专项市场；围绕着山东省乡村振兴示范镇的建设，打造旅游重点景区、精品项目和产品，提升经济效益；将蒋集建设成为宁阳旅游重点区域和泰安旅游新高地。

3. 远期：2031—2035 年为蒋集旅游"产业壮大期"

推进旅游品牌化、品质化和区域一体化发展，实现蒋集旅游的协调发展；以友邦田园为龙头整合镇域内的乡村观光、乡村休闲、乡村度假产品，申报打造 5A 级旅游景区，实现旅游产品多元化发展；蒋集旅游与小城镇建设、社会主义新农村建设相结合，实现城乡统筹发展；推进蒋集镇旅游转型升级和创新发展，做强做大旅游产业，实现蒋集旅游的跨越发展。

第二节 规划综合分析

一、上位规划分析

（一）《宁阳县乡村旅游总体规划（2014—2025 年）》

1. 空间布局——"一带三区"

根据宁阳县地形地貌特征、乡村旅游资源分布状况，结合宁阳县旅游发展总体规划的构想，依据空间邻近性、整体性、系统性、有机性的空间组织原则，将乡村旅游发展布局为"一带三区"的空间形态，通过水旱两路的网络化交通联系，形成"连接东西、沟通南北、活化乡村、整体联动"的一体化蒋集旅游格局，让宁阳县居民与游客能轻松享受到大汶河的绿色福利，同时又把散落一地的"珍珠"通过"一带三区"有机串联起来，形成整体组合优势。

汶河南岸乡村休闲带，为宁阳县大汶河沿岸的乡村风光带、风景带，亦即大汶河沿岸古文明保护带、大汶河沿岸观光农业带、大汶河沿岸乡村游憩带，包括鹤山镇、伏山镇、堽城镇、蒋集镇、磁窑镇五个乡镇，其中，鹤山镇是整个旅游风光带的龙头和重点。利用中皋岛、鹤山、皋山、琵琶湖、汶河湿地、禹王庙、堽城坝、古宅大院、白鹭生态保护区等资源，打造大汶河乡村旅游风光带，发展宁阳县乡村游憩带。

① 区位分析。该区位于宁阳县西北部、大汶河南岸，地势平坦，境内有鹤山、皋山、彩山等山头，历史文化悠久，与大汶河一起形成了一条休闲观景走廊，包括鹤山镇、伏山镇、蒋集镇、堽城镇、磁窑镇。

② 依托条件。省级地质公园——鹤山、白鹭湿地保护区，禹王庙，两处国家重点保护文物——堽城坝和颜林颜庙，三农文化博览馆，现代农业示范园，全国一村一品示范村——郑龙村等，大汶河（该段的大汶河景观最丰富，沙滩面积最大）。

③ 功能定位。河道观光、文化寻古、水上娱乐、岛上野营、滨水度假、户外运动。

④ 开发思路。汶河农耕文化、果蔬良种基地、太空蔬菜是该区的知名品牌。蒋

集镇南部以彩山带动周边的乡村旅游,中部以宁阳三农文化博览馆及设施农业为代表,北部以汶河白鹭栖息地带动郑龙村的乡村旅游发展。

2. 宁阳县蒋集镇乡村旅游发展导引

宁阳县蒋集镇乡村旅游发展导引表见表4-1。

表4-1 蒋集镇乡村旅游发展导引表

蒋集镇	白鹭家园三农示范镇	主要依托大胡村白鹭栖息地、三农文化博览馆、黄家大院、郑龙新三农示范区核心村、优质花卉种植基地等,发展大汶河沿岸文化生态休闲、民俗体验、农业观光体验旅游

(二)《宁阳县蒋集镇乡村振兴战略规划(2018—2022年)》

2018年10月,蒋集镇被列入山东省乡村振兴"十百千"工程,跻身全省100个示范乡创建之列,着力探索打造乡村振兴的蒋集模式。在新的时代背景下,蒋集要全面对接中央、省、市、县乡村振兴战略规划,加快实施乡村振兴"一二三四"战略。以打造"富美乡村"为目标("一个目标"),以游学小镇、农旅蒋集建设为特色路径("两大特色"),以发展现代农业产业园、彩山田园综合体、南部山区林果经济带项目为重点("三个重点"),推进农村党建提升、乡建人才集聚、美丽乡村改造、村集体经济增收("四项支撑"),推动蒋集乡村振兴走在全省前列,探索形成乡村振兴的"蒋集模式"。

① 一个目标。以绿色发展为引领,按照统筹规划、体现特质、提质增效要求,推动生产生活生态深度融合,全面提升生态宜居的农村环境,放大蒋集作为"宁阳之眼"的区域优势,深入挖掘蒋集丰富的生态、农业、文旅资源,打造全省乡村振兴的"蒋集模式",让蒋集成为全省乃至全国极富特色、令人神往的"富美乡村"。

② 两大特色。在坚持经济社会全面发展的基础上,逐渐推动蒋集特色产业发展。充分利用蒋集自然风景优美、农文旅资源丰富的优势,进一步推进生态蒋集和美丽乡村建设,加快发展现代特色农业和农业龙头企业,整合蒋集文化旅游资源,打造蒋集旅游文化特色品牌,推进"农旅蒋集"建设;结合彩山田园综合体项目,利用黄家大院、民俗馆、阙陵城遗址、大槐树、八音古钟等历史文化资源,培育一批游学项目,打造精品三条游学线路,推进"游学小镇"建设。

③ 三个重点。第一个重点是彩汶现代农业产业园建设。以绿色蔬菜、苗木花卉、畜禽养殖三大产业为主导,不断完善上下游产业链条。在已有农业产业品牌基础上,依托产业龙头企业,发展高效生态特色农业和品牌农业,推动形成和壮大一批农业产业品牌。推进农文旅产业融合发展,最终形成高标准的省级现代农业产业园。第二个重点是彩山田园综合体项目。依托蒋集绿水青山、田园风光、乡土文化等资源大力建设集"农业+旅游+教育+文化"于一体的彩山田园综合体。力争项目融入省会城市经济圈和泰山-曲阜黄金旅游线,成为独具宁阳特色的国家4A级景区,采取特色吸

引,错位跟进,满足旅行团队和自驾游的需要,吸纳承载大中城市旅客的休闲观光互动体验,带动蒋集及宁阳的经济发展。第三个重点是南部林果经济带的发展。按照山区农业旅游的总体要求,沿环山路上下科学布局,完善水电路等配套设施,选择核桃、榛子等耐旱林果作为主导果木。不断推动林果经济发展,到2020年实现林网全覆盖,沿环山道再发展经济林10000亩,努力建成南部林果景观道、花果山。

二、区域旅游发展格局分析

山东省的中西部,由北而南绵延着一条享誉世界的旅游路线,就是由济南、泰山、曲阜为中心构成的山水圣人旅游线。

山水圣人旅游线在短短一百多公里的距离内,聚集了两处世界自然文化遗产,四座国家级历史文化名城,两个5A、17个4A级旅游景区,在全国都是绝无仅有的。

蒋集镇要充分发挥它在山水圣人旅游线居中的区位优势,在山水圣人旅游线中进行准确的定位,与泰山等景区进行差异化联动发展。

三、发展条件分析

(一) 规划区概况

蒋集镇辖32个行政村,面积约65平方公里,平原、山区、丘陵各占三分之一。紧邻京沪高速、104国道、京沪铁路,交通便利,区位优势明显,素有"花生之乡"的美誉,先后荣获山东省文明乡镇、泰安市农业产业化先进单位、"五个好"乡镇党委等荣誉称号。

蒋集镇区域内自然条件优越,镇域地处泰莱平原,气候适宜,属北温带大陆性半湿润季风气候区,四季分明,雨量充沛。

蒋集镇是汶阳田所在地,创立了闻名全国的土地流转"郑龙模式",素有"生姜大镇""花生之乡""白鹭之乡"的美誉。蒋集有三张名片,有"一山一水一名人",即彩山、汶水和历史名人黄恩彤。

(二) 蒋集镇区位交通条件

1. 地理区位——汶河之畔,山水圣人旅游线居中区位

蒋集镇区位优势较为明显,处于交通节点,北依泰山、南临曲阜,"山水圣人"中华文化轴中间位置,大汶河之畔。

2. 交通区位——交通便利,可达性高

蒋集镇东距京台高速7公里。

在镇域范围内，G342 国道贯穿镇域东西，是主要交通通道。横向道路还有北部的汶河路、南部的环山大道，纵向道路有黄沙路、岗彭路、槐胡路、镇东路、西周路等。初步形成了"三横五纵"的交通体系。

(三) 产业基础

1. 现代特色农业深入发展

蒋集镇以有机蔬菜、畜禽养殖、苗木花卉、经济林等为主导产业。有机蔬菜、花生、生姜是特色农产品，素有"花生之乡"的美誉。花生常年种植面积 2 万余亩，生姜常年种植面积 5000 余亩。发展经济林近万亩、苗木花卉 2000 亩、有机蔬菜 3000 亩、养殖小区 20 个。彩汶农业产业园现有企业 13 家。

2. 工业效益稳步提高

初步形成了装饰建材、房车制造、化工肥料、食品加工等支柱产业，有规模工业企业 7 家，其中，国家级高新技术企业 1 家。

3. 服务业深入发展

蒋集交通便利，仓储物流、餐饮、住宿等三产服务业发展有天然条件。

(四) 旅游发展现状

从总体上看，蒋集镇旅游资源开发刚刚起步，旅游"六要素"无论在硬件或软件上都不能满足基本的接待需求，没有专门的旅游管理机构和旅游行业机构，缺乏对外宣传力度，在很大程度上阻碍了蒋集镇总体的旅游发展。

镇内成熟景区少，目前蒋集镇旅游资源主要以友邦田园为主打品牌。友邦田园 2019 年 5 月 1 日试营业，截至 2020 年底，已接待游客 45 万人次。

四、旅游资源分析

蒋集镇南部山区是黄淮的分水岭，滔滔汶水孕育了蒋集镇久远的历史和厚重的文化。

(一) 人文资源

蒋集镇悠久的历史形成了浓重的文化底蕴。这样浓重的文化底蕴带来的丰富人文资源为蒋集镇发展旅游产业奠定了良好的基础，是宁阳旅游业发展的重要资源。汶水是齐鲁文化交汇处，蒋集镇地处其间，人杰地灵，名人辈出，如唐朝诗人刘沧、晚清黄恩彤等。历史名人古迹丰富，如黄家大院、黄氏祠堂等。进入现代，蒋集镇有以"股份＋合作"土地流转模式为代表和现代农业产业园为主体的"三农"文化代表，如"全国一村一品示范村"郑龙村等。

(二)自然资源

1. 彩山

彩山,宁阳境内的名山,因宁阳境内诸山皆青,此山独赭,故称彩山。彩山位于山东省宁阳县蒋集镇东部、北依泰山、南偎曲阜、西傍水泊梁山,东邻104国道、京台高速公路和京沪铁路,蒙馆公路在山前穿过。

生态环境优美,森林覆盖率达98％以上,山高林密,蜿蜒曲折,面积广阔,气势雄伟,资源丰富。

山上天然景点众多,让人流连忘返,是休闲旅游的理想去处。清代名人黄恩彤笔下的《彩山赋》写尽彩山胜景。

2. 苗河一、二号水库

苗河一号水库位于蒋集镇肖傅村东南,是一座以防洪为主兼有农业灌溉等综合利用的小(一)型水库。灌区设计灌溉面积800亩,有效灌溉面积800亩。主要功能和作用:拦洪蓄水、灌溉农田、涵养地下水源。建成以来发挥了重要的社会效益和经济效益。

苗河二号水库位于蒋集镇前彭庄南,是一座以防洪为主,兼顾灌溉等综合利用的小(一)型水库。灌区设计灌溉面积1万亩,有效灌溉面积1万亩。主要功能和作用:拦洪蓄水、灌溉农田、涵养地下水源。

3. 大汶河

大汶河发源于山东旋崮山北麓的沂源县境内,汇泰山山脉、蒙山支脉诸水,自东向西流经莱芜、新泰、泰安、肥城、宁阳、汶上、东平等县、市,汇注东平湖,出陈山口后入黄河。

大汶河是全国最大的倒流河,河岸线约10公里,白鹭栖息地及湿地保护区位于大汶河的南岸。

(三)资源分析与评价

1. 资源分类

根据国家标准《旅游资源分类、调查与评价》(GB/T 18972—2017),结合调研组现场考察情况统计结果,整理出蒋集镇旅游资源如表4-2所示。

表4-2 蒋集镇旅游资源分类统计表

主类	亚类	基本类型	主要资源	数量
A 地文景观	AA 自然景观综合体	AAA 山丘型景观	彩山、骆驼山、杏山	3
		AAC 沟谷型景观	大汶河河谷蒋集段	1
		AAD 滩地型景观	大汶河	1
	AC 地表形态	ACD 沟壑与洞穴	仙人屋、圣人洞	2
		ACE 奇特与象形山石	福寿石、仙人屋、圣人洞、一剑天、五音石	5

续表

主类	亚类	基本类型	主要资源	数量
B 水域景观	BA 河系	BAA 游憩河段	大汶河	1
		BAB 瀑布	彩山瀑布、彩山跌水	2
		BAC 古河道段落	龙鱼泉古河道	1
	BB 湖沼	BBA 游憩湖区	苗河一号水库、苗河二号水库	2
		BBC 湿地	汶河湿地、白鹭生态保护区	2
	BC 地下水	BCA 泉	神龙泉（彩山）	1
		BCB 埋藏水体	蒋集汤沸珠玑	1
C 生物景观	CA 植被景观	CAA 林地	杏树园、核桃林、苹果林、山楂林	4
		CAB 独树与丛树	彩山松树、蒋集古槐、千年柏树	3
	CB 野生动物栖息地	CBA 水生动物栖息地	白鹭生态保护区	1
		CBB 陆地动物栖息地	彩山、骆驼山	2
		CBC 鸟类栖息地	汶河	1
D 天象与气候景观	DA 天象景观	DAA 太空景象观赏地	彩山	1
	DB 天气与气候现象	DBA 云雾多发区	彩山	1
		DBB 极端与特殊气候显示地	彩山	1
E 建筑与设施	EA 人文景观综合体	EAA 社会与商贸活动场所	蒋集集市	1
		EAB 军事遗址与古战场	黄家庵阙陵城遗址	1
		EAC 教学科研实验场所	友邦田园、泰安金利葡萄种植基地、千秋春	3
		EAD 建设工程与生产地	悦美客食品有限公司、泰安子泰食品有限公司、山野特房车、蒋集粮所	4
		FAE 文化活动场所	友邦田园、友邦智慧农业产业园	2
		EAF 康体游乐休闲度假地	友邦田园	1
		EAG 宗教与祭祀活动场所	华佗庙（彩山）、黄恩彤墓、黄家林、周仓墓、天齐庙、黄氏祠堂	6
		EAI 纪念地与纪念活动场所	公会杞侯莒子盟于曲池、张家圩子遗址、冯绍草堂、龙鱼泉遗址、曲水亭、古汶阳城遗址、曲池、阙陵城、栗家楼	9
	EB 实用建筑与核心设施	EBA 特色街区	郑龙村、张龙村、大胡村、小胡村	4
		EBB 特性屋舍	黄恩彤墓、黄家林、周仓墓	2
		EBC 独立厅、室、馆	友邦田园	1
		EBG 堤坝段落	苗河一二号水库堤坝	2
	EC 景观与小品建筑	ECA 形象标志物	八音古钟	1
		ECE 雕塑	白鹭雕塑	1
		ECF 碑碣、碑林、经幢	黄氏世德碑记碑、徐孟功德碑、黄家庵石碑、龙泉河碑桥	4
		ECL 水井	龙泉河	1

续表

主类	亚类	基本类型	主要资源	数量
F 历史遗迹	FA 物质文化遗存	FAA 建筑遗址	黄家大院、知青屋、铁道游击队建队旧址、彩山书院	4
	FB 非物质类文化遗存	FBA 民间文学艺术	彩山赋	1
G 旅游购品	GA 农业商品	GAA 种植业产品及制品	泰山豆腐宴、鲁菜、蘑菇炖柴鸡、泰山三美汤	4
		GAB 林业产品与制品	板栗、核桃、山楂、灵芝、何首乌、紫草、人参、枸杞	8
	GC 手工工艺品	GCB 织品、染织	十字绣	1
H 人文活动	HA 人事活动记录	HAA 地方人物	刘沧、冯绍、黄恩彤、黄恩澍、丁兆海	5
		HAB 地方事件	2019年11月成功举办2019泰山研学旅行国际交流会	1
		HBA 宗教活动与庙会	华佗庙朝拜、每年正月初九的华佗庙会	2
		HBB 农时节日	腊八、小年、除夕、春节、元宵、二月二、清明、端午、中元、中秋、重阳	11

经统计，蒋集镇旅游资源有：8主类，16亚类，45个基本类型，116个资源单体。

根据表4-2统计结果，对蒋集镇旅游资源总量评价和类型分析如下（表4-3）。

从资源总量来看，在8个主类，31个亚类和155个基本类型的旅游资源汇中，蒋集镇的旅游资源：8个主类，16个亚类，45个基本类型，116个资源单体。

表4-3 蒋集镇旅游资源类型统计

类别	主类	亚类	基本类型
全国	8	31	155
蒋集	8	16	45
比例/%	100	51.6	29

从资源的基本类型和单体分布情况来看，蒋集镇旅游资源的详细构成如表4-4，总的看来人文资源所占比例高于自然资源，人文资源占68.9%，自然资源占31.1%，人文资源中所占比例最高的是建筑与设施（37.4%），其次是人文活动（16.3%）。

表4-4 蒋集镇旅游资源单体构成情况表

序号	资源类型	数量	所占比例/%
A	地文景观	12	10.3
B	水域风光	10	8.6
C	生物景观	11	9.4
D	天象与气候景观	3	2.5

续表

序号	资源类型	数量	所占比例/%
E	建筑与设施	43	37.4
F	历史遗迹	5	4.3
G	旅游购品	13	11.2
H	人文活动	19	16.3
合计	—	116	100

2. 资源评价

按照《旅游资源分类、调查和评价》(GB/T 18972—2017)的评价标准，针对蒋集镇旅游资源现状，选取有代表性的旅游资源单体，以旅游资源的要素价值、资源影响力、资源利用条件、附加值等作为评价因子，进行赋值打分，并根据评价因子的权重，得出旅游资源评价等级（表4-5）。

表4-5 蒋集镇旅游资源分级评价

等级		数量	资源单体
特品级旅游资源	五级	—	—
	四级	5	友邦田园、彩山、白鹭生态保护区、黄家大院、友邦智慧农业产业园
优良级旅游资源	三级	6	栗家楼、华佗庙、黄氏祠堂、大胡村、小胡村、泰安子泰食品有限公司
普通级旅游资源	二级 一级	15	彩山书院、铁道游击队建队旧址、泰安金利葡萄种植基地、黄家庵阙陵城遗址、彩山赋、苗河一号水库、苗河二号水库、龙泉河、大汶河、悦美客食品有限公司、知青屋、郑龙村、张龙村、蒋集古槐、千年柏树

从表4-5可以看出：规划区特品级旅游资源为友邦田园、彩山、白鹭生态保护区、黄家大院、友邦智慧农业产业园。围绕这些独特的资源进行创意性的旅游开发，开展农业研学文化体验、森林康体休闲养生、湿地生态休闲、名人文化体验等特色旅游产品。

优良级旅游资源包括栗家楼、华佗庙、黄氏祠堂、大胡村、小胡村、泰安子泰食品有限公司等，这些资源具有一定区域特色，开发价值大。

普通级旅游资源主要包括彩山书院、铁道游击队建队旧址、泰安金利葡萄种植基地、黄家庵阙陵城遗址、彩山赋、苗河一号水库、苗河二号水库、龙泉河、大汶河、悦美客食品有限公司、知青屋、郑龙村、张龙村、蒋集古槐、千年柏树等，这些资源有利于观光休闲旅游产品的开发。

3. 旅游资源综述

蒋集镇山水人文资源丰富，有友邦田园、彩山、白鹭生态保护区、黄家大院、友邦智慧农业产业园，栗家楼、华佗庙、黄氏祠堂、大小胡村、泰安子泰食品有限公司、彩山书院、铁道游击队建队旧址、泰安金利葡萄种植基地、黄家庵阙陵城遗址、彩山赋、苗河一二号水库、龙泉河、大汶河、悦美客食品有限公司、知青屋、郑龙村、张龙村、蒋集古槐、千年柏树等,这些资源为蒋集旅游打下了坚实的基础。

蒋集镇旅游以友邦田园为核心和龙头联动整个蒋集镇域其他旅游资源点共同发展,并与泰山、曲阜进行联动,融入山水圣人旅游线,实现客源共享。

五、旅游市场分析

(一) 主要客源地消费能力与休闲方式分析

2020年泰安居民人均可支配收入30937元,首次突破"3万元大关",比上年增加1247元,增长4.2%。2020年,泰安全体居民人均消费支出18601元,同比增加499元。

济南居民人均可支配收入43056元,比上年增长3.8%,其中,城镇居民人均可支配收入53329元,增长2.7%;农村居民人均可支配收入20432元,增长5%。济南有约500万的出游游客量。

(二) 旅游客流量预测分析

旅游消费的弹性较大,出游目的地选择决策主要受到三个因素的影响:一是旅游资源的规模与品位,二是旅游产品的价格,三是旅游宣传促销力度。对蒋集镇旅游进行准确、独特的定位,增强旅游产品的适应性与多样性,把握市场趋势和人们的旅游偏好、消费心理,可以提高游客的到访率。假定蒋集镇旅游规划落实较好,开发措施得力,宣传营销效果好,2021—2035年游客接待量预测如下:

以2021年为预测期,第一个五年为快速增长期,年增长率为17%~25%;第二个五年为腾飞期,年增长率为14%~17%;第三个五年为稳定增长期,年增长率为6%~9%。

蒋集镇的旅游接待人次由友邦田园和其他景区两部分构成,2021年,友邦田园接待游客预计可达60万人次,预计7年后的2027年达到设计容量163万人次。其他景区2021年接待游客10万人次。经综合平衡,将2025年、2030年、2035年预测接待游客分别确定为144万人次、203万人次、221万人次。

近期(2021—2025年):蒋集镇旅游重点项目的发展阶段。以泰安、济南市场和山东省内城市市场为依托和突破口,拓展京津冀豫苏北等自驾车出游市场,借助各种市场拓展方式,推广蒋集镇研学、休闲旅游的新形象,扩大蒋集镇旅游的市场影响力。

中远期(2026—2035年):蒋集镇研学、休闲、度假旅游的稳步发展、全面建设阶段。随着旅游示范效应和波及效应,在稳固泰安本地、山东省内城市和山东周边重点城市市场的基础上，拓展和挖掘山东周边省市一般城市居民市场，打响蒋集镇研学、休闲旅游的品牌。

客源人数 $\qquad P=P_a(1+R)$

式中，P 为预测年的游客人数；P_a 为基础年的游客人数；R 为平均年增长率。

蒋集镇旅游接待人次预测见表4-6。

表4-6 蒋集镇旅游接待人次预测表　　　　　　单位：万人次

年份/年	增长20%	年份/年	增长15%	年份/年	增长8%
2021	60+10	2026	142+23	2031	163+43
2022	72+12	2027	163+26	2032	163+47
2023	86+14	2028	163+30	2033	163+50
2024	103+17	2029	163+34	2034	163+54
2025	124+20	2030	163+40	2035	163+58

（三）旅游市场定位

根据蒋集旅游产品特色及市场现状，目标市场定位为：立足泰安、济宁、济南，吸引省会城市群研学旅游、休闲游憩市场，逐步辐射省内其他城市的机会客源以及山水圣人黄金旅游线的分流游客。

1. 一级客源市场

一级客源市场即泰安本地市场及省会城市群市场。主要包括泰安，以及济宁、济南等城市的中小学研学旅游市场，政府机关、公司企业等素质拓展、培训教育、商务会议市场，城镇居民的亲子游市场，山水圣人旅游线的分流研学游客市场。

2. 二级客源市场

二级客源市场包括半岛城市群、周边省市及高铁沿线城市市场。以研学旅游为主要目的，依托周边著名旅游景区，形成互补促进、联动发展的旅游格局。

3. 三级客源市场

三级客源市场主要是国内中远距离城市市场，旅游人群主要包括回忆过往历史的知青，中高收入的老年人群，参加培训的学生家长以及一些慕名前来的人。

六、旅游发展SWOT分析

（一）旅游发展优势

1. 区位优势

蒋集在空间上处于山水圣人黄金旅游线路的重要节点，随着山水圣人黄金旅游线路的不断升温，蒋集的旅游发展面临着重要的历史机遇。

2. 旅游资源优势

蒋集镇拥有山（彩山）、河（大汶河）、水（苗河水库）、研（友邦田园）、名人（黄恩彤）五大旅游资源，五大旅游资源组合性良好，为旅游开发奠定了资源基础优势。

3. 农业产业优势

蒋集镇农业特色产业突出，农产品和特色商品丰富。花生、姜、灵芝、葡萄等种植规模大，形成了独特的地域品牌，产品质量得到消费者的广泛认可，具有比较大的产业优势。

4. 市场潜力巨大

蒋集镇位于山东省中部，临近济南都市圈，潜在客群较大；山水圣人黄金旅游线路的重要节点，泰山、曲阜之间的必经之路，每年数百万的客流经过蒋集镇，市场潜力巨大。

（二）旅游发展劣势

1. 资源挖掘深度不够

白鹭保护区、黄恩彤故居等具有较高义化、旅游等价值，目前资源均处于待开发状态，挖掘深度远远不够，将资源深度挖掘和呈现出米是将集旅游开发面临的重大课题。

2. 文化资源载体缺失

黄恩彤故居（黄家大院）、白鹭保护区（生态文化）、古楼民宅（厉家寨等乡村文化）、汶阳田农耕文化等各类文化资源的载体缺失，未能较好地呈现给游客。

3. 特色产品不突出

蒋集镇的旅游资源丰富，类型多样，除了友邦田园形成特色鲜明的研学旅游品牌之外，其他的景区景点尚未形成特色突出、具有较高吸引力的旅游产品。

4. 品牌带动效果不明显

蒋集镇提出打造研学小镇，友邦田园作为研学旅游的核心，对蒋集镇镇域内的其他旅游资源带动作用弱，未能在旅游线路组合等方面进行差异化联动发展，品牌带动效果不明显。

5. 旅游集群发展程度低

目前蒋集的旅游资源均为"单打独斗"，未能较好地结合各自的特色优势形成差异化联动，旅游集群发展程度低，并未与周边的景点形成集群式的发展模式。

6. 旅游人才缺乏

旅游经营管理人才和服务人才缺乏。多数从事旅游服务的人员文化素质有待提升，需要进行规范的培训，从而提升整体接待服务水平。

(三) 旅游发展机遇

1. 政策机遇

国家、山东省出台了若干促进旅游业发展的政策。国务院《关于促进旅游业改革发展的若干意见》与《中华人民共和国旅游法》等，这些都为蒋集旅游的发展提供了政策机遇。

教育部、国家发展和改革委员会等11部门联合印发了《关于推进中小学生研学旅行的意见》，随后教育部发布《中小学综合实践活动课程指导纲要》，研学旅行纳入小学、初中、高中阶段的必修课，为研学旅游提供了巨大的机遇。

2. 带薪休假制度的落实

鼓励机关、团体、企事业单位引导职工灵活安排全年休假时间，完善针对民办非企业单位、有雇工的个体工商户等单位的职工的休假保障措施。加强带薪年休假落实情况的监督检查，加强职工休息权益方面的法律援助。在放假时间总量不变的情况下，高等学校结合实际调整寒、暑假时间，地方政府可以探索安排中小学放春假或秋假。这些措施使得蒋集旅游发展面临重要的市场机遇。

3. 旅游行业复苏明显，增速回归

尽管2020年—2022年我国旅游业受不利因素影响，但我国旅游业面临的重大机遇和基本环境没有改变，旅游业总体发展趋势也不可能改变或逆转。我国经济社会发展的基本面没有改变，旅游业发展的动力依然强劲。我国对外开放不断扩大，各项改革稳步推进，城乡居民收入继续增长，居民旅游消费需求潜力依然巨大。改革开放40余年奠定的坚实基础，将有力地支撑我国旅游业发展。

4. 城乡居民旅游的休闲化

城乡居民收入快速增加和带薪假日浮出水面，使得近距离的休闲度假旅游将日益成为日常生活的组成部分。城市居民以回归自然、休闲娱乐、放松身心为目的的郊游（休闲、娱乐、寻幽、健行、自驾、会议、度假）将会成为日常需要而大量产生，全面小康进程中的农民也会逐步加入旅游休闲者行列。

（四）旅游发展挑战

1. 土地指标

旅游开发需要配套一定的建设用地，蒋集旅游资源丰富的地区，如彩山、华佗庙、知青点等地处山区和丘陵地带，建设用地规模较小，或者处于基本农田和一般农田地区，建设用地受到限制，因此在旅游开发规模与用地规模之间存在一定的矛盾，难以就地平衡资金投入，增加了对外招商引资工作的难度。

2. 同质化竞争

一方面，由于蒋集和相邻县市乡村旅游资源相近或相似，可能导致在旅游产品开发的定位和形式等方面雷同，带来外部同质旅游产品竞争的威胁；另一方面，由于蒋集境内不同乡村景点旅游资源相近，可能导致几个乡村旅游景点争着做雷同或近似的产品，带来内部同质竞争的威胁。

3. 旅游开发过程中生态破坏风险加大

随着乡村旅游的开发，资源持续利用和旅游可持续发展将受到一定威胁。

第三节　规划战略定位

一、规划发展战略

（1）打造精品、品牌带动

蒋集镇的旅游发展必须走"精品打造，强势突破"的道路，要重点培养几个资源品质好、市场符合度高的景区和产品，其中包括友邦田园、彩山、白鹭自然保护区、黄家大院等，通过高水准的打造，使之成为能够代表蒋集镇旅游形象的品牌产品，进而能够带动和辐射其他旅游景区，推动全域化旅游大发展，形成"一轮明月，群星璀璨"的发展格局，以精品树立蒋集镇旅游品牌，以品牌实现蒋集镇旅游的突破。

（2）联动发展，区域共赢

借势发展，充分发挥它在山水圣人线区位居中的优势，与周边泰山、曲阜形成旅游发展联动网络格局，带动蒋集镇旅游快速发展，形成区域客源互换格局。

（3）形象驱动，重点推广

推出鲜明的旅游形象——游学小镇、农旅蒋集，以形象为驱动，从市场运营的角度，形成蒋集镇品牌，并贯彻到蒋集镇旅游发展及城镇发展的各个方面，指导蒋集镇镇域形象和旅游形象的整体塑造。

（4）远近兼顾，统筹发展

旅游目的地的建设发展关系到整个区域社会经济的发展，是一个持续的过程，绝非一日之功。针对蒋集镇旅游资源丰富而区域经济基础薄弱的现状，在旅游开发中应避免一哄而上、平均使用力量，最后又落入平均发展、不温不火的状态。为了高效利用有限的旅游开发资金等资源，必须充分利用自身优势，根据市场需求变化，坚持循序渐进、稳扎稳打、分步发展、逐步推进的原则，实施渐进发展战略，即分清主次、明确步骤、留有余地、循序渐进地进行开发，实现规划的科学性、前瞻性、指导性和可操作性的统一。

（5）龙头带动，品牌培育

蒋集镇在旅游开发建设项目的具体实施上要做到宏观控制，突出重点，先易后难，分步实施，留有空间，滚动发展。要在"保护、整合、提升、发展"的前提下，分期分批实施规划任务，对优势资源、特色资源进行重点开发，精心打造，隆重推出，一举成功。避免一哄而上和遍地开花，避免乱上项目和上平庸项目。

结合全镇旅游发展目标，把握主次关系，明确政府和企业职责，以大项目开发为龙头，带动中小项目发展，坚持重点突破，对资源好、交通优势大的先开发，以点连线，以线带面，做到重点突破，以大项目带动全局，推动全域化发展。

以"农旅为主、生态优先、三产融合"理念为引领，通过友邦田园项目带动旅游发展，实现镇域经济的转型升级，从而带动经济社会的全面协调发展，实现蒋集镇乡村振兴，带动一、二、三产业的融合发展。

特色是旅游区的灵魂，旅游开发的过程也是展现资源特色的过程，只有突出了特色，才能使旅游资源有效转化为旅游产品。要突出蒋集镇自然生态优美、历史文化悠久、产业资源突出的特色，设计和开发具有特色的研学旅游产品。以市场为导向，积极引导社会资金、技术、人才向蒋集镇的优势特色旅游资源和发展方向聚集，打造独特的蒋集镇旅游品牌。

(6) 市场导向，持续发展

旅游产业发展的直接服务目标就是市场。市场需求的类型、特点、规模和档次，直接关系到产品开发的层次及经营状况。尊重市场、面向市场、服务市场是制定和实施本规划的基本出发点。

良好的旅游生态环境可以富民，保护生态就是对旅游发展的促进，美化环境就是提高旅游开发的竞争力。注意保护旅游生态环境，保护自然风貌和历史文化遗存，在保护的前提下进行开发和建设，防止破坏性建设。把严格保护、统一规划、科学开发和加强管理纳入法治化轨道。选择合理的发展模式和消费方式，注重人与人之间、人与自然之间的和谐共进，实现经济、社会和生态效益的统一。

(7) 政府引导，多方参与

蒋集旅游发展需要政府积极引导和大力支持，国家出台的一系列乡村振兴和旅游发展的政策法规，也明确了政府在乡村振兴和旅游业发展中的职能和作用。因此，蒋集要强化部门服务职能，协调政府相关部门，在规划、政策、资金、土地等方面积极引导和扶持旅游发展。同时，要发挥市场配置资源的决定性作用，强化农民在乡村旅游发展中的重要地位和关键作用，鼓励推广"农户＋景区、农户＋公司、农户＋合作社、农户＋协会"的经营方式，充分调动农民参与乡村旅游的积极性，尊重当地农民权益及主体性，实现旅游与乡村的共赢发展。

(8) 镇景合一，全域发展

在"全域旅游"思想的指导下，整个蒋集作为一个大旅游区，必须以"镇景合一"的理念指导全镇旅游建设。规划过程中，充分依托生态环境资源优势，结合各景点资源禀赋、区域定位实施，精细化打造，将具有集聚性的区域按照组团集群的理念进行发展，促进各区域功能要素聚集整合，实现规划区域旅游资源的充分开发、合理配置、协同增效。

(9) 主题聚合，集群发展

发展旅游首先要挖掘和凝练主题，整合和协调旅游各要素，创新旅游发展模式和经营机制，完善旅游产品体系，摆脱旅游"小、散、弱"的局面。同时要因地制宜，根据各自的特色和优势，实行差异化开发，错位发展。鼓励发展各类特色旅游村、特色乡村旅游景点等新型业态。

围绕研学旅游特色小镇和初步形成的旅游产业集群苗头，需要将单个看起来不起眼的一地"珍珠"进行有效串联整合，打造成为"悬挂在山水圣人旅游线脖颈的非常漂亮的珍珠项链"。

在全面深入挖掘每个村落历史文化内涵的基础上，尽可能打包开发，相邻村落或者文化特色相近的村落集中打造。考虑到蒋集现有的以友邦田园为中心的研学项目，可以把研学项目拓展到大胡小胡、黄家大院、黄氏祠堂、龙泉社区、白鹭保护区等区域，开展各种文化类研学项目，打造中西合璧的特色研学基地（友邦田园体现西方特色，文化类研学体现中国特色）。

利用好蒋集镇的自然山水、文化名人、特殊区位、特色乡村，打造特色浓郁的农旅集群小镇、研学旅行大本营，真正形成山水蒋集、文化蒋集、研学蒋集。

(10) 明确定位，联动发展

第一，明确友邦田园和蒋集镇的关系。友邦田园（齐鲁彩山研学小镇）为整个蒋集镇域的集散中心、服务中心、组织中心和核心节点，以友邦田园为核心联动镇域其他景区景点。

第二，明确友邦田园与泰山、曲阜的关系。友邦田园是山水圣人线中体验泰山文化和曲阜儒家文化的窗口，泰山和曲阜是相关文化的深度体验区域。因此，友邦田园与泰山、曲阜为窗口和深度体验的关系，从而实现窗口和深度体验联动发展。

同时，友邦田园在山水圣人线中可以承担第一站与落脚点的功能定位，以友邦田园为落脚点与集散地，然后前往泰山与曲阜。

二、规划发展定位

（一）总体定位

蒋集镇旅游规划总体定位为：研学旅游引导下的乡村振兴融合示范区、实践区、先行区。

在乡村振兴战略指导下，遵循严格的生态保护政策，依托蒋集镇山水林田湖村历史名人等优越的基底条件，构建以研学旅游为先导、产业为支撑、乡居养生度假为配套的乡村振兴示范区。通过一二三产业融合发展从而实现蒋集镇乡村振兴，将蒋集镇打造成为山东省乡村振兴的样板和示范。

蒋集镇乡村振兴示范区包含三个层面：第一，研学旅游开发；第二，产业聚集；第三，乡居配套。

1. 研学旅游开发

打造特色浓郁的农旅集群小镇、研学旅行大本营；做大做强友邦田园，打造彩山、黄家大院、白鹭自然保护区等，通过优化空间格局，整合核心游线，极点突破，以点带面，梯次推进精品项目建设，构建研学旅游为主题特色的旅游目的地。

2. 产业聚集

以研学旅游产业为导向的多种产业聚集，包括林果业、土特产与工艺品加工、养生、康疗、会议等；进行泛旅游产业整合，突破研学旅游产业链式结构，构建产业集群，实现多产业聚集效应。

3. 乡居配套

田园综合体、旅游民俗村、村居驿站等。

（二）产业定位

1. 蒋集经济发展的朝阳产业

发展旅游可以将农业产业、工业与服务业有效对接和融合，发挥旅游业产业关联度强、带动作用大的优势，完善"吃、住、行、游、购、娱"等旅游产业链条，增加第三产业在经济体中的比重，把旅游业培育成为蒋集经济增长的朝阳产业。

2. 城乡统筹发展的动力产业

农村和城镇是相互联系、相互依赖、相互补充、相互促进的，农村发展离不开城镇的辐射和带动，城镇发展离不开农村的促进和支持。近几年，蒋集十分重视城乡统筹发展，通过非农手段，转移农村劳动力，增加农民收入，推进城镇化发展。未来，通过大力发展研学旅游，推动产业"接二连三"，实现以旅促农、以镇带村、产业融合，促进城乡统筹协调发展。

3. 新农村建设的导引产业

研学旅游发展可以充分利用田园风光、民俗文化、农业特色产业等乡村资源，为城镇居民提供旅游产品和服务，实现农业产业结构调整，增加农民收入，发展农村经济。通过发展研学旅游，改善村居环境，加强乡村文明建设，提高村民素质，从而引导蒋集加快社会主义新农村建设。

4. 实现和谐富民的民生产业

乡村旅游是促进农村经济发展、富农惠农的民生产业。乡村旅游的开发主体，可以是独立经营的农户，也可以是集体或私营的企业。独立经营农户，以采摘、农家乐、垂钓园等方式，直接为游客提供服务。农村集体企业提供的具有一定规模和一定档次的旅游休闲服务，不仅就地消化了农产品，吸收农民就业，而且带动了区域的发展。乡村旅游还可以增加城乡交流，促进城乡居民和谐共处。

（三）形象定位

旅游区性质定位和形象设计在很大程度上影响旅游者的出游决策，是旅游地的灵魂,是形成市场竞争优势的关键。鲜明的旅游市场形象不仅便于旅游者识别,而且能突出旅游地的独特个性,从而吸引更多的旅游者。蒋集镇的旅游性质定位是对本镇旅游形象的总体认识和本质概括,旅游形象设计使旅游地政府和旅游者对本地旅游的核心资源、产品定位和发展目标有更清楚的认识,使旅游地在众多的同类产品中以鲜明的姿态出现在旅游者面前。蒋集的形象定位:"游学小镇、农旅蒋集!""山水圣人线上有个蒋集游学小镇!"首先打造友邦田园(齐鲁彩山研学小镇)4A级景区,以齐鲁彩山研学小镇为龙头和核心,通过研学旅游线路来整合辐射联动其他的景区景点,整合整个镇域资源,打造5A级旅游景区,最终将蒋集打造成为国内著名的研学旅游目的地。

第四节　空间布局规划

一、空间结构规划

(一) 空间布局原则

1. 主题突出原则

在空间布局上,将根据将集各种资源的不同主题和资源分布现状以及资源特点,在空间上最大限度地整合同类旅游资源,以突出不同的资源特点和主题,为品牌营造和市场营销创造良好条件。

2. 适度集中原则

根据蒋集旅游资源特点、市场发展方向和旅游者的游览偏好,将相同或类似的旅游资源适度集中,将分散的、零星的或者体量小的、资源禀赋一般的组合到一起,形成较大集群,发挥集团优势,把蒋集旅游做大做强。

3. 协调发展原则

蒋集旅游的"山水林田湖村历史名人"资源齐全,但又各具特色,分布相对独立。在空间布局中,将通过道路交通、游线组织、产业融合、设施建设等加以整合,使蒋集旅游中研学、乡村体验、休闲度假、康体养生等多重功能协调发展,保障蒋集旅游的完整性和丰富性。

4. 体现资源特色,充分合理分区

分区要充分体现资源的特色,不同功能区主打的旅游产品不同,但都与自身的功能相互协调一致。同时,要依据资源的现状和与周边区域的关系,合理分区,充分提升对资源价值的利用。

5. 遵循产业集聚的原则

旅游空间布局应在特定的地区,形成一种集中化的旅游产业布局,集中发展,打造规模较大的大项目，提升区域竞争力。

（二）空间结构与功能分区规划

结合旅游发展总体规划的构想、开发理念与思路，以及蒋集地形地貌特征、项目发展现状、资源分布状况，依据邻近性、整体性、系统性、有机性的空间组织原则，将旅游发展布局为"一核三片多组团"的空间形态，通过网络化交通联系，构建"核心带动，片区联动，组团支撑"的蒋集旅游格局，通过友邦田园研学旅游带动镇域旅游发展，蒋集北部、中部、南部联动发展，把散落一地的"珍珠"有机串联起来，形成整体组合优势。

1. 核心带动

构建研学旅游核心，友邦田园为整个蒋集镇域的集散中心、服务中心、组织中心和核心节点，以友邦田园为核心联动镇域其他景区景点，带动整个蒋集镇域旅游的发展。

2. 片区联动

南部片区以彩山森林康体养生、历史感悟、滨湖休闲为主，中部片区以智慧农业与工业观光研学为主，北部片区以汶河白鹭湿地研学游憩、三农文化研学、黄恩彤文化研学为主。南部、北部、中部三大片区功能互补，差异化联动发展。

3. 组团支撑

南部彩山森林康体养生组团，历史感悟与滨湖休闲组团；中部智慧农业与工业观光研学组团；北部汶河白鹭湿地研学游憩组团，三农文化研学组团；西北黄恩彤文化研学体验组团。通过组团来支撑整个项目的发展。

二、项目体系规划

蒋集旅游产品要考虑资源禀赋、市场需求、交通区位等多种因素集约化开发，避免遍地开花。要开发类型多样的旅游产品，增强产品的休闲性、参与性、体验性，打造功能多元化的旅游产品集群，建设集研学科普、观光、休闲、度假于一体的综合休闲旅游地，形成具有竞争力的旅游产品体系。蒋集镇研学旅游项目体系见表4-7。

三、项目规划布点

根据蒋集镇镇域的地形地貌、交通条件、存量资源状况、增量资源发展潜力以及市场需求，形成了蒋集镇南部、中部、北部三大研学旅游发展片区。南部研学旅游片区主要由历史感悟与滨湖休闲组团、彩山森林康体养生组团、友邦田园研学核心组团构成；中部研学旅游片区主要由智慧农业与工业观光研学组团构成；北部研学旅游发展片区主要由黄恩彤文化研学体验组团、汶河白鹭湿地研学游憩组团、三农文化研学组团构成。

表 4-7 蒋集镇研学旅游项目体系

蒋集南部研学旅游发展片区				蒋集中部研学旅游发展片区			蒋集北部研学旅游发展片区			
友邦田园研学核心组团	彩山森林康养养生组团	历史感悟与滨湖休闲组团		智慧农业与工业观光研学组团	汶河白鹭湿地研学游憩组团		三农文化研学组团			黄恩彤文化研学体验组团
研学友邦	康养彩山	渔乐肖堌	感悟怀古	工业研学	白鹭家园	生态大胡	知礼小胡	改革郑龙	泉润张龙	厚德添福
1. 青少年活动中心 2. 友邦颐养部落	1. 自驾车营地 2. 知青博物馆 3. 林下产业种植基地 4. 悬空玻璃观光台 5. 彩山堂 6. 山地运动拓展公园 7. 生态停车场 8. 森林课堂 9. 星海银河夜游道 10. 夜间幻影森林 11. 森木七养	1. 休闲垂钓园 2. 浑水摸鱼乐园 3. 渔家乐 4. 水库打渔体验	1. 柏树怀古 2. 大槐树怀古 3. 栗家楼村史文化馆	1. 友邦智慧农业产业园 2. 子秦工业观光工厂 3. 悦美客食品观光工厂	1. 汶河白鹭栖息家园 2. 露营基地 3. 白鹭驿站	1. 农家养生主题餐厅 2. 乡村驿站 3. 农家采摘园 4. 葡萄采摘园 5. 乡愁体验馆 6. 特色交通工具 7. 白鹭文化广场 8. 游客服务中心 9. 瓜果采摘园 10. 乡村创意公园 11. 家庭庄园 12. 田园课堂	1. 中国宁阳灵芝小镇 2. 开心牧场 3. 乡村动物园	1. 郑龙村史馆 2. 农业研学基地 3. 七彩采摘园 4. 大地创意景观 5. 郑农场	1. 张龙民俗街 2. 二日农 3. 张龙驿站 4. 农耕体验园 5. 农家主题餐厅 6. 工坊部落 7. 租赁农庄 8. 农家部落 9. 原乡酒吧	1. 黄家大院修复 2. 黄氏祠堂修复

第五节　分区项目规划

一、友邦田园（齐鲁彩山研学旅游小镇）研学核心组团

（一）项目范围

项目范围北至 G342 国道，南至彩山环山路，西至蒋集镇蒙八路，东至宁阳经济开发区彩山大道，涉及蒋集镇守安村、八大庄村、赵庄村，经济开发区羊栏村、枕河村、彩山村等，规划面积为 5000 亩。

（二）发展状况

2019 年 5 月 1 日友邦田园项目试营业以来，已接待游客超过 45 万人次，2019 年 11 月成功举办 2019 泰山研学旅行国际交流会，被国际营地协会指定为"第十二届世界教育营地大会（ICC2020）泰安分会"和"2022 亚太营地教育大会"承办单位，是"中国营地教育泰山论坛"发起单位和永久会址，已形成品牌效应并不断提升国际影响力。

目前友邦田园项目已与某教育投资集团签订战略合作协议，每年安排 7 万名中小学生来营地研学；列入泰安市青少年研学实践基地，每年约有 5 万名中小学生研学生源；周边游、亲子游、休闲游等主要辐射到泰安、济南、济宁等 2～3 小时车程的游客；泰山文化、儒家文化具有较高的国际影响力和吸引力，友邦田园位于泰山、曲阜之间，不到 1 小时车程，其农耕文化与两大文化形成互补，对国内外游客具有一定吸引力。

（三）发展定位——全国一流的青少年示范性综合实践基地

依托"山水圣人"中华文化轴、泰山曲阜黄金旅游线，最终将友邦田园打造成国际知名教育营地，国家级田园综合体，创建独具特色的国家 5A 级风景区，全国一流的青少年示范性综合实践基地，成为乡村振兴"齐鲁样板"新亮点、"好客山东"新名片、研学旅行新地标。

（四）规划思路

1. 开展合作，拓展研学旅行市场

随着世界营地大会的召开，行业和品牌影响力逐步提升，通过与国内高端研学机构和国外营地机构合作，拓展中小学生研学旅行市场。

2. 空间扩容，做大做强自身，联动辐射周边

① 建设青少年活动中心（梦幻中心），深入挖掘、展示齐鲁文化。

② 空间扩容。借助八大庄村农家院旧址，村庄内古井、池塘、原生树木，在原有村落格局得到较好保留的基础上对八大庄村农家院进行升级改造，使乡村自然风光得到原汁原味的呈现，成为泰安市乃至山东省展示农耕文化的特色民宿村。生活和农业相结合，游客可在此体验田趣，满足都市人回归田园牧歌的理想；设置家庭菜园，供康养人士体验农耕劳作。

③ 借助彩山资源发展森林康体养生产品。

④ 联动周边的农作物产业，如山楂，打通山楂种植、加工、推广产业流程，形成独特品牌。

⑤ 以友邦田园为龙头，通过研学联动蒋集镇域其他的景区景点，以全域旅游为理念，打造研学旅游目的地。

二、南部彩山森林康体养生组团

（一）规划思路

对接城市居民周末休闲康体养生市场需求，打造集观光采摘、特色餐饮、休闲娱乐、科普教育、拓展培训等为一体的旅游产品体系。依托南部山区防火通道建设，带动周边农家乐等乡村旅游，带动南部山区增收致富。

赋予南部山区休闲娱乐功能，开发军事研学项目，重点发展军事拓展、野战兵生存法则训练等。规划自驾车营地、知青博物馆、山地运动拓展公园、悬空玻璃观光台、彩山亭、星海银河夜游道、夜间幻影森林、森林课堂、森林七养等休闲娱乐项目。

（二）规划项目（部分介绍）

1. 自驾车营地

自驾车营地是自助或半自助服务的休闲度假区，是集休闲、娱乐、居住、服务于一体的综合性旅游休闲度假场所。

营地服务区既是车辆的主入口，也是综合的配套服务区，对进入营地的车辆和游人进行有效管理，主要包括管理中心、加油和维修中心、医疗服务中心、生态餐厅和汽车旅馆、超市、娱乐中心等。

自驾车营位为普通的家用轿车提供停车及休闲服务。

房车营位配备 AC 电源插座、水龙头，设露营车专用污水排放系统，相连停车位之间畅通无阻。

木屋采用实木建设，体现原生态；门窗正对的方向，要确保至少一面景观良好。

2. 知青博物馆

知青博物馆以知青文化为主题，依托老知青居住地，进行保护性开发，通过知青年代实景、知青时代文物、知青蜡像展示，再现知青上山下乡工作场景。同时设置知青文化主题餐馆、知青客栈、知青休闲吧、知青商品店等。

3. 林下产业种植基地

充分利用彩山的树林资源，大力发展林禽、林药、林苗、林菜等林下产业。种植中草药，如何首乌、四叶参、紫草、黄精等，既有经济价值，又形成一道亮丽的景观。

4. 悬空玻璃观光台

将玻璃观光台悬于岩壁之上，既是一个景观标的物，又是游客游览途中休憩体验的重要节点，游客来此既可以全方位欣赏美景，又可以感受脚下悬崖的惊险刺激。

5. 彩山亭

依托登山步道，于风景秀美之处，设计休憩观景平台"彩山亭"。观景平台的设置及设计要遵循游客心理感知，注重景观的多样化统一，观景平台的空间距离相对合理等。

6. 山地运动拓展公园

以地形为依托，建设山地运动拓展公园，以满足户外拓展、旅游观光等多种需求。山地运动项目主要由崖壁秋千、空中滑索、森林滑行等部分构成。

7. 生态停车场

规划多个生态停车场，生态停车场要求绿化高、透水性好、草的成活率高。车位间种植杨树、柳树等高大乔木，树木充当车位与车位之间的隔离，同时夏天可以给车辆遮阴，减少太阳暴晒。

8. 森林课堂

依托彩山树林资源，开展森林课堂研学活动，主要引导孩子记录和观察森林里的动植物，同时利用树林环境中的自然材料进行艺术创作，培养孩子们的动手制作能力。

9. 星海银河夜游道

打造夜游项目"星海银河夜游道"。选择人流量密集的百米游步道，在游步道的铺设材料上选用夜光石，绘制出一道绚丽的"星海银河画卷"。

10. 夜间幻影森林

选择合适的区域，依托茂密的树林，采用灯光照明设备，营造如梦如幻的夜间童话世界场景，开展夜间旅游，延长游客停留时间。

11. 森林七养

依托彩山良好的森林植被条件打造森林养生项目，设置七个休闲场地对应七个养生主题，分别是养心、养体、养眼、养肺、养神、养性、养情，通过游步道和游线进行串联，构建一条养生主题游线。

三、南部历史感悟与滨湖休闲组团

(一) 肖傅渔家风俗风情村

1. 规划思路

依托苗河二号水库及肖傅村,形成一个以渔业养殖、渔业观光、垂钓、渔业休闲、特色渔餐为主的渔家生活体验特色村。

利用周边山乡水韵的乡村意境,体验泛舟打渔体验,与渔民"同吃、同住、同打渔",吃渔家饭、住渔家院、享渔家乐,体验渔民的生活。

开发休闲渔业、渔家住宿、湖鲜美食、滨湖娱乐、垂钓等项目,完善相关配套设施,营造舒适、自然的旅游环境,打造以住渔村、赏渔俗、吃湖鲜、坐渔舟、戏湖水、买湖货等为主要活动内容的原生态渔家风俗风情区。

2. 规划项目

(1) 休闲垂钓园

依托苗河二号水库,在靠近岸边合适的区域打造休闲垂钓园,针对不同的游客诉求,设置休闲垂钓区、竞技垂钓区。通过举办垂钓比赛来提升知名度和影响力,通过垂钓比赛构建一个对鱼爱好者、钓手、赞助商以及游客开放的以渔业为基础的娱乐平台,以鱼会友、以友增技。

(2) 浑水摸鱼乐园

小溪里捉鱼、捉螃蟹是很多游客的童年乐趣和乡愁记忆,因此规划浑水摸鱼乐园,针对亲子、团队市场。设计抓鱼比赛活动的池塘,定期举办比赛活动,吸引周边的游客,让参与者尽享浑水摸鱼之乐。

(3) 渔家乐——全鱼宴

游客将自己捕捉到的鱼选择自己喜欢的吃法来进行烹饪,打造特色全鱼餐饮项目。

以苗河水库鱼为原材料,以土、鲜、清为特色,打造特色餐厅。

(4) 水库打渔体验

培训渔民,保证游客水库活动安全的前提下,开展"做一天渔民"活动,让游客跟随渔民一起坐渔船下网捕鱼,亲身体验渔民生活,学习渔业生产知识,领略渔村风土人情。

(二) 大槐树村怀古

1. 柏树怀古

依托大槐树村千年柏树进行观光怀古。一方面,对古柏树进行严格保护,设置围栏,安装摄像头;另一方面,对古柏树的历史脉络进行深入挖掘,并用标识牌以文字方式呈现给游客，对中小学生起到科普教育作用，也能使人们感悟到大自然沧海桑田的变迁与生命的顽强。

2. 大槐树怀古

依托大槐树村古槐树进行观光怀古。第一，对古槐树进行严格保护，设置围栏，安装摄像头。第二，将古槐树的历史脉络进行深入挖掘，并用标识牌以文字方式呈现给游客，对中小学生起到科普教育作用，也能使人们感悟到大自然沧海桑田的变迁与生命的顽强。第三，提升槐树周边的景观，种植乡土特色的花和菜。第四，在古槐树旁边建一座小庙，承载游客祈福祭拜、文化寻根功能。第五，将院落石头墙换成围栏，打通游客景观视线。

（三）栗家楼村史文化馆

规划栗家楼村的村史馆，展示栗家楼村的历史渊源；采用当地传统建筑形式，外观古朴，内部将传统农业技术、物候与节气、农产品加工、民间艺术和技艺、民间节庆等方面进行集中展览展示，供游客参观。

四、中部智慧农业与工业观光研学组团

（一）友邦智慧农业产业园（宁阳三农文化博览馆）

1. 发展现状

友邦智慧农业产业园中的宁阳三农文化博览馆是以"三农"为主题的文化博览馆，建筑面积4200平方米，以中华农耕文化及宁阳三农的悠久文化为底蕴，是集知识性、科学性、趣味性和互动性于一体的综合性展陈展示场馆。

2. 提升思路

针对青少年客群，开展研学科普活动，在现有展馆的基础上，利用博览馆的室内空间，运用VR等可视化技术手段，设置多种互动项目，包括VR体验区，全息立体体验区，时光穿越区等。设置影视中心，进行影视展示和研学授课。

（二）泰安子泰蔬菜观光工厂

1. 工厂概况

泰安子泰食品有限公司成立于2018年5月，是一家集种植、加工、销售农产品于一体的综合性企业。工厂占地约27000平方米，加工车间面积约7000平方米，冷冻库约4800平方米。主要产品涵盖：鲜果蔬、大蒜、姜、山药、胡萝卜、苹果、梨等；有机冷冻果蔬，毛豆荚、毛豆仁、西兰花、白花菜、菠菜、蒜米、蒜丁、青刀豆、各类混合菜等。产品主要销往日本、美国、加拿大、欧盟等国家和地区。

2. 规划思路

在不影响工厂生产的基础上,依托现有的观光通道打造食品观光工厂,针对青少年客群开展科普研学活动,一方面起到科普教育的功能,加深对蔬菜深加工的认知;另一方面扩大企业的知名度和影响力。

(三)悦美客食品观光研学工厂

1. 工厂概况

泰安悦美客食品有限公司于2014年12月23日成立,主要经营速冻米面食品(生制品)、速冻其他食品(速冻肉制品、速冻果蔬制品等)等。

2. 规划思路

在不影响工厂生产的基础上,规划观光通道打造食品观光工厂,针对青少年客群开展工业研学活动,一方面起到科普教育的功能,另一方面扩大企业的知名度和影响力。

五、西北黄恩彤文化研学体验组团

1. 现状分析

黄家大院位于大汶河南岸蒋集镇的添福庄,是以黄恩彤为代表的黄氏家族庄园,现存有黄家故居和家祠。

2. 存在问题

故居和家祠已多年失修,破败不堪,以往的宏大建筑格局不复存在,古建筑周边的传统风貌遭到破坏,代之而起的是缺乏时代气息的现代化的民居民房。

3. 发展定位

名人故居观光休闲、历史怀古、科普研学、文化体验。

4. 规划要点

(1)保护性修缮黄家大院,申请省级重点文物保护单位

近期,利用部分恢复、典型恢复和适当仿造的办法,扩大宅院空间,主要建设黄氏主宅、私塾、待客院等功能空间。远期,逐步调整周边的宅基地,恢复完整的黄家大院,向人们展示真实的黄氏家族的兴衰。

(2)深入挖掘"黄家大院"文化

从历史文化、名人文化、民俗文化、宗教文化、建筑文化、艺术文化等角度出发,对添福庄文化进行深入挖掘、系统展示。

整旧如旧,重塑历史印记,恢复原有旧貌,按照以往规格,进行黄家大院、黄氏祠堂及牌坊、黄家学堂、黄家商铺、黄家后花园等修复工程,从整体布局到每一个建

筑、每一个景观，将黄家的文化思想和理念贯穿其中。

（3）美化乡村环境

在不改变硬件设施的基础上，运用树林、花、草、雕塑以及民间器物、工艺、美术等，对主要游线、重要节点、重点建筑等进行全方位、立体式的装饰。

（4）活化乡村生活

将添福庄的传统生活延续、发扬，通过挖掘、整理，提高文化娱乐生活和休闲生活的比重，恢复部分典礼、仪式活动。

（5）完善旅游功能

古村内部增加观光、休闲、娱乐、购物功能，外围扩展休闲度假功能，完善多元化的产品体系，选择村西侧的空地，开辟住宿空间，可仿照黄家大院的建筑形式，建设几处大院作为酒店，酒店内的堂屋按照大院样式建设，中间为客厅，两侧四间为客房，东西厢房作为小型会议室和娱乐室，打造功能完备的乡村休闲酒店。

六、北部汶河白鹭湿地研学游憩组团

（一）白鹭湿地保护区

1. 概况

蒋集白鹭栖息地及湿地保护区作为江北最大的白鹭生态保护区，始建于2006年，位于宁阳县蒋集镇北部的国有大胡林场东部，大胡、小胡、西周三个行政村北，面积约3000亩，主要有白鹭、灰鹭、池鹭等6个品种。

宁阳县蒋集镇白鹭栖息地及湿地自然保护区是候鸟南北迁徙的必经之地。每年春季的2月下旬至4月上旬，以及秋季的10月上旬至12月中旬，大批的候鸟在此停歇，补充食物和能量，以完成长距离的迁徙。因此，该区域是鸟类顺利完成长距离迁徙不可缺少的中转站和停歇地。

2. 定位

打造江北最大、最美的白鹭生态保护区。

3. 总体目标

在全面保护的前提下，积极开展科研监测和宣传教育活动，加强村庄共管，发展村庄经济，建设集保护、科研、宣教于一体，功能区划合理、基础设施完备、管理水平高效、科研监测手段先进、区域协调发展的省内外知名且有特色的自然保护区。

4. 开发思路

① 申请国家级湿地公园。

② 保护白鹭栖息地，维持良好生态环境。

良好的生态环境是发展白鹭文化旅游的基础和载体。影响比较突出的是分布在林区外围的大小采沙场，影响鸟类的栖息、繁殖。建议采取更严格的控制措施，使其不会对保护对象产生大的影响。

进行湿地恢复建设。在规划保护区域内禁止采沙，对汶河骨干河道进行排污清淤，营建以芦苇为主的河床水域，同时截留污染物，缓解水土流失。

③ 核心区严格保护，实验区的划分应在保护主题的前提下，以"保护促发展，发展促保护"的良性循环实现可持续发展，留出教学实习、生态旅游和多种经营用地。设置观鸟屋，建停车场，建免水冲环保型厕所，设置垃圾箱，树立旅游宣传牌、景点引导牌。

5. 规划项目

（1）汶河白鹭栖息家园

每年收割芦苇期间都要保留部分，且加大防护林、经济林建设，为停留在此的水鸟提供栖息和隐蔽地。北部汶河里的鱼虾为水鸟提供了一定的食物来源。

（2）露营基地

依托保护区的河道、沙滩、林地、白鹭等元素，规划建造帐篷露营基地。帐篷营位选取干燥而平坦的地面，营位分区块集中提供供电设施，配备良好的给排水系统。

（3）白鹭驿站

建设白鹭驿站。在建筑风格上，白鹭驿站采用茅草和木料等天然建筑材料。白鹭驿站的外观为古朴的原木色，屋顶上覆盖着茅草作为装饰，与自然环境融为一体。可利用白鹭驿站举办白鹭观鸟文化节。

（二）宁阳县蒋集镇生态大胡村——白鹭村

1. 概况

大胡村北靠汶河，南望彩山，毗邻白鹭区，自然环境得天独厚。

2. 规划思路

（1）打造游客综合服务中心

将目前的广场及周边打造成为综合服务中心，配套生态厕所、特色商品售卖点、停车场、大胡村乡愁体验园、白鹭观鸟驿站，承载综合服务、游客集散、车辆停放、住宿调配、购物餐饮、投诉管理、民俗体验、观鸟休闲等功能。

（2）大胡民俗街

第一，对民俗街的景观进行提升，种植格桑花以及农家的蔬菜，形成乡土景观。

第二，丰富文化内涵，提升文化品位，突出白鹭特色，按白鹭品种分类，在墙面展示白鹭的画面，建设部分鹭鸟雕塑普及白鹭知识，增强人们爱鸟护鸟的意识，形成白鹭文化一条街。

第三，民俗街打造餐饮、工坊体验的民俗特色一条街，挑选3户村居进行试点改造，并予以挂牌，成功之后再进行推广。

第四，在泰安金利农业科技有限公司葡萄种植基地开展葡萄采摘活动，丰富游客体验。

第五，大胡村集体成立开发合作社，统一运作。主要通过会员管理的方式产生收益，吸纳餐饮、住宿、油坊、商店等消费类工商企业加入，入社会员每年缴纳会费，可享受村里定点推荐服务。

3. 规划产品

(1) 农家养生主题餐厅

以乡村原生态的蔬菜水果为原材料，在餐饮名称、就餐环境、菜品特色等方面体现乡村特色，同时积极开发乡村特色土菜，如土鸡炖蘑菇、凉拌野菜等，形成丰富多样的乡村养生菜系。

(2) 乡村驿站

对现有民居进行改造包装形成乡村驿站，驿站外立面通过乡村乡愁元素的植入形成具有浓郁乡村风情的建筑，民居内部按照旅游休闲度假的需求，配套休闲度假设施。

(3) 农家工坊

打造非遗文化主题工坊街，挖掘具有鲁中特色的手工艺、农耕文化、特色饮食、历史文脉等，通过如木艺坊、油坊、陶艺坊、糕点坊、豆腐坊等来集中展览展示，工坊采用前店后坊的形式，游客不仅可以品尝，还可以动手参与，打造集工坊体验、民俗休闲、特色购物功能的非遗文化主题工坊街。

(4) 葡萄采摘园

①依托泰安金利农业科技有限公司葡萄种植基地，规划一定面积的采摘区以吸引游客。②完善葡萄培育基地的标识系统，合理布局数量充足、标识醒目的解说牌，包括苗圃、果树的产地、中文学名、拉丁学名、科属、生活习性、作用功效、储存方法等，让游客在采摘的同时，了解相关科普知识。③在现有的品种基础上，争取引进新品种，形成早、中、晚熟组合配套、错季销售的格局。④开展"葡萄架下绘童心"亲子活动，采用网络报名形式，邀请20~30名8~12岁小朋友及家长在美丽的葡萄架下，挥洒童真，收获快乐。

(5) 田园课堂

利用该片区良好的田园环境，丰富室外植物的种类，引入农作物科普课堂、农事体验课堂、动物科普课堂、园艺课堂、生态系统课堂等一系列自然教育课程。

(6) 大胡村乡愁体验园

打造大胡村乡村体验博物馆、鲁中山区乡愁体验基地。乡村体验博物馆依托废弃的老房子打造。园内（馆内）以鲁中地区传统的乡愁文化为特色，构建集民俗体验、农事体验、童年游戏体验、美食体验等功能于一体的综合体。

(7) 特色交通工具

引进乡村特色交通工具，包括单人、双人、多人自行车；还包括驴拉车、牛拉车、羊拉车、马拉车；以及特色越野车、滑索等。

(8) 白鹭文化广场

提升白鹭文化广场成为节庆人流聚集区域，同时承载游客集散功能。广场周边设计景观小品，提供人性化的休闲空间。

(9) 游客服务中心

游客服务中心内部设有信息咨询台、投诉建议处、医疗室、小超市等，具有游客集散、引导、服务、游憩、解说、信息咨询、景区导览、旅游纪念品销售、医疗服务等多种功能。

(10) 瓜果采摘园

规划瓜果采摘园，游客可亲自动手体验采瓜、摘果，以及果树的嫁接、修剪、套袋等活动，享受田园乐趣，形成春季赏花、夏秋采摘的休闲田园。

(11) 乡村创意公园

运用各种废弃的农作物材料制作稻草人，同时联合地方艺术类学校，提供场地让艺术类学校的学生参与创作和展示。

(12) 家庭庄园

结合鲁中地区的农耕文化打造家庭庄园。家庭庄园内以特色木屋为主，每栋木屋都配套有1~3亩风情田园。家庭庄园实行管家式服务，配备电子导览系统、监控系统、动态视频管理系统，为业主提供专业服务。

(三) 知礼小胡村——奶牛场

1. 概况

小胡村北临大汶河，南临蒙馆公路，西临大胡村，全村耕地面积3330亩，村奶牛场占地100余亩。村民800余户，3000余人。

2. 规划思路

(1) 中国宁阳灵芝小镇

在已有灵芝种植的基础上，扩大种植规模，成立宁阳县小胡泰宝中药材专业合作社，同时与大学合作共建灵芝研究院，研发相关系列产品。

(2) 开心牧场

进行招商引资，以蒙牛奶站为龙头，带动发展小胡奶牛养殖，形成牛奶生产、销售一条龙。同时借鉴休闲农业的开发模式，打造开心牧场，开发丰富的体验活动，如挤牛奶，给小羊羔喂奶，丰富游客的体验。

(3) 乡村动物园

① 项目构思。农场里散养（适当围栏）一些乡村常见动物或萌宠动物，可以跟游人亲密互动；将一些小动物围合起来，可以开展表演等活动。

② 项目运营。大门票运营模式，内部设置若干互动体验项目，如剪羊毛、挤牛奶、观看动物表演等。

③ 项目盈利点。饲料购买收入、互动体验收入、宠物购买收入。

七、北部三农文化研学组团

(一)新农村样板——改革郑龙

1. 现状分析

郑龙村总人口 1260 人,耕地面积 1220 亩。2006 年以来,该村探索实行"股份+合作"的土地流转模式,至 2012 年,从一个负债 38 万元的落后村发展成村集体经济收入 200 万元的先进村,人均纯收入突破 12000 元。该村 1220 亩土地除了一些零散地外全部流转,成为合作社的"股份",并辐射带动周边基地蔬菜种植面积达到 8000 余亩。

郑龙村是宁阳县"新三农"事业示范区的核心村,积极探索村企合作共建新农村、新社区的发展模式。2011 年,郑龙村被农业部认定为"全国一村一品示范村",按照"公司+合作社+基地+农户"的经营模式,探索出了"群众自愿、土地入股、集约经营、收益分红"的发展路子,形成了"股份+合作"的土地流转模式,发展有机蔬菜规模种植,辐射带动周边 12 个行政村走上增收致富的路子。大力发展高效设施农业,建设高标准冬暖式大棚 30 个、小型拱棚 220 余个,发展食用菌养殖和反季节蔬菜种植,采取当前先进的大棚沼气池技术,大大提高了蔬菜质量和产量。

2009 年 3 月 18 日,中央电视台《新闻联播》以"山东泰安:'股份+合作'走出农民致富新路"为题报道了郑龙有机蔬菜合作社的经验做法。郑龙村被中央委员会宣传部列为全国近期农村改革发展六项成就之一,在中央电视台等八大央级媒体进行了报道。

农村土地制度调研组就土地流转、农民专业合作社到蒋集镇郑龙有机蔬菜专业合作社调研,给予了很高评价,"宁阳模式,惠及三农"。

2. 规划思路

依托郑龙村是宁阳县"新三农"事业示范区的核心村,积极探索村企合作共建新农村、新社区的发展模式。打造郑龙村史馆,以时间为轴,采用传统展示手法和现代数字虚拟影像等技术展示郑龙村艰苦奋斗,敢为人先,先行先试的发展历史。

将基本农田和农业种植作为旅游开发的载体,通过农业研学基地、郑龙农场、大地创意景观、瓜果采摘园等项目打造,将田园区域植入农业科普研学、农庄休闲、农业创意、瓜果采摘等功能,打造田园观光休闲示范村。

3. 规划项目

(1) 郑龙村村史馆(农耕文化博物馆)

郑龙村村史馆兼顾村史、农耕文化介绍。村史部分主要讲述郑龙村艰苦奋斗,敢为人先,先行先试的发展历史,农耕文化部分以时间为轴,采用传统展示手法和现代数字虚拟影像等技术展示中国和世界主要农业国家农业发展史、古代农耕文化和现代高科技农业知识,融知识性、科学性、休闲性于一体,通过眼看、耳听、动手操作,从中可以了解传统的农耕文化,了解克隆、转基因、太空农业等新概念,在休闲环境中享受生动的农业科普大餐。

(2) 农业研学基地

规划农业研学基地,依托农事活动开展研学科普教育,诸如挖花生、种菜、锄草、摘水果等,在参与农事劳作过程中培养孩子们的劳动能力,同时让孩子们了解乡村,热爱乡村。

(3) 七彩采摘园

规划特色瓜园、樱桃园、花圃、苗圃等,游客可入内采瓜、摘果、移苗,享受田园乐趣。

(4) 大地创意景观

通过创意性手法,将农田规划设计成具有创意性的农业大地艺术景观。采用彩色麦田种植技术,在最佳观景点设置观景平台,通过招商,吸引企业投资。

(5) 郑龙农场

主要为中小学生提供与环境有关的教育,为孩子们创造一种真正在乡村生活和学习的体验。编制农业、资源、生态、环境和可持续发展等理论课程,以户外课程为主要特色。发展年级菜园、学校菜园,带领学生们耕种、收割,教会学生们做饭,使学生们深刻体会"谁知盘中餐,粒粒皆辛苦"。

(二) 泉润张龙——同吃,同住,同劳动,同赶集

1. 概况

张家泉龙村地处大汶河南畔,地貌呈南高北低、东高西洼。辖区龙泉河自东向西,且有小支流6条,故地表层水源丰富,极利于农业发展。张家龙泉村盛产小麦、玉米、花生及各类蔬菜,植被覆盖率约为75%。村内街道四纵四横,道路两旁花木扶疏,绿荫婆娑。村内干净整洁,住房全部为中国北方传统四合院,且多二层小楼,红瓦白墙。

2. 规划思路

挖掘张龙村的乡村文化底蕴,以当地民俗文化为特色,重点发展民居观光休闲、特色民俗体验等旅游产品,打造山东知名民俗休闲聚落、山东省著名民俗接待乡村。

住农家屋、吃农家饭是游客乡村旅游和体验的重要环节,在现有建筑形式、外观不能大改的情况下,通过院内廊架(葡萄架、丝瓜架、扁豆架等)改善局部小环境特色。提高餐厅房间的设备和卫生条件,切实保障饮用水和食品安全。

3. 规划项目

（1）张龙民俗街

在张龙村元宝湾一侧，利用现有民房，改建5户民居，引进小磨坊、小加工、柳编等非遗文化产业，打造工坊体验和创意集市，增加游客与村民的互动。同时可设置赶集购物的项目，让更多的人从生活层面了解农村生活。

（2）二日农

乡村的生产生活对城市游客来说既陌生又好奇。设置二日农项目，让游客做两天的农民，体验农民的日常生活，感受中国传统的小隐隐于野、诗酒田园的农耕生活。

（3）张龙乡村驿站

规划前期通过1~2户的打造产生示范效应，然后引导居民发展特色民宿。鼓励村民将自家院落空余的房屋开辟为客房，包装成乡村驿站。张龙村成立"张龙乡愁驿站合作社"，对客房统一管理，统一卫生标准，根据服务与管理状况对张龙客房评定星级，为客人提供干净、方便的住宿服务，让游客感受富有特色的住宿体验。

对现有院落进行升级改造，完善休闲度假功能，外立面采用乡土文化元素进行点缀，形成统一的乡土主题民宿风貌；同时完善现代休闲度假功能，保持院落整洁干净。

（4）农耕体验园

规划一定范围的农用地打造农耕体验园，使游客在参与劳作的过程中放松身心，体验农耕文化。

（5）农家养生主题餐厅

打造农家养生主题的餐厅，就餐环境的布置方面体现浓郁的乡村气息，原材料采用原生态的蔬菜水果，菜品打造方面结合现代养生主题和理念，构建独具特色的乡村餐饮品牌。

（6）工坊体验部落

针对亲子客群，挖掘具有地域特色的非物质文化遗产等，开发陶艺制作、剪纸、木头工艺等亲子工坊群，游客既可参与体验，又可以购买带走，构建工坊体验部落。

（7）租赁农庄

将大块土地划分为小块土地供旅游者认领，用于都市居民休闲度假和农事体验。租赁农庄主要由农耕体验区、农事服务咨询中心构成。经营方式有两种：一是租地给游客，农场提供种子、肥料和农具，游客自己耕种；二是市民如果没有时间耕种，可以托管给农庄。

（8）农耕部落

通过完善相关旅游服务配套设施，营造舒适、自然、安全的旅游环境，游客来到这里，与农民同吃、同住、同劳动、同赶集，吃农家饭，住农家院，干农家活，赶农家集，满足游客农耕体验、休闲娱乐的需求。

（9）原乡酒吧

规划中远期游客量达到一定规模，尤其过夜游客达到一定的基数，规划建设原乡酒吧，满足过夜游客休闲娱乐需求。

第六节　道路交通与配套服务设施规划

一、道路交通系统规划

（一）道路现状

蒋集镇东距京福高速公路、京沪铁路和104国道约7公里。

S333省道（蒙馆路）贯穿镇域东西，是主要交通要道。横向道路还有北部的汶河路、南部的环山大道，纵向道路有黄沙路、岗彭路、槐胡路、镇东路、西周路等。初步形成了"三横五纵"的交通体系。全镇行政村硬化路通村率达100%。

（二）存在问题

区域内交通干线缺少通往旅游景区、景点的交通标识系统；交通网络不完善，通达性不足。

（三）规划原则

① 围绕旅游办交通，与全镇交通规划相衔接；
② 按照"进得来、出得去、散得开"的要求进行线路布局；
③ 注重协调，以建立综合旅游交通网络为目标，提高"可入出性"，形成便捷的综合旅游交通体系。

（四）旅游交通规划

1. 融入山水圣人旅游线的交通体系

依托友邦田园，通过G104、G3加强蒋集与泰安、曲阜等地景点的联系，加强蒋集与山水圣人旅游线的合作与交流，促进蒋集与山水圣人旅游线上诸城市的联合开发、一体化发展。

2. 实现与主要出口的对接

加强蒋集各旅游点与京台高速公路泰安出口的联系，打造旅游干线，实现高速公路与景区的有效、便捷连接。

3. 构建便捷、完善的乡村旅游交通网络

做好旅游区与外部道路的衔接，沟通内外部联系；完善各乡村旅游点与主要交通干道之间的道路连接，改善乡村道路路况，构建休闲绿道体系，健全旅游交通设施，完善交通管理和运营机制。

4. 道路设施服务于生产和旅游发展的要求

根据活动内容、环境容量、运营量、服务性质和管理需要，综合确定道路建设标准和建设密度。道路设计要满足旅游发展、农业生产、农产品观光采摘等多方面的需要，保证旅游、生活、生产所需的物资、原材料和垃圾能够运进和运出。

5. 注重乡村风味的保持，增加旅游乐趣

乡村道路的建设应尽可能保持原有的田园风光、自然风貌，从游客乡村旅游体验的角度出发，选择富含乡土气息的特色交通工具，增加乡村旅游的乐趣，如牛车、羊车、独轮小推车等。

6. 旅游交通标识系统

完善乡村旅游道路标识系统，如旅游标识、交通标示、安全警示、路牌路标、夜间引导、安保工程系统等，给游客清晰的旅游导向，使出游更加便捷，同时也能为培育健康、休闲、个性、便捷的自驾旅游市场奠定基础。

7. 主干道

蒋集镇旅游主干道主要功能是联系各游览区，主要有S333省道（蒙馆路）。横向道路还有北部的汶河路、南部的环山大道等。

近期规划建设：在通往各游览区的主要街道、交通路口设置游览区道路指示牌、里程牌、导游指示牌或游览区导游图等。

为了反映风景区的景观特色，接近风景区的路段，种植行道树，行道树选择具有当地特色的乡土树种，不同路段可选用不同树种，形成优美多变的植物景观。局部有条件的路段可形成具有一定宽度多层次的道路景观绿化带，增加行车的愉悦性。

8. 次干道

有条件的地块建设生态绿地，提前给游客营造视觉氛围。沿途可设置便民服务接待设施。

次干道是游览区内连接各个景区的旅游道路，也是各景区疏散游客的主要通道。各次干道都应当与游览区主干道相连接，以保证各游览区的可进入性。规划次干道宽度应为6米，为双向两车道混凝土或沥青道路，满足小型车对向行驶需求。

9. 游道

游道的职能是连接同一景区内不同景点，规划成环状结构，互相联结。游道只允许行驶小型车及电瓶车。规划游道宽度为4～5米，一般为水泥路，应满足消防车的通行要求，局部可扩宽至6米。

10. 步游道

步游道为供游人行走观景的小型道路，不允许机动车通行。规划宽度为1～2米，可采用不同质感的多种材质铺砌，如石板、卵石、碎石等。

11. 特色交通

如栈道、自行车、溜索等。栈道规划宽度为0.8～1米，采用木质材料搭建，两侧设置绳索或木质护栏。

12. 停车场

停车场是旅游道路交通系统的重要组成部分，景区内停车场采取集中与分散布置的手法，结合环境，用绿树掩映，全面设计和建造生态型停车场。

停车场主要分布于重要景观节点和乡村旅游集中的村落。建议采用生态停车场，避免空旷单调的铺面；停车场绿化造景除具备吸热及绿化效果外，风格设计也需要与乡村旅游区的整体造型相协调，与周边农业景观相融合。

二、旅游线路系统规划

（一）旅游线路规划原则

在组织蒋集镇旅游线路时，必须客观评估旅游资源数量和比较优势，对景区旅游景点进行优化组织，避免所选旅游景点雷同，防止旅游消费负效应的产生。同时设计搭配合理、主题突出、特色鲜明的游览线路，以适应客源市场多种需求。

1. 市场导向原则

根据市场需求，从区域竞合的角度出发，坚持市场导向原则，结合旅游景区景点，有针对性地组合旅游线路。

2. 区域互动原则

将蒋集镇旅游资源与泰山、曲阜区域旅游资源进行整合、优势互补，联合组织设计区域旅游线路，并进行联合促销。

3. 点线结合原则

以旅游点、旅游区、旅游集散地（友邦田园）为依托，以主要交通线为纽带，合理组织旅游线路，点式突破，以点带线、点线结合的原则进行旅游线路规划。

4. 动态发展原则

根据主要旅游目标市场的需求动态发展，结合周边类似项目的发展态势以及自身的旅游区（点）的开发建设状况动态调整，及时更新完善旅游线路组织。

5. 主题突出原则

旅游线路应具有鲜明的旅游主题，通过鲜明的主题提高旅游线路的可识别性和市场号召力，从而影响游客的决策和出行行为，最终形成有竞争力的知名旅游线路。

6. 多元层次原则

针对目标市场需求层次的多样性，区域内单一旅游线路应具有不同类型的产品组合；同时，区域内整体旅游线路应在消费层次、游程长短、交通方式等方面体现出层次感，以拓展旅游市场适应面。

(二)蒋集镇研学旅游线路开发现状

蒋集镇研学旅游尚处于起步阶段,绝大多数旅游区(点)尚未真正开发。研学旅游有待形成特色突出、功能完善的旅游线路。

(三)研学旅游线路组织规划

1. 区外研学旅游线路组合

① 济南—泰山—蒋集—曲阜。

② 泰山—蒋集—曲阜。

2. 区内研学旅游线路组织

(1)三日研学游旅游线路

第一日,友邦田园;第二日,彩山—华佗庙—知青屋—栗家楼;第三日,白鹭自然保护区—大胡村—小胡村。

第一日,友邦田园;第二日,彩山—华佗庙—知青屋—栗家楼—黄家大院;第三日,友邦智慧农业产业园—郑龙村—张龙村。

(2)两日研学游旅游线路

第一日,友邦田园;第二日,彩山—华佗庙—知青屋—栗家楼。

第一日,友邦田园;第二日,黄家大院—友邦智慧农业产业园。

第一日,友邦田园;第二日,郑龙村。

第一日,友邦田园;第二日,张龙村。

第一日,友邦田园;第二日,蒋集古槐—千年柏树—泰安子泰食品有限公司。

第一日,友邦田园;第二日,苗河一号水库。

(3)一日研学游旅游线路

友邦田园—彩山。

友邦田园—白鹭湿地保护区。

友邦田园—黄家大院。

友邦田园—郑龙村。

友邦田园—张龙村。

友邦田园—泰安子泰食品有限公司—悦美客食品有限公司。

3. 专项研学旅游线路组织

蒋集镇研学类型多样,如以汶阳农耕为主要功能的农业研学线路;以郑龙为代表的农业改革研学线路;以特色农产品为特色的农产品研学线路;以农业产业为特色的农业产业研学线路;以黄恩彤历史文化与山水文化构成的文化研学线路;以郑龙村、张龙村、大小胡村构成的乡村振兴研学线路;以黄家大院和栗家楼构成的民俗研学旅游线路;以企业构成的工业研学旅游线路;以白鹭自然保护区与大胡村构成的湿地研学旅游线路;以彩山、华佗庙、知青屋构成的生态研学线路等。具体路线如下:

① 湿地研学游：友邦田园—白鹭自然保护区—生态大胡村。
② 农业研学游：友邦田园—郑龙村—张龙村—泰安金利葡萄种植基地。
③ 民俗研学游：友邦田园—黄家大院—栗家楼。
④ 生态研学游：友邦田园—彩山—华佗庙—知青屋。
⑤ 工业研学游：友邦田园—泰安子泰食品有限公司—悦美客食品有限公司。

（四）旅游线路建设对策

① 改善镇至旅游区（点）交通状况，连接断头路，建设旅游环线，并与周边其他地区形成区域旅游环线。

② 完善交通干线、旅游区支线的旅游标识和解说系统，使各层次旅游线路畅通、便捷。

③ 加强与周边地区的旅游合作，共同培育中长线旅游线路。

三、配套服务设施规划

（一）环卫设施规划

为更好地服务蒋集镇旅游区客群，完善环卫设施，合理布局公共厕所、垃圾箱等，满足环境卫生诉求。

1. 垃圾处理设施

① 设立垃圾桶、垃圾暂存处、垃圾处理中心三级处理系统。垃圾桶的分布在游客高密度区每70～100平方米一个，沿游道200～500米放置一个。每个景区至少设一个垃圾暂存处，每个游览区要建立一个垃圾处理中心。

② 垃圾桶的尺寸、形状、外观、色调要求和景观环境、旅游形象相协调，并要始终保持美观、整洁。

③ 要在导游图、游览须知、警示牌、垃圾桶等位置，标明指导游客保护环境、保护基础设施、保持环境整洁等亲善性语言；环卫人员除做到垃圾流动清扫、日产日清外，还要以身作则，树立维护整洁环境的榜样，并可善意地提醒和阻止游客的不文明行为。

2. 公共厕所

公共厕所是反映景区卫生的管理水平和人文关怀的主要标志，要重视公共厕所的布局、建设和管理，为游客提供最大的方便。

① 厕所外观、色彩、造型与景观环境要协调一致，尽可能按景观氛围设计独具特色的厕所。

② 厕所定位为中等档次，保持洁净、无污垢、无堵塞、无滴漏、无破损、无污迹、无异味，并尽可能免费开放。

③ 派专人对厕所进行管理和清洁，以达到国家规定的卫生检测标准，向游客提

供优质、便利、卫生的服务。

3. 医疗设施

医疗设施布局要合理，数量要充足，能够满足游客的医疗、急救需要。住宿机构要有专门的医疗室，景区、景点在旅游旺季要设立临时医疗服务点，并免费提供日常旅游药品。与各景区所在的镇级医院、城区各大医院实行联动，提供快捷的旅游医疗救护。

(二) 安全、指示系统规划

为了确保游客进入蒋集镇各旅游景点的人身、财产安全，景区内要设置齐全的安全设施和明显的指示系统。

各景区（景点）要有醒目、齐全、规范的安全警告标志、标识。在危险地带要设置安全防护设施，在特殊地段（恶劣气候条件下易突发灾情）要有必要的警示标志、防护设施和安全处置措施，为游人提供安全的游览环境。

要在旅游经营单位、旅游景点设置指示标志和消防设备、设施，在水上景区（点）设置救护设备，各景区（林区）要具备必要的防火设施和措施。

建立完善的旅游区安全制度与措施，配备数量充足的安全保卫人员，对景区进行安全巡查和定期检查。对景区内开展的滑索等特种旅游项目，要经有关主管部门共同验收，合格后方可开展活动。

蒋集镇各旅游景区主干道的特殊地段，设置限速标志牌、反光镜等标志和设施，确保旅游车辆、游客安全通行；在景区内住宿、餐饮等服务设施内要安装消防报警系统，以确保客人的安全和营业的安全。在住宿接待点设医疗服务处，对游客进行卫生防疫等服务。

第七节 旅游产业要素规划

一、旅游住宿规划

(一) 旅游住宿现状

蒋集镇目前的旅游住宿主要集中在友邦田园，主要有友邦花园酒店、营员公寓、太空舱等，住宿业数量及接待能力基本能满足目前市场需求，但与未来蒋集镇旅游业的快速发展相比，还有一定差距。

(二) 规划思路

在扩大友邦田园住宿规模的基础上，大力发展其他类型的乡村住宿；同时加强政府引导,规范行业管理。通过建立住宿行业协会、星级评定等手段规范旅游住宿,促进旅游住宿产业水平的提高、经营业绩的改善。

(三) 未来旅游住宿重点发展方向

1. 乡村民宿

乡村民宿主要指以村庄农户自有住宅作为游客住宿接待场所的住宿方式。乡村民宿的接待房间量一般在5间以下(特殊地区15间以下)。目前主要有两种形式:一种是农户将自有住宅的一部分空闲居室出租给游客。农户可在不耽误自住的同时,以"副业方式"赚取收益。这种形式投资相对较少,加上"改厨改厕"的政策扶持,较容易推广实施。户主还可以通过为游客提供原汁原味的"乡土菜",介绍当地的风俗环境,带领游客体验各种农事活动等方式赚取更多收益。另一种是农户将整座自有住宅出租给游客使用。整租房一般要在保持乡土气息的同时,做到干净、整洁、有独特风貌。房屋整租投资相对高一些,收益也高。这种形式主客之间的交流虽较少,但能为游客提供更私密、自由和放松的空间。游客可根据自己的意愿体验乡村风情风貌,安排休闲时光。

2. 乡村客栈

乡村客栈指在乡村中建设的、专门向旅客提供的、具有乡村风格特色的住宿营业场所。乡村客栈通常客房量在6~50间,以大众群体为主要客源。乡村客栈须保证良好的卫生条件。在此基础上,有条件的客栈可配置适应乡土风格的电视、制冷/热设备、网络等适应现代旅游群体的设施设备,也可提供特色餐饮。

3. 户外营地

户外营地指各类可以进行露营地方,包括非经营性自然露营地、公共休闲游憩地露营点,以及经营性的自驾车露营中心(露营地)、景区/点露营点等。

非经营性的露营地/点一般以优美的乡村自然风光为依托,适用帐篷、房车等可移动式露营设备。

经营性的露营场所除了依托乡村自然风光外,通常还要配有多种乡村休闲活动,如采摘、喂养、户外游戏、特色餐饮等。这类露营场所适用帐篷、房车、可移动式露营屋、固定式露营屋等。

二、旅游餐饮规划

餐饮业收入约占旅游总收入的11.6%(海外游客)~16.8%(国内散客),在旅游产业中占有一定地位。旅游餐饮业除具有一般餐饮业的特点外,还具有地方性、风味性、文化性、多样性等特点。

品尝美食是旅游过程中不可缺少的重要环节,蒋集农林果产品以及山珍极为丰富,且多为有机食品,为餐饮业提供了丰富的原料,是蒋集旅游业深度开发的重要基础。

（一）发展现状

目前蒋集镇旅游餐饮主要场所为友邦田园的营员餐厅，其他区域因游客量未能达到一定的规模，因此尚未提供旅游餐饮服务。

（二）存在问题

① 餐饮品种不够丰富。蒋集镇物产丰富，有不少具有特色的风味小吃，但在旅游餐饮方面，众多的地方风味、绿色食品等尚未开发成为旅游食品和菜肴。

② 餐饮的旅游品牌有待加强。饮食不仅仅是为了充饥，尤其是旅游餐饮，更是品味地方深刻文化底蕴的途径。蒋集镇具有悠久的发展历史，历史文化、民俗文化丰富，有不少地方特色饮食。但尚没有与旅游餐饮有机结合起来，给游客留下深刻的印象的具有地方特色的餐饮项目还没有建立起来。

（三）餐饮规划

在餐饮发展目标上，充分挖掘当地饮食文化与食品特色，结合现代饮食潮流，在品种、质量、风味、档次上下功夫，培养和建立更能适应游客需求和当地居民消费需求的旅游餐饮业，强化餐饮的旅游吸引力。

1. 加强餐饮管理

无论是宾馆饭店餐饮、社会餐饮，还是景区景点餐饮，都要进一步加强管理，加大管理力度，逐步实现旅游定点餐饮挂牌制度。对于旅游定点餐厅，必须制定严格的卫生标准，改善就餐环境，落实服务规范，改进餐饮服务。

（1）部门协同，加强乡村餐饮的行业监管

餐饮作为旅游的重要环节，必须加强监管。与食品药品监督管理局、工商局、物价局、卫生局等相关职能部门加强协作，加大对餐饮的食品安全、环境卫生、产品价格和服务质量的监管，让游客"吃得放心、吃得明白、吃得开心"。

（2）实施标准化战略，全面提升餐饮水平

依托山东省乡村旅游相关标准，在乡村餐饮的文化、环境、菜品、服务、安全等方面，打造"蒋集人家"餐饮服务标准，申报山东省地方标准，推进餐饮上层次、上台阶。

（3）培训服务技能，提高服务水平

采用送教上门、办培训班等形式，派出专门人员深入乡村，对乡村餐饮从业村民进行经营创新、标准要求、礼貌用语等方面的培训，从而提高从业村民的服务技能和服务质量。

2. 景点餐饮方便化

景区景点餐饮宜在方便上下功夫，蒋集镇的景区景点规模较小，不适宜设置规模较大的就餐设施，从方便游客和绿色环保两方面考虑，可设置一些规模较小、用餐方便的餐饮设施，提供一些方便速食食品。设施的设置与游客的小憩相结合，既美观又实用。

3. 加强餐饮文化建设

餐饮文化包括三个层次：一是就餐环境文化；二是菜式菜品文化；三是服务程序文化。要在突出地方特色的基础上，把握好主要菜式和配套菜式的关系，通过人员的介绍、菜单的展示、菜名等来完整地表达餐饮文化的内涵，使游客在就餐过程中感受浓郁的文化氛围。

4. 有机绿色食品系列

蒋集镇旅游餐饮应突出以下几个系列：

① 农特产品餐饮系列。以野菜、玉米、大豆、花生等为原料制作的面食、炒菜、凉菜等。

② 畜禽产品餐饮系列。以当地土鸡等为原料制作的炒菜、凉菜、汤菜等。

③ 野生蔬菜系列。要突出"天然、野生、保健、绿色"等特点，以汶河湿地和彩山周边采集的各种天然野菜为原料制作的绿色菜肴。

5. 农家小厨系列

围绕着农家、田间、乡俗等乡土元素，开发乡土性、原生态的饮食菜品。农家田地里的原生态的玉米、小麦、红薯可以直接加工成烤玉米、烤红薯、玉米渣等原生态健康食品。村民的菜园中的黄瓜、韭菜等蔬菜和山野中的各类野菜、山花等，用农村最简单最传统的烹饪方法，制作菜品，游客还可以亲手采摘烹饪，在参与、体验、美食中感受快乐。

6. 规划建设多种餐饮接待设施

为满足不同类型游客的餐饮消费诉求，构建高档、中档、低档相结合的餐饮服务设施体系，形成精品餐饮、大众餐饮、特色餐饮等种类丰富的旅游餐饮供给体系。打造包括中高端酒店餐饮、主题餐厅、休闲街区餐饮、农家餐饮、营地自助餐饮等不同类型餐饮服务接待场所。

三、文化娱乐规划

（一）现状

目前，蒋集镇的文化娱乐业总体发展水平偏低。友邦田园主要是研学拓展，除此之外的景区景点仅限于观光层面，缺乏参与性的游乐活动，缺乏具有修身养性功能的时尚娱乐设施。众多地方特色的文娱表演及民俗活动，基本上停留在内部交流阶段，尚未得到有效的组织与开发，缺乏"大众亲和力"。

(二) 规划思路与目标

1. 规划思路

以表现现代时尚文化和地方传统民俗文化为准则，加强对现有文化娱乐场所的管理，积极引导地方民俗活动，推陈出新，挖掘、弘扬地方特色表演；合理规划，逐步扩大文娱设施规模，提高设施水准，在全镇范围内形成特色鲜明、参与性强、品位较高、类型齐全、管理规范的旅游文化娱乐接待体系。

2. 发展目标

在游乐项目的配置上针对不同类型的游客推出不同的项目；提高各个景区活动项目的参与性；深入挖掘传统民俗文化，迅速提高全镇旅游业的文娱接待能力。着重提高全镇各类旅游文娱设施的品位和档次，增强旅游娱乐设施的参与性、文化性、娱乐性。

(三) 文化娱乐业发展规划

1. 丰富景区活动项目

根据景区的景观特色与主题形象、自身规模和环境容量，在景区增设适量参与性、运动性、趣味性、科学性的康乐运动设施，结合现有的旅游节庆活动（如庙会），吸引大众游客参与。

2. 发展夜间娱乐休闲活动

在友邦田园增加夜间活动场所和文化娱乐项目，包括夜间小剧场、与餐饮相结合的演出等形式，积极推动夜生活的发展。

3. 尊重传承民间文化遗存

蒋集镇悠久的历史文化留下了众多民间的休闲娱乐习俗，在进行旅游休闲娱乐活动创意设计时，应当遵守以悠久文化遗存为基础，深刻挖掘，并对其进行传承的原则。可设计文艺演出剧目，在剧场、戏台等表演场所进行表演，丰富游客夜生活，展示蒋集镇传统文化。

4. 提升旅游节庆娱乐活动

举办乡村采摘节、彩山登山节等节庆活动，对节庆开展积极宣传和营销，以提高知名度，促进地方经济的发展，对外树立良好的旅游目的地形象。

四、旅游商品规划

旅游购物作为旅游产业要素之一，在旅游收入中占有很重要的地位，旅游发达国家和地区，游客购买旅游商品的消费可占旅游消费总额的 40%～60%，我国热点旅游区也可占到 20%～40%，旅游商品的开发、设计与销售越来越受到旅游业界人士的重视。

蒋集的旅游商品应充分挖掘蒋集特色资源，突显地方特色，开发满足各个年龄阶段消费者购物需求的商品，展现蒋集优美的山水风光、浓郁的民俗风情和名人文化，并提高商品的工艺价值、文化内涵和实用价值，增加旅游收入。

在旅游商品设计中，应本着便携、乡土气息浓厚为原则，并适度延长产业链。各重点旅游村可以依据本村特色建立旅游商品出售区，请本村村民一边展示制作过程一边出售，游客还可体验自己制作。也可以与文化创意机构、高校专业研究机构合作，进行旅游商品及其外包装的开发设计或采取多种合作方式同相关生产企业合作，进行旅游商品的生产。

1. 购物场所多样化

为方便游客购买旅游商品，购物场所需要多样化，主要分为旅游购物商店、私营摊点、自动售卖机三种。旅游购物商店以景区经营或者定向招商为主；私营摊点可以出租给当地农民来销售当地的农副产品，自动售卖机主要在景区入口处，以销售日常矿泉水和饮料等生活用品为主。

2. 鼓励社会参与，给予政策优惠

旅游商品的开发涉及诸多环节，主要包括四个方面：第一，旅游商品要有特色，要具有工艺品或者艺术品的属性；第二，旅游商品价格定价不能太高，要具有价格竞争优势；第三，旅游商品需要进行推广，让游客知道商品；第四，旅游商品还需要有销售渠道，将商品交付到消费者手中。旅游商品的开发周期较长，中间环节较多，存在一定的风险，因此，政府应给予旅游商品开发的企业和个人优惠政策，包括税收减免等，也应注重知识产权保护，打击仿造等。

3. 突出蒋集特色，体现蒋集文化

突出地方特色，造型、原料质地、流程设计、工艺技巧和包装装潢等方面要充分体现蒋集的民俗文化特色，反映景区的特点环境与风貌。设计区域形象与标志，并将其应用于区域旅游商品的制作中。这种个性鲜明的旅游商品对游客有极大的吸引力，且不易被模仿。

4. 注重对旅游产品的包装

艺术性与纪念性是旅游商品能够为游客所喜爱的重要特征，旅游商品的包装性越强，就越能诱发游客的购买欲望，开发中赋予日常实用品以工艺美学性，并强化其旅游纪念意义，精工细作，寓用于乐。

5. 邮游一体化，推进农产品 OTO 模式

"OTO(online to offline)"，即"线上到线下"，通过遍布城乡联系千家万户的快递物流,把农家的商品带到线上,把线上的消费者带到现实,在线支付购买乡村旅游的商品和服务,再引导到线下旅游体验。

第八节　环境保护与安全系统规划

一、旅游资源保护规划

重点对蒋集镇全域旅游资源聚集区、服务基地、交通干线及彩山的植被和水土保持等方面进行保护。

把重点资源分为自然景观资源、历史文物、非物质文化遗产三大类,进行分类保护。

1. 自然景观资源保护

加强对自然景观的保护,主要采取以下措施:

① 划定保护范围,严格控制土地使用项目审批。

② 严格控制生态环境容量,严禁开山炸石、砍伐树木、捕杀保护动物等活动。

③ 加大保护资金投入,将森林水体景观及环境保护投入纳入财政预算。

2. 历史文物保护

主要保护蒋集镇内的历史文化和遗迹,主要采取以下措施:

① 划定保护范围和监控地带,并严格控制保护范围内土地利用及新建项目的审批,定期对各遗址等巡视,发现问题立即处理。

② 加大保护投入力度,鼓励公民、法人和其他组织通过捐赠等方式设立文物保护基金,专门用于文物古迹保护。

③ 在各遗址等处设保护标志碑,在上面注明文物保护的级别、公布机关、公布日期,以及关于文物历史及保护要求的说明文字。

3. 非物质文化遗产保护

对蒋集传统的非物质文化遗产进行重点保护,采取的措施有:

① 进一步做好非物质文化遗产的普查、认定和登记工作,全面了解和掌握非物质文化遗产资源的现状及存在的问题。

② 抓紧征集具有历史、文化和科学价值的非物质文化遗产实物和资料,建立非物质文化遗产资料库及陈列展示场所。

③ 尊重和保护民间艺人,关注他们的生存状态,提高他们的社会地位和经济地位,支持和保障民间艺人传承活动的开展。

二、生态环境保护规划

（一）植被保护

以增加森林覆盖率，提高山地植被覆盖率，丰富植物层次，建立绿化景观体系为工作目标，根据区域保护的需要，重点做好旅游区和交通干线周边的植被保护。主要保护措施有：

① 建立以生态公益林建设为主体的生态安全体系，构建比较完整的生态屏障，满足社会和经济发展的生态需求。全面推进城乡绿化建设，加强森林资源培育，不断提高森林资源质量；扎实开展山区生态林建设、水系生态林建设、通道绿化和城镇绿化工程，快速推进城镇绿化建设，持续推动全镇生态环境进一步改善和提高，提升人居生活环境，促进人与自然和谐发展。

② 以国道、省道、乡道等交通干线为重点，建立交通沿线绿色廊道，选用当地乡土树种和花卉，美化沿线。

（二）水土保持

按照水土保持综合治理要求，控制水土流失，改善小流域生态环境，提高抵御洪涝灾害能力，整治措施有：

① 做好河道的清理和生态保护，严禁在山洪易发区段乱砍滥伐和非法采矿，防止山洪暴发和泥石流灾害造成巨大损失。

② 大力植树造林，对森林病虫害应严密监测，并有计划地进行治理，确保植被健康，提高生态环境质量和景观环境质量。

③ 加强旅游开发建设活动中的环境管理，强化水土流失治理，将生物措施、工程措施和农艺措施相结合进行综合防治。

（三）水体保护

应进一步整治苗河一、二号水库区周边各种水污染行为，加大治污基础设施建设力度，切实治理生活污染和经营性污染，加强生态建设与环境保护，逐步减少农业面源污染；严格控制库区周边开发，推进库区周边产业与水源保护协调发展，改善入库河流水质；积极推动建立库区及周边"保护、建设、补偿、利用、监管"五位一体的政策体系，逐步形成环境保护科学化、法制化和规范化的长效机制。

① 严禁在水域附近建设化工厂及采矿。

② 严禁向水体内排放污染物，防止水源污染。

③ 划定保护范围，在保护范围内严禁工程建设。

④ 提高区域周边植被覆盖率，涵养水源。

加强农村面源污染治理，重点加强对农村化肥、农药、畜禽养殖、土壤等的污染处理。建立健全主要污染物有偿排放制度和排污权交易制度，推进生态补偿机制的建立。

（四）生态保育措施

1. 原生物种保护措施

保护原生物种的生态环境，尽量保持原状，排除人为干扰；在退耕还林区补植原生物种；提倡使用当地物种，引进外来物种时一定要慎重考虑其对原生物种生境的影响。

2. 生物多样性保护措施

确定保护物种；根据其生活习性（生长条件）划定核心栖息地（生长区）；加强环境保护，扩大和恢复栖息地（生长区）；加强各生境之间植被的延续性，确保生态廊道的形成和延续；提高异质性，遵循自然演替途径。保护区内禁止砍伐森林，捕猎动物；鼓励采用电能等清洁能源；促进公众参与，提高公众素质，增强人们的自然保护意识；严格遵守《水产资源繁殖保护条例》《森林和野生动物类型自然保护区管理办法》。

（五）垃圾清运

加强垃圾无害化处理设施建设，加强固体废弃物收集和无害化处理，做到日产日清。在重点景区、旅游通道重要节点设置公厕和垃圾箱，集中收集处理，其他可与农、林等结合，转运、处理成为肥料用于农林业生产。加强旅游垃圾转运站、处理站、填埋场等设施的规划建设。

（六）噪声防治措施

① 旅游区内各种服务设施噪声不得超过国家规定标准。
② 消除、减少和减弱噪声，从根本上对声源加以控制。禁止在旅游区内鸣放高音喇叭，应使用隔音或低音设施以及营造隔音林带防治噪声。
③ 除特殊条件下，旅游区观光车不得使用高音喇叭，任何娱乐场所都不得使用大功率音响，以减少噪声污染。

三、旅游安全系统规划

旅游区内的消防重点主要是森林防火、村建筑物防火和服务中心防火。

1. 旅游安全急救系统

结合蒋集镇旅游的实际情况，建立旅游安全急救系统，增强抵御风险和应对突发事件的能力。

① 救援指挥中心　对整个旅游安全急救工作进行协调、整体统筹。

② 安全救援机构　涉及很多部门，如医院、消防部门，以及与救援工作有关的其他部门。

③ 安全救援的间接外围机构　主要包括保险机构、新闻媒体和通信部门。这些部门虽然不参加直接的救援工作，但是对救援工作的顺利开展起着非常重要的作用。

2. 旅游安全保险体系

①由保险公司为进入蒋集镇重要旅游区的游客及旅游从业人员量身定做综合保险保障产品；②建立旅游保险服务信息平台；③设立呼叫服务中心；④建立紧急救援中心；⑤建立理赔服务中心；⑥设立旅游保险基金。

第九节　市场营销规划与规划分期

一、市场营销规划

（一）营销目标

通过卓有成效的营销策略和营销措施，在较短时间内大幅度地提高蒋集旅游的知名度，将"游学小镇·农旅蒋集"旅游品牌打造成为知名度、美誉度和忠诚度完美统一的旅游强势品牌，使其在旅游市场竞争中占据较高的市场份额，为蒋集镇旅游带来最大经济效益、最佳社会效益和环境效益，同时促进游客总量的稳定增长。

（二）市场营销战略

1. 整合营销战略——整合各种资源，统一进行营销

以打造蒋集游学小镇旅游品牌为目标，整合各级政府、旅游要素、旅游企业、旅行商、旅游代理商和经销商、媒体、社会等各方面的力量，发挥协同效应，谋求最大的营销效果。广告、公关、促销、人员推销应互为补充，形成品牌冲击力。近期重点做好"三个一"工程：叫响一句旅游宣传口号；编写一本旅游手册；绘制一张旅游地图。

2. 品牌营销战略——培育游学品牌，提升旅游形象

蒋集旅游发展的重要突破就是建立和打造蒋集旅游品牌，它包括旅游产品品牌、旅游服务品牌和节庆活动品牌。应积极参加各类旅游交易会，以较高的起点和明确的目标，吸引更多的高消费客源；有计划地针对机关、企事业单位的工会，退休者协会等社会团体促销，扩大旅游者的数量；邀请客源产出地的旅行商代表和新闻媒体代表对蒋集旅游资源进行品牌宣传，增强品牌的传播力。

面向社会广泛征集旅游宣传口号，拍摄宣传片，在高速公路和104国道两侧树立广告牌，增强外界对蒋集旅游资源的认可度。

3. 差异营销战略——细分旅游市场，差异化营销

根据消费者的不同需求，对整体市场进行细分，分别设计不同的旅游产品，采取不同的营销手段，以满足每个市场的个体需要，从而占领多个细分市场。稳定亲子市场，扩大老人和青少年市场，开发自驾游、自助游、乡村体验和休闲度假游等专项市场。

4. 创新营销战略——运用新兴媒体，进行多元营销

旅游营销要吸收各行各业的闪光点，进行嫁接、借鉴和整合，创造出新的营销方式。顺应现代信息传播手段，积极应用网络等新型营销方式。

5. 捆绑营销战略——捆绑周边景区，寻求市场合力

借助泰山和曲阜黄金旅游线，与旅行社开展合作，扩大市场份额，将游学小镇纳入黄金旅游线路，与泰山、曲阜旅游进行联动，借"力"整合。

（三）市场营销渠道

1. 传统媒体

（1）借助目标客源地传统媒体

借助目标客源地报纸、杂志、电视、广播、户外广告等传统媒体宣传旅游区的旅游形象及旅游产品，不断扩大宣传推广范围提高旅游区知名度。

（2）分发旅游宣传册等材料

在参加各种国内外旅游会展或在目标客源城市举办旅游推介会和说明会时，向当地旅游业界人士和游客派发旅游宣传册、促销宣传页、旅游地图等各类宣传资料。

（3）在专业旅游杂志上发表宣传文章

在专业策划的基础上，与国内重要旅游杂志合作，形成一定量的宣传文章，不断传播曝光旅游形象。

2. 网络媒体

充分发挥新媒体的作用，应对不断变化的市场状况。新媒体在选择上主要分为三类：网络新媒体、移动新媒体和数字新媒体。

（1）网络新媒体

网络新媒体主要包括各大门户网站、电子邮件/即时通信、对话链、博客/播客、网络文学、网络动画、网络游戏、网络杂志、网络广播、网络电视等。重点关注社交网络媒体的传播方式。

（2）移动新媒体

智能手机应用程序、手机短信/彩信、手机报/出版物、手机电视/广播等。

（3）数字新媒体

数字新媒体广告投放包括数字电视、IPTV、移动电视、楼宇电视、城市多媒体终端等。在一级目标客源市场的火车站、飞机场、大型购物中心、重要的景区景点和

旅游咨询中心等地，开展旅游营销宣传。

3. 公共关系渠道

（1）公关营销

利用各种政府公关活动、会议、合作组织等进行市场推广。

（2）名人营销

聘请名人担任蒋集旅游形象大使；邀请名家名人前来指导，利用名人效应进行营销。

（3）关系营销

加强与各类车友会和俱乐部、独立的零售商、各类企事业单位、社会团体、学校等的联系；加强与相关旅游节目的合作。

（4）会议营销

积极主办高规格会议，利用会议效应形成旅游宣传的亮点；精心准备，参加主要市场和重要旅游交易会。

（5）旅行社营销

与知名旅行社合作推广精品线路，借助知名旅行社的渠道，分销旅游区的旅游产品；与目标客源市场的知名旅行社建立良好的合作关系，定期组织旅游考察，让其了解旅游区的特色；同时针对不同类型的旅行社提供不同的优惠套餐，最大限度将旅游产品纳入旅行社线路组织。

（四）营销活动创意

1. 节事营销

旅游节事活动既是旅游产品，又是重要的营销手段。蒋集要开发一系列主题突出、内涵丰富、参与性强的节事活动，集聚人气，吸引游客，带动蒋集旅游发展。依托蒋集的旅游资源，办好各种瓜果采摘节、彩山登山节等节事活动，力争形成旅游品牌。积极创办新型有影响力的研学旅游节事活动。

2. 网络营销

借助网络渠道，充分利用新型传播营销途径，打造新媒体时代的营销方式。例如邀请关注蒋集旅游官方微博，举办蒋集旅游微信平台转发抽奖活动，微电影大赛等。

3. 跨界营销

跨界营销是新型的营销方式，跨越行业的界限，发挥协同作用，创造出新的竞争优势。如与金融机构合作推出旅游信用卡；与百货公司合作，提供独特优惠等。

4. 蒋集旅游年卡或乡村旅游通票

旅游年卡（旅游通票）是一种新型"旅游营销模式"的产物，它整合了旅游区主要旅游景区门票，是很好地融合"年卡"概念的全新旅游产品。就蒋集来讲，可整合镇域内的优质旅游要素，包括景点、星级餐馆、农家乐、度假场所、购物超市等，形成竞争力联盟。游客以极低的价格购买旅游通票后，可以免费游览通票内的众多旅游点，并享受到旅游餐饮、住宿、购物的折扣优惠。

5. 事件营销

审时度势，策划有影响力的"旅游新闻事件"，进行"事件营销"，提高知名度和影响力。

6. 体验营销

邀请新闻记者、旅游方面的专家学者、社会名人、专业体验师等，对蒋集的新开发的旅游产品考察、体验，通过他们向广大游客推介。

邀请作家、摄影家、画家等进行文学艺术创作，开展采风活动，举办征文比赛、摄影或绘画作品展览等一系列活动。

与自驾车协会、自行车俱乐部、驴友组织、钓鱼协会等社会团体和机构合作，邀请他们到景区和乡村休闲体验。

二、运营模式

为保证蒋集镇旅游产业能够顺利发展，在运营模式上，采取"政府引导＋大投资运营管理公司＋次级开发商＋农民"即（G＋1＋X＋Z）的开发模式，走"政府支持、市场运作、农民参与"的发展模式。

关于（G＋1＋X＋Z）的说明：G指地方政府，即蒋集镇人民政府和宁阳县人民政府；1指大投资运营管理公司（友邦田园）；X指次级开发商；Z指广大农民。

宁阳县和蒋集镇政府从行政管理职能与社会公共服务等方面予以支持，包括基础设施建设、旅游服务设施配套、城乡统筹建设、旅游产业发展规划。

友邦田园作为开发运营的主体，上承政府意志、下与市场对接，包括次级招商引资、蒋集镇镇域旅游景区景点的整合、运营、管理服务等内容。

次级开发商是指具有专业能力的产品提供商，比如房车营地、汽车营地、特色餐饮、知名民宿品牌、卡丁车等。

农民参与强调的是农民参与旅游的开发运营，分享旅游发展带来的收益，从原来从事第一产业（农业）转化为从事第三产业（服务业），提高农民收入。

三、规划分期

本规划期限为2021—2035年，共15年。规划分为3期：

规划近期为2021—2025年，5年时间，蒋集旅游"培育成长期"；规划中期为2026—2030年，5年时间，蒋集旅游"整合成熟期"；规划远期为2031—2035年，5年时间，蒋集旅游"产业壮大期"。

（一）近期：2021—2025 年为蒋集旅游"培育成长期"

进一步做大做强齐鲁彩山研学小镇，一方面挖掘和展示齐鲁文化；另一方面重点开展彩山周边乡村康养民宿和森林康养旅游，申报 4A 级旅游景区。联动白鹭自然保护区与张龙村、郑龙村等社会主义新农村的乡村旅游，大力开展宣传促销，开拓客源市场；完善基础设施和服务设施，建立健全保障体系；引导蒋集旅游"起好步、走好路"，取得良好的经济和社会效益，在宁阳旅游发展中发挥先行和示范作用。

（二）中期：2026—2030 年为蒋集旅游"整合成熟期"

优化整合旅游资源和产品，培育重点项目和景区；完善乡村旅游营销体系，在巩固周边市场的基础上，积极开拓远程市场、专项市场；围绕着山东省乡村振兴示范镇的建设，打造旅游重点景区、精品项目和产品，提升经济效益。预计中期将蒋集建设成为宁阳旅游重点区域和泰安旅游新高地。

（三）远期：2031—2035 年为蒋集旅游"产业壮大期"

推进旅游品牌化、品质化和区域一体化发展，实现蒋集旅游的协调发展；以友邦田园为龙头整合镇域内的乡村观光、乡村休闲、乡村度假产品，申报 5A 级旅游景区，实现旅游产品多元化发展；蒋集旅游与小城镇建设、社会主义新农村建设相结合，实现城乡统筹发展；推进蒋集镇旅游的转型升级和创新发展，做强做大旅游产业，实现蒋集旅游的跨越发展。

蒋集镇项目开发时序表见表 4-8。

表 4-8　蒋集镇旅游项目开发时序表

开发分期	开发组团	开发产品
近期开发（2021—2025 年）	友邦田园研学核心组团	青少年活动中心、友邦颐养部落
	南部彩山森林康体养生组团	自驾车营地、华佗庙、知青博物馆、林下产业种植基地、悬空玻璃观光台、彩山亭、山地运动拓展公园、生态停车场、森林课堂、星海银河夜游道、夜间幻影森林、森林七养
	南部历史感悟组团	柏树怀古、大槐树怀古、栗家楼村史文化馆
	北部汶河白鹭湿地研学游憩组团	汶河白鹭栖息家园、露营基地、农家养生、主题餐厅、乡村驿站、农家工坊、白鹭驿站、葡萄采摘园、乡愁体验馆、特色交通工具、白鹭文化广场、游客服务中心、瓜果采摘园、乡村创意公园、家庭庄园、田园课堂、中国宁阳灵芝小镇、开心牧场、乡村动物园
	中部智慧农业与工业观光研学组团	友邦智慧农业产业园、子泰工业观光研学工厂、悦美客食品观光研学工厂
	北部张龙村三农文化研学组团	张龙民俗街、二日农、张龙乡村驿站、农耕体验园、农家养生主题餐厅、工坊体验部落、租赁农庄、农耕部落、原乡酒吧
中远期开发（2026—2035 年）	西北黄恩彤文化研学体验组团	黄家大院修复、黄氏祠堂修复
	北部郑龙村三农文化研学组团	郑龙村史馆、农业研学基地、七彩采摘园、大地创意景观、郑龙农场
	南部滨湖休闲组团	休闲垂钓园、浑水摸鱼乐园、渔家乐、水库打渔体验

四、近期行动计划

(1) 做大做强友邦田园,联动辐射周边

第一,建设青少年活动中心(梦幻中心),深入挖掘、展示齐鲁文化。

第二,借助八大庄村农家院旧址,在原有村落格局得到较好保留的基础上将八大庄村农家院升级改造,将乡村自然风光原汁原味呈现,让游客感知田园生活。将八大庄村打造成为泰安市乃至山东省展示农耕文化的特色民宿村。

第三,依托彩山发展森林康体养生产品。借助彩山的自然环境及附近林地、山地、田地,建设大自然栈道、彩山阁、观景平台、移动房车营地、森林浴场、森林乐园、度假木屋等休闲观光项目,赋予彩山康体娱乐功能,吸引游客在彩山进行游览观光、森林休闲、康养养生。

第四,以友邦田园为龙头,通过研学联动蒋集镇域其他的景区景点,如彩山、白鹭自然保护区、黄家大院、友邦智慧农业产业园、栗家楼、华佗庙、黄氏祠堂、大胡村、小胡村、苗河一号水库、苗河二号水库、知青屋、郑龙村、张龙村,以全域旅游为理念,打造研学旅游目的地。

(2) 加强招商引资,制订营销方案

通过各种途径为蒋集旅游发展招商引资,加大宣传推介力度,把优秀的旅游资源集中起来向外推广,使其发挥示范、引导和带动作用。

加强与媒体合作进行旅游线路推介;举办蒋集旅游形象评选活动;强化区域旅游合作;参与旅游推介会与交易博览会。在此基础上制订营销方案,包括营销推广策略、产品定价策略、渠道整合策略、网络渠道、媒介宣传策略、公关促销策略、节事营销策略、宣传品策略等,在开发景区的同时开展营销,两手都要抓,两手都要硬。

(3) 蒋集旅游点实行标准化管理

在贯彻《山东省旅游特色村评定标准》《山东省旅游强乡镇评定标准》《山东省好客人家农家乐等级划分与评定标准》等系列标准及山东省特色景观旅游名镇(名村)、"山东省好客人家农家乐"星级评定等工作的基础上,结合蒋集当地特色,创新乡村旅游新业态,加速推进蒋集旅游从初级观光向高级休闲、从同质开发向差异发展、从单体经营向集群布局、从粗放经营到示范先行的转变。

第五章

山东肥城小王村布金山景区旅游总体规划

第一节 规划总论

1. 规划范围

该项目位于泰安市肥城市边院镇小王村。本规划地块是小王村村落及西侧的布金山景区，总规划面积约3.86平方公里（布金山景区约2600亩，小王村约3200亩）。

2. 规划期限

本规划期限2019—2030年，共12年，分两个阶段：

近期（2019—2020年）：建设起步期，重点规划布金山观光休闲度假区、田园休闲游乐区和亲水休闲娱乐区，进行生态环境的整治及基础设施的建设。

中远期（2021—2030年）：快速发展期，重点进行小王村民俗文化体验区建设、新农村的开发和旅游区整体服务品质的提升。

3. 规划目的

为了科学合理地开发利用肥城布金山和小王村，通过规划，打造国家4A级景区，促进产业结构优化升级，使旅游区环境、经济、社会效益得到统筹发展。

4. 指导思想

旅游规划应满足长远发展前景，合理开发定位，充分利用现有旅游资源，增加有吸引力的项目，将文化体验、科普教育、休闲娱乐有机结合起来，实现社会效益、经济效益的协调发展和整体统一。

第二节 发展条件分析

一、上位规划分析

肥城市乡村旅游空间布局为"一核、两带、三区"，一核为"中部桃园文化旅游核"，两带为"北部肥国山乡生活体验带"与"南部汶阳田园农业观光带"，三区为"望鲁湖山水渔村休闲区""泰安泰山植物生态园区""牛家庄画中古村生活区"。北部肥国山乡生活体验带位于肥城北部山区一带，这里集中大量的优质乡村旅游资源，其主要依托八道岭原态乡村、双泉峪生态园、条水涧青少年乡村生活体验基地、黄叶高科技农业村、双峪村野茶长寿谷和张家花峪的茶叶种植园，未来主要发展乡村观光、农家乐、果品采摘、环境养生等乡村旅游产品；边院镇处于汶阳田园农业观光带之中，是肥城市四个重点旅游乡镇之一。

二、区位条件分析

(1) 地理区位

众多城市交叉辐射、叠加共振，区域旅游发展优势凸显。项目地处山东重要城市济南、泰安、聊城、济宁的中心区域，以上四市经济发展条件良好，人均收入高，居民出游意愿明显。小王村位于肥城市城区东南约15公里，边院镇驻地西北方向约4公里处。小王村是一个北、东、西三面环山的小山村，西侧为布金山、东侧为宝金山、北侧为横山，小王村位于布金山的东麓高台上，东临金沙河。

布金山旅游区受众多城市交叉辐射、叠加共振，区域旅游发展优势凸显。

(2) 交通区位

离尘不离城，城区后花园。

目前，小王村东临潮汶公路，南接泰东公路，东接京福高速公路，西连济微公路，交通较为便利。项目地距离泰安主城区半小时车程，交通条件便利，通达性良好。近而畅通的区位交通条件，是本项目开发的重要前提与基础。

三、资源本底分析

(一) 小王村概况

1. 历史沿革

小王村及周边区域积淀着灿烂的文化瑰宝。其中，西周遗址位于小王村西山坡，属市级文物保护单位。汉古城遗址，又称羽父城遗址，位于小王村东500米，古城村北，在断崖处，有古城墙残壁，是一座古城址，其属市文物保护单位。

2. 社会经济概况

小王村总面积约5800亩，其中山地面积约2600亩。近年来，小王村立足丰富的资源优势，探索实施"生态立村、文化兴村、旅游强村"三大战略，积极推进生态农业、文化、旅游三位一体化发展，走出了一条符合自己特色的发展之路，形成了生态农业壮大、特色文化兴起、旅游兴旺发达的田园综合体。小王村大力发展现代农业，种植板栗、大樱桃、核桃等约1000亩，并投资120万元建成约200亩樱桃滴灌项目；每年"五一"举办布金山春季文化旅游节，"十一"举办布金山金秋文化旅游节，年接待游客3万人次以上，全村旅游收入超30万元，扩大了布金山的影响力，布金山也成为具有地方特色的文化旅游品牌，被评为国家2A级景区、山东省农业旅游示范点。

2016年小王村实现村集体经营性收入56万元，被授予山东省生态文明乡村等荣誉称号，2016年被纳入省级美丽乡村建设试点；2017年，小王村入选山东省第四批"美丽宜居小镇、美丽宜居村庄"。目前，泰安市有13个省级美丽村庄，而小王村与潮泉镇柳沟村是肥城市的2个省级美丽乡村。

（二）旅游开发现状

小王村的旅游开发始于2003年的一次山会活动，活动设有戏剧、歌舞等文娱节目，并设有餐饮、副食等100余个摊位，山会期间，每天赶会人数1万以上。

在此之后，多方筹资100万元，开挖河道3公里，在布金山修建环山公路5公里，建成金山阁、金山关、石门关、泰山行宫、聚龙亭等多处景点，并建成了集旅游、休闲度假、垂钓、娱乐、餐饮服务于一体的金泉山庄。2010年，小王村投入300万元，全力打造"金泉度假村"，配套完善了水寨风情园、文化广场、农家乐等休闲娱乐设施。

以"打造最美乡村、建设幸福小王"为目标，以"古灵红秀"为主题，以"一街一园一馆"为精品景点，带动村庄建设更好更美。修复村内老街，使老街呈现"石上草砖"四类老房子，复建春秋时期的"芙蓉城"古城门、古戏园；突出山水灵气，沿河建设一处山水文化公园，配套"亭台廊榭"，建设李白草堂；突出红色主题，建设革命纪念馆，展示徐向前等革命前辈在小王村的红色印记；突出村庄秀气风貌，进一步完善村庄绿化，栽植翠竹、垂柳、杏树等具有当地特色的绿化苗木。

2017年以来，投资500万元，在布金山上修建3条环山公路，总长度约10公里，相互贯通；建设景区牌坊、停车场、游客接待中心、餐饮部、住宿部、农家乐、景区道路安全标志等配套服务设施。

（三）小王村资源分析

1. 气候条件优越，生态环境良好

小王村属暖温带半湿润气候区，雨热同期，光温同步，四季分明，适宜居住。布金山主峰海拔447米，为全镇最高点，山地植被覆盖率接近90%，山上松柏"戴帽"，坡上板栗、核桃"缠腰"，生态环境优良。

2. 历史古迹众多，文化源远流长

小王村及周边区域自古以来就是人类的聚落发展之地，有商周遗址、汉古城遗址等，而布金山也是一座历史文化名山，名胜古迹颇多，文化蕴藏丰富，曾留下李白等历史名人的足迹。山顶有"云阳庵"，庵南有"大云寺"，以及"朝阳洞""张仙洞"等诸多景点。

3. 红色记忆鲜明，红色历史传承发扬

小王村留下徐向前、罗荣桓、陈光、段君毅、袁振等老一辈无产阶级革命家的足迹。

为使红色精神得以传承，小王村投资 20 余万元建设红色文化纪念馆，并且在村主街北建设了长 20 米、高 3 米的红色文化墙，手绘老一辈无产阶级革命家的革命事迹。

4. 完整的传统村落，特色的北方建筑

村子依山而建，农户院落错落有致，与地形、地貌巧妙结合，深巷、大院、高屋浑然一体，仍然保持着传统民居建筑风格。目前，村内已修复了老街，村落内自古至今的"石土草砖"四类老房子类型齐全，各具特色，错落有致。由于修建了堤坝，保证了村内的河流常年有水。

5. 丰富多彩的民间娱乐活动

开挖整治 3 公里河道，建设文化生态公园、水上长廊、垂钓园，复建了古戏园，组建了地方戏曲班子、武术队，利用古城戏台表演古彩戏法、马术，利用李家武馆表演传统武术，利用草棚建设"煎饼铺"，利用老场院、老碾、石磨加工面粉、小米，利用"老街夜市"交易布金山特产、中草药，利用农家院开发农家乐餐饮、发展民宿游，利用红色文化纪念馆进行革命传统教育。

项目地旅游资源分类系统及实体旅游资源统计见表 5-1。

表 5-1　项目地旅游资源分类系统及实体旅游资源统计

主类	亚类	基本类型	旅游资源实体名称	数量
A 地文景观	AA 自然景观综合体	AAA 山丘型景观	布金山、红叶岭	2
	AC 地表形态	ACB 峰柱状地景	小石林	1
		ACD 沟壑与洞穴	红叶谷、仙人谷	2
		ACE 奇特与象形山石	观音石、飞来石、龟石	3
B 水域风光	BA 河系	BAA 游憩河段	南湖	1
		BAB 瀑布	峡谷瀑布、流水飞瀑、刘全瀑布	3
	BB 湖沼	BBC 湿池	南湖、观音湖	2
	BC 泉	BCA 泉	行者泉、金线泉、金水泉、卧龙泉、流泉	5
C 生物景观	CA 植被景观	CAA 林地	松林、刺槐、核桃	3
		CAB 独树与丛树	樱桃树、核桃树、栗子树、松树、核桃树	5
	CB 野生动物栖息地	CBA 水生动物栖息地	观音湖、南湖	2
		CBB 陆地动物栖息地	布金山林地	1
D 天象与气候景观	DB 天气与气候现象	DBA 云雾多发区	布金山	1

续表

主类	亚类	基本类型	旅游资源实体名称	数量
E 建筑与设施	EA 人文景观综合体	EAB 军事遗址与古战场	115师旧址革命遗址、石门关遗址、汉古城遗址	3
		EAD 建设工程与生产地	山上度假木屋别墅、山下木屋民宿	2
		EAE 文化活动场所	游客接待中心、演艺中心、红色纪念馆、民俗馆、红色纪念馆、演艺场、打谷场、民俗院	8
		EAF 康体游乐休闲度假地	樱桃观光采摘园、水上乐园、垂钓中心、演艺场、民俗街、木屋别墅	6
		EAG 宗教与祭祀活动场所	泰山行宫	1
	EB 实用建筑与核心设施	EBG 堤坝段落	南湖	1
	EC 景观与小品建筑	ECB 观景点	迎客亭、接驾亭、观景台、风光亭、聚龙亭、花海	6
		ECF 碑碣、碑林、经幢	李白诗文、石门关、金山关	3
F 历史遗迹	FA 物质类文化遗存	FAA 建筑遗迹	云阳庵、金泉寺、大云寺、小王村新建芙蓉古城、小长城	5
	FB 非物质类文化遗存	FBB 地方习俗	婚丧嫁娶、农历六月初六嫁出去的闺女回娘家看望双亲的节日	2
		FBD 传统演艺	山东梆子、泰山皮影戏	2
G 旅游购品	GA 农业产品	GAA 种植业产品及制品	一品豆腐、泰安驴油火烧、泰安煎饼	3
		GAB 林业产品与制品	泰山板栗、大樱桃、泰山赤灵芝、泰山何首乌、泰山四叶参、泰山黄精	6
		GAC 水产品与制品	南湖鱼、糖醋黄河鲤鱼、扒原壳鲍鱼	3
	GC 手工工艺品	GCD 陶瓷	泰山陶艺	1
H 人文活动	HA 人事活动记录	HAA 地方人物	李白、姜太公、徐向前、陈光、观音、碧霞元君、罗荣桓、张志纯	8
		HAB 地方事件	抗日武装起义	1
	HB 岁时节令	HBA 宗教活动与庙会	庙会	1
		HBB 农时节日	春节、中秋节、元宵节	3
		HBC 现代节庆	布金山春季文化旅游节、布金山金秋文化旅游节	2

根据国家标准《旅游资源分类、调查与评价》(GB/T 18972—2017),结合调研

组现场考察情况,整理出布金山旅游区旅游资源如表 5-2 所示。

表 5-2　项目地旅游资源统计

序号		资源类型	资源单体数量
自然旅游资源	A	地文景观	8
	B	水域风光	11
	C	生物景观	11
	D	天象与气候景观	1
人文旅游资源	E	遗址遗迹	30
	F	建筑与设施	9
	G	旅游商品	13
	H	人文活动	15
总计	—	8	98

根据统计,项目地共有主要旅游资源类型有 8 个主类,17 个亚类,33 个基本类,共有资源单体 98 个。

总体来说人文资源种类总体上多于自然资源,由此可见项目地旅游资源种类丰富,组合度较好,可塑性强。

因此,未来旅游开发需要在依托自然旅游资源的基础上,更多进行人文资源旅游开发。

四、市场条件分析

(1) 主要客源地消费能力

2018 年泰安城镇和农村居民人均可支配收入分别达到 28100 元和 13400 元。2018 年济南市城乡居民人均可支配收入分别达到 39876 元和 14317 元。

泰安市和济南市城镇居民平均可支配收入远远超 2 万元,农民人均可支配收入超过 1 万元,且居民收入不断上涨。

(2) 客源市场预测

通过对肥城市近三年客源市场规模及肥城市发展较好的景区全年游客接待量数据的分析,结合项目地旅游市场情况,对布金山和小王村乡村旅游项目客源市场做出预测(见表 5-3)。

表 5-3　2019—2030 年游客接待规模预测

年份	2019 年	2020 年	2021 年	2022 年	2023 年	2024 年	2025 年	2026 年	2027 年	2028 年	2029 年	2030 年
游客接待量/万人次	10	12.5	16.25	20.47	24.97	29.97	35.37	40.67	44.74	49.2	54.1	59
增长率/%	—	25	30	26	22	20	18	15	10	10	9	9

项目现阶段处于开发建设提升阶段,采用拟定基数和增长率预测的方法,对规划期的游客量进行预测。基数的拟定采取参考周边景区和景区项目建设情况结合的

方法。

基数拟定：根据项目建设情况，项目采用"边建设、边营业、边投资、边盈利"的发展模式，2019年部分布金山游乐项目已可面向市场，相关的市场推广也已进行。

山东肥城市小王村项目的发展会经历快速发展、稳定增长、平稳发展三个时期，至2030年旅游接待人次预计将达到59万人次。

五、旅游发展SWOT分析

（一）旅游发展优势

1. 历史悠久，田园意境突出

小王村历史遗迹众多，具有很高的文物价值。村庄与布金山景区互为依托，融为一体，村居环境古朴恬静。此外，村庄依山傍水，农田、古树、山川、水库与村落有机组合，和谐一体，一派诗情画意般的景象，让人流连忘返。

2. 民俗风情淳朴，文化突出

小王村民俗风情淳朴，保存有众多具有地方特色的传统节日、手工技艺和传统风俗，这也是该村旅游资源的重要组成部分。

3. 经营管理优势，执行力强

小王村的突出特点是村风正，村民朴实、勤劳、诚信，村委班子团结、实干、上进心强，有很强的执行力，这是乡村旅游的最主要基础。并且村内的土地逐步收归集体经营，整个村的土地将由村集体掌控，避免了一些旅游区因土地权属问题所带来的纠纷。

4. 红色旅游资源丰富，周边组合条件较好

该区域红色旅游资源丰富，有马家堂后方医院、中共泰西特委旧址、一一五师驻地等；同时，周边还有布金山、大王村的樱桃基地等，初步具备形成旅游集群的基础。

（二）旅游发展劣势

1. 旅游配套设施偏弱

小王村的旅游开发已有多年，有了一定的旅游基础设施，现有的硬件设施已初步具备，但旅游配套设施还有较大差距。

2. 知名度不高，旅游形象尚待进一步突出

小王村虽是省级美丽乡村，但还不具备全国乡村旅游示范点等荣誉，市场知名度不高，目前客源主要是考察团队及少量慕名而来的游客。

3. 旅游人才缺乏

旅游业的发展必将对人力资源提出更高的要求，而目前小王村专门从事旅游管理和旅游服务的人员较少。从旅游队伍素质看，专业管理、策划、营销人才极度缺乏。

4. 民俗建筑符号保护不够，部分景观损毁，环境有待整治

由于常年无人居住，部分传统村建筑损毁严重；虽大部分新建筑分布于村西和村南，但仍有不少现代建筑耸立于传统建筑群中，与原有的建筑风格迥异，影响村落整体风貌。

（三）旅游发展机遇

1. 国家对乡村旅游日益重视

《国务院关于促进旅游业改革发展的若干意见》（国发〔2014〕31号）指出，大力发展乡村旅游。推动乡村旅游与新型城镇化有机结合，合理利用民族村寨、古村古镇，发展有历史记忆、地域特色、民族特点的旅游小镇，建设一批特色景观旅游名镇名村。目前，从中央到地方，对乡村旅游的发展给予了充分的重视，乡村旅游的发展面临前所未有的机遇。

2. 城市居民乡村游常态化

随着生活水平的提高、生活节奏的加快，城市居民越来越重视回归自然、返璞归真的乡村旅游，原汁原味的乡村旅游地越来越受到旅游者青睐。而现行休假制度的调整，使旅游业的发展在时间、空间等方面形成了新的格局，短途、近郊的休闲度假游获得了极大的发展，乡村旅游的需求更加旺盛。

（四）旅游发展挑战

1. 传统民俗文化面临消失，村庄"乡村性"变异

随着城镇化的推进，乡村也表现出了"城市化"倾向，传统的乡村风貌和意识逐渐淡化，乡村传统的民俗文化也被忽视，很多优良的传统民俗文化无人继承，无人发扬，不得不处于消失的边缘。

2. 青年人才的引流

乡村旅游的发展，需要足够的人才支撑。吸引青年人才回乡创业，在人力、智力上支持乡村旅游的持续健康发展，是小王村发展乡村旅游面临的巨大挑战。

3. 同质性乡村旅游的竞争

目前乡村旅游开发已呈遍地开花之势。就山东而言，以临沂竹泉村为代表的乡村精品旅游开发早、发展快，形成了良好的旅游品牌，而泰安市地域的里峪村已建设成为中国美丽休闲乡村，新泰市掌平洼村、肥城市仪阳镇鱼山村等也已开发，这些村落与小王村一定程度上具有同质性，已经占领了一定的乡村旅游市场份额，对小王村旅游发展是一大挑战。

第三节 旅游发展战略与定位

一、旅游发展思路

提升观光、增加游乐、配套度假、产业复合。第一步，提升观光，提升布金山和小王村旅游的观光功能；第二步，增加游乐，增加布金山及小王庄项目的游乐功能，注重参与性、互动性和体验性；第三步，配套度假，配套度假休闲产业项目，承载综合服务功能；第四步，产业复合，泛旅游产业聚集，实现消费聚集。

二、旅游发展战略

（1）市场导向战略

准确进行市场的定位和划分，主要针对基础市场和核心市场，积极争取机会市场，只有针对游客的诉求进行精准的产品和服务供给，才能赢得游客的认可，才能具有吸引力和竞争力。

（2）区域联动战略

从区域发展的角度来审视布金山旅游区的发展，站在区域的角度突出自己的竞争比较优势，与其他区域进行差异化联动发展，主题差异，功能互补，优势组合，形成区域整体，统一对外推广营销。

（3）特色化战略

特色化是项目的核心吸引力，有特色的产品和服务才能对游客产生号召力和影响力，通过挖掘项目的特色，然后进行呈现、包装、推广和营销，形成独具特色的品牌。

（4）系统整合战略

任何一个项目都是一个系统，需要进行内外整合，进行系统整合，通过游线将功能不同的产品、配套的服务设施进行整合。同时，立足自身与其他的景区景点进行联动，形成旅游集群，统一对外推广和营销。

三、旅游发展定位

（1）总体定位

依托布金山和小王村秀美的山水环境及深厚的文化底蕴，以生态保护为前提，提升布金山和小王村旅游观光休闲功能，增加休闲游乐项目，配套康体度假项目，形成产业复合聚集区,打造一个集生态观光、休闲娱乐、红色记忆、文化体验、养生度假、田园互动体验、研学科普等功能于一体的国家4A级景区和山东省著名的乡村旅游休闲度假目的地,积极融入区域旅游线路。

(2) 形象定位

形象定位:悠游布金圣境 醉卧江北水乡。备选:山水圣境 江北水乡;山水布金 大美胜境。

项目地既有代表北方粗犷雄浑壮观的布金山,又有江南幽雅妩媚秀丽的小王庄,被人们誉为"江北水乡",名副其实的山水胜境,大美之地。

(3) 市场定位

立足中短距离的近郊游,拓展山东省其他区域客群。

① 一级客源市场。项目地的一级客源市场主要定位于肥城市、泰安市的周末家庭休闲、乡村休闲度假、红色旅游、研学客群。

② 二级客源市场。项目地的二级客源市场主要定位于济南市、聊城市、济宁市等区域的周末家庭休闲、乡村休闲度假、红色旅游客群。

③ 三级客源市场。项目地的三级客源市场主要定位于济南都市圈其他地区的周末家庭休闲和乡村度假客群。

(4) 产业定位

小王村应以乡村旅游开发为契机,带动生态林业、生态农业、生态养殖业等生态产业的发展。将小王村乡村旅游业培育成为小王村经济新的增长点,以发展乡村旅游为突破口,改善当地经济环境,促进本地产业结构转型、优化升级、扩大就业,塑造本村旅游品牌形象,提升小王村乡村旅游的知名度、美誉度。

第四节 旅游发展布局与分区

一、旅游发展功能分区

(一) 功能分区原则

1. 依托资源原则

资源禀赋特点是功能分区的依据,因此必须依托资源的比较优势进行功能分区的划分,最大限度挖掘主要资源的价值。

2. 体现不同功能原则

根据各功能区特点,规划不同活动内容,打造独特的旅游产品,使其形成互补关系,避免重复建设和盲目开发,体现不同的旅游功能。

3. 完整性原则

功能分区的划分既要考虑各分区资源的内在性质不同,又要兼顾各个分区的相互配合和补充,考虑各分区之间的连接,形成景区统一的旅游概念。

4. 突出主题原则

功能分区既要有各自的主题,又要有景区整体的主题,各分区主题将是景区主题的诠释,旅游项目将是各分区主题的诠释。

(二)功能分区构想

根据小王村资源现状及地形地貌条件,结合该村开发思路,充分考虑各个项目功能特色、可操作性、开发建设步骤的科学合理性,把项目地功能分区定为"一心四区"。

1. 一心

由于村内地形限制,规划将入口服务中心建在村广场和广场南侧的荒地,易于村内的布局建设和活动项目的开展。广场南侧主要是建设生态停车场、游客服务中心、农家食坊街。主要功能包括:生态停车、游客服务、游客集散地、餐饮购物。

2. 四区

① 亲水休闲娱乐区。充分利用现有的河道,规划滨水乐园、鱼乐园、休闲垂钓项目,架设荡桥,打造亲水休闲游乐项目。

② 田园休闲游乐区。规划主要将小王村周边樱桃园和田园作为旅游开发的载体,充分利用现有的果园和村内的空闲地开发休闲农场等。主要功能:田园观光游乐、农耕文化体验、林果采摘等。

③ 布金山观光休闲度假区。设置参与性、互动性、体验性项目,利用已有的木屋群打造休闲度假设施,树丛中设置拓展项目,开展山地康体运动项目,如设置山地滑道等。

④ 小王村民俗文化体验区。对小王村现有的项目进行提升改造,打造乡村民宿、农家乐,采用先期试点、政府引导、村民参与的模式。

根据场地现状、交通条件、资源禀赋、市场需求,形成规划布局和空间落位。

二、旅游发展项目体系

旅游产品要考虑资源禀赋、市场需求、投资收益等多种因素。开发具有观赏性、休闲性、参与性、体验性的旅游产品,建设集观光休闲、亲水娱乐、田园休闲游乐、民俗文化体验于一体的综合休闲旅游地,形成具有竞争力的旅游产品体系。布金山景区旅游重点项目体系见表5-4。

表 5-4 布金山景区旅游重点项目体系

入口服务中心	布金山观光休闲度假区	亲水休闲娱乐区	田园休闲游乐区	小王村民俗文化体验区
1. 游客服务中心	1. 野战游戏	1. 沉鱼走廊	1. 樱桃部落	1. 民俗接待村
2. 生态停车场	2. 萌宠乐园	2. 休闲垂钓园	2. 瓜果采摘园	2. 樱桃人家乡村驿站
3. 文化广场	3. 艺术家创作基地	3. 鱼乐园	3. 田园童话世界	3. 乡土主题精品民宿
4. 农家食坊街	4. 观景平台	4. 荷园	4. 农耕体验园	
5. 特色交通工具	5. 五彩山乡画廊	5. 水岸游乐园	5. 布金山农场	
6. 红色教育基地	6. 营地世界	6. 工坊体验街	6. 大地艺术景观	
	7. 林间创意乐园	7. 儿童乐园	7. 跑马场	
	8. 山地拓展运动基地	8. 荡桥	8. 花海卡丁车	
	9. 儿童拓展娱乐园	9. 村史馆	9. 猕猴桃采摘园	
	10. 森林七养	10. 农耕展馆	10. 小王农产品展销中心	
	11. 林中滑索			
	12. 水游乐园			
	13. 文物古迹修复			
	14. 森林滑行			
	15. 停车场			
	16. 研学木屋营地			
	17. 林间瞭望木屋			

三、旅游发展分区规划

（一）入口服务中心

入口服务中心在小王村的入口处，主要有游客服务中心、生态停车场等，形成综合服务接待中心，承担游客集散、票务、游客咨询、车辆停放、住宿调配、购物餐饮、投诉管理等功能。

1. 游客服务中心

将文化广场东侧的民房改造成游客服务中心，内部设有售票处、信息咨询台、投诉受理处、医疗室、小超市、旅游厕所等，具有游客集散、引导、服务、游憩、解说、门票售卖、信息咨询、景区导览、旅游纪念品销售、医疗服务等多种功能。

2. 生态停车场

文化广场南侧按照国家 4A 级标准设置生态停车场。在公路两边规划多处分散的应急停车位，以解决节假日停车位紧张状况。

3. 文化广场

规划文化广场成为举办庙会等大型活动的聚集区域，同时承载游客集散功能，广场采用乡土石板进行铺装，形成打麦场式样的乡土气息集散广场。

4. 农家食坊街

将东侧及北侧的民居打造成"农家食坊街",为游客提供餐饮服务,将乡村生产的有机食材与传统乡村饮食相结合,打造乡村绿色美食体系,形成"布金味道"农家食坊街区。

5. 特色交通工具

打造小王村特色交通体系,包括滨水休闲游船、儿童卡丁车、马车、牛车、电瓶车、骑行自行车(单人、双人、多人)等,作为代步工具的同时,让游客感受特色的交通方式。

6. 红色教育基地

充分利用现有的场馆,主要展示小王村及周边的抗战历史,包括抗战时期办公场景、同敌人斗争的场景、著名人物事迹的展示以及特定历史事件的场景展示;场景展示的方式包括蜡像展示、模型展示、视频展示、实物展示和人物活动再现展示等。

(二)布金山观光休闲度假区

1. 野战游戏

依布金山地形和地势,完善野战游戏的场地要求,让游客在游戏中体验乐趣,也可培养团队的团队精神和合作意识。

2. 萌宠乐园

面向家庭亲子市场,建设萌宠乐园,饲养兔子、羊、荷兰猪、孔雀和羊驼等,观赏之余,还可喂养动物与动物互动。例如:

① 兔子乐园。饲养各种兔子,游客可认养、喂养、拍照等。

② 孔雀园地。饲养若干孔雀,游客不仅可以欣赏孔雀开屏的景象,也可以喂养孔雀,亦可与其拍照等。

③ 羊驼乐园。饲养若干羊驼,游客可以参与羊驼的喂养、剪毛、拍照等活动。

3. 艺术家创作基地

布金山视野较好,依托天然优美的生态环境,规划建设成为艺术家创作基地,定期开展艺术家创作,召开摄影、写生、绘画展览。

4. 观景平台

选择布金山具有一定高度、视野开阔、景色秀美之处规划观景平台,观景平台采用木质环保材料,注重与周边自然环境的融合,游客登临,感受大自然的壮丽风景。

5. 五彩山乡画廊

在布金山目前单一绿色林相景观的基础上,通过植入枫树、三角枫、元宝枫、火炬树等彩叶植物，构建丰富多彩的景观林相。金秋时节，构建五彩山乡画廊。

6. 营地世界

依托良好的生态环境，以低碳、生态、健康、环保为开发理念，配套多样化的活动设施、休憩平台等，完善服务设施，打造露营地聚集的大本营，满足游客休憩、露营等需求。例如：

① 木屋群。充分利用现有的木屋，赋予其餐饮、住宿等功能，面向家庭度假市场。

② 星空营地。选择地势平坦且景观效果极佳区域规划星空营地，以开阔的景观视觉效果和户外野宿体验为旅游核心吸引力，同时配套管理中心、生态厕所等一系列营地旅游配套设施。

③ 帐篷营地。在平坦地段和视野开阔处打造帐篷营地，形成特色户外度假体验地，同时将帐篷营地以木质栅栏的形式围合起来，形成相对私密的户外休闲度假空间。

7. 林间创意乐园

依托现有林场较为平缓的森林谷地，结合当地的历史文化故事和传说，在此打造以"乐活林间，童话世界"为形象的"快乐森林谷"；同时，以"快乐六品，童趣五味"构建整条沟谷的产品体系。

8. 山地拓展运动基地

针对学生和企业客群，规划山地拓展运动基地，主要由户外拓展基地、青少年运动营构成。青少年运动营可以满足不同年龄和不同层次的学生，给他们提供社会实践和团队活动的场地；针对企业客群的户外拓展基地，通过功能齐全的拓展娱乐项目，满足企业团建活动和拓展训练的需求。

9. 儿童拓展娱乐园

针对儿童专门设置拓展娱乐活动项目，设置障碍长廊、走钢丝、走晃桥、臂力通道、高架攀绳、荡麻绳等。增加研学功能，通过户外生态障碍设施，锻炼儿童及青少年敢于争先的探索精神，以及相互协作的团队能力。

10. 森林七养

依托布金山良好的森林植被，打造森林养生项目"森林七养"。通过七个不同的主题对应养眼、养心、养肺、养体、养神、养性、养情七种不同养生方式，通过游线将七个节点串联起来形成森林养生主题游线。

11. 林中滑索

引进林中滑索项目，游客通过林中滑索穿越山谷和树林，在感受飞跃激情的同时，感受壮观的美景。

12. 水游乐园

打造夏季水上游乐园，设置儿童戏水区，吸引亲子客群前来戏水游乐。

13. 文物古迹修复

对于文物古迹原则上不再修复，设置解说牌，对于恢复的景观建筑进行做旧处理。

14. 森林滑行

在木屋群的东侧设立空中滑道起点，利用蜿蜒的山路，架设林中滑道，终点在布金山入口处。游客在林中树梢之上穿行，犹如游龙，结合山势滑行下山。

（三）亲水休闲娱乐区

1. 沉鱼走廊

沉鱼走廊是设置在水体中的休闲长廊，人在长廊中行走，两边是透明玻璃制作成的挡水墙，通过玻璃可以观赏到湖里的水草和鱼，从远处看人如同鱼儿一样沉浸在水中。

2. 休闲垂钓园

依托湖面规划休闲垂钓园，休闲垂钓园分为大众的休闲垂钓区和专业人士的竞技垂钓区。竞技垂钓区通过联系垂钓协会举行各类垂钓比赛，增加收益的同时，扩大垂钓园的知名度。

3. 鱼乐园

规划鱼乐园，为游客打造一个回味童年的休闲体验空间。亲子客群可以参与网鱼、摸鱼、钓虾、捕泥鳅等，同时可以体验喂鱼活动。

4. 荷园

打造莲藕种植、莲藕采挖、荷花观赏于一体的荷园，夏季呈现荷塘月色的唯美意境，在此期间，举办荷花节吸引游客前来观光休闲和文化体验。

5. 水岸游乐园

充分利用现有的湖面和河道，建设水岸游乐园，主要针对亲子和情侣市场宣传营销，提供脚踏船和木舟等游乐设施，让游客感受水岸游乐园的亲水乐趣。

6. 工坊体验街

挖掘具有地域特色的手工艺、特色饮食、非遗文化、历史文脉等，打造非遗文化工坊群，通过木艺坊、陶艺坊、糕点坊、豆腐坊等集中展览展示，工坊采用前店后坊的形式，游客可参与互动，打造集乡愁体验、民俗休闲、特色购物的非遗文化主题工坊群落。

7. 儿童乐园

利用小岛开发儿童娱乐项目，空地种植高大的乡土树种，形成树林，林中设置相应儿童游乐项目，与城市中的游乐园项目区别开来，不提供任何机械游乐项目或者现代化的光、声、电游乐项目，项目设备以木质为主。因陋就简，提供乡村味道十足的儿童娱乐项目，场地内草坪绿化选用耐踩踏的草种，为儿童提供柔软、舒适的活动场地。同时划定相应的活动区域，做好安全提示。儿童乐园边界用以常绿树种和绿篱环绕做围墙。

8. 荡桥

岛屿之间、岛屿与河岸通过荡桥进行连接，可设置不同样式的荡桥，供游客休闲娱乐，荡桥既是通行的交通设施，也具有游客参与体验的功能。

9. 村史馆

规划建设村史馆，通过文字、模型、标本等的展示介绍小王村的历史、家族兴衰史、名人事迹等。

10. 农耕展馆

利用现有的旧民房进行改造，以传统的乡村生活为主题，展馆展出传统的农业生产工具及方式，如织布机、纺纱车、牛拉车、犁具、石磨、石碾子等，同时表演并教授游客如何使用传统的工艺进行生产加工。展馆还可系统介绍先辈们的农业耕作制度及人民生活习俗，评说传统农业中处理生态环境的合理部分，对比现代生态农业发展及应继承的部分，启迪人们要重视人与自然、人与环境的关系，要走可持续发展道路。还可以让村里的能工巧匠制作精致的迷你农具工艺品，也可以让游客参与体验。

（四）田园休闲游乐区

1. 樱桃部落

依托樱桃等果林，开发赏花、采摘、农耕园、田园摄影等旅游产品，围绕樱桃设计樱桃宴、樱桃主题民宿客栈、樱桃创意坊、休闲驿站等要素，并通过举办节庆活动如樱桃采摘大赛、品尝大赛、樱桃文化节、樱桃摄影节等，增加旅游人气。

2. 瓜果采摘园

依托小王村现有的桃树、杏树、梨树等果树开展春季赏花、秋天采摘活动，树下还可以种植红薯，丰收时节亲子家庭参与其中，体验瓜果采摘的乐趣。同时可参与果树的嫁接、裁剪、套袋等活动，也是一个科普研学、体验果农生活的好项目。

3. 田园童话世界

创新农业景观，借鉴稻田艺术的模式，在农田中打造田园动漫城，将稻田、蔬菜地等转化为具有艺术美感的景观。同时，利用农业生产和生活资源，打造乡村主题家庭游乐项目，让游客在体验农业文化的同时，享受到家庭欢乐的氛围，以满足现代人亲近土地、返璞归真的心理诉求。

4. 农耕体验园

将一定范围的农用地规划为农耕体验园,游客可体验传统的农耕文化。

5. 布金山农场

规划布金山农场,将土地集中管理,分割成块,方便游客租种,聘请当地农民作为农场管理人员,加强农场日常田地及农作物管理,设置田园代管、果蔬直邮等服务。同时开通线上微信公众号,方便游客随时了解农场发展动态。线下由当地农民为城市居民提供定制化农产品种植服务。

6. 大地艺术景观

依托开阔土地资源,种植特色花卉,打造四季花海景观片区。依托四季花海,开展以婚庆为主题的浪漫系列旅游产品。

7. 跑马场

针对亲子客群,规划跑马场开发马上旅游体验项目。同时针对马术爱好者群体成立马术俱乐部,提供含马具、装备、教学、野外骑乘、组织活动等"一条龙"产品服务,为马术爱好者提供马匹骑乘、骑术训练等课程。

8. 花海卡丁车

通过种植不同色彩的花卉,形成独特大地艺术花海景观,景观中设计卡丁车路线,让游客感受在绚丽多彩的花海中一路驰骋的速度与激情。

(五)小王村民俗文化体验区

住农家院、吃农家饭是游客乡村旅游体验的重要环节。在现存建筑结构、建筑形式不能大幅度调整的情况下,强化院落内外景观的乡土风情和乡愁元素,院内通过廊架(葡萄架、丝瓜架、扁豆架、小葫芦架等)改善局部小景观环境特色。完善餐厅的服务设备,提高卫生条件,切实保障饮用水和食品安全。

鼓励村民将自家院落空余的房屋开辟为民宿客房,为游客提供乡村住宿服务。小王村成立"小王客栈合作社",借鉴江浙地区民宿的先进管理经营理念,对客房统一定价、统一管理、统一卫生服务标准,根据服务与管理状况对客房民宿评定星级,为游客提供干净、方便、安全的住宿服务。

1. 民俗接待村

挖掘小王村以及鲁中地区乡村特色民俗文化资源,重点发展民居观光休闲、特色民俗体验等旅游产品,打造山东知名民俗休闲聚落,使民俗接待村成为鲁中地区民俗文化的展示平台、交流平台、体验平台、传承平台。

2. 樱桃人家乡村驿站

依托小王村恬静祥和的田园环境和乡村聚落,针对泰安、济南的都市家庭客群,对现有乡村民居进行改造,在不改变原有民居格局的情况下,配套完善休闲度假功能,外立面统一采用乡土文化元素进行点缀,形成统一的乡土主题民宿风貌;

院子整洁干净，种植石榴、枣树、国槐、樱桃、绿竹等形成优雅休闲度假氛围，对房间内部、厕所、洗浴间、厨房进行改造，满足游客休闲度假需求，内部的房间装饰采用乡愁主题元素。每户民居可以整体进行出租，也可以以房间为单位进行分割出租。

游客来到这里，与农民同吃、同住、同劳动，感受农耕体验，打造樱桃人家乡村驿站。

3. 乡土主题精品民宿

村民可将闲置的民居打造成乡土主题精品民宿，提供农家餐饮、住宿服务。民居改造以风貌改造为主，加强清洁能源的利用，注重庭院生态景观环境的整治力度，为旅游接待服务提供绿色、安全、闲适的接待空间。精品民宿客房内部采用乡土元素点缀，游客居住在此，感受浓浓的乡土气息和农耕文明。

第五节 旅游专项系统规划

一、道路交通系统规划

（一）道路交通现状

1. 外部交通现状

项目所在地缺少高速公路和国道，规划修建的青兰高速将大大提高项目地的可进入性。小王村目前对外的主要交通路线是S331省道和潮汶路（县道），衔接主干道路的乡村路，路面较窄。

2. 村内道路存在的问题

① 村中道路部分是土路，易遭雨水冲刷，需要以石铺面，在有些地方需要夯实加固。

② 村内游路系统缺少必要的摄影点、休息平台、服务点等，无专门的旅游停车场地。

③ 有些道路还存在安全隐患；主干道路两旁缺少绿化，道路的景观效果较差。

（二）道路设施规划

1. 外围道路设施规划

在景区外部设置完善的景区宣传及指示系统，即在济南市、泰安市和肥城市至景区的各主要道路出入口、交叉口设置景区指示系统，引导游客从不同方向进入景区。

潮汶路的小王村入口的南北侧50米处设置景区导向牌。

2. 对外连接道路

现有的对外连接道路路面较窄，缺少绿化，规划拓宽路面至 6 米，两侧种植行道树。

3. 村内游览道路规划

村内道路由车行主干道与步道组成。车行主干道是现有的穿村柏油路，主要通行小排量的景区管理服务用车和电瓶车。村庄内部的道路主要由可行电瓶车的村内环线和呈网状分布于村中的步行道组成。

（1）车行主干道

主干道以行车为主要功能，道路两侧种植芙蓉树作为行道树。

（2）村内环线

村内环线主要是作为步行观景、骑马骑驴、开电瓶车之用。规划沿路每隔 60 米设一个装有太阳能电池板的景观路灯，路灯风格应尽量凸显山乡风貌；对路面进行整修，将土质路面铺设自然石块或者砂石路面。

（3）村中步游道

村中步游道呈网格状分布，路面应较平整，在道路交叉地点，应设置景观指示牌。路宽 1.2～2 米，石头铺面。

二、旅游服务设施规划

（一）餐饮设施规划

1. 餐饮服务食品现状

该区域生态环境优良，绿色食品和有机食品丰富。

2. 餐饮服务设施规划

根据景区特性、游客容量预测和景区游览线路特点，以住宿接待地为辅助，规划餐饮服务区，满足游客的餐饮需求。在餐饮业位置布局上，选取在村中滨河地段和布金山山中设置相应的旅游餐饮设施。

餐饮特色，以绿色食品和土特产品的开发为主，包括特色菜、农家菜、山野菜等，融入当地的饮食文化，突出地方风味，打造乡村旅游餐饮品牌。

（二）住宿接待设施规划

1. 住宿设施现状

小王村的旅游开发正在进行中，新建了一批木屋，初步具备了接待游客的能力。

2. 住宿设施规划

根据景区客源情况提供接待形式，有以下两种，一是研学、度假、郊游、考察等集体形式；二是以家庭为单位或者个人的形式。

住宿设施根据多样化的市场需求，形成功能齐全、布局合理、高、中、低档结合的乡村旅游住宿体系。中高端度假以木屋养生度假基地为主，低端度假以传统民居为主。

（三）旅游商品开发规划

为充分利用当地资源，在旅游商品开发中应注意以下几点：

1. 土特产品要突出地方特色

小王村要利用当地优势资源，如重点开发有机小米、有机玉米、有机绿豆、有机地瓜、大樱桃、板栗、核桃、野菜、山鸡、无公害农副产品等。

2. 注重深加工

山村自然资源丰富，要充分利用山地物产资源，深加工以提高产品附加值，如开发小包装农产品、药膳等。

3. 增加保健养生产品的利用与开发

重视女性和老年客源市场的消费，开发当地具有健康养生特性的食品，扩大消费对象和群体。

（四）购物设施规划

根据景区游路设计、景点分布和便于游客采购的目的，规划的购物服务设施主要分布如下：

综合服务中心为景区人流集散地，设置旅游购物点，与游客服务中心结合，这些购物市场主要综合经营各类旅游用品、旅游纪念品和土特产品。

河流东岸的步行街，每个作坊设小型购物点，购物面积10～20平方米，以经营各类土特产、乡土工艺品等为主。

三、环卫设施系统规划

环卫设施主要有垃圾箱和旅游公厕两大类。规划要求在村内的游路沿线及入口地段上，均匀布设垃圾收集箱，以方便游客放置垃圾和环卫人员的收集，从而保持游线与游览区的清洁。

垃圾箱的设置标准为：沿游览步道每间隔200米设置一处垃圾箱，在重要景点沿主要道路每间隔100米设置一处垃圾箱。垃圾箱的外形可采用农村篓子的样式。为便于收集转运村内垃圾，要求在停车场西侧的隐蔽处，设置垃圾收集点。

旅游公厕是景区不可或缺的环卫设施，在现代旅游服务中，对旅游公厕的要求越来越高，其不仅要具有先进的使用功能和很高的环保卫生标准，而且还要具有美观的造型。根据小王村的具体情况，现有的主要是水冲式厕所，应注意厕所的卫生，建设相应规模的化粪池。旅游公厕分布在四大功能分区中，共计建设 4 处生态厕所（每个功能区各 1 处），厕所外观采用石头装饰。

四、旅游解说系统规划

（一）解说系统设计的理念、功能和规范

① 解说系统应具备以下功能：管理功能、服务功能、教育功能、保护功能、参与功能和交流功能。

② 解说系统的规范：遵循系统化配套、形式多样化、简洁清晰和乡土化。

（二）景区解说系统设计

1. 建立解说中心

游客解说中心一般设在入口综合服务中心处，游客解说中心的规划设计要注意其外形的独特性，与景区的环境背景相协调。解说中心免费提供景区的导览地图并配备专业的工作人员，回答游客咨询的问题并接受投诉。解说中心提供景区及其周边其他景区的游览信息、交通信息、餐饮住宿等配套服务信息。

2. 设置标示解说系统

（1）全景标示解说

全景标示是小王村景区的整体形象展览展示，是策划、规划、设计重点，制作应精致大气，以环境地图形式出现。全景标示在小王村主要体现为全景图，全景图展示小王村景区的总体游览结构和景点、道路、服务设施（小商店、旅游公厕、医务室、垃圾箱等）的分布。全景标示设在综合服务中心大门处。

（2）导引标示解说

规划设置在岔路口、内部各景区、景点之间道路旁，导引标示解说上标明前进方向、距离（或到达时间）。材料统一为木质或石质，色彩与环境相协调，造型可活泼多样，如植物、动物、人物造型等。

（3）景点解说牌

景点解说牌用以说明单个景点的概况、性质、历史等信息，文字应简洁、清晰、易识、悦目、精确，尽量不用难懂的学术用语。在各景点入口设景区解说牌，根据景区的设计需要选择墙面固定式、地面固定式两种固定方法，解说牌载体结构一定要坚固，保证安全性和可靠性。

（4）忠告标示解说

忠告标示解说主要是告知游客安全注意事项和禁止游客的各种不良行为的标示。如在滨湖、山上、山底等潜在危险地点，以"游客须知"等形式设立安全警告标示，提醒游客注意人身安全。忠告标示解说摆放在醒目及事故易发生地点。

(5) 植物、石头标牌

在小王村的古树和名贵树木、地质遗迹旁，可设立植物标识牌，注明各物种的名称（学名、俗名）、产地等。

（三）人员解说

根据小王村各景区、景点的特性和不同层次的游客选择针对性的解说方式：拉家常式解说；逻辑性解说；儿童式解说。聘请旅游院校的专家编写导游词，语言要简洁、准确、生动、活泼。导游人员服饰要规范，讲解要自信，做到礼貌周到、微笑服务、应答耐心。导游人员应熟悉景区景点，规范认真讲解，不可随意篡改导游词。

第六节　运营体系规划与效益分析

一、运营模式

为保证布金山小王村旅游产业能够更好发展，必须选择科学合理的发展模式，在发展模式上，采取"政府＋村集体成立管理公司＋次级开发商＋农民"即（G＋1＋X＋Z）的开发模式，走"政府支持、市场运作、农民参与"的科学发展道路。

关于（G＋1＋X＋Z）的说明：G指地方政府；1指村集体成立管理公司；X指次级开发商/旅游设备供应商；Z指广大农民。

肥城市和边院镇政府从行政管理职能、社会公共服务、基础设施建设等方面予以支持。小王村村委会成立旅游开发公司作为开发运营的主体，上承政府意志、下与市场对接，包括对外招商引资、资金筹措、运营管理服务等，整体运营整个景区，同时对接次级开发商和各种旅游设备供应商，以及通过旅游开发公司吸纳当地村民就业，让村民参与到乡村旅游发展中，分享旅游发展收益。

二、营销体系

（一）市场营销渠道

1. 传统媒体

(1) 借助目标客源地传统媒体

借助目标客源地报纸、杂志、电视、广播、户外广告等传统媒体宣传旅游区的旅游形象及旅游产品。

(2) 分发旅游宣传册等材料

在参加旅游会展或在目标客源城市举办旅游推介会时，向当地旅游业界和游客派发旅游宣传册、促销宣传页、旅游地图等各类宣传资料。

(3) 与专业旅游杂志合作，形成营销软文

在专业策划的基础上，与国内重要旅游杂志合作，形成一定量的营销软文，营造正面舆论环境，不断传播小王村旅游形象。

2. 网络媒体

充分发挥新媒体的作用，应对不断变化的市场要求。新媒体在选择上主要分为三类：网络新媒体、移动新媒体和数字新媒体。

3. 公共关系渠道

(1) 公关营销

充分利用各种政府公关活动、会议、合作组织等进行市场推广。

(2) 名人营销

邀请一一五师的后代前来指导，利用名人效应进行营销。

(3) 关系营销

加强与各类车友会和俱乐部、独立的零售商、各类企事业单位、社会团体、学校等的联系；加强与相关电视旅游节目的合作。

(4) 会议营销

积极主办高规格主题会议，利用会议效应形成旅游宣传的亮点。

4. 专项营销渠道

(1) 旅行社营销

与济南市、泰安市、淄博市的旅行社进行合作推广精品线路，借助当地知名旅行社的客源渠道，销售景区的旅游产品；与一级和二级目标客源市场的旅行社建立良好的合作关系，定期组织旅行社进行景区项目线路考察，让其了解景区的特色项目和亮点产品，以求最大力度吸引旅行社将景区推介给游客。

(2) 行业协会营销

与旅游行业协会建立良好的关系，邀请协会负责人到景区游览参与体验，利用旅游行业协会的渠道进行精准推广销售。

5. 结对营销

与岱岳区的里峪、肥城的五埠村等结对营销，结为友好乡村，形成乡村联盟，互相宣传推介，实现联动发展、客源共享。

6. 基地营销

针对济南、泰安、淄博等城市的高校和专业院校，签订战略合作协议，联合建立写生和专业实习基地，作为校外定点的写生、实习基地。锁定高校专业市场，提高景区知名度。

(二) 营销策略

1. 旅游产品策略

（1）分期开发，逐步推出产品

一期重点开发投资小、吸引力强、投资回收期短、投资风险可控的旅游项目，主要是特色旅游新产品。对于投资偏大、风险偏高、有一定吸引力的项目可定向招商，或联合开发，或根据未来市场的变化安排在中远期开发，减少资金沉淀，降低开发风险，延长产品生命周期。一期开发的内容必须能够吸引游客，迅速扩大知名度，较快占领市场，同时根据游客量配套一定的餐饮和住宿服务设施。

（2）强调个性化和人性化

在小王村进行旅游产品开发的过程中，除了提供餐饮和住宿等常规服务，还需要挖掘当地的文化脉络和民俗风情，融入旅游产品项目打造中，形成更多的特色化和个性化的产品；在给游客提供服务的过程中，还需要给予游客更多人性化的关怀，让游客体验到宾至如归的服务。

2. 销售渠道策略

旅游产品的销售渠道策略涉及一个旅游企业怎样以最低的成本，通过最合适的途径，将自己的旅游产品及时送到旅游者手中的重要问题。具体实施：加强促销攻势，结合灵活的价格策略与各地旅行社建立良好的合作关系，鼓励大中型旅行批发商进行经常性的业务促销，授权其代理销售本景区的各种产品。针对不同地区、性质、规模的旅行社，制订不同的分销策略，以渠道建设为前提，建立完善的分销渠道，保障旅游产品流通顺畅。

分销网络体系的建立对于小王村旅游形象推广和产品推广是非常重要的，可选择如下的分销渠道：

① 市场导入期，重点与泰安市、济南市的旅行社开展合作。
② 市场成长期，与省会都市圈的相关城市的重点旅行社展开合作。
③ 市场扩展期，跟省内重点旅行社和周边省市重点旅行社展开合作。加强与旅游行业内专业门户网站、各大门户网站旅游频道的合作。

3. 旅游促销策略

（1）报刊促销

积极谋求在《齐鲁晚报》《泰安日报》等核心市场的各类报刊介绍小王村旅游资料与旅游产品，发布招商引资信息的机会。设计发行并赠送小王村的风景画册、挂历、台历、景点导游图、手提袋等。

（2）节事、活动促销

景区可以挖掘本地资源优势和特色，利用一些民俗节事等，开展促销活动。根据节事旅游活动选取的主题，分为以下几点：以"红色记忆"为主题的节事活动，如小王村爱国主义教育活动月等活动；以"文化"为主题的节事活动，如"戏曲文化主题月"等活动；以"民俗风情"为主题的节事活动，如小王村民俗文化节等。

(3) 网络促销

利用新媒体加强促销活动是越来越迫切和重要的事项，会越来越成为主流渠道。一是利用好手机网络平台，特别是微信平台，图文并茂，快速传播小王村的旅游形象和详细信息；二是建设"网上小王"，形成较为详细的网上搜索资料库，便利网民平时尤其是出游决策咨询期间的网上搜索。

(4) 口碑促销

"金杯银杯不如游客口碑"，以游客为中心，处处体贴游客，为游客着想，以一流真诚的服务打动人、感染人，"以游客满意而获利"是乡村旅游的基本准则。让游客个个成为宣传员、促销员。

(三) 营销推广

借助分享游历故事、旅游体验等方式，通过社交平台传播口碑，提高营销效率，提升营销效果。

三、规划分期

综合考虑布金山小王村旅游区开发建设成本及运营周期，根据地块面积、功能分区等因素，规划建议本旅游区分两期开发：

一期开发（2019—2020年）：塑造品牌形象，引爆市场需求。建设起步期重点进行布金山观光休闲度假区、田园休闲游乐区和亲水休闲娱乐区的提升，引爆市场需求；生态环境的整治及基础设施的建设；完善公共服务配套，打造生态停车场、游客服务中心等。

二期开发（2021—2030年）：强化旅游特质，提高综合消费。快速发展期重点进行小王村民俗文化体验区建设和旅游区整体服务品质的提升，从而提升旅游区综合价值，提高综合消费。

旅游产品开发分期见表5-5。

表5-5 旅游产品开发分期

开发分期	开发板块	开发产品
一期开发 （2019—2020年）	入口服务中心	游客服务中心、生态停车场、文化广场、农家食坊街、特色交通工具、红色教育基地
	布金山观光休闲度假区	野战游戏、萌宠乐园、艺术家创作基地、观景平台、五彩山乡画廊、营地世界、林间创意乐园、山地拓展运动基地、儿童拓展娱乐区、森林七养、林中滑索、水游乐园、文物古迹修复、森林滑行、停车场、研学木屋营地、林间瞭望木屋
	田园休闲游乐区	樱桃部落、瓜果采摘园、田园童话世界、农耕体验园、布金山农场、大地艺术景观、跑马场、花海卡丁车、猕猴桃采摘园、小王农产品展销中心
	亲水休闲娱乐区	沉鱼走廊、休闲垂钓园、鱼乐园、荷园、水岸游乐园、工坊体验街、儿童乐园、荡桥、村史馆、农耕展馆
二期开发 （2021—2030年）	小王庄民俗文化体验区	民俗接待村、樱桃人家乡村驿站、乡土主题精品民宿

四、效益分析

(1) 产业效益

多产业融合,形成产业聚集区。布金山旅游区将形成文化产业、研学教育产业、旅游休闲产业,相关产业之间相互影响和相互驱动,延伸产业链条,拓展产业空间,最终形成产业聚集区,实现产业之间的互融与共荣。

(2) 文化效益

构建城市文化品牌系统,打造城市文化名片。通过发展布金山小王村旅游,构建肥城市文化品牌系统,打造具有文化内涵的旅游区,为肥城建设文化强市做出重要贡献。

(3) 生态效益

优化区域环境,打造低碳示范区。在建设与运营中,利用建筑科技、环保照明、太阳能、地热能、绿色交通等绿色节能减排措施,提高布金山小王村旅游区节能减排环保水平,构筑低碳示范区。

(4) 社会效益

搭建交流平台,构建乡村旅游典范。布金山旅游区的建设,实际上是在搭建一个高品质的交流平台,为肥城提供对外文化交流展示的窗口和优质平台,在开发建设的过程中,将布金山小王村旅游区开发与城乡统筹有机结合,充分关注"三农"问题,特别强调社区参与的原则,使区域人民融入区域产业体系,分享区域发展效益,构建乡村旅游典范。

参考文献

[1] 何景明，李立华. 关于"乡村旅游"概念的探讨［J］. 西南师范大学学报（人文社会科学版），2002（9）.

[2] 唐代剑，池静. 中国乡村旅游开发与管理［M］. 杭州：浙江大学出版社，2005.

[3] 刘德谦. 关于乡村旅游、农业旅游与民俗旅游的几点辨析［J］. 旅游学刊，2006（3）.

[4] 刘锋. 新时期中国旅游规划创新［J］. 旅游学刊，2001（5）.

[5] 余佳雨. 乡村旅游产品深度开发研究——以四川夕佳山旅游区为例［D］. 成都：成都理工大学，2007.

[6] 苏平，等. 国外城市旅游规划研究述评［J］. 国外城市规划，2000（3）. 10-12，43.

[7] 国家旅游局人事劳动教育司. 旅游规划原理［M］. 北京：旅游教育出版社，1999.

[8] 吴必虎. 区域旅游开发 RMP 分析——以河南省洛阳市为例［J］. 地理研究，2001，20（1）：103-110.

[9] Freeman R Edward. Strategic Management：A Stakeholder Approach［M］. Boston：Pitman Publishing Inc，1984，46.

[10] 周玲. 旅游规划与管理中利益相关者研究进展［J］. 旅游学刊，2004（6）：53-59.

[11] 张广瑞. 关于旅游业的 21 世纪议程［J］. 旅游学刊，1998（2）：50-54，（5）：50-53.

[12] David Weaver，Martin Oppermann. Tourism Management［M］. John Wilev&Sons Australia，Ltd.

[13] 胡志毅，等. 社区参与和旅游业可持续发展［J］. 人文地理，2002（2）.

[14] 唐代剑，池静. 论乡村旅游项目与游览组织［J］. 桂林旅游高等专科学校学报，2005（3）.

[15] 王宁. 乡村振兴背景下红色乡村旅游规划设计研究——以通渭县榜罗镇为例［D］. 兰州：兰州交通大学，2021.

[16] 薛美丽，薛威振，蔡帅军. 红色文化在乡村旅游规划中的传承与再生研究［J］. 当代旅游，2021，19（3）：46-47，97.

[17] 马力，段然. 全域旅游视角下的乡村旅游规划的思考与探索——以嵊州市贵门乡上乌山村为例［J］. 宁波工程学院学报，2020，32（1）：61-65.

[18] 李晶，宋建军，王倩雯，等. 湖南省乡村旅游规划实施存在的问题与对策研究［J］. 现代园艺，2019（3）：52-54.

[19] 王瑞. 基于产业融合背景下的望江县凉泉乡乡村旅游产业发展规划研究［D］. 合肥：安徽农业大学，2018.

[20] 孙博. 乡村旅游规划模式分析——以恩施百草池为例［D］. 武汉：湖北工业大学，2015.

[21] 刘晨辰. 环巢湖沿线乡村旅游规划设计探索——以庐江县同大镇灵台村为例［J］. 城市旅游规划，2019（7）：82-83.

[22] 唐建兵. 试析"反规划"理论在成都乡村旅游规划中的应用［J］. 绿色科技，2012（12）：224-227.

[23] 韩云霞. 乡村旅游发展规划理论与实践探究［J］. 现代农业研究，2022，28（6）：7-10.

[24] 肖剑锋. 基于大市场营销理论逻辑的乡村旅游规划研究［J］. 中国商论，2022（10）：053-057.

[25] 李烨. 国土空间规划背景下乡村旅游规划编制的探索［J］. 山西建筑，2021，47（16）：21-22.

[26] 何晶晶. 苏州三山岛体验式乡村旅游规划研究［D］. 苏州：苏州科技大学，2021.

[27] 刘玮芳，徐洪武，方宇鹏. 基于"反规划"视角下的乡村旅游规划理论研究［J］. 上海商业，2021（4）：172-173.

[28] 陈文捷，段湘辉. 基于"反规划"视角下的乡村旅游规划理论研究［J］. 老区建设，2020（2）：16-22.

[29] 张立诚，蔡家瑞. 基于轻旅游概念的乡村旅游规划设计——以四川宜宾市高县新寨村为例［J］. 城市旅游研究，2020（5）：84-85.

[30] 慢旅游理念下乡村旅游规划设计研究——以云南腾冲市荷花乡为例［D］. 合肥：合肥工业大学，2017.

[31] 曾鸣. 原真性视角下的乡村旅游规划研究［D］. 武汉：武汉工程大学，2019.

[32] 唐代剑，池静. 论乡村旅游项目与游览组织［J］. 桂林旅游高等专科学校学报，2005（3）.

[33] 王云才，刘滨谊. 论中国乡村景观及乡村景观规划［J］. 中国园林，2003（1）.

[34] 熊凯. 乡村意象与乡村旅游开发刍议 [J]. 桂林旅游高等专科学校学报, 1999 (3).

[35] 韩帅, 陈曦. 乡村旅游规划发展策略探寻 [J]. 旅游与摄影, 2022 (3): 10-12.

[36] 刘雨欣. 吉林省乡村旅游规划探究 [J]. 合作经济与科技, 2021 (7): 40-41.

[37] 李双英. 近年来国内乡村旅游发展规划分析研究 [J]. 旅游与摄影, 2021 (10): 25-26.

[38] 苏毅, 祖振旗, 宋子涵, 等. 融合自然疗愈的乡村旅游建设规划探索——以京郊密云金叵罗村为例 [J]. 小城镇建设, 2021, 39 (5): 49-56.

[39] 杨明, 赵朝丛. 精准扶贫视角下的乡村旅游规划研究——以重庆石柱县为例 [J]. 农场实用技术, 2021 (11): 111-112.

[40] 张淑娟. 探析乡村旅游规划发展策略——以溧阳市曹山乡村旅游项目为例 [J]. 四川水泥, 2020 (4): 66.

[41] 李倩. 慢旅游理念下乡村旅游规划设计研究 [J]. 农村科学实验, 2020 (7): 17-18.

[42] 朱鹏亮, 邵秀英, 翟泽华. 资源同质化区域乡村旅游规划差异化研究——以清漳河流域为例 [J]. 山西农经, 2020 (2): 37-38+40.

[43] 尹振华. 开发我国乡村旅游的新思路 [J]. 旅游学刊, 2004 (5).

[44] 李永文, 王培雷, 孙本超. 乡村旅游开发刍议 [J]. 焦作大学学报, 2004 (1).

[45] 陈文君. 我国现代乡村旅游深层次开发探讨 [J]. 广州大学学报 (社会科学版), 2003 (2).

[46] 周玲强, 黄祖辉. 我国乡村旅游可持续发展问题与对策研究 [J]. 经济地理, 2004 (4).

[47] 郭焕成. 发展乡村旅游业, 支援新农村建设 [J]. 旅游学刊, 2006 (3).

[48] 罗永常. 民族村寨社区参与旅游开发的利益保障机制 [J]. 旅游学刊, 2006 (10).

[49] 郑群明, 钟林生. 参与式乡村旅游开发模式探讨 [J]. 旅游学刊, 2004 (4).

[50] 唐琦. 全域旅游视角下乡村旅游规划研究——以芜湖市繁昌区平铺镇为例 [D]. 绵阳: 西南科技大学, 2022.

[51] 胡梦子, 周嘉仪, 蒋正容. 湖州四联村乡村旅游规划设计 [J]. 山西建筑, 2021, 47 (22): 12-13.

[52] 郭隽瑶, 张妍. 乡村振兴战略背景下乡村旅游规划现状与优化路径 [J]. 农村经济与科技, 2021, 32 (10): 49-51.

[53] 刘玮, 王婷, 谭晓军. 区域协同发展视角下的景区依托型乡村旅游规划研究——以重庆市巫溪县为例 [J]. 小城镇建设, 2021, 39 (5): 32-40.

[54] 商丹妮. 基于海南地域文化背景下的乡村旅游规划研究——以海南罗驿古村为例 [D]. 海口: 海南大学, 2021.

[55] 郭培, 周晓路, 张川. 全域旅游导向下乡村旅游规划方法探索与实践——以常州市武进区乡村旅游规划为例 [J]. 小城镇建设, 2019, 37 (7): 82-88.

[56] 向然禹. 田园综合体乡村旅游规划策略研究——以武都镇黑宝彩谷田园综合体为例 [D]. 绵阳: 西南科技大学, 2020.

[57] 王红山. 河北省乡村旅游景观规划设计研究——以抚宁县乡村旅游规划为例 [D]. 保定: 河北农业大学, 2014.

[58] 刘斐. 精准扶贫背景下乡村旅游规划路径与方法探析——以福建省福清市一都镇为例 [D]. 南京: 南京大学, 2018.

[59] 霍松涛. 乡村振兴战略下的乡村旅游产业规划研究 [J]. 中国果树, 2022 (3): 49-51.

[60] 王晶晶, 刘清泉, 司端勇. 乡村振兴视角下基于地方特色资源开发的乡村旅游规划研究 [J]. 中国市场, 2020 (34): 46-48.

[61] 洪占东, 殷滋言. 基于乡村振兴背景下的合肥三十岗乡村旅游规划研究 [J]. 安徽建筑, 2020, 27 (2): 22-23.

[62] 石斌. 基于社区营造理念的乡村旅游规划策略研究 [J]. 住宅与房地产, 2019 (8): 215.

[63] 刘琛. 基于研学旅行背景下的乡村旅游规划设计研究——以临武紫薇天下乡村旅游规划设计为例 [D]. 长沙: 湖南农业大学, 2020.

[64] 胡世伟. 乡村旅游规划的环境承载力测算关键因子体系构建研究 [J]. 环境科学与管理, 2019, 44 (4): 165-169.

[65] 徐妍婷. 基于游客体验的乡村旅游规划研究 [J]. 农村科学实验, 2019 (4): 114-115.

[66] 孙瑞桃, 李庆雷. 三生共融型乡村旅游规划编制研究 [J]. 曲靖师范学院学报, 2018, 37 (5): 66-71.

[67] 卢珊珊. 现行乡村旅游规划编制体系研究——基于规划文本的内容分析 [J]. 旅游纵览, 2017 (3): 53.

[68] 郑容. 度假民居视角下的乡村旅游规划——以张家界"五号山谷"为例 [J]. 城市地理, 2016 (16): 249-250.

[69] 徐彩球, 金姝兰, 黄建男, 等. 鄱阳湖流域典型矿区乡村旅游规划设计 [J]. 上饶师范学院学报, 2014, 34 (3): 95-99.

[70] 邱慧. 乡村旅游规划的社区参与机制研究——以郑州樱桃沟为例 [D]. 郑州: 郑州财经政法大学, 2013.

[71] 魏有广. 乡村旅游规划协调体系研究 [J]. 旅游规划与设计, 2013 (2): 80-85.

[72] 侯志强. 旅游发展规划理论探讨 [J]. 华侨大学学报 (哲学社会科学版), 2002 (4).

[73] 王云才. 乡村旅游规划原理与方法 [M]. 北京: 科学出版社, 2006.

[74] 侯志强. 旅游发展规划理论探讨 [J]. 华侨大学学报 (哲学社会科学版), 2002 (4).

[75] 卢晓. 上海旅游资源产品化的一般模式研究 [J]. 旅游科学, 2000 (1): 17-19.

[76] 石玲. 法国农会及其推行的旅游观光农场情况介绍 [J]. 旅游调研, 2003 (12): 51-57.

[77] 窦银娣, 李伯华. 县域乡村旅游产品内部差异化设计——以宜都市乡村旅游为例 [J]. 沙洋师范高等专科学校学报, 2007 (5).

[78] 赵岚鞞. 关于体验经济时代的旅游产品开发研究 [J]. 内蒙古民族大学学报 (社会科学版), 2007 (4).

[79] 王云才, 郭焕成, 等. 乡村旅游规划原理与方法 [M]. 北京: 科学出版社, 2006.

[80] 邝强. 风景名胜区景点建筑生态化技术设计优化的探讨——以湖南东江湖风景名胜区为例 [J]. 广东建材, 2007 (7).

[81] 丁炜, 金剑波. 生态技术与理念在蟠龙云水生态技术园规划设计中的应用 [J]. 南京工业大学学报 (自然科学版), 2006 (2).

[82] 姚伃茂, 薛家莲, 等. 乡村旅游驱动下万溪冲村的发展历程研究 [J]. 经济与管理, 2022 (5).

[83] 宋章海, 马顺卫. 社区参与乡村旅游发展的理论思考 [J]. 山地农业生物学报, 2004 (10).

[84] 曹洪珍. 浅谈发展乡村旅游 [J]. 辽宁经济, 2004 (1): 60-61.

[85] 孙殿武, 张弘. 关于环境保护规划的概述 [J]. 环境保护科学, 1995, 21 (1): 31-33.